RIGHT TRACK READING LESSONS

A Highly Effective Step-by-Step
Direct Systematic Phonics Program

Second Edition

Easy-to-use multisensory tools for parents and teachers
to get children on the right track to proficient reading!

By Miscese R. Gagen
©2010

ISBN 978-0-9763290-2-2

Second Edition
September 2010

Published by Right Track Reading LLC
Livingston, Montana
www.righttrackreading.com

Printed in the U.S.A. by
Morris Publishing®
3212 East Highway 30
Kearney, NE 68847
1-800-650-7888

Acknowledgements

With grateful appreciation, I would like to thank:

- ❖ My Mama who taught me to read the right way all those years ago.

- ❖ My three precious children, Mike, Jessica and Kayla. My son's request of "Mommy, show me how to read" sparked my ever expanding adventure and passion in teaching children how to read. My own children were my first and best instructors in teaching me how children learn to read.

- ❖ The children I have the privilege of working with on reading instruction and reading remediation. These children have shown me how to effectively teach reading. They taught me many details on the specific types of errors children make and helped me learn how we need to instruct children to avoid problems, build necessary skills, and insure reading success. Their proud smiles and enthusiasm for reading showed me without a doubt how specific instruction methods have a dramatic influence on success. These individual students are my motivation for publishing this book. We can help students achieve success by developing necessary skills. We can improve reading proficiency one student at a time!

- ❖ The parents and teachers who believe in the potential of their children and spend the time and effort to help their children learn. This book is designed to empower you with effective tools to help your child or student achieve reading success.

- ❖ My friend Sally. Over cups of coffee with kids playing in the background, she encouraged me to get the first edition of this reading program published. She also helped me with some of the details of self publishing and was kind enough to take the red pen to my first draft.

- ❖ And most importantly, I would like to offer a special thanks to my wonderful husband, Mike, who always supports and encourages me in everything I do. His constant love and unwavering support made this book possible. Without his support and encouragement this book would have just remained an idea. More important than this book, his hard work and commitment to his family allowed me to be at home with our children and share many adventures including teaching them to read. I am truly blessed.

TABLE OF CONTENTS

PREFACE

Congratulations! This easy to use, direct-systematic-phonics program gives you the tools to get your child on the right track to reading success. *Right Track Reading Lessons* is specifically designed for teaching children to read in a one-on-one situation. This complete step-by-step program is easy to use for parents who have never taught reading before as well as for seasoned educators. This program empowers you with tools to teach your child how to read proficiently.

Right Track Reading Lessons directly teaches specific skills necessary for proficient reading. Research clearly shows direct systematic phonics programs are the most effective method of teaching children to read, and these phonologic based programs actually develop proficient reader neurologic processing pathways. *Right Track Reading Lesson's* carefully designed multisensory activities are based on the research and science and intentionally develop phonologic processing pathways by directly teaching the child to convert print to sound. In addition, these activities are 'kid tested' for both usability and effectiveness. The program explicitly builds skills in phonemic awareness, knowledge of the complete phonetic code, proper tracking, smooth blending, careful attention to detail, and correct phonologic processing. Importantly, this program also provides sufficient practice integrating and applying these skills.

This reading program evolved out of my passion for teaching children to read. My son's innocent request "Mommy, show me how to read" triggered this passion. My experiences teaching my children, studying significant quantities of valid research on effective reading instruction, learning from the fascinating neuroscience on proficient reading, observing many bright children who were not learning to read, scrutinizing ineffective instruction, and successfully tutoring children fueled my passion. As I learned more about effective reading instruction and prepared to teach my youngest daughter to read, I searched for the ideal effective program. Unable to find an affordable program meeting my expectations, I put together instructional materials that became the first draft of *Right Track Reading Lessons.* My newly developed reading program was extremely effective with my youngest daughter and with the struggling children I was asked to tutor. I used, refined, and improved the program and began sharing it with friends searching for a way to teach their children to read. I recognized the need to share this effective, easy-to-use direct systematic phonics program with more than a few friends and the small number of children I could personally tutor. Therefore, in 2004 I published *Right Track Reading Lessons.* Subsequently, I worked with older students, adapted instructional material to meet their unique needs, and published *Back on the Right Track Reading Lessons* in 2007. This 2nd revised edition of *Right Track Reading Lessons* continues my mission to help individual children learn to read proficiently by providing parents and teachers with effective, affordable and easy-to-use programs. We can improve reading proficiency rates in this country one child at a time.

This updated and revised 2nd edition *of Right Track Reading Lessons* builds on the strength of the original program by expanding decodable word lists and sentences, clarifying instructions, adding illustrations, providing helpful tips, including supplemental activities, and tweaking activities to reflect the insight and experience gained from six additional years of experience tutoring children. Improvements were also made based on feedback from parents and teachers as well as incorporating and applying recent findings from the neurobiologic research on reading. In addition this new edition contains links to the free information, articles and resources found on the **www.righttrackreading.com** website.

We have learned much from the neuroscience of proficient reading and scientifically valid research on effective reading instruction. The research reveals the importance of phonologic processing to proficient reading, the effectiveness of explicit phonologic based instruction, and the evidence programs utilizing multisensory structured language techniques can help children learn to read. We now hold the 'map' to proficient reading. The child needs to convert print to sound and develop phonologic neural processing pathways. However, the key is translating this 'map' into concrete actions parents and teachers can use to actually help their children travel the path to proficient reading. The direct instruction, multisensory activities, and structured techniques of *Right Track Reading* offer parents and teachers easy-to-use, effective and affordable implementation tools to lead their children to reading success.

This book empowers you with tools to help your child or student achieve reading success!

*Note: In this book sounds are indicated between slashes / /. For example, the letter **m** has the sound /m/.

OVERVIEW OF READING

A. Introduction

We all want our children to read proficiently. They need to be able to look at black squiggly marks on a page and translate this written code into our English language. Reading is the key that unlocks the door to the vast wealth of information and literature. Reading is critical to a successful education. If children struggle with reading, they suffer in other areas of education because they cannot easily access information contained in our written language.

Unfortunately, difficulty reading is a significant problem throughout our country. If your child struggles with learning to read, he or she is not alone. In 2009, 67% of the 4th graders in this country were NOT at a proficient level. Even more alarming, 33% of our nation's 4th graders were below the basic level. [1]

The fact is many students in the United States struggle learning to read proficiently. While the various testing measures can be debated, the undeniable proof of this prevalent reading failure is reflected in the adult literacy rates. Difficulty reading is far greater than the limited scope of a student's ability to read stories, complete classroom assignments or pass a standardized test. The end result is limited literacy skills that handicap an individual's educational potential, future employment opportunities, earning potential, and ability to function as a fully productive member of society. Approximately 93 million American adults have limited literacy skills. Literacy is now measured by the adult's ability to perform three different real life literacy tasks; prose literacy (reading materials arranged in sentences and paragraphs such as newspaper articles), document literacy (reading tasks not organized in sentences such as bills, maps, bus schedules and prescription labels) and quantitative literacy (activities requiring simple calculations such as written checking statements or tax forms). In prose literacy, 43% of adults are either below basic (14%) or at basic level (29%). In document literacy 34% are at or below basic level. In quantitative literacy 55% of adults are at or below basic level. [2]

The purpose of this book is not to debate the challenges within our education system in teaching students to read or to discuss the serious consequences of poor literacy rates, but rather to provide parents and teachers effective tools to help individual children learn to read proficiently. The bottom line is that learning to read is not easy for many children. It is critical to get these children on the "right track" to reading success. We can effectively help a child learn to read proficiently by intentionally teaching exact necessary skills in a direct, systematic and complete manner. This program tackles and solves the literacy issue from the bottom up, by effectively teaching one individual at a time how to read.

B. Important Background Facts About Our Wonderful English Language

1. Written English is a phonetic system: English is a phonetic language, meaning words are made up of sounds blended together. English words consist of various combinations of 44 sounds. The alphabetic characters, the 26 different artificial black squiggly marks, are the way we show this phonetic language on paper. The printed letters and combinations of letters represent specific sounds. The linguistic fact is written English is a phonetic alphabet, not a pictograph or other symbolic writing system. In linguistic history, written phonetic alphabets replaced pictographs precisely because there were too many words to represent by pictures. Written English is a phonemic code and we need to approach it as such. When the complete code is known, the vast majority of English words are decodable. In addition, even irregular words are mostly decodable. Written English is based on printed phonemic symbols representing sounds. To read, we need to translate or decode these written symbols back into the sounds that blend to form specific words.

2. Written English is NOT simple. It uses a complex code: Unfortunately, English phonetic writing is not limited to a simple one-to-one relationship between a single printed symbol and one unique sound. English contains numerous complexities. The 26 written symbols and combinations of these symbols represent 44 sounds. There is overlap where a single sound is represented by more than one symbol (/k/ can be written 'c', 'k', 'ck' or even with the Greek 'ch'). Specific symbols often represent multiple or alternate sounds (c=/k/ & /s/; o= /o/, /oa/ & /u/, y=/y/, /ee/, /ie/). Symbols combine in consonant digraphs and vowel combinations to represent different sounds than the individual components (t=/t/ h=/h/ but th=/th/, o=/o/ i=/i/ but 'oi'=/oy/). Many of the combinations of symbols represent multiple sounds (ow=/ow/ & /oa/; ea = /ee/, /e/ & in a few words /ay/). Some symbols influence and modify other symbols creating new sounds (w+a; w+or, a+l;

[1] The 2009 National Assessment of Educational Progress (NAEP) Reading Report Card www.nces.ed.gov/nationsreportcard/reading
[2] The 2003 National Assessment of Adult Literacy US Department of Education National Center for Education Statistics http://nces.ed.gov/NAAL/

and the r-controlled vowel combinations). To top it off, the English language has assimilated components of Greek, Latin, German, French, Spanish, Native American, and other languages. While this diversity adds to the richness of English, it does complicate reading. To read proficiently the student needs to learn these complexities.

3. Reading is a complex artificial skill: Reading our complex artificial system of recording the English language on paper is absolutely NOT a part of natural biologic development. While speech is a natural biologic process, reading our man-made arbitrary system of artificial black squiggles is not innate. All components of writing and reading our language are contrived. For example, even the basic left-to-right directional processing of print is not natural. Think about it. In the natural world, the best way to gather information is to look all over. In contrast, to read English you must process the alphabetic symbols in an artificial, straight-line, left-to-right manner. Other languages apply up-to-down or right-to-left processing rules. While we obviously use our biologic functions of vision and hearing to read, learning to read print is not a natural biological developmental process. Therefore, children do not necessarily acquire skills or biologically 'grow into' reading. Like all complex learned skills, reading it is best taught step-by-step with practice and mastery of individual steps before moving on to advanced skills.

4. Children are naïve about how reading works and can easily end up on the incorrect track: Not only is reading unnatural but children are also naïve about written language. Much of what skilled readers take for granted is *not* evident to children. From a child's point of view, print is simply abstract squiggles. Many are not aware of how our artificial alphabetic system functions with letters representing sounds blended into words of our language. Children can easily adopt incorrect strategies which lead to reading difficulty. Many children fail to learn with reading instructional programs that are incomplete, include incorrect strategies, fail to teach all necessary skills, or teach skills using analytical, embedded, implicit and indirect instruction. While *some* children figure out the necessary process and become good readers under any reading program, *many* do *not* learn. If a child gets on the "wrong track" on his approach to reading, he faces serious and persistent difficulties. The reason some children do not succeed has nothing to do with intelligence or ability, but rather with how different children learn and process information. Many children struggle with reading because they fail to acquire necessary skills. It is risky to leave it to chance for a naïve child to acquire the complex skills necessary for proficient reading on his own.

5. To read English, children must decode the print: While 'reading' obviously is more than decoding, this ability to translate printed symbols into sounds of the words of our language is a necessary foundational skill. The decoding needs to be effortless and accurate so the child has mental energy left over to achieve comprehension, enjoyment, content learning, critical analysis and the other higher level objectives of reading. Although proficient decoding is not the reason why we read, it is a foundational skill essential to reading success. To read written English, the child must learn how to decipher this complex phonemic code by translating or decoding the print to sound. The more advanced skills in fluency and comprehension are dependant on first mastering phonetic decoding.

Try to read a puzzle where familiar letters are replaced with unknown symbols such as the simple sentence, "⌂∞⅄ɸЦⴰꙄ ⅄ⴰ ⴹⴰᲢⴰ€ ζⴰ ⌘€ɸ∞ Ц⅋ ⴰ€⊠ ∞⅄⅋ⴰⵝ." The importance of deciphering the code is clear. A young child looking at unknown squiggles of the English alphabet faces a comparable challenge. To solve the 'puzzle' of reading, the child needs to learn the code. By the way, the puzzle answer is "Reading an unknown code is not easy."

C. Biologic Process of Proficient Reading & Difficulty Reading/Dyslexia

The scientific research on neurological processes involved in proficient reading is fascinating. Scientific advances allow neuroscientists to view images of the brain as it reads and map out these neural functioning pathways. Amazingly, researchers can actually see how the brain reads! We are learning much about the distinct neural processes involved with both proficient reading and difficulty reading. Sally Shaywitz describes this information in her book *Overcoming Dyslexia A New and Complete Science-Based Program for Reading Problems at Any Level.* [3] I highly recommend this informative book for learning about the science of reading or for anyone who has a child struggling with learning to read. In addition, a selection of informative research summaries and articles on neural imaging/phonologic processing, dyslexia and phonologic based reading can be found at **www.righttrackreading.com/page7.html**. This section lists a few of the key findings from the nueroscientific research.

---

[3] Shaywitz, Sally. *Overcoming Dyslexia A New and Complete Science-Based Program for Reading Problems at Any Level.* New York: Alfred A Knopf, 2004.

1. Neuroscientists have learned proficient readers use phonologic pathways: Thanks to the extraordinary advances in science and functional MRI technology, scientists have actually mapped out neural functioning pathways involved in proficient reading. Researchers discovered proficient readers convert print to sound using phonologic processing pathways. In contrast, struggling readers have difficulty turning print to sound and aren't using phonologic processing pathways. We now have biologic proof that the key to proficient reading is phonologic processing. Scientists learned these neural processing pathways necessary for proficient reading first form in beginning readers. Scientists are also learning how fluent reading develops word by word and is dependent on accurate phonologic processing. While actual neural processing is complex and involves multiple areas of the brain, the bottom line is that proficient reading requires phonologic processing of print. By converting print to sound the child taps into the brain's natural systems for efficiently processing spoken language. Phonologic processing is literally the pathway to proficient reading. This fascinating brain imaging research has given us the 'map' to proficient reading. To read proficiently, the child must develop and use the brain's phonologic processing pathways and turn print into sound.

2. Neurobiologic discoveries on dyslexia/reading difficulties: Dyslexia is defined as a problem learning to read despite normal abilities and intelligence. In other words, it is when someone with no specific physical or mental limitations has persistent difficulty reading. Researchers determined these frustrating problems learning to read have nothing to do with intelligence or ability but rather with how the person processes print. Thanks to the scientific advances, we now have neurobiologic evidence of why individuals have difficulty reading. The researchers discovered dyslexic readers use different neural pathways than proficient readers, and these improper neural pathways form because the individual does not recognize the sound structure of words, and does not process print phonetically. *Dyslexics have problems turning print into sound* and consequently do not develop phonologic processing pathways necessary for skilled reading. Researchers are learning dyslexia is a disorder within the phonologic processing component of the language system. Brain imaging shows struggling/dyslexic readers fail to process print phonologically.

3. Neural processing pathways form in beginning readers: Researchers determined neural processing pathways are created in *beginning* readers. Children who convert print to sound are literally on the correct neural processing pathway to develop proficient reading. Conversely, individuals who fail to develop correct phonologic 'proficient' reading processing pathways in the beginning continue to face serious and persistent difficulties learning to read. This helps explain the evidence showing that most children who fall behind in reading never catch up. Difficulty reading persists because from the beginning these struggling readers failed to develop necessary phonologic processing pathways.

Sometimes children 'get by' with incorrect processing in the lowest grades (K, 1st). The easy reading material, illustrations, context clues, oral directions and limited depth of content disguise difficulty decoding print. For example, if a child looks at the picture or memorizes repetitive text, it appears he can 'read'. However, children who fail to develop necessary phonologic processing rapidly run into problems as vocabulary expands. Incorrect strategies of 'whole word' visual memorization, word guessing, context clues, and predictable text fail as reading level advances. This is why 'reading problems' often become evident in 2nd or 3rd grade. In reality, the 'difficulty' processing print already existed because the child never developed necessary phonologic processing pathways. To read proficiently, the child must process print phonetically. Students who don't develop phonologic processing pathways face persistent difficulty reading. These neural processing pathways first form in beginning readers.

4. Effective Phonologic Based Reading Programs Create Proficient Reading Neural Pathways: The most exciting element of the fascinating science of reading research is the neurobiologic proof direct-phonologic-based reading programs can actually develop the neural pathways for proficient reading in both children and adults. The brain imaging studies have shown effective phonological based reading instructional programs that specifically taught letter-sound correspondence not only improved reading skills in struggling/dyslexic readers, but actually changed neural activity from incorrect neural pathways to 'correct' phonologic pathways used by good readers. We have scientific evidence effective direct systematic phonics based reading instruction builds the necessary proficient reader phonologic processing pathways. We can intentionally help children form the proficient reader neural pathways that lead to reading success.

5. Summary of the Neurobiological Research: The key to proficient reading is the development of phonologic processing pathways. Proficient readers use phonologic neural pathways to convert print to sound. In contrast, struggling/dyslexic readers have difficulty turning print to sound and do not use phonologic processing pathways. Direct systematic phonologic based reading programs can actually create proficient neural processing pathways.

D. Effective Reading Programs Can Develop Proficient Reading

We have neurobiologic evidence effective direct systematic phonologic based reading instruction builds the neural processing pathways necessary for proficient reading. This brain imaging research supports the existing results-based evidence. For years, valid results-based research has shown direct systematic phonics programs are the most effective approach for teaching children to read. The neuroscientific research reveals *why* these direct systematic phonics programs work. In addition, the neurobiologic details on how proficient reading functions provide a wealth of information on how to design effective reading instruction. By directly teaching the child to convert print to sound you can intentionally develop proficient neural processing pathways.

The valid evidence based research clearly demonstrates the effectiveness of systematic and explicit phonics instruction in helping students learn to read. This research reveals "systematic and explicit instruction in phonics produces significant benefits for children from kindergarten through sixth grade and for children having difficulty learning to read".[4] Systematic and explicit phonics instruction is effective for children from various social and economic levels and is particularly beneficial for children who are having difficulty learning to read. Systematic and explicit phonics instruction significantly improves children's reading comprehension. The research also clearly reveals systematic explicit phonics instruction was significantly more effective than non-systematic or no phonics instruction. Direct systematic phonics instruction was not only effective, it was more effective than other approaches to reading instruction. "Students taught phonics systematically outperformed students who were taught a variety of nonsystematic or non-phonics programs, including basal programs, whole language approaches and whole-word programs." [5] Direct systematic phonics instruction provides the most effective approach to directly help children achieve reading success!

Direct systematic phonics programs of reading instruction are proven to help students develop correct phonologic processing pathways and build proficient reading skills. Scientific evidence clearly shows the specific program of reading instruction has a significant effect on rates of reading success. There is a "right way" to teach reading and to ensure the correct proficient reader neural pathways are activated. The brain research reveals why many children fail to learn to read with the popular methods of reading instruction such as 'whole language', 'literature based', and 'balanced' approaches. These well intentioned methods allow and often encourage development of incorrect neural pathways or at best fail to intentionally develop correct pathways. If children fail to convert print to sound and form phonologic processing pathways they face difficulty learning to read. Additional information is found in the article *Why Parents and Teachers Should Use Direct Systematic Phonics Programs* at **www.righttrackreading.com/directphonicsworks.html**

Effective direct systematic phonics reading programs intentionally teach children to convert print to sound and directly help children acquire specific necessary skills to develop proficient reader neural pathways. We have proof, both validated results-based evidence and findings from the neural imaging studies, direct systematic phonics programs are effective in helping young children learn to read proficiently and in helping struggling children and adults overcome reading difficulty. It is like railroad tracks leading from a beginning point; if the child accidentally gets on the 'wrong track' he most likely will never make it to the proficient reader station, unless direct appropriate intervention occurs. In contrast, effective phonologic based programs can 'wire' the brain for reading success and ensure the child is on the "right track" to reading proficiency.

Right Track Reading Lessons is specifically designed to help children acquire necessary skills and develop proficient reader neural pathways so they get on the 'right track' to reading success. *Right Track Reading* uses the train track image and analogy to represent this ability to directly help your child develop phonologic neural processing pathways in order to get your child on the 'right track' to reading success. Just as the correct track leads trains to their desired destination, the development of phonologic processing pathways literally gets your child on track to the desired destination of proficient reading. *Right Track Reading Lessons* is an effective direct systematic phonics program that gives you the tools to help your child develop proficient reading.

---

[4] National Reading Panel's "Teaching Children to Read" Summary Report www.nationalreadingpanel.org/publications/summary.htm
[5] National Reading Panel's "Teaching Children to Read" Summary Report www.nationalreadingpanel.org/publications/summary.htm

SKILLS NECESSARY FOR PROFICIENT READING

This section lists and describes individual skills and elements necessary for developing proficient reading. The child needs to master, integrate, and apply these skills in order to develop proficient reading. Reading is a complex learned skill. The most effective and efficient way to ensure a child learns is to directly teach all necessary skills to the child. **Figure 1** on page 15 depicts the necessary skills and integration of these skills in the process of proficient reading.

The list of essential skills necessary for proficient reading was compiled from validated scientific research found in the National Reading Panel's "Teaching Children to Read" Summary Report (**www.nationalreadingpanel.org/publications/ summary.htm**), the University of Oregon "BIG IDEAS in Beginning Reading" (**http://reading.uoregon.edu/**), and various articles on the amazing neuroscientific research on how the brain functions in proficient reading. In addition, this list was supplemented by the author's experiences carefully observing children learning to read, evaluating specific errors struggling students made, and learning techniques to help children achieve reading success.

A. Fundamental Skills Necessary for Proficient Phonologic Processing

1. Phonemic Awareness: Phonemic awareness is literally 'sound' awareness. It is the ability to understand words are made up of sounds and to be able to hear, recognize, and manipulate individual sounds of a word. Phonemic awareness (PA) is an auditory skill of distinguishing and recognizing the sound structure of language. For example, PA is realizing the word 'puppy' is made up of the sounds /p/ /u/ /p/ /ee/ or the word 'shape' is formed by the sounds /sh/ /ay/ /p/. Phonemic awareness, or developing an 'ear for sounds', is critically important to reading and spelling success.

Individuals vary greatly in their natural ability to hear sounds within words. Some individuals have a definite phonological weakness and do not realize the words they hear break apart into smaller chunks of sound. Hearing the individual sounds within a word *is* difficult because spoken language is seamless. When we speak, we naturally and effortlessly blend all the sounds together to say and hear the overall word. The natural ease of seamless speech hides the phonetic nature of our spoken language. For example: The child says and hears the word "puppy" as one seamless word /puppy/ and does not recognize or distinguish the separate sounds /p/ /u/ /p/ /ee/ that make up the word.

Research shows children with poor phonemic awareness struggle with reading and spelling. Individuals who do not distinguish and recognize the sounds within spoken words have difficulty developing the necessary link between print and sound critical to proficient reading and spelling. It is important to realize natural phonological abilities are not related to intelligence. Highly intelligent individuals can have phonological weakness that leads to reading difficulty. In addition, tendency for phonologic weakness may be an inherited trait as it appears to run in families.

Although some individuals have a definite natural phonological weakness, the good news is phonemic awareness can be taught and learned. We have validated scientific evidence that PA instruction has a significant positive effect on both reading and spelling.[6] You can directly help children develop the necessary phonemic awareness skills.

PA development /instruction should include the following specific skills:

- The ability to isolate and distinguish individual sounds (fish starts with /f/, 'cat' ends with /t/)
- The ability to identify phonemes ('bat' and 'boy' start with the /b/ sound, 'tall' & 'toy' start with the /t/ sound)
- The ability to categorize similar sounds and recognize phonemic patterns: this includes the ability to recognize rhyming words (cat, mat, fat, and sat rhyme) and the ability to recognize similarities and differences in a group of words (bake and bike start with the same sound but they do not rhyme) or (in the group of words 'bug', 'rug', 'run' and 'hug', the word 'run' is different)
- The ability to segment phonemes in a word (the word 'cat' is made of the sounds /k/ /a/ /t/, the word 'shake' is made up of the sounds /sh/ /ay/ /k/)
- The ability to blend sounds together (the sounds /h/ /or/ /s/ put together make the word 'horse')
- The ability to delete phonemes. (Say 'train' without the /t/ & the child says 'rain' or 'mud' without the /d/ is /mu/)
- The ability to manipulate phonemes making changes/substitutions (What would the word 'milk' be if it started with the /f/ sound instead of the /m/ sound? and the student can say '/filk/')

---

[6] National Reading Panel's "Teaching Children to Read" Summary Report www.nationalreadingpanel.org/publications/summary.htm

It is important to realize oral PA instruction alone is not sufficient. Research shows PA instruction is most effective when children are taught to manipulate sounds *with letters*. In other words, the greatest effectiveness in helping children learn to read occurs when oral PA training (recognizing the sounds) is linked directly to the printed letters (knowing the specific black squiggles). The child needs to recognize the word 'fire' starts with the /f/ sound AND know this /f/ sound is represented by the printed letter 'f'. To read, the child must link oral PA skills directly to the printed phonemic code.

2. Knowledge of Complete Phonetic Code: The complete phonemic code is the entire set of printed symbol=sound relationships written English is based on. The child needs to acquire knowledge of the *complete* phonetic code. Knowing the basic alphabet is not sufficient to read our complex English language. The child needs to learn all the phonograms. Phonograms are the distinct printed letters or combinations of letters symbolizing specific sounds within written words. Depending on classification, there are between 70 to 80 distinct phonograms. In addition to 26 single letters of the alphabet, the child needs to learn the consonant digraphs (th, sh, ch, wh, ck...), vowel combinations (ee, oa, oe, ai, ay, oi, oy, ea, ow, ou....), r-controlled vowels (ar, or, ore, er, ur, ir, air...), the 'bossy' letters that modify adjacent sounds (w+a, a+l,...), the multiple or alternate sounds for many phonograms (s = /s/ & /z/ , ow = /ow/ & /oa/...), and other complexities (ph, igh, ough...). It is no surprise vowel combinations and complexities are frequently a source of reading and spelling difficulties. Many children lack necessary knowledge of the complete phonetic code. We often fail to teach these complexities or teach them in an indirect, incomplete or haphazard manner. Although it *is* complex, English is not random chaos. When *all* sounds are learned and patterns practiced, most words *can* be phonetically decoded.

To read proficiently, the child must process print phonetically by converting printed letter(s) directly to correct sound. The child needs to learn the sound the letter represents, not the letter name. For example, for the letter 'h' the sound is /h/ not the letter name /aych/. Correct pronunciation is also important. For example the letter 'd' has a quick sharp /d/ sound not a long /duh/. The child also needs to accurately convert the printed phonograms directly to sound. Avoid indirect processing as it is inefficient and makes reading harder for the child. Indirect processing relates print to a known object or word, then extracts the sound from that word. For example if you see 'oy' in 'destroy' and have to think 'oy' is in the word 'boy' and therefore determine indirectly the 'oy' must have the same /oy/ sound instead of directly processing 'oy'=/oy/. Other indirect approaches link printed letters to a word/object ('b' = book), or to a picture ('b' = 📖) instead of direct print to sound (b=/b/). Efficient processing requires a direct *accurate print = correct sound* relationship.

The goal is for the child to automatically know the printed alphabetic character(s) sound association for the complete phonemic code. The child effectively learns this '*printed letter=sound*' association through direct instruction *and* repeated practice. When a sound is automatic, the child does not have to expend effort consciously recalling the sound and can then concentrate on higher reading skills. It is comparable to learning how to type. In keyboarding, you learn the association of finger movement for a specific letter. At first, a beginner looks at both the keyboard and their hands. After drill, he can type without looking by concentrating on what finger to move. With additional direct practice, the typist improves in proficiency to the point where keyboarding is automatic. When you are no longer spending mental energy on remembering finger placement, all your concentration can then focus on the material. The same concept applies to reading. The objective is for the child to establish direct automatic print=sound code knowledge. The most effective way to ensure children acquire knowledge of the complete phonemic code is to directly teach them all the phonograms.

3. Directional Tracking: In English, we read and write from left-to-right. Proper directional tracking of looking at and processing all the letters *in order from left-to-right* is essential for reading success. Although this simple sub-skill may appear self evident, many children do not apply this essential element. Remember, scanning left-to-right in a straight line is *not* a natural process. Instinctively, looking all over is a superior way to gather information. Left-to-right processing is one of the arbitrary artificial components of written English the child must learn and automatically apply. Knowing the individual sounds is not sufficient. For accurate reading, the child *must* process sounds *in order from left-to-right*. The following words demonstrate the importance of processing order: (stop-pots-tops) (thorn-north) (no-on) (miles-limes-smile) (step-pets-pest) (every-very) (felt-left). Poor readers frequently make errors processing letters out of order. They often exhibit erratic eye movement as they jump around searching for 'whole words', familiar parts or word families. These incorrect tracking strategies contribute to reading difficulty. To read proficiently, the child must not only know the individual sound but must process all letters in order left-to-right. The most effective way to ensure the child acquires this essential skill is to directly teach and require proper directional tracking. A detailed article on directional tracking is found at **www.righttrackreading.com/tracking.html**

4. Blending: To read proficiently, the child needs to learn to blend individual sounds smoothly together into words without choppy pauses between the sounds. This essential blending skill does not come easily and automatically for some students. Some children's inability to blend smoothly creates a hurdle that blocks reading development. If a child segments or chops sounds apart he is not able to put all the sounds together to 'smoothly' say the word and build fluency. The child might know the sounds in isolation but is unable to 'hook' the sounds together. He may initially get by with short words but quickly runs into trouble with longer words containing four or more sounds. To avoid potential difficulty, it is important to directly teach smooth blending skills from the beginning. For example, this is teaching the child to read the word 'mast' with smoothly blended sounds /mmaasst/ instead of a choppy /m/..../a/..../s/..../t/. When sounding out it is essential the teacher demonstrates the correct blending skills of not stopping between the sounds. Teach smooth blending skills from the beginning and specifically work on this skill with any child that has difficulty blending smoothly. A detailed article on blending can be found at **www.righttrackreading.com/blending.html**

5. Attention to Detail: Attention to detail is carefully looking at all the letters/sounds in a word. The details are critical to accuracy. Skilled reading involves focus on the internal details of the word. The child must process all sounds in order, without skipping, adding or changing any sounds. Words are too similar (insist-insect-inspect) (stain-strain) (form-from) (tree-three-there) (then-than) (change-charge) (strange-strong-string). Only 26 letters make up over a quarter of a million distinct words. Listen to children who struggle with reading and you will quickly observe numerous errors because they fail to process details. Despite some erroneous claims, the fact is children can *not* learn to read by only looking at the first and last letter. Skilled readers pay attention to the details. Not only are details critical for accurate reading but careful attention to detail is also essential in forming the accurate neural model of the word that allows development of fast/fluent reading. You can help a child develop the attention to detail skill critical to reading success. Paying attention to detail is closely intertwined with proper tracking and correct phonologic processing.

B. Combining Fundamental Skills To Develop Correct Efficient Phonologic Processing

Correct phonologic processing is a complex process and requires integration of many different fundamental subskills. Children need to convert print to sound so they can tap into the brain's phonologic processors designed for effortlessly processing spoken sound. To do this efficiently the child must recognize the sound structure of language (phonemic awareness), directly and automatically know the phonemic code including the complexities (knowledge of the complete phonemic code) and learn how to read by sounding out the word. The child needs to smoothly blend sounds together (blending), process print from left-to-right (tracking) and pay close attention to all the letters in the words (attention to detail). Learning the individual components in isolation is *not* sufficient. The child must not only master these individual skills but also integrate and automatically apply these skills when he reads. As with all learned skills, sufficient practice 'sounding out' words with correct phonologic processing is essential to developing proficiency. **Figure 1** on page 15 shows integration of these skills in the process of proficient reading

In summary, to become a skilled reader the child needs to develop a foundation of proficient phonologic processing. Parents and teachers can use effective instruction and targeted activities to directly help their children acquire the necessary foundational skills, learn to convert print to sound, and intentionally build phonologic processing pathways. When teaching beginners, it is imperative to directly help the child acquire skills and to also provide sufficient practice applying these skills. Help your child establish a strong phonologic processing so he can advance to skilled reading.

C. Advancing to Skilled Reading

Obviously proficient reading is more complex than simply establishing correct phonologic processing. While correct phonologic processing provides the essential foundation for accurate and effortless decoding, this is only the beginning. Children must also develop higher level skills in fluency, handling multisyllable words, expanding vocabulary, and improving comprehension. Children need to acquire these higher level skills to advance from the beginner level to skilled or proficient reading. The most effective way to ensure a child acquires important higher level skills is to establish a strong foundation of correct phonologic processing and then directly teach and develop the specific advanced skills. See **Figure 1** *"Overall Processes Required for Proficient Reading"* on page 15.

1. Fluency: Fluency is 'fast' or 'automatic' reading. Fluent readers are able to read quickly and accurately without effort. Fast oral reading with proper expression is a trademark of fluent reading. Fluency is critical to skilled reading and comprehension. By appearances, the student knows words instantly and reads the 'fast way' without slowly sounding out the word. It seems by 'knowing' the words the individual reads easily and quickly. However, it is important to realize appearances do **not** reveal the actual process involved in fluent reading. To help children become fluent readers, we need to study the specific process of fluent reading and understand how fluent reading is developed. The necessary information lies in the amazing field of modern neuroscience.

The remarkable advances in neural imaging research allow scientists to examine the process of fluent reading and how fluent reading is developed. Researchers are learning fluent or 'fast' reading utilizes a neural 'expressway' to process words. This 'fast reading area' of fluency is different from the slow phonologic processing pathways used by beginning readers. With fluent reading, a quick look at the word activates a stored neural model that allows not only 'fast' reading but also includes correct pronunciation and understanding of the word.

Importantly, neuroscientists are learning how fluency is developed. Fluent reading is established after the individual reads the word *at least* four times using accurate phonologic processing (slow accurate sounding out). Fluency is build word by word and entirely dependent on repeated, accurate, sounding out the specific word. Fluency is *not* established by 'memorizing' the appearance of a word but rather by developing a correct neural-phonologic model of a word. Therefore, reading a word over and over will *not* develop fluency *unless* the student is processing the print phonetically. The initial process of repeated sounding out 'engraves' a neural model of the word that then is stored in the 'fast reading area' available for rapid retrieval. Fluency is not visually recognizing an entire word but rather the retrieval of the neural model created by proper repeated phonologic processing. Neuroscience has revealed the initial stage of repeated slow 'sounding out' is the essential precursor for developing the advanced 'fast' neural pathways of fluent reading.

Neuroscientists also discovered dyslexic readers have not developed these fluent or 'fast reading' systems. Children who lack the essential foundation of phonologic processing fail to develop the 'fast' or fluent reading pathways. Because they don't sound out words, the neural phonologic 'engraving' of the word is never made and fluent reading is not developed. This is why struggling readers can see a word hundreds of times and never develop fluency on that word. Fluency is completely dependent on phonologic processing. Without express reading pathways, reading remains slow and laborious. These children may work hard and eventually learn to read accurately but they will not achieve the quick and almost 'effortless' process of skilled reading.

Effective reading instruction can directly help a child develop fluent neural pathways. First, intentionally establish the essential foundation of phonologic processing. Then, provide guided practice so the child repeatedly sounds out individual words consequently expanding his storehouse of neural models available for rapid retrieval. Fluency is developed word-by-word and is absolutely dependent on repeated accurate print to sound (phonologic) processing.

2. Skill in handling multisyllable words: Multisyllable words *are* harder to read than single syllable words. The majority of English words are multisyllable so it is critical children learn to read them effectively. Syllables are the chunks of sound within a spoken word said with a single puff of air. Every syllable has at least one vowel sound with or without surrounding consonant sounds. Multisyllable words are made up of a combination of these distinct sound chunks. To read multisyllable words the child has to break the word down by distinguishing and clumping appropriate sounds to form the correct syllables and then smoothly combine these correct sound chunks with the adjacent syllables into one fluid word. The child needs to capture *all* the appropriate sound chunks in the word without missing one or adding one that should not be there. It is tricky and takes application of proper strategies and practice to master this complex skill.

Some children automatically develop proper strategies for reading multisyllable words but many do not. Handling multi-syllable words is a complex skill and beginning readers can run into problems handling these longer words. These children need to learn strategies for handling multisyllable words. The general rule of thumb is 1st graders need to easily read 1 syllable words, 2nd graders 2 syllable words, 3rd graders 3-syllable words and 4th graders need to easily handle 4 or more syllables. It is also important to realize, this more advanced skill of reading multisyllable words can not be proficiently mastered until *after* the child is able to automatically decode and blend the individual sounds. You can help a child develop proficiency in reading multisyllable words with direct instruction in strategies to handle these longer words and by providing guided practice in reading multisyllable words.

3. Vocabulary: As can be expected, vocabulary knowledge is important to reading development. Expanding a child's knowledge-bank of words he understands is important to reading comprehension. The greater the student's vocabulary, the easier it is to make sense of and understand text. Vocabulary refers to understanding individual words where 'comprehension' generally refers to understanding larger parts of text. Vocabulary and comprehension are interrelated.

Vocabulary knowledge is distinct from the skill of decoding print. A student can fully understand words he is not able to read/decode. For example a five year old has a much larger speaking and understanding vocabulary than a printed reading vocabulary. He may not be able to decode the printed words 'gorilla', 'vacation' or 'chocolate' but has the vocabulary knowledge to understand exactly what these words mean. In contrast, a child may be able to correctly decode a strange word perfectly and still now know what it means. For example, the child may correctly decode the words 'kelp', 'placid' or 'leviathan' but have no idea what these words mean. This lack of understanding is a vocabulary knowledge issue. Of course for comprehension, the child needs to both accurately decode the word *and* know what the word means. Expanding a child's vocabulary knowledge is important to reading development.

4. Comprehension: Comprehension is deriving meaning from the text. Comprehension goes beyond decoding the text to actually thinking about, relating to and understanding what the text means. Obviously, comprehension is vital to the development of skilled reading. Comprehension is an active process requiring thoughtful interaction between the reader and text. Comprehension is the goal of reading instruction.

Remember, to achieve comprehension, the student must *first* develop accurate phonological decoding skills and build fluency. Fluency and accuracy are critical to reading comprehension. If the child struggles with accurate fluent decoding, this inability to easily convert print into language will continue to limit reading comprehension. If decoding takes significant effort, the child has little energy left to devote to thinking about what he is reading. When the child easily, accurately and fluently decodes printed text, he then is able to focus energy on higher level comprehension skills.

Reading comprehension is a complex higher level skill that needs to be developed. It is important for children to develop comprehension strategies. Comprehension strategies focus on teaching students to understand what they read. While readers acquire some comprehension strategies informally, explicit or formal instruction in the application of comprehension strategies has been shown to be highly effective in enhancing understanding.[7] In other words, you *can* take specific actions to help students develop comprehension strategies and skills.

D. Summary of Skilled Reading

Skilled reading requires the mastery, integration, and application of numerous skills and knowledge. The child needs to establish the strong foundation of phonologic processing and then build advanced skills in fluency, handling multisyllable words, vocabulary and comprehension. An effective direct-systematic-phonics program explicitly teaches children to convert letters into sounds and blend the sounds into words to develop proficient phonologic processing of print. However, it does *not* constitute a complete curriculum or entire reading program. A direct-systematic-phonics program provides the essential foundation of accurate effortless decoding so the child can begin to achieve the higher goals of reading. In addition to requiring practice to build proficiency, a comprehensive reading program needs to include vocabulary, fluency, and comprehension development. Other essential language curriculum areas in spelling, grammar, creative and technical writing, exposure to literature, appreciation of writing, and ability to research and extract information from multiple sources are absolutely essential to education. The importance of these educational elements is *WHY* you must *first* get *all* children on the right track to reading proficiency. With the help of this effective direct, systematic phonic program, you can get your child on the right track to reading proficiency so he or she will be able to obtain the higher skills and greater objectives.

Figure 1 on the following page visually represents the necessary skills and integration of these skills in the process of proficient reading

---

[7] National Reading Panel's "Teaching Children to Read" Summary Report www.nationalreadingpanel.org/publications/summary.htm

Overall Processes Required for Proficient Reading (Figure 1)

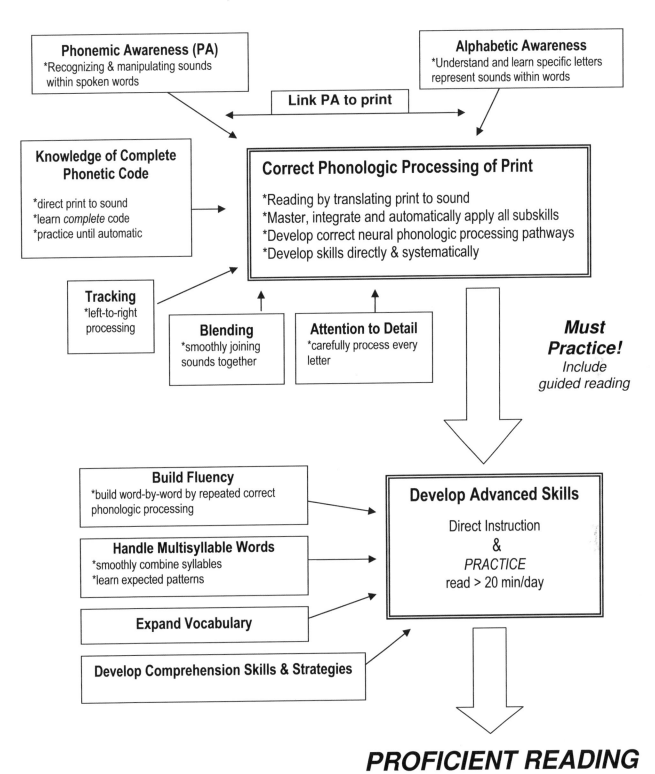

Phonemic Awareness (PA)
*Recognizing & manipulating sounds within spoken words

Alphabetic Awareness
*Understand and learn specific letters represent sounds within words

Link PA to print

Knowledge of Complete Phonetic Code

*direct print to sound
*learn *complete* code
*practice until automatic

Correct Phonologic Processing of Print

*Reading by translating print to sound
*Master, integrate and automatically apply all subskills
*Develop correct neural phonologic processing pathways
*Develop skills directly & systematically

Tracking
*left-to-right processing

Blending
*smoothly joining sounds together

Attention to Detail
*carefully process every letter

Must Practice!
Include guided reading

Build Fluency
*build word-by-word by repeated correct phonologic processing

Handle Multisyllable Words
*smoothly combine syllables
*learn expected patterns

Expand Vocabulary

Develop Comprehension Skills & Strategies

Develop Advanced Skills

Direct Instruction
&
PRACTICE
read > 20 min/day

PROFICIENT READING

For illustration purposes, this diagram simplifies the complex process of reading. Skills are not isolated tasks. The foundational skills must be mastered, integrated, applied and PRACTICED! The correct phonologic processing of print is an essential foundation. The advanced skills in fluency, multisyllable words, vocabulary, and comprehension are also critical to developing skilled proficient reading.

ELEMENTS OF AN EFFECTIVE READING PROGRAM
These elements are part of *Right Track Reading Lessons*

You can directly help your child achieve reading success by using an effective direct systematic phonics program and explicitly teaching all skills necessary for the complex task of reading. Elements of an effective reading program include:

1. Must Be an Effective Direct Systematic Phonics Based Program: The child needs to learn to read by using phonologic processing. The most effective way to ensure children convert print to sound and develop the phonologic processing necessary for proficient reading is to teach them with a strong direct systematic phonics-first program. Explicitly teach children to convert letters into sounds and blend these sounds into words. Validated research shows this type of direct-systematic-phonics instruction has significant benefits for children in K through 6th grade and in children having difficulty learning to read. [8] In addition, researchers have provided neurobiological proof that instruction with direct-phonological-based reading programs develops neural pathways for proficient reading in both children and adults.

Effective phonics based programs teach students printed letters represent specific sounds and how to blend these sounds into words. They teach the child to approach reading by sounding out words. To maximize effectiveness, you need to teach the student *explicitly* and *directly* in a *systematic* and *complete* manner. An important note: this absolutely is *not* a blanket endorsement for all 'phonics' programs. Many programs labeled 'phonics' use indirect, embedded methods, are incomplete or rely on indirect memorization of long complex lists of rules. In addition, many so called 'phonics' programs are in fact whole word or literature based programs with a token addition of a few sounds.

Parents and teachers should use direct systematic phonics based instructional programs in teaching children to read because these programs give us the tools to directly develop the phonologic processing necessary for proficient reading. All reading instructional approaches are NOT equal in effectiveness. Direct systematic phonologic based instructional approaches are more effective than other approaches to reading instruction. This is not opinion. This is clearly revealed by the neurobiological science as well as proven by valid evidence based research. The article *Direct Systematic Phonics Instruction Proven Effective! Why Parents & Teaches Should Use Direct Systematic Phonics* contains further details and links to research. This article is found at **www.righttrackreading.com/directphonicsworks.html**.

2. Teach All Skills Directly: Always explicitly teach children exactly what they need to know. Never leave it to chance for a child to self discover essential elements. Direct instruction prevents situations where children do not learn because they inadvertently missed essential information. While some students may be able to learn with indirect, analytic, embedded or incidental approaches, many do *not* acquire necessary skills. At best, indirect and embedded instructional methods are inefficient. To maximize effectiveness and efficiency, directly teach all skills. Ensure your child learns!

3. Teach In a Systematic Manner: Present information in a deliberate, pre-planned, carefully controlled manner. Reading is a complex learned skill. This step-by-step instruction allows the child time to practice and master individual skills before additional information and complexities are taught. Start simple. Introduce new skills and knowledge a bit at a time, adding complexity as the child learns. Examples of systematic instruction include teaching sounds a few at a time, teaching the simple sounds before adding in complexities, teaching blending with easier consonant-vowel-consonant words before adding in the harder consonant blends, and beginning with simple single syllable words before adding in multi-syllable words. The English language is complex. Systematic presentation helps children manage and master the complexities. A carefully designed program that directly teaches the *complete* code and progressively builds skills and knowledge in a direct systematic manner prevents the chaos and confusion created when you toss the entire English language at the child at one time. Carefully controlled systematic presentation helps children make sense of and learn our complex written language.

4. Always Provide Immediate Correction: Immediate correction is essential in beginning reading so the child learns and develops proper skills. It is a disservice to allow a child to learn, perform and practice skills incorrectly. It is always easier to learn correctly than to go back and unlearn incorrect habits. If the child can not correct himself or doesn't understand, stop and teach the missing skill. As the teacher, it is your job to ensure the child learns correctly. Correction is NOT a negative action but rather a positive opportunity to help the child learn.

---

[8] National Reading Panel's "Teaching Children to Read" Summary Report www.nationalreadingpanel.org/publications/summary.htm

5. Develop Phonemic Awareness and Link this Phonemic Awareness to Print: Directly develop phonemic awareness skills. Although some individuals have a definite natural phonological weakness, phonemic awareness (PA) can be taught and learned. The scientific evidence proves PA instruction has a significant positive effect on both reading and spelling. Directly teach children how to hear, recognize and manipulate sounds within words. To maximize effectiveness for reading, this PA training needs to directly link the oral PA skills to print.

6. Develop and Engrain Proper Tracking: To read proficiently the child must automatically process *all* the letters in a word *in order from left-to-right.* It is important to directly teach and emphasize proper directional tracking to beginning readers. Many young children make frequent tracking errors where they look at all the letters at once or hop around searching for letters or portions of words they recognize. Preventing these incorrect strategies requires direct work on proper tracking skills. Require the child to physically point and move their finger left-to-right. The multisensory benefits of the finger movement (kinetic motion) develop and engrain this essential subskill.

7. Teach Smooth Blending: The skill of smoothly blending individual sounds together into words is critical. The child needs to learn how to say the sounds smoothly without pausing between sounds. Choppy/segmented sounding out makes it difficult for children to hook the sounds together into a word. They might know all the individual sounds but by the time they get to the end of the word with separated choppy sounding out they forget what sounds they just said or add in extra sounds when they try to put it all together. If the child keeps sounds smoothly 'hooked' together, the word doesn't 'fall apart'. Directly teach smooth blending so the child masters this essential skill. In addition, the instructor needs to *always demonstrate and require the correct smooth blending technique* of not pausing between the sounds.

8. Teach the Complete Phonetic Code: The child needs to look at the black printed letter(s) and immediately and directly process the correct sound for the *complete* phonetic code. A well designed direct systematic phonics program teaches the direct print-to-sound relationship for the complete phonetic code including the multiple sounds for the vowels, the consonant digraphs, vowel combinations, r-controlled vowels and other complexities. Although it is best to start with the simple and most frequently encountered sounds, it is not adequate to stop there. It is essential to teach the complete code necessary to master our complex phonemic based written English language. The sound knowledge needs to be direct, automatic, and phonetically correct print-to-sound. Effective programs directly and systematically teach the accurate print=sound relationships and allow sufficient practice to build automaticity.

9. Provide Sufficient Practice Sounding Out *Decodable* Words To Develop Phonologic Processing: An effective direct systematic phonics program needs to do more than tell the child to convert letters to sound and blend sound together when reading. The program must provide adequate practice with correct phonologic decoding of words. The child *must* practice applying phonologic processing by reading **decodable** words in guided instruction with feedback.

In reading instruction, the term **'decodable'** refers to words containing only the phonetic code the child has already learned. To determine if text is decodable you need to *evaluate the phonetic structure of the words and compare it to the code knowledge the child has already acquired.* We often think of 'decodable' text as phonetically simple words and text. Although decodable text is simple in the beginning when the child has limited knowledge of the phonemic code, decodable text expands as the child learns more of the phonemic code.

In beginning reading, it is critical for the child to read phonetically decodable text because it allows the child to apply correct phonologic processing skills. If the child reads text that is NOT decodable (contains sounds child has not yet learned) he is unable to use correct phonologic processing and therefore often applies incorrect reading strategies that lead to reading difficulties. To become a proficient reader, the child *must develop and practice correct phonologic processing.* Decodable text allows the child to actually build correct print-to-sound phonologic processing pathways.

The purpose of having the child read simple decodable text such as 'The map is flat.' or "The pup will swim in the pond' is to intentionally help the child establish essential phonologic processing pathways. Decodable text is a temporary restriction to help the child build necessary skills. The use of decodable text in beginning reading does not limit children, but rather is the effective tool to build vital skills so they become proficient readers and can later access the vast opportunities of skilled reading. Having a child read decodable text is similar to teaching a child to play the piano. You don't ask a beginner to play complex pieces of music. The beginner starts with individual notes and simple songs. As the child learns more notes, practices and advances she is able to play more songs correctly. Similarly, as the child learns more sounds, the material that is decodable rapidly expands. Before long the child is able to read any appropriate book.

The requirement for beginners to read decodable text absolutely does NOT mean you need to avoid reading engaging books to your child. The use of decodable text *only* applies to the material *the child reads to you* when the child is first learning how to read! This prudent use of decodable text never limits the text *you read to your child*. You definitely should be exposing your child to a wide range of books and true literature. Use of decodable text to help your child develop and practice reading skills never prevents or limits access and exposure to wonderful children's books.

As with all learned complex skills, practicing correct phonologic processing of decodable words is essential. Correct phonologic processing requires integration and application of phonemic awareness, knowledge of the code, proper tracking smooth blending and attention to detail in the process of sounding out words. Lots of practice reading decodable text is essential for helping children build proficiency.

10. Use Targeted Multisensory Processes: Multisensory processes refer to utilizing the different senses to aid learning. The general concept is we learn and remember more when we involve multiple senses including visual processes (pictures, 'seeing' images), auditory/oral processes (listening and talking), and physical/kinetic processes (motion, hands on, doing). Multisensory instruction applies two or more of these senses to enhance learning. *However*, to be effective in developing reading skills these multisensory activities must be carefully targeted. Multi-sensory approaches in themselves will not help a child learn to read *unless* they directly build the exact skills necessary for proficient reading. Effective multisensory activities directly teach correct directional tracking, develop phonemic awareness, create a direct and automatic link between print and sound, teach smooth blending, and establish correct proficient phonologic processing. It is not the multisensory process itself but the application of these multi-sensory processes to the development of specific skills that is key to enhanced learning.

For instance, neural research clearly identifies directly converting print to sound is necessary to develop proficient reading pathways. This direct link between printed letter and correct sound is the skill activities must target. An effective multisensory instructional activity is to have the child write the printed letter while saying the sound. This simple action directly links the motion of forming the printed letter (kinetic), image of the completed letter (visual) to saying and hearing the correct sound (auditory). This targeted application and integration of the multisensory processes is highly effective in helping the child learn the necessary skill.

In contrast, multisensory activities not targeted to develop necessary skills (based on the science of proficient reading) have limited benefit. Activities can even be detrimental if they unintentionally create incorrect processing or utilize energy for indirect efforts. A jumping jack, dance or hand sign are misguided application of the kinetic process because these motions are unrelated to skills necessary for reading print. These activities may actually develop indirect, inefficient processing. We know auditory and oral processes of saying and hearing sounds are critical to phonologic processing. However, orally chanting words or singing songs without linking them visually to the printed letters will not directly develop necessary skills of converting printed letters to their correct sound, blending these sounds into words and developing phonologic processing pathways. Similarly, looking at objects or images, color coding, and other unrelated visual activities are misguided. Teaching a child to visual 'recognize' words by overall appearance (sight word approach) is detrimental because it undermines the phonologic processing essential for proficient reading. Remember, to be effective, multisensory activities *must* focus on developing necessary skills.

Mixed in with multisensory instruction, there is often discussion about 'multiple intelligences' and 'multiple learning styles'. These terms refer to theories how individuals have specific strengths and how some children learn better with certain styles. This theory professes views such as a child with strong 'visual intelligence' learns better with visual instructional approaches and a child with strong 'auditory intelligence' learns best with oral instructional methods. It is very important to realize while individuals absolutely do have specific strengths, this does not mean that proficient reading is achieved by many different pathways. The neural science is clear. To read proficiently the child *must* convert print to sound and develop phonologic processing pathways. An assumption such as strong visual learners would best learn to read using visual processing completely ignores and contradicts the science of proficient reading. In fact, this false assumption is most detrimental to children with the naturally strong 'visual intelligence' and weak phonemic awareness as these children are least likely to develop the necessary phonemic processing on their own. Instruction that encourages the use of visual processing actually leads these strong 'visual' children further down the incorrect processing pathways. Reading instruction needs to be designed to develop the specific skills necessary for proficient reading.

An individual's unique strengths and weaknesses make it even more important to directly develop necessary skills. It is especially important to specifically teach, emphasize, and develop strong phonemic processing skills in children who are naturally weakest in these areas. Left on their own, many children with poor phonemic awareness rely on their natural strengths and fail to develop necessary phonologic processing pathways. It is also important to realize, building children's skills for proficient reading never negates or minimizes their other natural strengths. For instance, if a child has strong visual skills, developing his phonemic awareness and teaching him to read with phonologic processing will not eliminate his strong visual skills. It simply teaches him to apply phonologic processing when reading print. Effective reading instruction is not designed to match an individual's existing strengths but rather designed to intentionally develop and build skills and processes necessary for proficient reading.

In summary, multi-sensory activities are effective tools in helping students learn to read. However, these activities must be carefully designed and targeted to directly teach and reinforce the skills and knowledge necessary for proficient reading. While children may naturally have specific learning strengths and weaknesses, proficient reading requires the development of phonologic processing pathways. Effective reading programs use a variety of carefully designed and targeted multi-sensory activities to directly teach and develop these skills.

11. Emphasize Attention to Detail: To read proficiently, the child needs to learn to pay attention to detail. Teach the child to carefully look at all the sounds within a word and stop him immediately if he skips details. This emphasis on attention to detail is important in beginning reading to establish the essential habit of processing all details necessary for creating accurate neural models of words. Proper tracking is also intertwined into the attention to detail skill. An effective reading program directly teaches, develops and reinforces attention to detail essential to proficient reading.

12. Ensure Phonologic Processing - Avoid Sight/Whole Word Reading: It is important to avoid teaching a sight word approach where the child learns to "read" by trying to recognize what whole words "look like". Students who adopt this incorrect 'whole word' visual word-recognition strategy will struggle with reading. Effective instruction *must* prevent this detrimental process of trying to visually recognize entire words.

A 'whole word' approach to reading fails because there are too many words and words are too similar to learn by overall visual appearance. The linguistic fact is our written language is NOT made up of whole word "pictures" but sounds that blend together to form spoken words. Initially, a limited list of visually different words can be successfully "read" by whole word strategies and guessing. (For example, 'a, the, cat, ball, house, green') This whole word identification "instant reading" may be exciting at first but can encourage children to develop incorrect reading strategies where they equate "reading" to identifying what the word looks like, recognizing a few letters, and then "word guessing". Some children, especially those with strong visual memory skills, excel at this in the beginning. However, as vocabulary expands, visually similar words are encountered. *The student who has adopted a whole word reading strategy is certain to fail.* There are absolutely too many words. A child starts school with something like a 24,000 word speaking and listening vocabulary. His vocabulary is up above 40,000 by 3rd grade. It is impossible to learn such an extensive vocabulary visually as whole words. Words are also too visually similar. Only 26 letters make up all those words. To read proficiently, the neural imaging studies confirm the child must look at each letter in order and process it phonologically.

Difficulties are apparent when observing children who were instructed in whole word methods and adopted 'whole word' visual reading strategies. Their reading errors clearly reflect how they look at appearance or physical structure of the word, look only at a few letters or at part of the word, mix up the order of letters, or simply make wild guesses. These children say "very" for the word every, "made" for dim, "doctor" for describe, "sleep" for speed, "smell" for small, "volume" for value, "have" for van, "poured" for sprout, "mile" for lime, "nice" for since, and "soft" for often. They wildly guess un-common learned words like "chimp" for chart and "prehistoric" for plenty. Frequently, the errors and 'guesses' are words they visually memorized. They look at very simple phonetic words like "rod" and "fat" and say, "I don't know the word". They cannot read simple phonetic words yet can recognize a word like 'elephant'. All these are actual observed examples. In closer evaluation, these children often have poor phonemic awareness, do not know many necessary sounds, do not track letters in order left-to-right, do not process all letters, and have poor blending skills. Sadly, they never learned HOW to read and instead adopted a strategy of trying to memorize the appearance of words - a strategy guaranteed to fail. The brain imaging research on dyslexia confirms and explains why whole word approaches fail. Proficient reading is dependant on phonological analysis. While some words are not completely phonetic and are read partly by "sight", visual recognition sight word/whole word reading should *not* be taught *as a reading strategy*.

13. Teach Phonetically Accurate Representations of Print - Avoid teaching "word families" and "blended consonants" as unique units: Teach the child phonetically accurate representations of print. Avoid inaccurate representations of print such as word families (at, ig, it, am & hundreds of other possibilities) and blended consonant clusters (bl, cr, fl, st, sl, bl & other 60+ possible beginning and ending blends) *as* unique letter/sound units. It *adds hundreds of additional combinations* for the child to learn. Teach the necessary single sounds and blending skills and the child can then read all possible combinations. For example by knowing and blending 6 sounds (a e m n d t) the child can sound out 10 different common combinations (am, an, ad, at, and, em, en, ed, et, end). At best, teaching blended consonant and word family units is an inefficient and indirect way to teach blending skill. However, the serious concern is these incorrect representations actually may create reading difficulties in *some* students. Problems arise when children adopt a strategy of memorizing the cluster groups as visual units instead of processing each sound. Not only is the sheer number of combinations overwhelming but the visual similarities between the clusters make "what it looks like" strategies difficult for a child to master (such as bl, pl, lb, ld). In addition, if children hop around within words searching for familiar clusters and word families, they often confuse left-to-right tracking and sounding out skills. They inappropriately pull out word family combinations such as 'it' from wait, 'in' from coin, and 'ag' from page. These blended consonant clusters and word family units encourage some students to skip processing all letters. Children who learn with consonant clusters frequently insert blended sounds when they are not present. They read camp as 'clamp', tack as 'track', fake as 'flake', tide as 'tride', and set as 'sent'. Because they learned the cluster as a unit they actually 'see' the cluster when it is not there. These difficulties are all actual errors made by children taught with word family and consonant cluster techniques.

It is simpler, more effective and prevents potential reading problems to teach children necessary sounds and develop phonemic awareness and blending skills to combine all sounds. Children do need direct practice handling blended consonants sounds. Practice blended consonants as processing and blending the individual sounds NOT by clusters. For example, teach 'flap' as blending /f/ /l/ /a/ /p/ NOT /fl/ /a/ /p/. Same with "word families"; teach blending individual sounds /s/ /a/ /t/ NOT /s/ /at/. Word families and blended consonant clusters are inaccurate representations of our language. These shortcuts can bypass the process of careful attention to detail, and unintentionally create reading difficulties in some children. Attention to phonetic accuracy is important in building a strong foundation for reading success.

14. Guided Oral Reading is Essential: Guided reading is reading out loud to an adult, or other proficient reader, with feedback. It is *not* independent silent reading. The key component is 'guided'. Correction and instruction help the child learn and improve skills. Validated research shows guided out loud reading has significant beneficial impact on word recognition, fluency and comprehension across a range of grade levels.[9] Guided reading benefits both good and struggling readers. In contrast, silent independent reading may *not* actually improve reading skills for beginning readers. Numerous studies show the best readers read the most and poor readers read the least. However, these studies are correlational. Good readers may simply spend more time reading. Although it sounds like a good idea to have students read more alone, there is *no* research evidence showing *independent silent reading* improves reading skills. If children sit flipping pages and making errors, their skills will not improve. In contrast, *guided* oral reading helps children improve skills. This is NOT saying children should not read to themselves, or there are no benefits for children looking at books, or students do not need to read more. Rather, it says *to improve skills*, particularly in learning stages, children need to read *out loud with feedback*. At more advanced levels, silent reading does improve the higher skills of fluency, comprehension and vocabulary. Guided reading has a *significant* beneficial impact on developing reading skills and should be a part of reading instruction. Guided reading is an integral part of the *Right Track Reading Lessons*.

15. Develop Fluency: Fluency is the 'fast' or 'automatic' reading where words appear to be almost instantly recognized. Fluent readers read quickly and accurately without effort. Fluency is the objective of phonologic decoding. The critical information to keep in mind for effective reading instruction is fluency or 'fast reading' is developed word by word based on repeated accurate phonologic processing of specific words. To build fluency, the child must *first* read by correct, accurate phonologic processing (sounding out the word). This foundation of correct phonologic processing is the essential precursor to develop fluency. Children do not become 'fluent readers' overnight but rather build fluency word-by-word over time. With repeated practice correctly reading individual words, the child adds to his storehouse of 'fast'/fluent words. Guided reading builds fluency. Practice to build fluency is incorporated into the *Right Track Reading Lessons* as words are repeatedly included for reading practice in the word lists and sentences.

---

[9] National Reading Panel's "Teaching Children to Read" Summary Report www.nationalreadingpanel.org/publications/summary.htm

16. Teach Strategies for Handling Multisyllable Words: It is more difficult to process multisyllable words than simple one syllable words. The majority of English words are multisyllable so it is critical for children to acquire strategies to read them effectively. A reading program should include both direct instruction and guided practice in handling multisyllable words. Direct practice with common affixes is also effective in helping students learn how to handle multisyllable words. Spelling can also be used as an effective tool for learning how to process these longer words.

17. Expand Vocabulary Knowledge: Expanding a student's vocabulary knowledge is important to reading development. Vocabulary instruction leads to gains in comprehension. A comprehensive reading program needs to include vocabulary development. Children acquire vocabulary both incidentally through exposure and through direct vocabulary instruction. It has been shown various techniques designed to directly build vocabulary are effective in expanding vocabulary knowledge and improving reading comprehension. Optimal learning occurs when vocabulary instruction involves a combination of different techniques.

18. Directly Develop Reading Comprehension Skills: Comprehension if deriving meaning from text. Parents and teachers can take direct actions to help children develop specific comprehension skills and strategies. While readers acquire some comprehension strategies informally, explicit or formal instruction in the application of comprehension strategies has been shown to be highly effective in enhancing understanding.[10] These strategies help children think about, remember, and understand what they are reading. Comprehension strategies are effective for non-impaired readers. Remember, if the child has decoding difficulties you need to *first* establish the necessary fundamental decoding skills of proficient phonologic processing. Otherwise the difficulty decoding will likely inhibit the development of the more advanced comprehension. Children may have no difficulty decoding but struggle with comprehension and need direct instruction in developing comprehension skills. Reading programs should include direct instruction in developing comprehension skills. The majority of comprehension development can be accomplished as a part of guided reading.

19. Practice reading: Read! Read! Read! Daily reading is essential. Children should read a *minimum* of 20 minutes a day. Of course, more is better! In learning stages the majority of reading time should be guided reading (out loud with feedback) of decodable text. As the child's skills develop, reading will shift primarily to independent silent reading.

In general children should read level appropriate material. Obviously, 'appropriate' is a relative term and a child's reading level will change and advance as age and skills advance. The appropriateness of material also varies, depending if the child is reading alone or reading outloud with feedback. Multiple formal methods and systems for evaluating and rating 'reading level' exist. Most are based on readability factors such as vocabulary, number of multisyllable words, sentence length and structure, grammar, and complexity of story plot. A few rating systems consider suitability of the content. Many of these systems provide numerical ratings to evaluate and compare books. These technical methods attempt to provide objective information on the actual 'reading level' of a particular book. The reading level needs to be considered relative to the individual's skills to determine what is 'appropriate' for the child. In addition to the formal methods, you can simply listen to your child read and then adjust material to fit. The following simple rule of thumb can be used to help you determine if a book is the appropriate reading level for a particular student at a certain time and situation:

Independent level: This is material the student can read with few errors. If the student makes only a few errors on a page the material is at the independent level. This 'easy' or independent level is ideal for silent reading.

Instructional level: The learning level material is where the student reads with some errors and skill building. If the student makes 4 or more errors per page the material is considered instructional level. This instructional or learning level is ideal for guided reading so you can help the child develop skills.

Frustration level: This is where the material is really 'too hard' or advanced. The student makes frequent errors in every paragraph. It is best to avoid frustration level material by selecting another book. If frustration level material must be read, it is should be read as guided reading with assistance.

When a child learns to read proficiently, he should be able to read all grade level material. In other words, a 2nd grader might not be able to read *Eragon* but should be able to read *My Father's Dragon*. A 6th grader may have difficulty reading a college level physics textbook but should not struggle with her middle school science textbook or other classroom material. If grade level material is consistently not 'appropriate' for your child, chances are the child is lacking necessary decoding skills and need direct instruction in developing the necessary phonologic processing skills.

---

[10] National Reading Panel's "Teaching Children to Read" Summary Report www.nationalreadingpanel.org/publications/summary.htm

20. Share the joy of reading: And as always, share the joy of reading. Reading is wonderful. Children have a natural excitement about reading that can be tapped into. Teaching your child to read using a direct systematic phonics program does not preclude enjoyment and excitement with reading. In fact, it is the ability to read well that removes roadblocks and provides the route to reading enjoyment. The often quoted observation 'good readers' like to read and 'poor readers' do not enjoy reading is absolutely true. However, this is a correlational, not cause and effect, relationship. This tendency to spend time and enjoy what we are good at is simply human nature. Rarely do we 'enjoy' an activity we struggle at, make frequent frustrating errors and can only accomplish with difficulty. When children learn how to read they then are able to become 'engaged' and 'excited' about reading.

An effective reading program intentionally develops necessary proficient reader skills. Structured reading lessons teach your student *how* to read. However, the lessons alone will not ensure your child achieves a love of reading. Parents and teachers absolutely need to encourage and promote a love of reading. Expose students to a wide variety of literature. Help them discover the amazing wealth of information contained in books. Encourage children to read. Go to the library frequently. If he loves trains, let him pick out 14 train books. Help your daughter unpack the box of well worn favorite horse stories her aunt sent her. Give your child a flashlight so she can re-read all the *Little House* books under the covers after lights out. Read all the *RedWall* books with him so you can discuss the details of how the brave mouse warrior and his woodland friends defeat the evil horde of vermin. Read the newspaper sports page at breakfast. Look up information on how to take care of kittens. Read a nightly Bible verse. Read the same favorite book over and over. Enjoy books! However, do not skip the important step of carefully teaching your child *how* to read. Help your child become a 'good reader' so he or she is able to enjoy reading. Skilled reading is a key that unlocks the doors to limitless knowledge, enjoyment and adventure. Give your children this key by getting them on the right track to reading proficiency!

****

Action Plan to Get Your Child on Track to Reading Success

If your child is:

➤ **Pre-reader / Preschool** - Begin developing phonemic awareness, print awareness and alphabetic awareness. See Appendix F and **www.rigthttrackreading.com** for additional information.

➤ **Beginning Reader Kindergarten/1st Grade** - Use *Right Track Reading Lessons* effective direct systematic phonics program to establish phonologic processing pathways and directly build skills to develop proficient reading.

➤ **Novice reader in 1st/2nd grade needing to advance to higher level skills** – Directly build skills with *Right Track Reading Lessons*. Many novice readers have a foundation with basic sounds yet lack knowledge of the complete code including vowel and r-controlled vowel combinations and can not handle multisyllable words. This complete systematic phonics program ensures foundational phonologic processing, directly teaches the complete code complexities, develops skills in handling multisyllable words and helps the child advance skills.

➤ **Struggling with Reading** - Struggling readers are lacking essential skills and need direct effective intervention to develop necessary skills and build proficient reader neural pathways. Do not wait for the child to 'outgrow' his reading problems. Research data reveals this rarely happens. As students get older, difficulty reading handicaps them further in all subject areas. Continuing to read the 'incorrect' way, additional practice of incorrect strategies, or repeating a program that failed the child the first time around will NOT help the child overcome his difficulties. Intervene immediately with an effective direct systematic phonics program. If your struggling reader is 1st, 2nd, or a young 3rd grader, use *Right Track Reading Lessons*. If your struggling reader is 3rd grade or older, use *Back on the Right Track Reading Lessons*, an effective reading remediation program targeted specifically for older struggling readers. This program directly helps your struggling reader build the skills necessary for achieving reading success. If your child is struggling with reading/dyslexic please see the detailed article *How to Help a Student Overcome Reading Difficulties and Achieve Success* located at **www.righttrackreading.com/helpstudent.html**

*Important Note: If you have any concerns about a child's hearing, vision, development or other medical concern, the child must be evaluated by a doctor or other appropriate professional. If the child has difficulty hearing (for whatever reason from an ear infection to a physical disability) it significantly impacts phonemic awareness and the ability to tap into correct phonologic processors. Children with uncorrected vision impairment will have challenges seeing the print. Any and all medical concerns need to be addressed by medical professionals.

EXPLANATION AND SPECIFIC INSTRUCTIONS FOR
RIGHT TRACK READING LESSONS

A. Overall Structure and Format of the Reading Lessons

This program is arranged into carefully designed lessons structured for one-on-one individual instruction. The lessons use a variety of targeted multisensory activities to directly teach skills necessary for proficient reading. The activities systematically develop skills in phonemic awareness, knowledge of the complete phonetic code, directional tracking, smooth blending, attention to detail, and correct phonologic processing. Effective multisensory word building activities and extensive practice reading decodable text are integral components of the program. Advanced sections teach children to handle multisyllable words, build fluency, expand vocabulary and develop comprehension. A spelling section is also included.

The lessons directly teach skills in a deliberately planned sequence. Basic sounds are presented in the first lessons, followed by alternate vowel sounds, vowel combinations, r-controlled vowel combinations and other complexities. Essential tracking, blending and phonologic processing skills are developed throughout the program. The program is cumulative. The decodable text includes newly introduced sounds as well as continued practice applying previous sounds. The systematic presentation allows time for the student to learn, apply, practice and master skills.

The lessons incorporate a series of specific activities including direct instruction and practice of the sounds, sound writing, word making activities, guided reading of word lists and sentences, and writing words. Review lessons periodically provide additional review and practice of sounds and skills learned to date. All these activities are carefully designed to systematically develop specific skills. Directions for all activities are listed in subsequent sections.

Schedule for Reading Lessons: There is no instant remedy for teaching a child to read. It takes time for the child to build and acquire specific skills. The time you spend working with your child with effective instruction directly helps him build these skills. When teaching children, a consistent schedule is necessary to establish correct skills. Appropriate length for a reading session varies with the individual child. Generally a 20-30 minute session is appropriate for kindergarten, a 30 minute session for 1st grade and 30-45 min session for 2nd or 3rd graders. Although there will be variation in session length for individual students, a consistent schedule should be used. It is best to teach the child 4 or 5 sessions per week.

The lessons do not have to be completed in one session. However, be sure to complete each lesson before moving on the next lesson. Lesson length varies and individual lessons may take more than one session to complete. It is not a race. The goal is to effectively teach your child to read, not to finish the program of study in a certain time period. Do not skip lessons. The program design systematically teaches skills. If you skip lessons, you may miss directly teaching a necessary sound or practicing on an essential sub-skill. The lessons are cumulative, incorporating practice of previously learned sound. If you skip or go too fast, the child will not have time to practice and master the skills. Observe your child and make adjustments to meet the child's individual rate of learning. Repeat a lesson or portion of a lesson if the child has not yet mastered a skill or if he needs reinforcement. On the other hand, if the child masters a skill proceed at a faster pace (don't skip).

Consistency and practice is very important in the learning stages. If you are unable to conduct reading sessions 4 or 5 times a week be sure and include daily practice of the sounds in some other way. For example, practice the sound cards, play other sound games or conduct other activities. If you have long breaks between sessions, especially in the young beginner stages, the child often forgets much of what he has previously learned. A consistent program helps the child learn. In addition, the more time you spend the sooner your child will develop necessary skills.

Example of schedules for effective reading instruction:
- 5 year old: 20-30 min reading sessions 4 to 5 days/week with supplemental sound games on 'off' days
- 6 year old: 30 min reading sessions 4 to 5 days/week
- 7 or 8 year old: 30-45 min reading sessions 4 to 5 days/week
- 9 years old: 45 min sessions 5 days/week

B. Materials Needed

By design this reading program does NOT require purchase of expensive or complex supplemental materials. Everything you need to complete the lessons and activities is readily available and affordable. In addition to this book, you will need the following materials:

1. Paper and Pencil: Use regular loose-leaf paper and standard pencils. With younger children, use the wider primary lined tablets with the dashed middle line or pre-printed tracer letter pages. Free pre-printed tracer letter pages for all the basic sounds are available at **www.righttrackreading.com/tracerletterpages.html**

2. Sound Cards: "Sound cards" are used to teach and practice the sounds. To make "sound cards" simply write the letter/phonogram on an index card. For the letters and "buddy letters" with multiple sounds it is helpful to note a little 2 or 3 in the corner to remind the child how many sounds that phonogram represents. Index cards are inexpensive, so you can make several sets for practice in alternate locations such as in the car. Keep cards in a zip-lock bag or bound with a rubber band. Make the cards as you proceed through the lessons.

3. Sound Tiles/ Sound Tile Kit: The sound tiles are an integral part of the *Right Track Reading Lessons* Program. The sound tiles are an effective multisensory tool for allowing the student to 'see' and learn the correct phonetic structure of our language. Directions for making a complete tile set are provided. This complete set provides necessary tiles for conducting all word making activities in the lessons as well as double tiles of most sounds for additional multisensory activities such as sound bingo, stack the sounds, sound memory and other supplemental activities. The 'sound tile kit' includes the sound tiles and a template for word making stored within a plastic organizer box.

Sound tiles are made by printing the phonograms on 2" ceramic bathroom tiles with a permanent black marker using lower case normal/block style letters.

2" square ceramic bathroom tiles – Basic white 2" ceramic bathroom tiles are available at home improvement stores for approximately $2.50 for a sheet of 36 tiles. You need a total of 132 tiles for making a complete sound tile set. Therefore, it requires purchasing four sheets of the 2"-tiles. Each sheet contains 36 2"-inch tiles attached in a 12"x12" sheet with rubber tabs. I found it is easier to first break the tiles apart by bending them back and forth. After the tiles are separated, carefully trim off the excess rubber connection tabs with a pair of scissors. You can make 'sound tiles' from other materials such as thick cardstock. However, paper and other thin materials are difficult for children to pick up. The 2" ceramic tiles are ideal for manipulation.

A permanent black marker: Use a permanent marker to write the correct letter(s)/phonograms on the tiles using lower case normal block print style. I use a fine point *Sharpie* marker.

Make "Sound Tiles": Make the complete tile set by printing the following sounds/phonograms on the 2" white tiles with the permanent marker. Neatly print lower case standard block print style letters.

Make 2 tiles for the following sounds: a e i o u y   b c d f g h j k l m n p qu r s t v w x z th sh wh ck ch ing ink ay ai oy oi ea ee ow ou oa ue ew ui oo au aw or ore oar er ur ir ear ar are air eer

Make 1 tile for the sounds: tch ie ei ey oe augh igh ph wr kn oor our ere ire

A plastic organizer box with compartments large enough to hold the 2" tiles (Optional but highly suggested): The storage box needs compartments large enough to fit the 2"-tiles. A carrying handle is also a desirable feature. I have located several affordable storage box options, including a $5 tackle box at the sporting goods section of a large discount store to a slightly larger and studier $10 hardware/screw organizer at a home improvement store. While this box is not mandatory it highly recommended. I tried using an old shoebox and it was difficult to find the tiles needed for a specific lesson or activity. An organizer box is well worth the $10 investment.

Small labels (Optional but suggested): It is helpful to label compartments with small sticky labels so you can quickly find specific tiles. This is a convenient feature to help the adult who is teaching the lessons.

Suggested tile layout/organization for sound tile kit:

The grids on the chart below represent the compartments of an 18 compartment storage box. The kit includes two of each sound tile except for the single tiles indicated with *. Layout varies depending on the size and configuration of the storage box compartments. I tend to group tiles by categories including vowels, consonants, consonant digraphs, vowel combinations and r-controlled combinations. I arrange the consonants alphabetically and separate other groups by sound structure (For example, placing /er/ sounds er, ur, ir, ear together in the same compartment). Label compartments to help locate necessary tiles.

a e i	o u y	b c d f	g h j k	l m n p	qu r s t
v w x z	th sh wh ck	ch tch* ing ink	ay ai oy oi	ea ee ie* ei* ey*	ou ow oa oe*
oo ue ui ew	au aw augh* igh* ph* wr* kn*	or ore oar oor* our*	er ur ir ear	ar are air	eer ere* ire*

4. Template for Word Making: Make a template for 'word making' activities. This can be made from a piece of poster board approximately 18" long by 6" wide. When 'making words', you need to place tiles next to each other with no gaps between sound tiles. However, there needs to be a small gap on the template lines. An easy way to make the template is to place 7 tiles next to each other in a straight line and draw template lines slightly shorter than the tiles as to leave a slight gap between the template lines. Draw a large directional arrow under the tile-template to reinforce tracking.

5. A Place to Work: Find a quiet spot with adequate room to work. A table with two chairs is ideal. Sit next to the child so you can *see* and *hear* the child and provide immediate feedback with both positive encouragement and corrective instruction.

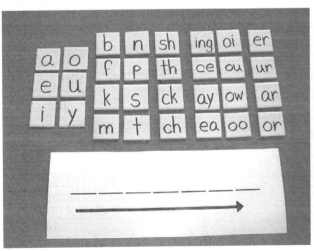

Sound Tiles and Template

Sound Tile Kit, Sound Cards & Template

C. General Instructions for the Lessons/ Apply Throughout all Activities

1. Always Make Immediate Corrections: Immediately correct any errors. Remember corrections are a positive action and a prime learning opportunity. It is essential to make immediate corrections so the child does not learn the wrong way. Ensure the child correctly performs the subskills of tracking, blending, and accurately pronouncing the sounds. All words need to be read correctly. When the child makes an error, stop him. Often all it takes is 'oops' or simply tapping the error on the page with a pencil so he looks closer at the word. If the child does not understand how to perform a skill or is lacking necessary sound knowledge then you must teach him before continuing. In beginning reading, correction is essential to help the child develop efficient processing pathways. Detailed explanations for correcting errors in the various activities are included in the next section (Section D Instructions for Specific Activities).

2. Use Understandable Terms: Remember, you are teaching children! When presenting information, always use understandable terms and explanations so the child comprehends the concept. Use terms such as 'sounds' and 'buddy letters'. Avoid the official technical linguistic terminology such as phoneme, digraphs, diphthongs, and phonograms that are meaningless to children as well as most adults. It is always clearer to say "this letter has the sound __" instead of "the alphabetic characters in this phonogram symbolize the phoneme __". It is better to say "please write the buddy letters 'sh' while you say the /sh/ sound" instead of saying "please encode the proper consonant digraph for the phoneme /sh/." This does not mean that you leave out all correct terminology, but rather you should explain in understandable terms and minimize unnecessary jargon. Keep it Simple! Help the child learn.

3. Directly and Systematically Teach 'Print = Sound' & PRACTICE These Sounds: Systematically present and directly teach the direct *printed letter(s) =sound* relationship. By design, the lessons include a variety of highly effective multisensory activities to help the child develop the automatic direct *print=sound* relationship necessary for efficient phonologic processing. Initial lessons directly teach the basic sounds, subsequent lessons add the vowel combinations, r-controlled vowel combinations and other complexities. The sound introduction, sound card practice and writing the sound activities all provide direct print=sound practice. The word making and word writing activities also reinforce this direct print=sound relationship. Remember this is not 'learning the alphabet'; it is the process of converting print to sound. Directly teach and practice the *printed letter(s)=sound* relationship. When practicing sounds make sure the child looks at the printed letter(s), pronounces the sound correctly, and tracks under the letter with his finger. Repeatedly practice this direct print=sound relationship until the child knows the sound(s) automatically. The *'printed letter=sound'* relationship must become automatic so the child can concentrate on higher skills. To achieve rapid retrieval/automatic knowledge, lots of direct print=sound practice, repetition, and reinforcement are necessary. Practice! Practice! Practice!

4. Pronounce all the Sounds Correctly: Correct pronunciation is critical. Always make sure *you can say the sound correctly* before teaching it to the child. This needs to be the sound the letter represents in our language NOT the letter name. The sound pronunciation table is found in Appendix A. The child needs to learn correct pronunciation.

5. Engrain Proper Left-to-Right Tracking: It is critical the child learns to always look at and process *all* letters *in order* from left-to-right. To develop proper tracking, this program requires the child physically follow under the words with his finger or another pointer. This physical tracking motion is crucial to help beginning readers engrain this essential skill and not make errors in processing order. In addition, the act of pointing helps the child focus attention on individual sounds.

Tell younger children to "Get out your reading finger" or "Use your finger". Explain to the child that their finger is a terrific tool for learning to read. If the child is uncomfortable using his finger, he can use a toothpick, pencil, or another pointer. However, always require the child to physically move his finger or pointer under the letters from left-to-right in all reading. This kinetic finger motion is the effective multisensory technique to directly establish proper tracking.

Directly teach, require and reinforce proper left-to-right directional tracking throughout the entire *Right Track Reading Lessons* program. In word making activities, have the child make words in order left-to-right. Never let the child make or write words out of order. When reading word lists and sentences have the child physically track under the words with his finger. Require the child to read word lists left-to-right across the rows. Do not let him read down the columns or skip around. After the reading program is completed, proper tracking is automatically applied and the child makes no tracking errors, the child 'outgrows' the need for physical tracking and the requirement for physical movement can be dropped.

6. **Directly Teach Smooth Blending Skills:** Smooth blending is an essential subskill to proficient reading. Many children automatically and easily blend sounds together smoothly. However, others need specific work to master this vital skill. *It is essential the child masters smooth blending in the initial stages.* If the child can not blend smoothly it will handicap his ability to process print phonologically and to develop fluency. In the beginning, take the time to ensure the child understands and develops smooth blending. Require the child to smoothly blend sounds together in all reading.

In the beginning, explain to the child the importance of smoothly blending sounds together when reading. Use age appropriate terminology. Blending can be explained as 'keeping sounds hooked together' or not 'chopping up' the sounds. For younger children who like trains, make an analogy to train cars coupled together. When train cars come 'unhooked' the train falls apart. Words are the same way, when we 'unhook' the sounds the word 'falls apart'. For older students, the straightforward explanation of 'smooth blending' is sufficient. Use whatever terms you wish, just be sure the child understands he must keep sounds hooked together so the word does not 'fall apart'. Demonstrate the *correct blending technique* of not pausing between the sounds. Say something like "listen to how you need to keep the sounds together without stopping when you sound out" and then sound out several words for the child.

It is vital the teacher always demonstrates correct smooth blending skills. Pay attention to how you sound out! Many adults inadvertently chop or segment sounds without realizing the child may pick up incorrect techniques. Always keep sounds hooked together smoothly. If the child does not remember an individual 'sound' point to and say the individual sound in isolation. Don't segment all sounds.

If the child is separating/chopping the sounds apart instead of smoothly blending them together, immediately *stop the child* and work on this critical skill. Never let the child learn and reinforce the detrimental habit of chopping sounds apart/segmenting sounds when reading. From the beginning, require smooth blending in all reading. Remind the child to 'hook the sounds together' when sounding out. Tell the child to 'take a breath' before sounding out a word. Intentional inhaling before starting a word helps the child get through the word before he has to pause for a breath. This reminder to 'take a breath' before starting to sound out a word is a temporary step to help the child develop blending. If that does not work, have the child *sing* the word to you. When the child sings the word, it is impossible to segment the sounds. I would like to thank my friend Sally who shared this simple yet highly effective technique with me. Singing is fabulously effective with children who struggle with blending. Singing forces the child to 'hook the sounds together' and helps the child develop smooth blending skills. If the child can not blend, STOP and work on supplemental oral sound blending exercises found in Appendix E. It is essential to develop smooth blending in the beginning.

When blending, remember sounds must always be pronounced correctly. Make sure the child does not distort sounds when 'stretching out' the word. Some sounds can be easily stretched out (m, f, s, a, i, o, e, l, n, r, v). Other sounds can *not* be stretched out (the 'fast' sounds b, d, t, h, k, g, p, ch) and must be hooked quickly to the next sound. Learning to smoothly blend these sounds is more difficult for some children and must be practiced. The lessons are designed to teach blending in a systematic manner. The initial lessons teach blending of simple consonant-vowel-consonant words followed later by two-consonant clusters. The trickier 3-consonant clusters are not added until Reading Lesson # 24.

7. **Directly Develop Phonemic Awareness (PA) Skills:** The lessons directly teach the child to recognize and distinguish the individual sounds within words and to link this phonemic awareness to print. Phonemic awareness segmenting skills are directly developed in the word making and word writing activities. The sound tiles are especially helpful in developing PA as the child is able to physically 'see' and physically manipulate the accurate sound structure of language. In all PA activities, help the child learn how to distinguish the sound structure within words. Specific instructions and corrections for developing PA are given in the directions for the word making and word writing activities

There is a progression of difficulty in developing PA skill. Help the child develop the simpler skills in distinguishing sounds and then systematically build the more difficult PA tasks. It is easiest to distinguish beginning sound. Then ending sounds followed by the middle sounds. Sounds that can 'stretch out' including /m/, /s/, /f/, /a/, /r/, /l/, /n/, /o/, /sh/ are easier to distinguish than the 'fast' or 'quick' sounds such as /t/, /d/, /b/, /k/, /g/, and /p/. Single consonants are easier to distinguish than blended consonants. The blended consonants with 'fast' sounds are the most difficult to distinguish. Children need direct practice on hearing and segmenting sounds within these more difficult combinations. Phonemic awareness skills to distinguish the individual sounds within these blended combinations is directly developed in the word making activities and in the word writing/spelling activities

8. Use Normal Print for Teaching Sounds and Writing: Use normal block print or similar straightforward manuscript print styles for all reading instruction activities. When writing letters on the sound cards and sound tiles, use lower case standard block print. Do not use cursive, italics or any loopy script crossover styles. This program uses the Zaner-Bloser manuscript print but other comparable styles are similarly effective.

The reason why it is best to use standard block print is primarily because the vast majority of reading material uses standard manuscript print styles. To read, children need to decode this standard print. For an adult proficient reader, changing print styles and fonts is irrelevant. However, for children who are just learning the code and have not developed neural processing pathways, alternative print styles create unnecessary complications and challenges. Teach the child in the same straightforward print styles he will encounter in the majority of printed material.

Straightforward manuscript print styles also prevent potential problems with letter confusion and related reading errors from confusing visually similar letters. In standard block print style letters remain fairly distinct from each other except for the notorious difficulties with visually similar b, d and p (Effective techniques for addressing, preventing and correcting this common letter confusion are found in Appendix C). In contrast, when loopy script cursive-crossover styles are used *additional* letters become harder to distinguish. Loopy script cursive-crossover print styles create additional letter confusion and can make reading more difficult for some children. I have observed numerous examples of letter confusion I strongly believe are created by this loopy style of writing. Children who learn a loopy-crossover 'k' often confuse k and h and consequently also mix up 'ch' and 'ck'. This is reflected in reading errors with mixing up /k/ & /h/ and /k/ & /ch/ sounds. Loopy-crossover print styles also create letter confusion with i, j and l. These letters are distinct in regular block print but appear similar and are a frequent source of confusion when loopy script *i j l* is used. I recommend avoiding the loopy cursive-crossover style of print because I have witnessed frequent letter confusion and reading errors made by children instructed in these styles. These specific types of letter confusion and related reading errors with k-h, ck-ch, and i-j-l rarely occur in students who learn block print. Make it easier for the child to learn and prevent problems with letter confusion and related reading errors by teaching standard block print.

9. Emphasize Lower Case Letters in Reading Instruction: This program directly teaches and uses lower case letters in reading instruction because in actual reading, most print is comprised of lower case letters. In a typical sentence only the first letter and proper names are capitalized. Reading predominately requires processing lower case letters. For example, in the previous section #8 on using manuscript print there are over 2,200 letters and only 28 are capitalized. In most reading approximately 98-99% of letters are lower case. Even in short simple sentences, around 90-95% of letters are lower case. Learning lower case print aids the child in processing the letters he will encounter in the majority of text.

Use lower case print for direct print=sound instruction, practice with sound cards, sound writing activities, and with sound tiles. Although this program uses lower case letters in the majority of instruction, the appropriate use of capital letters absolutely *is* incorporated into all word lists and sentences. From the very beginning, children need to be exposed to and learn appropriate use of capital letters. It is detrimental for learning to expose the child to incorrect usage. Always use capital letters to start sentences and proper names. In understandable terms, explain to the child the concept of capital letters and appropriate use of capital letters. While this program emphasizes lower case print for learning the sounds, the child does still need to learn their capital letters. I have found most children have learned or are learning their capital letters in other instruction. If a child does not recognize the capital letters, take the time and directly teach the child the required capital letters. Please see information for teaching capital letters in Appendix D.

D. Instructions for Specific Activities

Right Track Reading Lessons includes a variety of carefully designed multisensory activities to directly teach and develop skills necessary for proficient reading. The following summary gives specific directions on how to conduct these activities. This section is organized by activity and includes instructions for conducting the activity, an explanation of the specific skills the activity targets, and suggested corrections. A few additional activities are described so you can supplement the lessons and provide additional practice and reinforce skills. Note: Although lessons provide scripted wording, there is flexibility to use your own words as long as you do not alter the design of the program including direct instruction, correct sounding out, left-to-right tracking, proper blending, and immediate correction of errors. Scripted instructions help start you with correct techniques.

1. Teaching the Sounds

The lessons systematically introduce and directly teach the complete phonemic code. The initial lessons directly teach basic sounds, subsequent lessons add vowel combinations, r-controlled vowel combinations and other complexities. This activity introduces the printed letter (or partner letters) = sound relationship and directly links the visual image of the print to the oral and auditory process of saying and hearing the sound.

New sounds are listed at the beginning of lessons. When you first introduce a sound: Point to the print and say "This sound is __" or "this letter has the sound __". Teach correct pronunciation (See Appendix A). When you first introduce any multi-letter sound (such as th, ch, sh), explain how the letters are "buddies" that work together to make a sound. Use an understandable term such as "buddy letters" or "partner letters" so the child understands the concept. Once the child understands the direct relationship between print and sound you can skip explanation and simply point at the print and say the sound. Teach the sound to the child by saying the sound a few times as you follow under the print with your finger. Next have the child say the sound correctly, *as* he looks at the print and follows under the sound with his finger. He must be looking at the printed letter on the page *as* he says the sound NOT parroting the sound while looking at you. Directly link the visual image of the print to the oral and auditory process of saying and hearing the correct sound. If the child says the sound incorrectly, the correction is to stop the child and have the child repeat the sound correctly.

Directly teach the correct sound for each newly introduced phonogram:
- Tell the child the correct pronunciation of the sound.
- The child points at the print and says the sound correctly.

2. Practice Sound Cards OR other 'fun games' to practice print=sound

The next activity in most lessons is practicing sound cards (index cards with sound written on it). The sound cards directly teach and provide practice of the *printed letter=sound association*. Make a card for each new phonogram using lower case normal block print. Use these sound cards as flash cards. The child practices newly introduced as well as previous sounds until the print=sound knowledge is automatic. This simple but highly effective multisensory activity directly links the visual image of the print to the oral and auditory processes of saying and hearing the correct sound.

In all practice, the child must *look directly at the printed letter while saying the correct sound out loud.* To be effective make sure the child:
- Looks directly at the printed letter (visually processing the print)
- Says sound out loud with correct pronunciation (says and hears correct sound)
- Follows under the sound with directional finger tracking (tracking and focus)
- Practices all sounds. If the phonogram has alternate sounds, make sure the child practices all sounds and properly pronounces each distinct sound separately. For example the sounds for 'o' are /o/, /oa/ & /u/ NOT /o-oa-u/ together in one breath.

Practicing sounds in isolation helps the child acquire automatic print=sound knowledge so he can effortlessly apply this knowledge in the process of sounding out words. To develop automatic print=sound knowledge, the child *must* be looking at the correct print while saying/hearing the sound. Chanting the sound while looking out the window is not effective. Repeated practice and drill with these sound cards is necessary to achieve the goal of *automatic recognition and knowledge of printed letter=sound*. Index cards are inexpensive. Make several sets. Practice frequently. The more practice, the quicker the child gains automatic knowledge. Once a sound is automatically known, the child no longer needs to practice that sound in isolation and it can be removed from the practice stack.

Direct practice and drill with the printed letter(s) = sound can be accomplished with a variety of fun age appropriate games. Not only are these options are a terrific way to get young children to practice and build automatic knowledge of the phonemic code but they are also lots of fun. **Fun 'Sound Games' with sound cards and sound tiles include**:
- **"Fishing for Sounds"**: Cut out index cards or cardstock in the shape of fish. Write the letter(s) on the fish. Your child 'catches' the fish. If the child knows the sound, he can keep the fish. See how many fish he can catch. You can even make a 'fishing pole' with a stick, string and small clothespin.

- **"Catching Sound Butterflies"**: Cut out the index cards or cardstock in the shape of butterflies. Write the letter(s) on the 'butterflies'. Give your child a small goldfish net and let her 'catch' the sound butterflies. She can keep the 'sound butterflies' that she knows!

- **"Collecting Sound Cars"**: Cut out the index cards or cardstock in the shape of cars. Write the letter(s) on the cars. The child collects the sound cars when he says the correct sound!

- **"Herding Sound Horses"**: You guessed it! Cut out the index cards in the shape of horses. The child sees how big of a horse herd she can round up. All she needs to do to herd a horse is to say the sound correctly! She can even collect her herd in a 'corral' or 'barn'.

- **"Go Fishing Card Game"**. Write the sounds on the cards. Have the child ask "do you have an /__/" (say the sound). For example "Do you have a /s/?" No, go fish! Yes, hand it over!

- **"Stack the sounds"**: Turn the sound tiles over. Have the child pick a tile up. When the child knows the sound, he can keep the tile. See how high he can build his stack.

- **"Sound Memory"**: play the traditional memory game except the child needs to match sounds. Every time he turns over a tile, he must say the sound. When he locates the matching sounds he can keep the set.

- **"Sound Bingo"**: Make bingo cards with 3x3 or 4x4 grids with the letter(s) your child needs to practice written on the squares. Then call out the sounds (not letter names). For example, do you have /s/, do you have /m/, do you have /th/...etc. Use the 'sound tiles' or make 'bingo chips' with the letters printed on them. The child must find and match the correct 'sound tile' or bingo chip to the correct bingo square AND the child must say the correct sound!

Teaching with carefully targeted direct instruction activities absolutely can be fun. Use you imagination and come up with variations your child enjoys. If he likes basketball, write the sounds on paper 'basketballs' and let him 'dunk' the sounds he says correctly. If it a nice day, go outside with sidewalk chalk and play 'sound hopscotch'. Write sounds on the driveway and practice basketball dribble drills over the sounds. As long as the **child directly looks at the accurate printed letter(s) AND says the correct sound** the activity effectively builds the necessary print=sound relationship. Have fun with your child! The article *Free, Fun, and Highly Effective Games You Can Play With Your Child to Directly Teach Automatic Knowledge of the Phonemic Code* contains descriptions and photographs of effective games. This article can be found at **www.righttrackreading.com/funcodegames.html**

3. Write and Say the Sound

A highly effective multisensory activity for directly learning the *'printed letter=sound'* relationships is to write the letter while saying the sound. In this paper and pencil activity, the child writes each sound at least 5 times (or more) while saying the sound. This simple act of printing the letter(s) while saying the sound effectively and efficiently establishes a direct link between print and sound. To be effective the child must *say the sound* as he prints the letter. The sound writing activity teaches new sounds and allows practice of previous sounds.

The effectiveness of 'writing the sounds' cannot be emphasized enough. This simple yet highly effective multisensory activity forces the child to develop an efficient direct link between print and sound. The multisensory processes of the kinetic motion of forming the letter, the visual image of seeing the completed print, the oral process of saying the correct sound, and auditory processes of hearing the sound are all linked and targeted toward directly developing the essential automatic print=sound knowledge of the phonemic code necessary for proficient reading. Anytime the child does not automatically remember a sound, have him *repeatedly write the phonogram while saying the sound*. It works! As with sound cards, after sound knowledge is automatic the child no longer needs to practice writing the sound in isolation.

When 'writing the sounds', it is important to use standard block print styles and emphasize correct letter formation. For young children who are just learning their letters or have difficulty with accurate letter formation, I highly recommend tracing over pre-printed dashed tracer letters. It is much more effective for a child to trace letters correctly than it is for the child to write letters incorrectly. Emphasize correct formation and neatness will improve with practice and as fine motor skills develop with age. Tracer letters help the child learn correct formation form the beginning! Free pre-printed tracer letter pages for all the basic sounds are available at **www.righttrackreading.com/tracerletterpages.html**. Formation is especially critical with the similar appearing letters b, d and p. Explicit instruction and careful attention to how these letters are formed helps the child learn to distinguish the difference between these visually similarly letters and prevent the common confusion that occurs in both reading and writing. Please see the letter formation instructions in Appendix C.

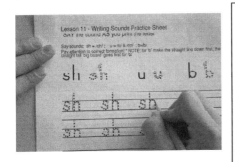

Although it does not replace essential paper and pencil practice, mix in supplemental sound formation activities. Go outside and have the child write the sounds with sidewalk chalk. Write the sounds with finger paint or in flour. Make and trace texture letters. Have fun with writing sounds. Just be sure letter formation is correct and the child says the sound while he writes or traces the letter.

4. Review Sounds

The sound review activity is periodically incorporated into the lessons. The sound review lists all the sounds previously learned. The child points under each sound with his finger or a pointer and says the sounds, rapidly working through the listed sounds. This activity provides the child additional direct practice and reinforcement of the sounds. This quick review is also designed to show the instructor which sounds the child may need additional practice with. If a child does not automatically know one of the sounds on the review list, provide additional practice for that sound (practice sound cards and practice writing/saying sound). Conversely, if the sound is automatic, it no longer needs to be practiced in isolation.

5. Making Words with the Sound Tiles

The word making activity with the 'sound tiles' is an integral part of the *Right Track Reading* program. 'Sound tiles' allow the child to actually 'see' and physically manipulate the accurate phonemic structure of our language. The word making activity provides a tangible way to learn correct phonological processing. This multisensory activity forces the child to develop phonemic awareness, visualize sounds as proper printed units and physically combine these distinct printed sounds into words. By design, these activities integrate kinetic, visual and auditory processes to develop correct phonologic processing of the print. 'Sound tile' activities are highly beneficial in beginning reading as they directly teach and intentionally develop correct phonologic processing. As a bonus, these 'sound-tile' word construction games are fun.

Tell the child he is going to construct or make words by putting sounds together. The child listens to a spoken word, and then makes or constructs that word with the sound tiles. This activity develops direct sound=letter knowledge, phonemic awareness of segmenting the separate sounds within a word, proper blending and tracking skills, and requires the child use correct phonologic processing.

Take out the appropriate sound tiles listed in the lesson and lay them above the template. It is helpful to sort the tiles into slightly separated groups of vowels, consonants, partner letters, and r-controlled vowel combinations. The child doesn't see the listed words but rather listens carefully as you tell him the word you want him to make. For the first lesson, demonstrate how to make one of the words correctly on the template with proper sounding, blending and finger tracking.

Say "Please make the word ____". Read the first word, speaking clearly and repeating the word at least once. If necessary, speak slowly and emphasize the sounds. The child repeats the word and then starts making it. Make sure he says the individual sounds as he lays down the tiles, makes the word in order and uses proper smooth blending skills. After he completes the word, have him sound out the word using finger tracking and smooth blending skills. Correct any errors and give short encouraging remarks. Clear all the tiles before reading the next word on the list to the child.

In all word making activities, ensure the child:
1) Says the individual sounds out loud as he picks up/lays down the appropriate tiles.
2) Always works from left-to-right. Never let the child make a word out of order.
3) Blends the sounds together smoothly.
4) Accurately sounds out the word with finger tracking after completing the word with the tiles.

The following illustrations demonstrate examples of the word making activity.

> Use Sound Tiles... u i ee ay d(2) g m n p r s t w ch ing
>
> Word List: speech midway greeting indeed stingray praying unseen

Lay out the template and the appropriate sound tiles listed in the lesson. Notice the separated grouping of vowels, consonants and partner letters. Separating/sorting tiles when laying them out helps the child find sounds.

Ask the child to make the first word on the list. For example, say "Please make the word 'speech'". The child does not see the printed word, he only hears it. The child 'makes' the word by translating sounds to print as he selects and places appropriate tiles on the template. The child says the sounds (not letter names) out loud as he makes the word in order from left-to-right. After completing the word, the child reads the word to you with finger tracking and smooth blending.

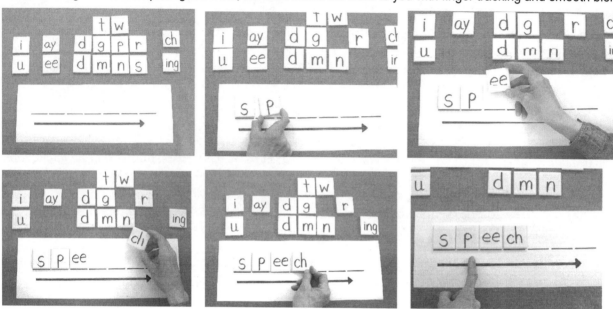

Clear the template completely and ask the child to make the next word on the list. For example, "Please make the word 'midway'". The child makes the word by translating sound-to-print in placing the correct tiles on the template. Once again when the word is completed, the child reads the word with finger tracking and smooth blending.

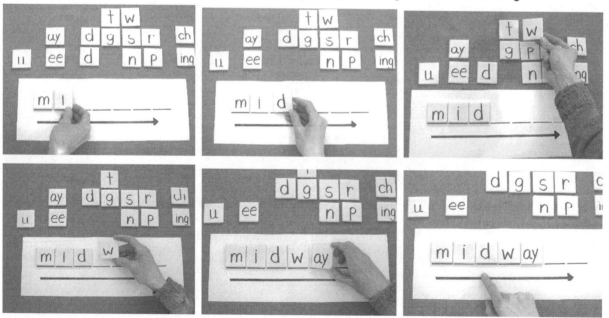

Stop and correct any errors as the child makes these words. Specific corrections are given on subsequent pages.

This effective multisensory word making activity directly helps the child develop correct phonologic processing of print!

Immediately correct any errors in the word making activity. It is essential to correct to help the child learn necessary skills. **The following section lists errors and effective correction techniques:**

- **Child has difficulty hearing the sounds**: Children with a phonemic weakness often have a difficult time hearing the individual sounds within a word. Help the child hear these sounds by speaking slowly and clearly and repeating the word at least one time. If necessary, slow the word down and emphasize sounds. By 'slowing down' the word, the child is better able to hear the individual sounds. I tell the child when a car drives by slowly it is easier to describe the car than when it drives by fast. Words are similar to cars. If you 'slow down' the word it is easier to hear the sounds. Remind the child to "listen carefully". Speak slowly and clearly. Individuals such as myself who tend to talk too fast need to intentionally slow down. Also make sure you keep the sounds smoothly blended together (continuous as one word). Do not segment the sounds. For example say 'run' slowly as /rrruuunn/ not a choppy /r/…/u/…/n/. You are stretching the word, not chopping it apart. Also be sure and pronounce sounds correctly when you slow down/stretch out the word. The 'fast' sounds can not be stretched out. As the child's phonemic awareness skills develop you can gradually return speaking rate back to normal speed.

- **Child has difficulty distinguishing specific sounds**: Certain sounds are harder for children to distinguish. These closely related sounds are especially difficult for younger children and children with weaker phonemic awareness. Examples of closely related sounds that are harder to distinguish include: /t/-/d/, /b/-/p/, /k/-/g/, /e/-/i/ and /f/-/v/-soft /th/. This is why in speaking young children will say 'baff' for bath or 'haf' for have. They have not yet developed the phonemic awareness to distinguish these closely related sounds. Please see the notes at the end of Appendix A on tips for sound pronunciation for some of these similar sounds. If the child makes a word with the incorrect closely related sound, stop the child. Say something like "oops, that was close. Listen carefully, you need to make the word ____" and repeat the word emphasizing the sound they are having a hard time distinguishing. Often if you simply say "listen carefully" and emphasize the sound it helps the child distinguish it correctly. For example, you give the child the word 'mess' and he makes the word 'miss'. Say "oops, you made miss", "listen carefully, you need to make the word 'mess'". Be sure and emphasize the /e/ sound when you repeat the word. Help the child learn to distinguish these sounds. For some of the sounds, it is helpful to have the child look at you as you say the word/sounds. This helps with the soft /th/-f-v sounds. Supplemental activities for distinguishing the tricky /e/ and /i/ are included in Appendix F. These types of activities can also be conducted with other sounds.

- **Child picks up incorrect tile:** If the child picks up the wrong tile stop him with an 'oops' and ask him what the sound tile says. Is he hearing the sound within the word incorrectly or does he not know the *letter=sound* relationship or did he just accidentally grab the wrong tile? In addition, require the child use the correct tile/phonogram. For example, if a word has the /th/ sound the child must use the 'th' tile not the 't' tile laid next to the 'h' tile.

- **Child makes word out of order:** Stop the child immediately. Say something like "oops, you have to make the word by sound'. Have him start over, saying the sounds as he lays the tiles down.

- **Child misses a sound in making the word or has difficulty with blended consonants:** When making words the child will often leave a sound out. These missed sounds frequently occur with the blended consonants. It is more difficult for a child to segment or split apart these sounds than it is to read/blend them together. The child may read the word 'trap' without hesitation but when asked to make the word he writes "tap". He needs work on hearing and segmenting these blended consonant sounds that are more closely 'glued' together. Specific attention needs to be given to the blended consonant combinations as it is more difficult to distinguish and segment these sounds, especially the blended sounds starting with "fast" sounds such as b, c, d, t (for example dr, tr, cl, br). If he leaves a sound out, stop him and have him read the word he made to you. For example, the child will make the word "string" as "sting". Say, "This word says 'sting' how would you make it say 'string'?" Help him learn to hear and distinguish the sounds. Make corrections so the student learns and weak skills are strengthened. Making words with blended consonants helps the child develop the phonemic awareness necessary for reading and spelling.

The child does *not* need to make all listed words in each lesson. Modify the word making activity to strengthen specific skills by selecting words from the list containing sounds the student needs to work on. Pick and choose words. If the child has difficulties distinguishing 'fast' blended consonant sounds then give words with those combinations. Include words with new sounds and words containing sounds the child is having difficulty with. The intent of this activity is to build specific skills. By selecting certain words you can modify the activity to best meet the child's individual needs. Likewise, if the child's skills with certain sounds are well established it is not necessary to make all the listed words. You may also supplement this activity by creating your own word building lists. Just be sure you include only sounds that have been previously introduced. Take care to avoid including confusing sounds on the same list/group (such as having c, k and ck all available for selection in same set). You never want the child to practice making a word incorrectly.

6. Sound Changing Activity (or other phonemic manipulation activities)

This is another word making activity with the sound tiles, except the child listens and determines how he needs to change the word one sound at a time instead of starting over. This sound changing activity gives the child direct practice in hearing and manipulating sounds, develops phonemic awareness skills, provides practice with the letter=sound relationship, and establishes correct phonologic processing. This also directly teaches the child how important each and every letter is in a word. The importance of attention to detail is demonstrated. One sound changes the entire word. Once again, the physical manipulation of the sound structure of language is especially beneficial in beginning reading.

Explain this sound tile activity is similar to the previous word making except instead of starting over each time, the child *listens carefully* and only changes one sound to make the new word. Remind the child to listen carefully so he hears what sound to change. The first time you conduct this activity, demonstrate what you are asking him to do.

Say, "Please make the word ___ for me". Tell the child the first word listed. Make sure he makes the word correctly using the techniques given in the word making activity. Then say something similar to "Great Job! You made ___." "Now please change a sound to make the word ___ (say the next word on the list)". Be sure the child says the sounds as he picks up the tiles, makes words from left-to-right, and blends the sounds together correctly. Make immediate corrections if the child makes an error. When the word is completed, have the child read the word to you. With this activity, do not clear the tiles. Leave the word in place and have the child make the necessary changes to make the next word.

For example, if the sound changing activity gives the words "bit > but > shut": The child would make 'bit' as described in the word making activity. After the child reads 'bit', ask the child to change it to 'but'. The child listens and makes the change removing the 'i' and replacing it with 'u'. The child points at the completed word and reads 'but' to you before you say the next word 'shut'. Once again the child listens and makes the necessary change, changing the /b/ sound to /sh/ by replacing the 'b' with 'sh'. This word changing continues through the list of words.

You can also conduct other sound changing activities with the tiles. Have the child make a word and then ask the child to make specific changes to it. For example: "Please make the word 'trap'. Now what word would you have if you changed the /a/ to /i/?" "Make the word "string", now what word would it be if you took out the /r/ sound". If you made the word 'paint' and then changed the 'ai' to 'oi' sound what word would you have. If the child needs extra work in developing phonemic awareness, these types of sound manipulation activities with the tiles are a terrific method to directly develop necessary phonemic awareness skills. When making your own sound changing games, be sure to only use decodable words made up of the sounds your child has already learned.

7. Reading Word Lists

The *Right Track Reading Lessons* program makes extensive use of decodable word lists to directly teach and provide guided practice of accurate phonetic decoding. These word lists are effective in beginning reading because they force the child to develop and use correct skills. Reading isolated words in a list develops necessary phonologic processing skills as the child must look carefully at all the sounds and use correct processing. Words cannot be guessed from pictures or context clues. Incorrect strategies will not work with random word lists. In other words, the child must sound out the words! Not only are the decodable word lists are an extremely effective tool for developing and practicing correct phonologic processing these word lists provide the guided practice essential to building proficiency.

The child reads *all* listed words in each lesson with your guidance and feedback. The words are decodable consisting only of sounds the child has systematically learned. The word lists are cumulative, incorporating all previously taught sounds. Guided reading of these decodable word lists is where the child learns and practices integrating and applying fundamental subskills in blending, tracking, knowledge of the code and attention to detail in the process of correctly sounding out the words. The child reads all the listed words in each lesson. To develop correct skills:

- **Directly teach and require proper directional tracking**. The student needs to physically follow under the word with either his finger or a pointer as he reads each word. Once again, this physical movement directly develops correct tracking skills and is especially critical with beginners who have not acquired this essential subskill of proficient reading. The physical pointing also helps the child focus on specific sounds. In addition, to reinforce proper tracking, always have the child read the word lists in order from left-to-right across the rows. Do not let the child read down the columns or jump around the page randomly reading words.

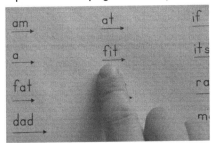 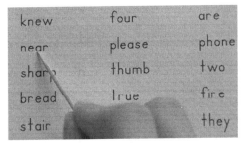

- **Directly teach and require proper smooth blending**. This word reading activity is where the child learns how to smoothly blend sounds together when sounding out words. Require smooth blending in all word reading. *Smooth blending is critical!* If the child has problems blending, have him take a breath before starting the word or have him 'sing' the word to you so that sounds do not fall apart. Do not allow choppy segmented sounding out. From the very beginning, be sure smooth blending is acquired, practiced and mastered. Please see the complete directions for #6 directly teach smooth blending on page 27. It is imperative smooth blending is established in the beginning!

- **Always require completely accurate decoding of all listed words. Teach careful attention to detail.** Emphasize accuracy in the word reading. The child must read the word correctly. If the child misses a sound or adds a sound, stop the child and have him look again. Even minor errors like saying 'run' for 'runs' must be corrected as the child needs to learn to carefully look at each and every sound. This emphasis on accuracy is critical for building proficient reader skills. By design the word lists help the child develop and practice attention to detail because random words cannot be read correctly without careful sounding out. Teaching the child to pay attention to details and decode accurately is critical for building proficient reader skills.

Immediately correct any errors. Make sure the child reads each word accurately! It is essential to stop the child as soon as he makes any error. A quick "oops", "stop" or simply tapping the word with your pencil is often sufficient to get the child to look carefully. The teacher should keep a pencil in hand during this word reading for pointing, corrections and assistance. The author personally prefers a mechanical pencil as the lead can be retracted and the fine point allows precise pointing at specific sounds. When the child makes an error, use the pencil tap as the silent "oops, look again" signal. Pencil marks can be used to help the child learn specific skills (for example d-b-p correction). After you stop the child, always have the child re-read the word correctly. Specific errors and suggested corrections are listed below:

- **Choppy sounding out:** If the child is segmenting sounds, stop the child immediately and teach him to smoothly blend the sounds together. See the directions for #6 Directly Teach Smooth Blending on page 27

- **Child says the sound incorrectly or does not know a sound**: If the child attempts to read a word and does not remember a sound or can not recall the sound without significant effort, he often says the sound incorrectly or pauses. Stop the child and have him look again. If the word contains a newly introduced sound the child does not yet know automatically, you may need to say 'remember this sound is __" as you point to the sound. If the child misses the same sound several times, stop reading the word list and go back and practice this particular sound in isolation. The child needs to know the individual sounds in order to correctly decode the word. Some children need a few days practicing a new sound in isolation before they can apply it in decoding words. If your child needs this additional practice, introduce new sounds and incorporate sound practice a few days prior to starting the lesson for that sound.

- **Attention to detail errors, missing sounds in the word or adding nonexistent sounds to the word or other minor mistakes:** When the child makes an error in the details of the word, stop the child and have him look again. You can tap the page or say 'oops' or 'look carefully' and point to the specific error. Attention to detail errors may include saying a sound that is not actually in the word (reading 'tip' as 'trip' or 'sting' as 'string'), leaving off details (reading 'runs' as 'run'), leaving out sounds (reading 'hunt' as 'hut') or other errors that are close but not quite correct (reading 'rot' as 'rat', or 'rust' as 'rush'). These types of errors can be summarized as not looking carefully at the word. If necessary, use your pencil tip to point at the exact sound that was missed or the specific error made. Always have the child re-read the word correctly. Correct so the child learns to pay attention to these details.

- **Child not recognizing buddy letters as a unit:** If the child is not recognizing the 'buddy letters' correctly within a word, stop the child and help him learn to 'see' the buddies. Signal 'oops-look again" with a tap. Then with your pencil lightly underline the phonogram. For example, if the child goes to sound out the word 'that' and starts by sounding out /t/+/h/ separately instead of /th/ or 'shop' as /s/+/h/ instead of the /sh/. Reach over and underline 'th' in 'that or 'sh' in 'shop'. The underline technique helps the child see these letters together as one sound. Also remind the child to "look closely at the buddy letters'". If the child makes repeated mistakes with newly introduced 'buddy letters', stop and practice writing the specific phonogram in isolation a few more times before reading the word list. If the child struggles with a new buddy letter combination, make several words with the sound tiles and have the child read these tile words before tackling the printed list. The child 'sees' the letters together as a unit on the single tile, making it easier to understand the 'buddy letter' concept and process these letters as one sound.

- **Errors with b, d, and p:** Switching the /b/, /d/ and /p/ sound are common errors caused by letter confusion between d, b and p. The child has not yet learned how to distinguish these visually similar letters. Correct to teach your child HOW to determine the difference between these letters. Stop the child with an 'oops' or tap and then take your pencil and trace either the 'doughnut'/round part for **d**, the 'board'/tall straight part for **b** or the ponytail/straight line going down for the **p**. By tracing and emphasizing these parts of the letters with pencil marks, you are showing the child to focus his attention on these distinguishing parts of the letter. Don't tell the child the correct sound. Have the child look at the motion you are making with your pencil, and determine the correct sound from this motion tracing the '/d/ doughnut', '/b/ board', or '/p/ ponytail'. Then have the child re-read the word correctly.

for **d**
Trace the round 'doughnut'

for **b**
Start at the top & trace the 'big board'

for **p**
Trace down the 'ponytail'

If the child makes repeated errors with d, p, and p, pick one of the letters (for example d) and have the child practice writing that letter using correct formation while saying the sound. Please see Appendix C describing how to teach the formation difference between these letters.

- **Particularly troublesome word:** In come cases, a listed word may be particularly troublesome. If the child struggles several times on the same word, stop the child. Either make the word with the sound tiles and have the child read the tile word to you or tell the word to the child and have him make this word with the sound tiles. Making the word with the tiles helps the child 'see' the phonemic structure of the word. Afterwards, go back and have the child read the word in the printed word list.

In addition to establishing foundational phonologic processing, the word lists are also designed to teach the child how to handle other complexities of decoding our complex English language. Guided reading of the word lists also incorporates direct instruction of the following skills:

- **Reading words with double letters:** When first introducing words with double letters explain and show the child how when two of the same letters are right next to each other we tend to say the sounds together as one sound. In the first few lessons where the child encounters double letters, specifically point out this pattern to the child. You can make a few of the words with the tiles to help demonstrate if that helps. The child needs to learn to correctly combine double consonants together. This is easiest to do with the 'stretchy' sounds such as /s/ and /f/. Errors with doubling the sounds are usually evident with the doubled letters in the fast sounds (/d/, /t/). If the child makes an error doubling a sound when sounding out, stop the child with a pencil tap or oops and remind him that since both letters have the same sound you say them together and have him re-read the word correctly. For example, if the child sounds out the word 'add' as /aaa..d...d/ (doubling the /d/ sound), stop him and give a reminder to say the /d/ together as one /d/ sound and have him re-read the word. Most children quickly pick up on this concept after a few encounters. If the child needs a little additional help, use your pencil to underline the double consonants and tell the child 'say these sounds together' and then have the child re-read the word correctly. The key is to correct so the child learns to process these double sounds together.

- **Reading words with blended consonants/Developing skills with these 'complex words':** The word lists included direct work and practice with blended consonant sounds. The child needs to apply smooth blending skills to be able to combine multiple consonant sounds. The reading lessons are organized to develop skills systematically. The initial lessons contain primarily single consonants and then systematically add 2-consonant blends into the mix. This provides the student sufficient practice with 2 consonant blends before tackling the harder 3-consonant blends. The trickier 3-consonant blends are not added until reading lesson #24 providing time for the student to develop the blending skills necessary to handle these harder blends. If the child misses reading a sound within a blended consonant combination, stop the child. Usually an 'oops' or the pencil tap signal is sufficient. Sometimes pointing to the specific sound that was missed with the pencil tip helps the child see a missed sound. In addition, smooth blending is essential. Remind the child to 'take a breath' before starting the word and to 'sing' if necessary. Have the child re-read the word smoothly blending sounds together.

- **Reading alternate sounds correctly/ Handling print with more than 1 sound:** The child needs to learn how to handle the complexities of the English code. Our printed phonemic code/letter(s) often represent more than one sound. For example s = /s/ in 'miss' and 'sit' but /z/ in 'has' and 'his' or o=/o/ in 'not' but '/oa/ in 'no' and 'most'. The child needs to learn how to handle these alternate sounds. The program manages the complexities by systematic presentation. The initial lessons include decodable words with only the short vowel sounds. Subsequent lessons systematically incorporate the alternate sounds. As complexities are added, the child needs to learn when to use what sound and acquire knowledge of the expected patterns. When alternate sounds are first applied in Reading Lesson # 27, explain to the child he will begin using the other sounds for some of the letters. Tell the child it takes a little practice but he will soon know which sound to use in a word. When the child decodes a word and applies the incorrect sound, stop the child, remind him to use the other sound, and have the child re-read the word correctly. For example, if the child reads the word 'has' as /hhass/ using the /s/ sound instead of the correct /z/ sound, the child has used correct decoding skills however he applied the incorrect sound for 's' in that specific word. Stop the child with a tap and say "good try but this word uses the /z/ sound for s" or "try the /z/ sound in this word" and have your child read the word again. Be sure to stop the child, remind the child to "use the other sound" or "use the __ sound" and require he re-read/sound out the word correctly. By practicing the word correctly with phonologic processing, the child learns to apply the correct sound/pronunciation for the specific word and begins to learn expected patterns.

- **Handling Multisyllable words:** The program directly teaches the child how to handle multisyllable words. The child needs to distinguish and group appropriate sounds to form the correct syllables and then smoothly combine these correct sound chunks with the adjacent syllables into one fluid word. Please read the Introduction/General Information portion of **Section 6 - Reading Multisyllable Words** for a complete explanation of multisyllable words. Two-syllable words are first introduced in Reading Lesson #25 after the child has established foundational skills necessary to tackle these longer words. The program incorporates guided reading with 2-syllable words and subsequently adds in a few 3-syllable words. The longer multisyllable words (3+ syllables) are addressed in Section 6.

The technique for helping a child learn how to handle longer words is fairly simple. As the child reads the words to you, have your pencil ready. *If* the child has problems with breaking words into appropriate syllables, place a light pencil mark slashes in the appropriate syllable breaks and make a comment such as "take another look" so he can better 'see' the syllables. For example: add light pencil slashes to indicate in/sect, fin/ish, or ex/pen/sive. These light pencil marks help the child 'see' the appropriate breaks. Remember to make the slash marks *only* when the child needs help. While some children easily handle the 2 syllable words without assistance, some need direct help in learning how to break these words.

Pronunciation can also be an issue with multisyllable words as the child needs to accent the correct syllable. Children tend to recognize and attain correct pronunciation with the common 2 syllable words. Pronunciation difficulties typically occur with longer multisyllable words and unknown vocabulary. Directly help the child learn correct pronunciation. When the child sounds out a word but doesn't get the pronunciation quite right, tell the child how the word is pronounced. Say something similar to "Good try, that was close but we actually pronounce the word _____". Then have the child re-read the word processing the print while pronouncing the word correctly.

- **Building Fluency on Common Words:** The word lists incorporate frequent practice of many common words. These frequently encountered words are included in the lessons after the necessary sounds are taught. Repeated and correct phonetic analysis of these common words helps the child develop accurate 'neural models' and achieve fluent 'fast reading' of these common words. Although the child needs to practice reading these common words, never have the child shortcut the correct sounding out/phonologic processing essential for developing true fluency.

- **Expanding Vocabulary:** The word lists are designed to develop phonologic processing not to build vocabulary. However, you can occasionally include incidental vocabulary instruction. As the child reads through words, he may ask the meaning of an unknown word. You can give a quick definition. Techniques for expanding vocabulary are covered in Section 10. Direct instruction on the meanings of common affixes is included in Section 6.

Additional Practice with Decodable Word Lists: Some children need additional practice to fully master reading skills. If the student has not mastered the smooth accurate decoding, provide additional practice by having the child read word lists more than once. The child can practice any list from previously completed lessons. When a sound is new to the child decoding is often slow requiring much effort. Repeating a word list after the child has had a few days to practice the new sound helps the child decode these words. You can also make supplemental word lists to provide additional practice. If you make your own word lists, be sure the words are decodable, only using previously taught sounds.

8. Reading Decodable Sentences, Paragraphs, and Short 'Stories'

The reading lessons include guided reading practice with decodable sentences and paragraphs. These sentences are decodable containing only sounds the child has previously learned so the child can practice and develop correct phonologic processing. The sentences allow the child to practice correct tracking, smooth blending and attention to detail in the process of accurately sounding out words. In addition to providing practice with accurate decoding, the sentences allow the child to learn how to smoothly read text at normal speed and begin to develop basic comprehension skills.

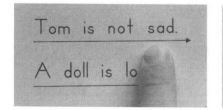

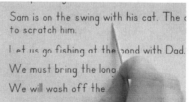

When the child reads the sentences, he must sound out the words, use physical tracking with his finger or a pointer, blend sounds smoothly and read words correctly.

- **Require Correct and Accurate Decoding:** The child reads the sentences sounding out words with finger tracking and smooth blending. Immediately correct any errors. Make sure *all* words are read correctly. Don't let the child misread *any* words, skip words, or substitute incorrect words even if they have similar meaning or are 'unimportant' such as saying 'a' for 'the'. Help the child learn careful, accurate reading where he always looks at each sound within a word and at each word within a sentence. To correct reading errors, tap the missed word with a pencil and have the child "look again". Correct specific decoding errors as explained in the word reading directions.

- **Help the child learn to read a sentence smoothly**: Explain how sentences contain a complete thought. Point out how sentences always begin with a capital letter and end with a period or other end mark. Help the child learn how to read sentences with a smooth natural flow and include appropriate pauses at the end of a sentence. In the beginning you may need to demonstrate to the child how to smoothly flow a sentence together. This ability to smoothly read a sentence at a natural rate improves and progresses as the child's decoding skills advance and he begins to build fluency on individual words. When children first start they tend to read word-by-word at a slower rate. When reading is choppy or when you stop the child for error correction, have the child re-read the sentence. After the child correctly decodes the words, ask the child to read the sentence again at a regular rate. Say something like "Good job, now read the sentence again all together". Reading the sentence again helps the child learn to apply this natural flow. In addition, the child needs to pause at the end of sentences. If the child runs sentences together, have him take a breath at the period. Point to the period with your pencil to help him 'see' the stop.

- **Develop *initial* comprehension skills:** Because comprehension is vital to skilled reading, this program uses the sentences to begin directly developing basic comprehension. Although comprehension is dependant on accurate decoding it doesn't automatically occur. Comprehension needs to be intentionally developed. At first this is just a simple process of making sure the child actually understands, can remember (as least for a brief moment) and recap what she read. It is also important for children to learn to go back and re-read a sentence or word when they miss or don't understand something.

To develop comprehension skills simply ask your child a *specific question* about what he read. Start simple and then ask more complex questions as his reading skills advance and as the sentence or story content becomes more complex. At first the simple questions just check if the child remembers the content of what he just read you. There is no required format for questions. Make up your own *specific* questions. The idea is to get the child to actually think about what he reads and to learn to re-read when necessary. Ask a few questions just to check the child understands what he is reading. If the child reads "The raft is at the pond.", ask "What's at the pond" or "Where is the raft?". If the child reads, "Pick up the trash on the grass.", ask "What did that say" or "What do you need to do?" If the child reads, "Kim's doll was lost", ask "What happened?" or "What was lost?".

Although the child must always decode each word accurately when reading the sentence, the child has leeway on how he answers the comprehension questions. As long as he understands the content, the exact wording is flexible. For example, if the sentence is "The gift is on the desk". He *must* read it *exactly* as it is written. But, when you ask "What was on the desk?" and he answers "The present was on the desk" that is fine because he understood what he read. In contrast, if he tells you " the kid is by the desk" then say something such as, "Oops you better read that again to see what it said" or "Are you sure? You better check that again". The purpose questioning is to get the child to pay attention to what he is reading. If the child does not know what he just read, simply have him re-read the sentence. You can use your pencil to point to the word or words the child needs to re-read. This visual cue helps the child learn the important skill of looking back at the text for an answer he doesn't remember.

Obviously, the decodable sentences/short passages are simple. This text is designed to develop phonologic processing. This is not meaningful literature. There is not much depth to a sentence like "The fish is in the pond". However, by asking questions you help your child *begin* to develop *initial comprehension skills*. Questioning from the beginning, helps him learn to think about and remember what he just read and learn the important technique of re-reading. This is only the very beginning of comprehension skill development. Comprehension is complex and much more must be done later. You can also work on additional comprehension activities with your child when *you* are reading more complex and exciting stories to him. Please see Section 9 Developing Reading Comprehension Skills.

9. Writing Words (Spelling) and Spelling Activities

The program utilizes 'writing words' or spelling words by sound as an effective technique to intentionally help the child develop phonologic processing. Reading and spelling are converse sides of the same process. If the child learns to listen to oral speech and translate those sounds into print it strengthens the reverse skill of looking at print and translating that back into the sounds of our language. Writing words is similar to the word making, except the child prints the word instead of making he word with the tiles.

Writing words or spelling by sound effectively reinforces essential 'printed letter=sound' relationships, strengthens phonemic awareness and develops correct phonologic processing. Writing directly links and targets the processes of saying the sounds (oral), hearing the spoken sound (auditory), physically forming the letter (kinetic) and seeing printed letters (visual) to help children effectively develop phonologic processing. Word writing by sound is also an effective tool in building fluency for individual words. Spelling activities are designed to develop foundational skills.

For writing the words/spelling to be an effective tool for reading development the child must *say the sounds as he writes the letters*. Teach the child to spell by listening to and writing the sounds of a word. Do *not* give the child the words to practice ahead of time. Select words from the lesson's word list (or other decodable words). At first spelling needs to be simple and phonetic. As the complexity increases, minimize confusion by telling the child what sound combination to use. Spelling lists for the initial reading lessons can be found at **www.righttrackreading.com/spelllistsforrtr.html**

Tell the child you are starting a word writing or spelling activity. Give the child some paper & pencil. Say "please write the word _____". Speak clearly. Repeat the word if necessary. Speaking clearly and repeating the word are especially important if the child is still developing phonemic awareness skills to properly distinguish sounds within words. Have the child use standard block print and immediately correct all errors. Stop the child, help him develop the necessary skill and provide assistance so the child learns and practices correct spelling. This is not a "spelling test". It is practice turning language into print. Always have the child write the word correctly. Remember the child is forming neural models of words. Never practice incorrectly. Corrections include:

- **Child misses writing a sound within a word**: If the child misses a sound, stop the child and help the child distinguish and recognize the missing sound and then write the word correctly. See the directions for child having difficulty hearing sounds and difficulty distinguishing specific sounds on page 33 under directions for word making.

- **Spelling correctly, Handling the complexities:** Spelling is tricky! Children can spell phonetically yet spell the word incorrectly. For example, spelling 'cat' as 'kat'. In these cases the child is converting print to sound, he just needs to use the correct phonogram for that word. The correction is to stop the child with an 'oops' and directly tell the child "in this word the /k/ sound is spelled with the letter 'c' and have the child rewrite the word correctly. When giving spelling words avoid mixing alternate spellings in a list and tell the child which pattern to use. For example tell the child "in these words the /k/ sound is spelled with the 'ck' buddy letters" and give him the words 'back', 'rock', 'stick' and 'luck'. Then tell him "in these words the /k/ sound is spelled with 'k' and give him the words 'milk', 'kid', 'skip', and 'kit'. Don't mix spelling patterns in the learning stages." Help the child spell correctly. Don't let the child practice incorrect spelling. At this stage you are teaching common spelling patterns not testing the child.

In addition to writing words, supplemental sound identification activities can teach spelling patterns and provide practice and reinforcement of phonetic analysis. These activities add variety to simply writing words. Provide a list of decodable words. Use this printed list to conduct sound identification activities. In the sound identification activity, the child identifies and underlines all the sounds in the word. For example in the word 'chain' he would underline ch ai n, in 'reading' he would underline r ea d ing. Another variation is to have the child underline a specific sound that you ask him to identify. For example, give the child a list of 'ea'=/ee/ words and ask the child to underline the /ee/ sound in the words and he underlines r<u>ea</u>ch, dr<u>ea</u>m, l<u>ea</u>st, l<u>ea</u>f, h<u>ea</u>t.

Later the child will need to practice the more complex spelling words, irregulars and memorize the actual "correct" spelling option for specific words. (The /ay/ sound is spelled 'ai' in rain, 'a' in rang, 'ay' in play, and 'eigh' in eight, so which spelling do you use for a specific word?) However, don't *begin* with advanced complexities where the student *approaches* "spelling" as memorizing a random collection of letters. Additional information is located in *Effective Spelling Instruction: Teaching Children How to Spell* at **www.righttrackreading.com/howtospell.html** and the Spelling Section starting on page 321. The spelling lessons teach expected patterns and helpful guidelines to help advance the child's spelling skills.

10. Reading Irregular Words

Irregular words are a part of our English language. Although most words are phonetic when the complete code is known, some words are not. While some words do not 'sound out' accurately and need to be learned partially by "*sight*", visually memorizing the whole word should absolutely *not* be taught *as a reading strategy*. It is important to realize even irregular words are partially phonetic and still apply left-to-right tracking. For example in the irregular word 'said' the 's' and 'd' are completely phonetic, /s/ is the first sound, followed by the 'irregular' /e/ and then the phonetic ending /d/. In the word 'busy' the only irregular portion is the 'u'=/i/. In 'what', only the 'a'=/u/ is irregular. The child needs to notice and process every letter in order, even with the irregular words ('from'-'form, 'was'-'saw' are not the same). The child needs to track properly and pay careful attention to detail to develop an accurate neural model of the word.

The program directly teaches common irregular words to the child by explicitly introducing them to the child as irregular or 'silly words' that we say differently than they should sound out. This would include common words such as said, of, to, do, was, want, one and two that are not entirely phonetic and common words containing sound combinations that have not yet been taught such as the word 'you' before the child has learned the 'ou' combination. The reading lessons systematically incorporate direct instruction in the common irregular words. After they are explicitly introduced, the common irregular words are included in the word lists and sentences for frequent practice.

An effective technique for teaching irregular words is to point at the word and say "This is one of those 'silly' or 'irregular words'. When we sound out the word it should be ___, but we actually say ___." and have the child practice reading the word several times. Point out the irregular portion and remind the child to look carefully at the letters as he says the sounds in this 'silly' word. If the child reads the word incorrectly by phonetically sounding it out, simply say "yes, that is how we sound it out but this is a silly word, do you remember how we say it? We say it _____." For example is the child sounds out 'was' as /w//a//s/ instead of /w//u//z/, say "Good sounding out but do you remember how we say this word?" Tell the child the pronunciation if he doesn't remember and then have the child re-read the word correctly. Word writing can also be used to help the child learn common irregular words. Have the child write the word several times, saying the sounds as he writes paying particular attention to the irregular portion of the word. These techniques help children learn common irregular words without developing incorrect strategies of visual memorization or whole word guessing.

When other irregular words are encountered, use the same technique to teach the child the word. Directly introduce the word as irregular. Specifically point out the irregular portion of the word to the child. Use the technique, "___ **is an irregular word, it should sound out ___, but we say ___**". Have the child read the word several times noting the irregular part. Practice writing the word several times, paying attention to the sound structure and spelling that is used.

11. Additional Guided Oral Reading Practice with Decodable Text

As previously explained, the child must practice reading decodable text. To review the importance of reading decodable text see #9 on page 17 and the article *Decodable Text Explained* at **www.righttrackreading.com/decodabletext.html**. Guided reading of decodable text is essential to build and advance skills. In addition to the decodable text incorporated in the reading lessons, supplemental practice with decodable text benefits reading development. The following summary provides several options for providing other decodable text for your child:

- **Create decodable word lists:** Word lists are effective tools for practicing correct phonologic processing. It is easy to create decodable word lists for additional practice. Simply list words containing code your child has learned. If selecting words from the reading lessons include words from the lesson your child is on or previous lessons.

- **Create simple decodable sentences:** It is also fairly easy to create a few simple decodable sentences. Once again, create sentences containing only code the child has learned or copy sentences from the reading lessons. Write the sentence on a blank sheet of paper and have the child read the sentence and illustrate the page.

- **Make your own decodable books:** A terrific and inexpensive alternative for younger children in the early stages is to make your own decodable books. Making your own decodable books is easy. All you need is a paper or a stack of 4x6 index cards. Print one simple decodable sentence per page and staple the pages together to make your own decodable story. Draw a few simple illustrations or better yet, have your child illustrate his own book after he reads the text. You don't have to be a talented author. This is not literature. List out the sounds the child knows and write up a few short sentences or copy sentences from *Right Track Reading* to make these simple decodable books.

41

- **Supplemental decodable stories:** In addition to the decodable text incorporated in the reading lessons, the Right Track Reading website contains supplemental decodable stories. These free decodable stories are located at **www.righttrackreading.com/decodablestoriesrtr.html**

- **Select Beginner Books with Decodable Text:** Carefully select decodable books for your child. To determine if a book is decodable evaluate the phonemic code used in the text and check if it meets your child's code knowledge. Always evaluate the vocabulary carefully! Do not rely on the grade level rating printed on the book. Many very simple children's picture books with only one or two words per page including numerous books actually labeled "early phonics readers" are full of words like 'rhinoceros' and 'laugh' that contain complex code or multisyllable word such as 'carnival' and 'investigations' that are not decodable by beginners. It is not simplicity of the text, but rather the phonetic structure of the words. Help your child find, select and practice reading appropriate decodable text.

In the very early stages it is often difficult to find a book that is entirely decodable based on your beginners limited code knowledge. As the child's code knowledge expands, it is easier to find books. Several decodable beginning reader series are commercially available (for example the 'Bob Books' series). When you purchase decodable books, check the sounds within the text match your child's knowledge of the code.

When code knowledge is still limited, you can expand options by reading a book with your child. Tell the child you are going to read a book together. You read all the words that contain unlearned code and when you get to a word the child can decode, point to the word and he reads this decodable word to you. This shared reading technique not only makes it easier to select books but it is a fun way to read with your child.

The use of decodable text in reading instruction does not mean more advanced books are off limits but rather the text *the child first reads to you* needs to be decodable. For example: If your child likes dinosaurs, go the library, head for the dinosaur section and check out a stack of books. Let him look through all the books. Sit down on the couch and study the illustrations. Read pages and pages of advanced text to him such as "The paleontologist discovered ancient fossilized relics of a Dromaeosaurus from the cretaceous period". However, when it is his turn to read to you, select decodable text and have him read the beginning decodable book "Tom dug up a big T-rex fossil."

Be sure to continue a *minimum* of 20 minutes of daily guided oral reading after Reading Lesson #98. At this point the child has directly learned the vast majority of the phonemic code (all but special -tion, -cial endings.) Guided reading where the child reads out loud with guidance and feedback is vital in the learning stages. In addition to strengthening phonologic processing skills and building fluency, guided reading provides the child an opportunity to develop reading comprehension skills and vocabulary. Detailed instructions for conducting guided reading are found in Section 7.

E. ADDITIONAL TIPS

Children are all unique. I learn something every time I work with a child. Students truly have been valuable instructors for helping me learn about teaching reading. In addition, a variety of knowledgeable individuals have shared suggestions and tips with me. Thanks to all my 'instructors', I have picked up a few tips and valuable ideas for helping children develop their reading skills.

- The instructor needs to keep a pencil in hand during lessons. A pencil makes is a helpful tool for pointing to focus the child's attention to a specific sound, for making corrections and for indicating necessary breaks in the multisyllable words. I personally prefer a mechanical pencil as the lead can be retracted when using as a pointer and the fine tip allows precise pointing at specific sounds. Often when the child makes an error, I don't say anything. I simply tap the pencil on the missed word. The child quickly picks on this silent 'oops-look again' signal. Somehow the pencil tap is more pleasant than a verbal correction.

- If the child has difficulty maintaining focus for longer lessons or activities, split the instruction into smaller tasks and intersperse variety to maintain interest/focus. Development of correct phonologic processing pathways requires practice. Don't eliminate necessary tasks but rather split them up into 'bite sized' portions. *Right Track Reading Lessons* includes a variety of activities. It is sometimes helpful to break the longer word lists into smaller sections and alternate the word reading with work making activities with the sound tiles. For example, if a child struggles with completing a 300 word list, have the student read 100 words, then switch to some word making activities with the tiles, then read another 100 words and then write some words. Take a 2 minute stretch break and then practice sounds for 2 minutes and make some more words with the tiles before completing the word list. Notice, the child still has to read all 300 words. Don't shorten the necessary practice just break the activity into smaller parts. When you are reading with children, monitor their attention/focus and appropriately manage activities.

- Having energetic children go outside and literally run a few laps immediately prior to sitting down for reading can be extremely beneficial. In addition, if you have an especially energetic student who has difficulty sitting still, try having the child stand next to you. I have successfully used this technique with several children. The child *must* stand right next to me, focus and pay attention to the lesson. Standing seems to utilize some of the excess energy. An article with tips for working with energetic students is found at **www.righttrackreading.com/tipsenergeticstudents.html**

- If a child has difficulty with writing (penmanship), I recommend the *Zaner-Bloser* manuscript handwriting program. Please see Appendix C for additional information.

- If a child has a speech difficulty, talk with a speech pathologist for specific recommendations. Most school districts have a speech specialist or can recommend a specialist. These specialists often can provide user friendly tips and methods of helping a student make specific sounds. Additionally, a collection of some 'sound pronunciation tips' are located at the end of Appendix A. While reading instruction absolutely does *not* replace the need for speech assistance, the individual instruction with specific sounds as a part of the reading program provides an opportunity to help a child work on particular sounds and supplement the speech instruction.

- In addition, when correcting the reading of a child who has a speech difficulty, inability to say a sound or mispronunciation due to a speech difficulty is NOT a reading error. If the child correctly identifies and attempts to say the sound, don't correct mispronunciation as a reading error. The instructor can repeat the word pronounced correctly and help the child practice sound pronunciation but do not treat it as a reading error. For example: If the child has difficulty pronouncing /r/ and says /stwing/ for 'string' the child read the word correctly even though he did not pronounce it correctly. Do not correct these types of pronunciation errors as reading errors. In contrast, if the child misses the /r/ sound altogether and says /sting/ you would stop him and have him re-read the word picking up the 'r'.

- It is helpful to use some sort of log to keep track of the child's progress. A progress log is located in Appendix B. Younger children often like to keep track of their progress with small stickers. Older students simply like to check the chart with handwritten date to track how rapidly they are progressing. If you are tutoring more than one student or have an intervention program where more than one adult is tutoring a child, progress logs are essential.

- In addition to a progress log, it is also helpful to keep brief notes. I record handwritten notes to myself on loose-leaf paper organized chronologically by date of the tutoring session. For each tutoring session, note information such as the exact sounds the child may need to work on, the specific errors or types of errors the child makes, skills that need further development, any skill the child seems to have fully mastered, or other pertinent information. There is no required format. These 'working' notes help the instructor modify and target instruction to best meet the student's specific needs. If you are working with more than one child or have several different instructors working with an individual student these written notes are vital. The notes and progress chart can be kept in an inexpensive two pocket folder labeled with the child's name. When you go to work with a student you can simply grab his folder.

Reading Lessons: Ready... Set... Go!

When starting the reading program, let your child know you are going to teach him to read. Give your child a quick summary. You can explain something similar to:

"You are going to learn to read. I am going to teach you how words are made up of sounds put together. Those sounds are written down on paper as certain letters. So the first step in reading is to learn the sounds that the letters represent. The secret to reading is learning the sounds! I am going to teach you these sounds and how to put them together and read them. Learning to read is lots of fun. It will take some work but you are very smart and in a short time you will be an awesome reader! Before we start I want to let you know that we will always practice the sounds and reading correctly. I will stop you if you start to do something incorrectly. We don't want to practice doing something the wrong way. It's my job to make sure together we learn the right way! You can even stop me if I make a mistake! Let's get started. Reading is so much fun."

OUTLINE OF READING LESSON CONTENT

For each lesson, this outline provides: **1)** the beginning page number, **2)** the sounds introduced or a brief summary of the lesson, **3)** the high frequency words included as the necessary sounds are introduced and **4)** the common irregular words introduced and included for practice.

Lesson #	Page #	Sounds Introduced Summary of Lesson	High Frequency Words Included for Practice	Common Irreg. Word Introduced
SECTION 1	48-114	**BASIC SOUNDS/SKILLS**		
1	48	**m t a**	am at	
2	50	**s d**	add	
3	52	**i f**	if, did, it, its	
4	54	Review & I, a	I, a	
5	55	**r th**	that this	
6	57	Review		is
7	58	**l o n**	in and on an not than man off stand last list still land	
8	61	**p e**	tell set spell self stop left plant let red	
9	65	Review & the		the
10	66	**h v**	him had help hand	
11	69	**sh u b**	us up but must run sun	
12	73	Review & to, do		to do
13	75	**k ck**	back ask black	
14	79	Review & said		said
15	82	**c g** (/k/ & /g/ sounds)	can get got long big act	
16	86	**j w**	will with just well jump	
17	89	Review & was		was
18	92	**ch tch**	much such	
19	96	**x z qu**	next box quick	
20	99	Review & of		of
21	100	**wh**	which when	
22	102	Review & what, who		what who
23	104	Review & Practice		
24	108	Blended Consonants & Review		
25	110	skill intro 2 syllable words	into little children until happen problem	
26	112	Review & Practice		
SECTION 2	115-145	**ADDITIONAL SOUNDS**		
27	115	**s** (/z/ sound)	as has his	
28	118	**e** (ee sound) pronunciation /i/ - e+n e+m	me we be he she when them then end men even begin began	
29	121	**o** (/oa/ sound) **o** (/u/ sound)	no go old so most both told open from month son	
30	124	Review & some, done, none		some done none
31	125	**i** (ie sound)	find kind behind	

Lesson #	Page #	Sounds Introduced Summary of Lesson	High Frequency Words Included for Practice	Common Irreg. Word Introduced
32	127	**a** (/ay/ sound) pronunciation a+l a+ll & w+a	all call small also walk talk wash watch	
33	131	**y**(/y/ sound) (/ee/ sound) (/ie/ sound)	yes yet only very study by my why	
34	134	Review, you & want		you want
35	136	**ing ink**	bring going think	
36	138	Review and Practice		
37	141	Practice & Silent Letters		
38	143	Review and Practice		
SECTION 3	146-212	**VOWEL COMBINATIONS**		
39	146	Intro Vowel Combinations		
40	146	**ee**	see three need keep free tree feet green between	
41	150	**oa oe**		
42	152	**ai ay**	rain wait main plain way may day say play away always	
43	155	Review & Practice		
44	157	Intro vowel-consonant-e		
45	159	**a_e**	make made came take name same late state	
46	161	**o_e**	home close those	
47	163	**i_e**	like time side line while life size	
48	165	**u_e**	use	
49	166	**e_e**	these complete	
50	167	practice all vowel-consonant-e		
51	170	**c** (/s/ sound = c+e,i or y) **g** (/j/ sound = g+e i or y)	place notice sentence since face city change page	
52	174	Review & Practice		
53	177	**u** (oo and uu sound)	put full pull	
54	179	**oi oy**	oil point voice boy	
55	181	**ea**	each mean read real teach eat please ready head great	
56	184	Review & Practice		
57	186	**ow**	now how down brown show low grow slow	
58	188	**ou**	out sound round about house found group young	
59	190	Review & would could should		would could should
60	193	**ue ew ui**	new few blue true	
61	195	**oo**	look good food book room soon took	
62	197	**ie ei**	friend	

Lesson #	Page #	Sounds Introduced Summary of Lesson	High Frequency Words Included for Practice	Common Irreg. Word Introduced
63	199	**ey**	they money	they
64	201	**au aw augh**	saw draw because	
65	203	Review & Practice		
66	205	**igh**	right high light night	
67	207	**s** (/z/ sound)	is was has his	
68	208	intro few 3 syllable words		
69	209	Review & Practice		
SECTION 4	213-249	**R-CONTROLLED VOWEL COMBINATIONS**		
70	213	Intro r-controlled vowel combo		
71	213	**ar** (/ar/ & /air/ sounds)	part large hard start far mark carry	
72	216	**w+ar** (pronunciation)		
73	218	Review & are		are
74	220	**or** (/or/ & /er/ sounds)	or for form story short north work word world	
75	223	**5 /or/ combinations or ore oar our oor**	or for more your more before your four	
76	226	Review & Practice		
77	228	**er**	her other number over after every under	
78	231	**5 /er/ combinations er ur ir ear or** (w+or & or ending some multisyllable words)	turn hurt girl bird earth, learn heard early (or) color	
79	236	Review & Practice, were		were
80	239	**/air/ combinations are ar air ear** (uncommon)	care air there where	
81	242	there & their Review & Practice		their there
82	244	**3 /eer/ combinations ear eer ere**	here ear year hear near	
83	246	review **ear** combination Review and Practice		
84	247	**ire** & Review		
85	248	Review & Practice		
SECTION 5	250-269	**OTHER SOUNDS & PRACTICE**		
86	250	Silent letter combos **dge mb**		
87	251	More Silent Letters **wr kn**	write wrong know knew	
88	253	one, two, any, many		one two any many
89	254	Greek Sounds: **ph** /f/ **ch** /k/ **y** /i/	school	
90	256	Infrequent Sounds **i** /ee/ **ai** /i/	again certain mountain	
91	257	Vowel Combos. **eigh ough**		

Section1: Learn Basic Sounds & Establish Foundational Skills

Lesson 1:

Teach Sounds: "I am going to teach you how written letters have certain sounds. Once you learn their sounds you will be able to begin to read. Learning the sounds of the letters is the secret to reading!" Follow under the sound with your finger and say the sound for your child making sure to pronounce the sound correctly. Demonstrate a few times and then have you child say it with you and then alone. Make sure the child says the sound correctly as he follows under the sound with his finger. **Complete directions are found on page 29.**

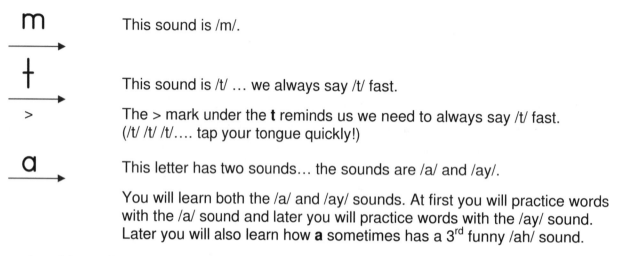

m — This sound is /m/.

t — This sound is /t/ … we always say /t/ fast.

> — The > mark under the **t** reminds us we need to always say /t/ fast.
(/t/ /t/ /t/…. tap your tongue quickly!)

a — This letter has two sounds… the sounds are /a/ and /ay/.

You will learn both the /a/ and /ay/ sounds. At first you will practice words with the /a/ sound and later you will practice words with the /ay/ sound. Later you will also learn how **a** sometimes has a 3rd funny /ah/ sound.

Give the New Sound Cards to Your Child:
Present the sound cards (index cards w/ sound written on it) to the child for these new letters. You will continue to add to this sound card collection as additional sounds are introduced. Make sure the child follows under the letter with his finger and says the sound correctly. **Practice the sounds: m, t, a   See page 29 for directions.**

Write and Say Sounds:
Tell the child you are going to show him a great way to learn the sounds. Say "You will write the letter and say the sound at the same time." Make sure your child forms the letter correctly AS he says the sound. If your child struggles with letter writing, have him trace over dashed letters. Free tracer letter worksheets for *Right Track Reading Lessons* are found at **www.righttrackreading.com/tracerletterpages.html**. Writing *and* saying the sound *at the same time* is critical. If he isn't saying the sound, tell him "Oops, make sure you say the sound as you write so I can hear you". **Write each sound m, t, a 5 times. See page 30 for complete directions.**

Getting Ready to Make Words:
Now that you know some sounds we are going to make words. Just like you make a train by hooking together train cars, we make words by hooking together sounds. Before we start making words there are a few things you must know.

1) "When making words we always start on the left and go to the right. We will follow the arrow and use our finger to help us learn this. Let me show you what I mean. Take the child's finger and run it down the directional arrow several times. We start here and go this direction." Words ALWAYS go left to right. Just like you never see a caboose pulling a train… you never make words backwards. We always go this way. (Show w/ finger movement). Now which way do words go? Have the child physically show you which direction words are made.

2) When we make and say words we need to keep the sounds hooked together. Words are like a train, except instead of train cars hooked together words are made of sounds hooked together. Just like when train cars come unhooked (or uncoupled for children who are train fans and insist on proper train terminology) the train falls apart, when we separate the sounds the word falls apart. We keep sounds hooked together so our word does not fall apart. Listen carefully and I will say a word with the sounds hooked together. Demonstrate the correct technique by saying a few words slowly with sounds connected. (fun, mom, sit). Please see the complete instructions for teaching smooth blending skills on page 27. Some children may need oral blending exercises. See oral blending exercises in Appendix E.

Word Making Game: Now it is time to make some words. Take out the sound tiles a, m and t and show the child how the sounds are written on the tiles. Have the child tell you the sound for each individual tile. Show the child the arrow and demonstrate how to build the first word. Say "I am going to make the word "mat". Demonstrate saying each sound as you make the word, keeping the sounds hooked together (blended properly) and proper tracking. After making the word, read the word to him, sounding it out with finger tracking. Then tell him "Now it is your turn to make a word! Please make the word _____" The child does not see the word but rather listens as you read the words one at a time to him speaking clearly and repeating it at least once so the child hears correctly. When he is making the word, be sure he says the individual sounds as he lays down the appropriate sound tile in order and is blending sounds properly. Immediately correct any errors. After he makes the word, have him read/sound out the word with finger tracking. When he reads the word, say "GREAT JOB, you are reading! You just read the word _____".
See complete illustrated directions starting on page 31.

  Use sound tiles: a   m   t
  Say "**Please make the word _____**": at   am   mat

Reminder for Reading Words: Now you are going to read some words. Remember, you need to use your finger (or toothpick) to follow along, look carefully keeping your eyes on the sounds, say the sounds, and make sure you smoothly hook the sounds together.

Reading Words: Have your child read the following words to you. He needs to sound out the words with finger tracking and proper blending. Correct any errors immediately. **Please see page 34 for complete directions.** It is essential to help you child establish the foundational skills when learning to decode. Directly teach essential skills in blending, tracking and attention to detail. Stop all errors. Helpful reminders such as "look carefully", "use your finger" and "keep the sound hooked together" are frequently needed in the early stages to help your child learn correctly.

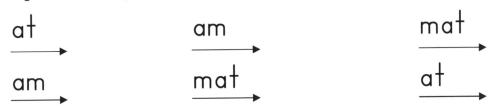

Lesson 2:

Teach Sounds:
"Now you are going to learn new sounds." Follow under the sound with your finger and say the sound for your child making sure to pronounce the sound correctly. Demonstrate a few times and then have you child say it with you and then alone. Make sure he says the sound correctly as he follows under the sound with his finger.

s →

This letter has 2 sounds.. The sounds are /s/ and sometimes /z/.

First you will practice words with the /s/ sound and later you will practice words with the /z/ sound. You will learn both the /s/ sound and the /z/ sound when s is naughty and steals the /z/ sound!

d →
>

This letter has the sound /d/… we always say /d/ fast.

The > mark under the d reminds us we always need to say /d/ fast.
** Specifically point out how the round part of the d comes first.
Round like a donut…. donut for dad…the donut/round part first.

Practice Sound Cards:
Add the new sound cards to your previous sound card collection and practice *all* the cards. Make sure the child follows under the letter with his finger and says the sound correctly. **Practice the sound cards for: s, d** + previous sounds **m, t, a**

Write and Say Sounds:
Tell the child "please write (or trace) the letters and say the sound when you are writing it". Make sure he forms the letter correctly as he says the sound. **Please write each of the sounds 5 times: s d m t a** Complete directions are on page 34

/d/ = doughnut

****Formation of the d is very important to prevent the child from confusing d, b and p. To help the child avoid confusion emphasize the formation. Emphasize you form the round portion first…around then up. A fun way to help the child learn this is to tell them to them remember the round part first…round like a donut…..a donut for dad! The round 'donut' first is /d/. Lots of tracing and writing d is important. This is a good letter to make into a large texture picture for the child to trace making sure they are starting at the correct spot, going around to make the donut first and then up to make the tall part. Make sure they form the round part first, then up.

Reminder on Getting Ready to Make Words:
Now that you know more sounds we are going to make even more words. Just like you make a train by hooking together train cars, we make words by hooking together sounds. Remember that when we make the words we always start on the left and go to the right. Track down the directional arrow with you finger and then have the child show you which way we start and make words.

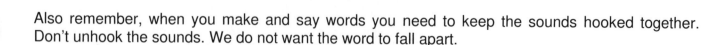

Also remember, when you make and say words you need to keep the sounds hooked together. Don't unhook the sounds. We do not want the word to fall apart.

Word Making Game: Now it's time to make some more words. Take out the appropriate sound tiles. Have the child tell you the sound for each of the individual tiles. For the first few lessons, show him the arrow and demonstrate how to build one of the words. Then tell the child it is his turn to make some words. Say "please make the word _____ for me". Read the list of words one at a time, speaking clearly and repeating the word at least once so the child is sure to hear the sounds correctly. When he is making the word, be sure he says the individual sounds as he lays down the appropriate sound tile in order. Immediately correct any errors. After he completes the word, have him sound out the word to you using finger tracking and proper blending skills. Correct any errors and give short encouraging remarks like good job, great sounding out, way to follow with your finger, ...etc. Clear all the tiles before reading the next word on the list to him. See complete directions starting on page 31.

"Please make the word _____":

Use sound tiles... a   d(2)   m   s   t
       at   am   sad   Sam   mad   mat   sat   dad

Reading Words: Have your child read the following words to you. He needs to sound out the words with finger tracking and proper blending. Correct any errors immediately. Please see page 34 for complete directions.

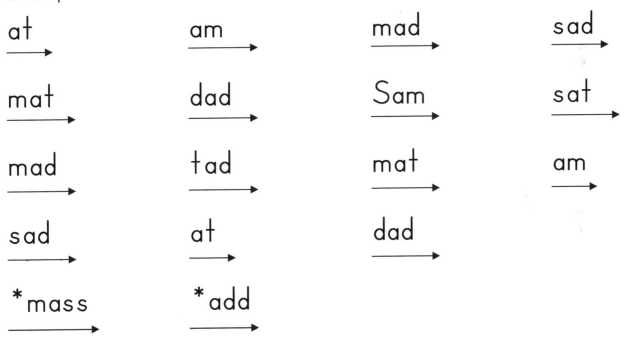

at	am	mad	sad
mat	dad	Sam	sat
mad	tad	mat	am
sad	at	dad	
*mass	*add		

* Teaching Note: The words 'mass' and 'add' contain double letters. Specifically explain to and show the child how when two of the same letters are next each other, we tend to say the sounds together as one sound. For mass, remind the child 'both these letters say /s/ so we can say the sounds together as one /s/. If the child sounds out the word as /m/ /a//s//s/...just remind him to say the /s/ sounds together and have them re-read the word as /mass/ **Please see 'reading words with double letters" on page 37 for complete directions.**

Lesson 3:

Teach Sounds: "Now you are going to learn some new sounds. This sound is ___." Follow under the sound with your finger and say the sound making sure to pronounce the sound correctly. Demonstrate a few times and then have you child say it with you and then alone. Make sure he says the sound correctly as he follows under the sound with his finger.

i →

This letter has 2 sounds. The sounds are /i/ and /ie/.

First you will practice words with the /i/ sound and later words with the /ie/ sound. You will learn both the /i/ and /ie/ sounds.

f →

This letter has the sound /f/.

Practice Sound Cards: Add the new sound cards to your sound card collection and practice *all* the cards. Make sure the child follows under the letter with his finger and says the sound correctly. **Practice the sound cards for: i, f** + previous sounds **m, t, a, s, d**

Write and Say Sounds: Tell the child "please write (or trace) the letters and say the sound when you are writing it". Make sure he forms the letter correctly as he says the sound. **Please write and say each of the sounds 5 times**: i f s d m

Reminder on Getting Ready to Make Words: Now that you know more sounds we can make even more words. Remember, when we make the words we always start on the left and go to the right. Show the child by tracking down the directional arrow with you finger and then have the child show you which way we start and make words.

Remember, when you make and say words you need to keep the sounds hooked together. Don't unhook the sounds. We do not want the word to fall apart.

Word Making Game: Now it's time to make some more words. Take out the appropriate sound tiles. Have the child tell you the sound for each of the individual tiles. Then tell the child it is his turn to make some words. Say "please make the word _____ for me". Read a word from the list, speaking clearly and repeating the word at least once so the child is sure to hear the sounds correctly. When he is making the word, be sure he says the individual sounds as he lays down the appropriate sound tile in order. After he completes the word, have him sound out the word using finger tracking and proper blending skills. Correct any errors and give short encouraging remarks such as "good job", "great sounding out", "way to follow with your finger". Clear the tiles before reading the next word on the list. **"Please make the word _____"**:

Use sound tiles... a i d(2) f m s t
      at if am it sad sit sat dim fit sam mad did mat dad fat
      fast mist mast fist

Reading Words: Have your child read the following words sounding out with finger tracking and proper blending. Correct any errors immediately. Please see page 34 for complete directions.

at	am	it	mat
if	fat	did	at
add	sad	dim	mat
Sam	did	sat	mitt
mad	Tim	fit	fat
dad	mat	at	sit
if	it	mass	am
its	sat	miss	sass
did	if	fast	mist
fit	dim	dad	fat
mast	fist	sad	sift

* note: for 'add', 'mitt', 'mass' 'miss' & 'sass' specifically show and remind the child when the word has double letters, we say the sounds together as one sound. Please see 'reading words with double letters" on page 37 for complete directions and corrections.

Lesson 4: Review

Review Sounds: Let's quickly practice the sounds you have learned! Have child follow under with their finger and say the sounds.

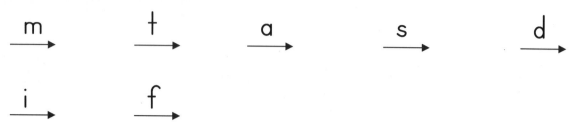

m   t   a   s   d

i   f

Word Reading: There are two words that only have 1 letter each. The sound of the letter lets us know what these words are. Let's read those words.

I   When you see a capital **I** by itself, it is the word I.

Like… "**I** am learning to read." "**I** am having fun".

Let's practice that word again!   I   I   I

a   When you see the letter a by itself, it is the word a.

"Please give me **a** cookie" "Sam has **a** kitten"
(You can teach the word as /ay/ or with the more typical /ə/ pronunciation. Once the child learns the word 'a' he reads it how he says 'a' in oral speech)

Let's practice that word again!   a   a   a

Let's practice reading words! Have your child read the following words sounding out with finger tracking and proper blending. Correct any errors immediately. See page 34.

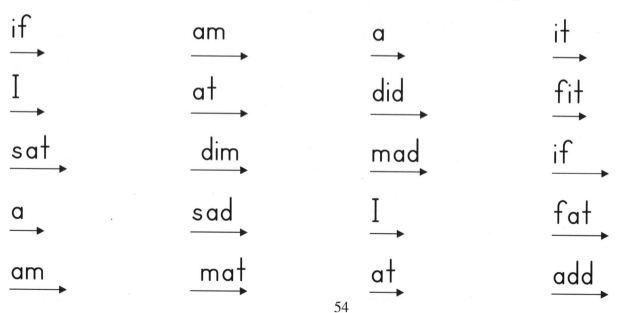

if	am	a	it
I	at	did	fit
sat	dim	mad	if
a	sad	I	fat
am	mat	at	add

Lesson 5:

Teach Sounds:
Now you are going to learn some more new sounds. Follow under the sound with your finger and say the sound for your child making sure to pronounce the sound correctly. Demonstrate a few times and then have your child say it with you and then alone. Make sure he says the sound correctly as he follows under the sound with his finger.

r   This letter has the sound /r/.

This next sound looks a little different. It is made up of 2 letters together. These letters are "buddies". When "buddy letters" stand together they work together to make a sound. We will learn the sound these buddy letters make.

th   These buddy letters have the sound /th/ and /*th*/.

The sounds are pronounced just a little differently in some words.
Listen so you can hear the sounds.
1) Most of the time we say /th/. Listen to the "tickle the tongue" sound
.....the…this…that…/th/
2) sometimes we pronounce th with a softer quieter sound that does not tickle the tongue. Listen to the quiet sound…./*th*/….bath, three, thin, math. We make both the /th/ & /*th*/ sounds by 'sticking your tongue out'.

Practice Sound Cards:
Add the new sound cards to your previous sound card collection and practice *all* the cards. Make sure the child follows under the letter with his finger and says the sound correctly. **Practice the sound cards for: r, th** + previous sounds **m, t, a, s, d, i, f**

Write and Say Sounds:
Tell the child "please write (or trace) the sounds and say the sound when you are writing it". Make sure he forms the letter correctly as he says the sound. **Please write each of the sounds 5 times**: **r th i   f   s   d**

Reminder on Getting Ready to Make Words:
Now that you know more sounds we are going to make even more words by hooking together sounds.   Remember, when we make the words we always start on the left and go to the right. (Track down the directional arrow with you finger and then have the child show you which way we start and make words.)

Remember, when you make and say words you need to keep the sounds hooked together so the word does not fall apart.

Word Making Game:
Make words with the sound tiles. Make sure the child says the individual sounds as he makes the words and uses proper blending skills. After he completes the word, have him read the word using finger tracking and proper blending skills. Correct any errors. **"Please make the word _____"**

Use sound tiles… a i d(2) f m r s t th
        at if am it sad sit rat dim this rid fit that rim mad ram mid did
        dad   math raft rift fast fist   mast mist

Reading Words: Have your child read the following words to you. He needs to sound out the words with finger tracking and proper blending. Correct any errors immediately. See page 34

it	am	at	if
I	a	fit	its
did	fat	Tim	rat
ram	dad	that	math
Sam	mat	this	rim
rid	fit	I	dim
sad	if	a	rid
ram	this	it	did
fat	math	at	am
that	rim	miss	mist
fist	fast	stiff	mast

Lesson 6:

Review Sounds:
Let's quickly practice the sounds you have learned! Have child follow under with their finger and say the sounds.

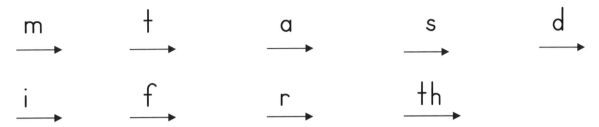

Reading Words:
We are going to learn a new word. Before we start we will practice the two sounds that make up this word.

i   the sound /i/ and /ie/ - In this word you will use the sound /i/.

s   the sound /s/ and /z/ - In this word you will use the second sound /z/.

Let's put the sounds together and practice sounding out our new word. Before the child starts, point to the **s** and remind the child "Remember to use the /z/ sound".

is   is   is   is

If the child reads the word as /is/ using the /s/ sound for s, simply say 'oops, remember this word uses the /z/ sound, and have the child reread the word correctly as /iz/.

Great job! Let's try our new word in a sentence.

Reading Sentences:
Have child read the following sentences. Make sure the child uses finger tracking and proper blending. Have him sound out words. Immediately correct any errors. **Please see complete directions 'Reading Decodable Sentences' on page 38.** After the child reads the sentence, ask him a simple question about what he read. Ask a specific question like… How did Tim feel? Who was mad? Who is fast? What did the rat look like?

Tim is sad.   Sam is mad.

Dad is fast.   This rat is fat.

Lesson 7:

Teach Sounds: Now you are going to learn some new sounds. This sound is _____."

l

This letter has the sound /l/.

o

This letter has 3 sounds! The sounds are /o/, /oa/ and sometimes /u/.

At first you will practice words with the /o/ sound and later you will practice words with the /oa/ and /u/ sounds. When you see the letter **o** you will learn it can have 3 sounds, /o/ /oa/ and the silly /u/.

n

This letter has the sound /n/.

Practice Sound Cards: Add the new sound cards to your collection and practice *all* the cards with him. Make sure your child finger tracks and says the sound correctly. **Practice the sound cards for: l, o, n** + previous sounds **m, t, a, s, d, i, f, r, th**

Write and Say Sounds: Tell the child "please write (or trace) the sounds and say the sound when you are writing it". Make sure he forms the letter correctly as he says the sound. **Please write each of the sounds 5 times: o l n r th i   f d**

Word Making Game: Make words with the sound tiles. Make sure the child says the individual sounds as he makes the words and uses proper blending skills. After he completes the word, have him read the word using finger tracking and proper blending skills. Correct any errors. **"Please make the word _____"**

Use sound tiles a i o d(2) l m n s t th
    on in lit not man dot tan thin lot moth that sod than did this math dad
    and last mist mast slim slot slam lost list

Use sound tiles... a i o d f l m n r t th
    on an not ran nod lot lit and thin that math tan rid rod dim lid
    fit rim rat ant tin ram lad fan than fin land raft rift loft lift land

Reading Words: Have your child read the following words sounding out with finger tracking and proper blending. Correct any errors immediately.

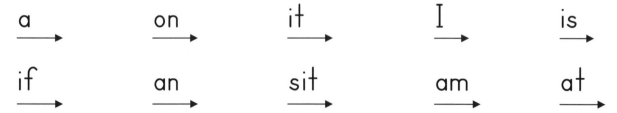

a   on   it   I   is

if   an   sit   am   at

in →	its →	not →	did →	lit →
dim →	and →	that →	if →	ant →
rod →	fin →	on →	tom →	ram →
did →	doll →	this →	than →	rot →
nod →	off →	fin →	and →	lot →
sod →	tin →	man →	math →	lad →
rim →	loss →	ran →	fill →	sin →
ant →	thin →	rot →	tot →	than →
rid →	is →	tan →	lid →	not →
slat →	raft →	slim →	this →	slid →
lost →	slam →	land →	trim →	fast →
fist →	mast →	mist →	loft →	slot →
lift →	not →	land →	last →	sand →

WOW! You just read 75 words. What an awesome reader!

Writing (Spelling) Words: Select some words from the list above for your child to write/spell. Please see the directions on how to conduct this activity in the "Writing Words/Spelling and Spelling Activities" section found on page 40)

Reading Sentences: Have your child read the following sentences. Make sure the child uses finger tracking and proper blending. Have him sound out words and immediately correct any errors. After the child reads the sentence, ask him a few questions about what he read. Ask a specific question like... How did you run? How does Tom feel? What happened to the doll? See page 38.

I ran fast.

Tom is not sad.

A doll is lost.

Did a ram sit?

That ram is fat.

That man is not last.

Sam is thin.

Tim is on this raft.

This man is mad.

Lesson 8:

Teach Sounds:

This letter has the sound /p/. We always say /p/ fast.

The little > mark under the **p** reminds us we need to say /p/ fast.
(/p/ /p/ /p/ pop your lips fast - like popping popcorn)
** Specifically point out to the child how /p/ goes straight down
like a ponytail, then up and around. The ponytail hangs down for /p/.

This letter has 2 sounds! the sounds are /e/ and /ee/.

At first we will practice words with the /e/ sound. Later we will
practice with words with the /ee/ sound. But when you see **e**
you will learn it has 2 sounds, /e/ and /ee/.

Practice Sound Cards: Add the new sound cards to your collection. **Practice the sound cards for: p, e** + previous sounds **m, t, a, s, d, i, f, r, th, l, o, n.** Make sure your child finger tracks under the letter and says the sound correctly.

Write and Say Sounds: Have the child write (or trace) each letter. Make sure your child forms the letter correctly and says the sound as he writes. **Please write and say each of the sounds 5 times: p e o l n r th d**

/p/ ponytail

> ****Formation of the p is very important to prevent the child from confusing d, b and p. To help the child avoid confusion emphasize formation. Emphasize you first go straight down then up and around to make the round portion. Go straight down first. A fun way to help the child learn this is to tell them to them remember the ponytail goes straight down first and then up and around.   /p/ /p/ ponytails always hang down.
>
> This is another letter where it is helpful to make a large texture letter to practice tracing. Just be sure the child is tracing correctly with going down first just like a /p/ ponytail then up and around.

Word Making Game: Make words with the sound tiles. Make sure the child says individual sounds and uses proper blending. After he completes the word, have him read the word using finger tracking. Correct any errors. **"Please make the word ____"**

Use tiles.... a e i o   d l m n p s t   th
pit and pat net pot not pan lap sip mop   this set tip met pet path sap
top map that let dip than land stop nest past spit pest plan sand
pond melt slap stand   stomp slant   stamp

Use tiles..... a e i o   d f l n p r s t
on lip red in pet rot sod let nod   fed lot led fin step spin drip spit spot
drop trip prod rest pond sift slip pelt nest flip left raft trap sped loft felt
flap strip print

Sound Changing Game: "Now we have a new word making game with the sound tiles. This time you will make a word and then listen to see what changes you need to make a new word. (Demonstrate an example to the child of how you make the word and then change one sound to make the new word). Please make the word _____. (first word on list). Be sure the child is saying the sounds as he puts down the appropriate tiles. When the child finishes the word, do *not* clear the tiles. After the child reads the completed word to you, say "good job, that word says _____. Now listen carefully. Please change the sound to make the word _____ (say next word on the list). Correct any errors immediately. **See page 34 for complete illustrated directions**.

Use tiles a i o f m n p(2) t
    map > tap > tip > tim > tom > top > pop > pip > pit> pin > fin

Use tiles a e i o f n p r s t
    net > not > rot > pot > pit > fit > fat >fan > fin > sin > sit > pit > pet > net

Use tiles.....a i o e f m p r s t(2)
    fast> fist > mist > mast > past > pest > rest > test

Use tiles..... a i th t s m n
    that > sat > mat > math > mat > that> than > thin

Reading Words: Have your child read the following words sounding out with finger tracking and proper blending. Correct any errors immediately.

if	is	a	am	in
at	it	an	on	I
did	not	and	its	dim
mop	that	doll	this	lit
sap	lip	met	top	lap
than	fed	pot	let	pan
tap	net	pad	lot	sip
tell	pod	fat	sod	map

rip →	red →	pet →	dad →	less →
thin →	mess →	rod →	pass →	fan →
math →	rip →	pit →	ran →	did →
let →	fin →	dip →	led →	ant →
set →	tip →	red →	till →	path →
off →	lot →	rim →	rap →	pet →
nip →	dot →	lap →	pep →	pit →
math →	pest →	snip →	land →	sled →
lost →	step →	test →	mist →	stop →
drop →	slip →	nest →	slim →	fret →
step →	flat →	plod →	trap →	flip →
slit →	melt →	this →	felt →	plan →
flat →	lamp →	spin →	past →	land →
pest →	spit →	tint →	fast →	slop →
loft →	sand →	trim →	slam →	pond →

slap   last   slot   lost   pelt

list   melt   trip   stop   that

pond   sped   left   spell   not

WOW! You just read 130 words. What an awesome reader!

Writing (Spelling) Words: Select some words from the list above for your child to write/spell. See page 40 for detailed directions on how to conduct this activity.

Reading Sentences: Have child read the following sentences. Make sure the child is sounding out with proper blending and finger tracking. Immediately correct any errors. After the child reads the sentence, ask him a few questions about what he read. Ask a specific question like…, What was on the path. Or what do you need to hand Dad? You can have him pick one of the sentences then you can copy it onto on a blank sheet of paper and have him illustrate the 'story' for him to read to someone special.

An ant is on a path.

Tim is in a pond.

I am lost.

Drop off a math test.

That is not a fat rat.

It is a thin rat.

I ran fast. I am not last.

Pam is on a trip.

This is a mess.

64

Lesson 9:

Review Sounds: Quickly practice the sounds you have learned! Have your child follow under with their finger and say the sounds.

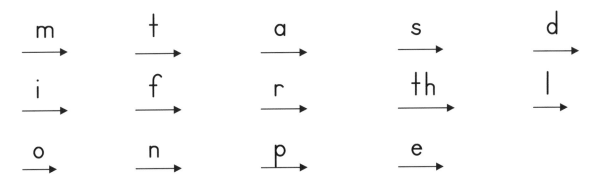

m   t   a   s   d

i   f   r   th   l

o   n   p   e

Reading Words: We are going to learn a new word. Before we start we will practice the 2 sounds that make the word.

th   the sound /th/... have the child finger track and say sound

e   the sound /e/ and /ee/, this word uses the second sound /ee/

         Have the child finger track and say the /ee/ sound

Let's put the sounds together and practice sounding out our new word. Point to the letters and tell the child "remember (point at th) the sound is /th/ and (point at the e) the e has the /ee/ sound. Note: You can teach 'the' as either /thee/ or /thə/. As the child learns, he will read/pronounce 'the' how he says it in oral speech.

the   the   the

Great job! Let's try our new word in a sentence.

The man is mad.

The ant is red.

The pet is lost.

The map is flat.

The rat is not fat.

The spot is on the rim.

Lesson 10:

Teach Sounds:

h

>

This letter has the sound /h/. We always say /h/ fast.
The little mark > reminds us to say /h/ fast. (Note: /h/ can be tricky. Have the child practice feeling the short puff of air with their hand in front of their mouth as he quickly says /h/.)

v

This letter has the sound /v/.
Notice how /v/ vibrates (shakes) your lower lip

Practice Sound Cards: Add the new sound cards to your collection. **Practice the sound cards for: h, v** + previous sounds **m, t, a, s, d, i, f, r, th, l, o, n, e, p.** Make sure your child finger tracks and says the sound correctly.

Write and Say Sounds: Have the child write (or trace) each letter. Make sure your child forms the letter correctly and says the sound as he writes. **Please write and say each of the sounds 5 times: h v p e o l n + any other sound the child needs to practice.**

Word Making Game: Make words with the sound tiles. Make sure the child says the sounds as he makes the words and uses proper blending. After he completes the word, have him read the word using finger tracking. Correct any errors. **"Please make the word _____"**

Use tiles.... a e i o   d h l m n p r t
      and hid hot him hit   had   hat red hop ham met nod not let mop help
      pet lip pod dip lamp pond   hint   hand   melt limp trap held land ramp

Use tiles..... a e i   d f l m n p r s t v   th
      vat vet van rest vest vast nest past drop spit drip stamp ramp prim
      hit fed this felt than   pelt   that slip flint damp math strip print

Sound Changing Game: Let's play our sound changing game again. Remember, I will tell you a word and you will listen carefully so you can hear the sound that changes. The child says the sounds as he picks up the tile and sounds out the word with proper blending. When the child finishes the word and reads it to you, don't clear the tiles. Say "good job, that word says ___, now can you please make ___ (next word listed). Correct any errors immediately. See page 34.

Use tiles a i o d h m p t
      him > hit > hid > had > hat > hot > hop > hip > him > dim
Use tiles.....a e i   h l n s t v
      vet > vat > van >
      hint > lint > list > last > vast > vest
Use tiles....a e   f l m p s t v
      felt >   melt > pelt > pest > vest > vast
Use tiles...a e i o f l p s t
      step > stop > slop > slip > flip > flop > flap > flat > slat

Reading Words: Have your child read the following words sounding out with finger tracking and proper blending. Correct any errors immediately.

am	if	at	on	an
I	in	is	a	the
lit	rod	and	not	him
had	hot	off	vet	dim
its	hat	led	hop	doll
red	did	ham	pin	this
let	nod	hiss	pad	fell
hit	pet	lot	that	red
pass	hip	path	sell	rat
net	lip	rap	him	mop
top	vet	nap	nod	tell
than	hid	van	moth	vat
fill	rim	fad	pot	hop
pin	lad	pop	lap	hip

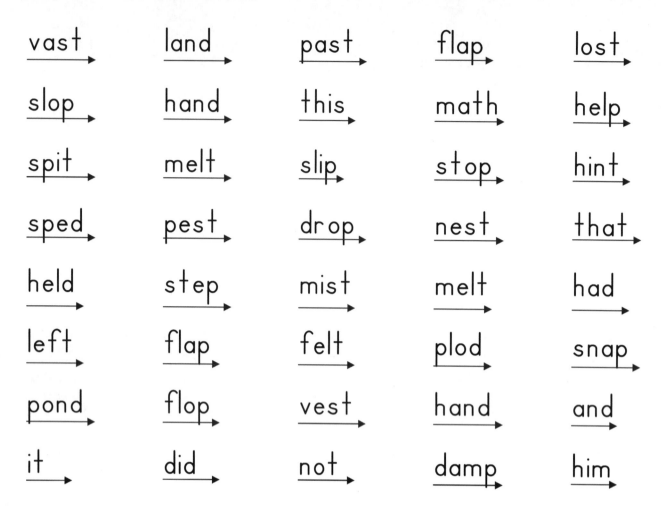

vast	land	past	flap	lost
slop	hand	this	math	help
spit	melt	slip	stop	hint
sped	pest	drop	nest	that
held	step	mist	melt	had
left	flap	felt	plod	snap
pond	flop	vest	hand	and
it	did	not	damp	him

WOW ! You just read 110 words. What an awesome reader!

Writing (Spelling) Words: Select some words from the list above for your child to write/spell. See page 40 for detailed directions on how to conduct this activity.

Reading Sentences: Have child read the following sentences. Make sure the child is sounding out, using finger tracking, blending properly. Immediately correct any errors. After the child reads the sentence, ask him a few questions about what he read. Ask a specific question like….Where was the raft? What was on the hill? …etc..

The raft is at the pond.

The ant is on the hill.

Hand Dad the mop. Mop this spot.

Slip past the red ant hill.

Tom had the last hot ham.

I left the net at the pond.

I lost the doll.

The doll had a red vest.

The sand is in the pot.

Tell him to step off the pad.

Lesson 11:

Teach Sounds:

sh

Remember when we learned about buddy letters! These 'buddy letters' work together to have the sound /sh/.
(Just like when your mom wants you to be quiet /shh/)

u

This letter has 2 sounds! The sounds are /u/ and /oo/. At first you will practice words with the /u/ sound and later you will practice words with the /oo/ sound. Later you will learn how it sometimes is silly and has a 3rd sound /uu/ but for now when you see the letter **u** you will learn the 2 sounds /u/ and /oo/.

b
>

This letter has the sound /b/. We always say /b/ fast.
The > mark under the b reminds us we always say /b/ fast.
** Specifically point out to the child how the /b/ first has a tall straight part like a board. The tall board is first, then the round part. In /b/ the big board for building tall buildings is first.

Practice Sound Cards: Add the new sound cards to your collection. Make sure your child finger tracks and says the sound correctly. **Practice the sound cards for: sh, u, b** + previous sounds **m**, **t**, **a**, **s**, **d**, **i**, **f**, **r**, **th**, **l**, **o**, **n**, **e**, **p,h**, **v**

Write and Say Sounds:
Have the child write (or trace) each letter. Make sure your child forms the letter correctly and says the sound as he writes. **Please write and say each of the sounds 5 times: sh u b h v e p o + any other sound the child needs to practice.**

/b/- big board

Formation of the b is very important to prevent the child from confusing d, b and p. To help the child avoid confusion emphasize b is a tall letter starting with a big straight part. You start at the top and go straight down making the tall/big straight part first, then go up and around to make the short round part. A fun way to help a child learn this is to tell the child to remember the b /b/ has the 'big board' for a big building first. You can even demonstrate with a real 2x4 to show the child boards make buildings, tall straight 'boards' make /b/-b! When writing b remember the /b/ big board for the building is first.

This is another letter where it is helpful to make a large texture letter to practice tracing. Just be sure the child is tracing correctly with starting at the top of the tall board, going down and then up and around. The big board for /b/.

Word Making Game:
Make words with the sound tiles. Ensure the child says the sounds as he makes the words and smoothly blends the sounds. After he completes the word, have him read the word using finger tracking. Correct any errors. **"Please make the word _____"**
Use tiles.... a i o u   b h m n p r s t   sh
  run rib but ash hush bus rub bun tub hut sub shin sun shut rash shop
  sash hunt bash ship must stub bunt ramp runt rush spin hump shrub
Use sound tiles... a e i o u   d f l m n p s t   sh
  fish nest fun shot sham mud dish shin shed lash mash lush mesh
  shun dash lump pelt dust slush lint plum melt flash punt flush dump

Sound Changing Game:
Remember with the sound changing game you listen and make changes to the word to make a new word.
Use sound tiles.... a i o u   b d r t
  tub > rub > rob > rib > rid > red > bed > bad > bud > but > bit> bat
Use sound tiles...... a i o u b h n p t sh
  bash > bat > bit > bin > shin > ship > shop > hop > hip> hit > hot > hut > shut
Use sound tiles...a u   h l n r t sh
  lash > rash > rush > hush > hut > shut> rut > run > rush > lush
Use sound tiles... a e u b h n s t v
  vet > bet > bat > hat > hut > but > bus > bun > ban > van

Reading Words:
Have your child read the following words sounding out with finger tracking and proper blending. Correct any errors immediately.

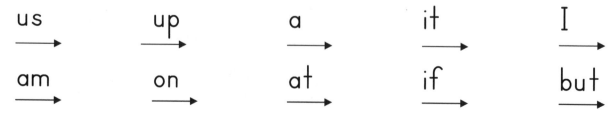

is	in	the	an	him
tub	and	its	ash	bit
bat	fun	that	rub	lap
pup	bet	fuss	let	pass
hut	had	but	run	hip
bus	lab	dud	hill	ship
hum	hid	rod	this	sun
bit	mash	bun	fed	bat
hum	bass	mud	rut	bad
did	shut	fish	tub	hut
bell	rob	bun	shell	nut
hush	bed	lash	shin	vet
dish	ship	rush	shop	rib
hunt	stop	dust	rash	shed
us	shut	nun	stub	hash

rust	vest	shush	mint	shrub
soft	drum	trip	bunt	must
band	plus	shrill	plum	slush
pump	help	best	shred	trash
held	plan	hint	bled	vest
dust	drum	melt	still	thump
silt	shift	belt	fresh	bless
nest	lump	mint	dump	plot

WOW ! You just read 125 words. What an awesome reader!

Writing (Spelling) Words: Select some of the listed words for your child to write.

Reading Sentences: Have your child read with finger tracking and proper blending. Immediately correct any errors. After he reads a sentence, ask a few specific questions.

The fish is in the pond.

Sam is last on the list. Sam felt sad.

The red rat is on the ship.

Fran held the drum.

Help us hunt the ram.

Stop at that shrub.

The sun is hot.

Mud is on the pup. Help him hop in the bath tub.

This math is fun.

Did I run fast?

It is fun to hop in the mud.

Pam fell in the mud.

Bill shut the lid on the tub.

Lesson 12:

Review Sounds: Let's quickly practice the sounds you have learned!

m	t	a	s	d
i	f	r	th	l
o	n	p	e	h
v	sh	u	b	

73

Reading Irregular Words: We are going to learn a few new words. These are kind of 'silly' or irregular words that we say differently than they should sound out.

to   /t//o/ is how this word should sound out but this word is a little "silly" or irregular.

We say **to**. Let's read **to** together. Finger track and say **to** with the child. Then have the child read to alone. If the child sounds out **to** as /t//o/ say something like "Stop, that's how we sound out the word. Do you remember how we say it? We say **to**."

Great job SAYING the word **to** correctly. I'll use our new word in a few sentences so you can hear the word. These sentences are strictly for the adult to read to the child. The child should not read these as they contain sounds not yet learned. When you read emphasize **to**: --Grandma gave the book **to** me. --I like to go **to** my friend's house. --Please go **to** the front of the line.

Now you can practice saying this word correctly. Have the child finger track as he says **to**.

to   to   to

Ok, here is another word that is also a little silly or irregular.

do   /d//o/ is how this word should sound out but this word is a little "silly" or irregular.

We say **do**. Let's read **do** together. Finger track and say **do** with child. Then have the child read it alone. If the child sounds out **do** as /d//o/ say something like, "Stop. That's how we sound out the word. Do you remember how we say it? We say **do**.

Let's practice saying this word correctly (have child finger track as he says the word)

do   do   do

Great job SAYING the word **do** correctly. I'll use our new word in a few sentences so you can hear the word. (These sentences are strictly for the adult to read to the child. The child should not read these as they contain sounds not yet learned. When you read emphasize **do**): --**Do** you like ice cream? --We **do** not throw rocks on the playground.   --Please **do** not run in class!

Let's practice saying those words one more time!

to   to   do   do

Great job! Let's try our new words in a few sentences. Have the child read these sentences. Make immediate corrections. If the child makes an error on the irregular words simply say "oops... do you remember how we say that word".

Hand this to him.   Run to Dad.

It is fun to fish.   Do not hit the pup.

Lesson 13:

Teach Sounds:

ck

Remember when we learned about buddy letters! These "buddy letters" have the sound /k/. We always say /k/ fast. The little > under the 'ck' reminds us we always say /k/ fast

k

This letter has the sound /k/. We always say /k/ fast.

The > mark under the **k** reminds us we always say /k/ fast.

I bet you noticed that both the **ck** and the **k** make the same /k/ sound. You are right! **ck** and **k** both make the same /k/ sound. When you start reading you will notice that **ck** is never used at the beginning of words, but rather mostly at the end of words that have the /a/ /i/ /o// /u/ or /e/ sound right before the /k/ sound (sock, back, lick, deck, luck). Directly point out this pattern as the child reads and makes words.

Practice Sound Cards: Add the new sound cards to your collection. **Practice the sound cards for: k, ck**, + previous sounds **m, t, a, s, d, i, f, r, th, l, o, n, e, p,h, v, sh, u, b** Make sure your child finger tracks and says the sound correctly.

Write and Say Sounds: Have the child write (or trace) each letter. Make sure your child forms the letter correctly and says the sound as he writes. **Write and say each of the sounds 5 times: ck k sh u b h e p + any other sound the child needs to practice.**

Word Making Game: As the child makes words with the sound tiles, ensure he says the individual sounds and uses smooth blending skills. After he completes the word, have him read the word using finger tracking. Correct any errors. **"Please make the word _____"**

**Directly point out to the child how 'ck' is used at the end of the word after the short /a/ /e/ /i/ /o/ or /u/ vowel sounds. Use sound tiles: a e i o u   b d f l m n p r s t ck
lock tick dock rub luck bed muck elf deck rib sick rock duck lack tuck lick sack bled black melt felt flack stack stick flick stuck track blot truck fleck trick blast unpack radish backup punish

Use sound tiles: a e i o u   d k l m n p r s t sh
kim ask elk kid run kin mud shin shop ted mash ramp desk kept task dusk skip silk skin skid must skim milk dust skit spin tusk silt

Sound Changing Game: Remember with the sound changing game you listen and make changes to the word to make a new word.
Use sound tiles... a i o u d k l m n p s sh
skid > skin > skip > slip > slop > slosh > slash > slap > slam > slum
Use sound tiles... a i o u b n p s t ck
stub > stun > stan > stab > stack > stick > stock > stop
Use sound tiles.... a i u b l p r s t sh ck
track > truck > trick > trish > trash > brash > brush > blush > slush > slash > slap > slack
Use sound tiles a i u b h k l m n p r s t
milk > silk > sulk > sunk > bunk > bunt > hunt > runt > rant > pant > past > mast > mask

Reading Words: Have your child read the following words sounding out with finger tracking and proper blending. Correct any errors immediately. Although the directional arrows are no longer included, *make sure the child still uses finger tracking.*

Directly teach the 'ck' spelling pattern: Tell the child to notice how the 'ck' spelling is never used at the beginning of words and how this 'ck' is used at the end of words that have the /a/, /i/, /o/, /u/, or /e/ sound right before the /k/ sound. Stop the child after he reads a 'ck' word. Ask him to point to where the 'ck' spelling was used in the word.

sock	back	lick	deck	luck
sick	dock	pack	thick	pick
lick	rock	sack	duck	lock

Read mixed word list including 'ck' and 'k' words

us	up	a	it	am
ash	in	is	at	kit
to	Kim	I	back	but
hut	sick	had	deck	and
ask	kid	ship	lock	to
sack	luck	not	nick	run
bus	dock	than	do	peck
tick	sun	kin	sock	rub
rock	and	mash	kick	fed
lick	shin	sack	but	rib
tub	shut	fish	this	hush

kill	deck	if	mud	did
tick	him	to	fun	luck
dish	lash	thick	shop	elk
kiss	bus	rush	tack	hush
pack	pick	that	tick	puck
rush	shock	duck	ask	shack
neck	bash	rack	shell	help
milk	stub	desk	skin	truck
hunt	kelp	dust	stop	bunt
skill	trick	silk	rust	mask
block	shrub	held	flick	slack
skip	slob	skid	drum	husk
stick	must	brick	plus	stack
flat	sunk	task	must	slam
risk	bunk	past	dump	skit
held	trick	shrill	fleck	track
dusk	tusk	black	flash	stuck
help	rock	than	had	let

- - - Begin reading words with 5 sounds. Remind child to 'take a breath' before starting and to smoothly blend the sounds together. Blending needs to be established to handle 5 sounds. - - -

slant	stand	stamp	plant	print
flunk	brand	stilt	blond	shrimp
stump	trust	stomp	trunk	slump

Writing (Spelling) Words: Select some of the listed words for your child to write. In these learning stages, don't mix 'k' and 'ck' spellings. Tell the child in these words the /k/ sound will be spelled with the 'ck' and give 'ck' words. Then tell him the /k/ sound in these words is spelled with 'k' and give the child 'k' words to spell.

Reading Sentences: Have your child read with finger tracking and proper blending. Immediately correct any errors. After he reads a sentence, ask a few specific questions.

Skim milk is on the list.

Ham is on the list.

Rush the back-pack to Kim. Kim's hat is in the pack.

Stop at the dock and pick up the shrimp.

The pup is sick. Hand this pill to him.

The red hat is in his left hand.

Do not run up the hill. Rush to the pond.
Dad is at the pond. Run to him.
Pick up rocks to toss.
It is fun to skip rocks on the pond.
But, do not hit the duck!

Lesson 14:

Review Sounds: Let's quickly practice the sounds you learned! Have your child follow under with their finger and say the sounds. Use the review to see what sounds your child may need additional practice with. Practice until the child knows these sounds automatically!

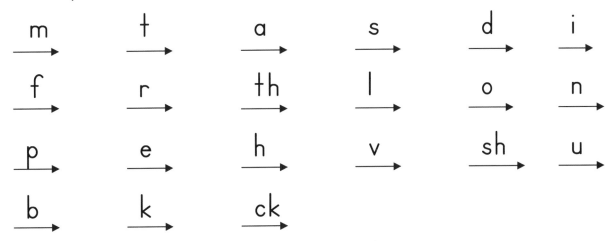

Great job! Look how many sounds you know!

Reading Irregular Words: We are going to learn a new word. This is a 'silly' or irregular word that we say differently than it should sound out.

said   /s//a//i//d/ is how this word should sound out but this word is a little "silly" or irregular.

We say **said**. Let's read **said** together. Finger track and say **said** with the child. Then have the child track and say it alone. If the child sounds out **said** as /s//a//i//d/ say something like "Stop, that's how we should sound out the word but do you remember how we say it? We say **said.**

Great job SAYING the word **said** correctly. I'll use our new word in a few sentences so you can hear the word. These sentences are strictly for the adult to read to the child. The child should not read these as they contain sounds not yet learned. When you read emphasize **said**:   --Grandma **said** she will come see me. -Mike **said**, "I love hot dogs". -I **said**, "You are becoming an awesome reader".

Now practice saying this word correctly. Be sure the child is finger tracking as he says the word 'said' correctly.

said   said   said   said

Reading Sentences: Ok, now it's your turn to read our new word in a sentence. Have child read the following sentences. Make sure the child uses finger tracking. Immediately correct any errors. If the child makes an error on the irregular words (to, do, said) simply say "oops… do you remember how we say that word".

Mom **said** to run to bed.

I **said**, "Kim is fast."

Tom **said**, "A duck is on the pond".

Jack **said** to pet the pup.

Mom **said** to pick up that red vest.

More Practice Reading Words: Have your child read the following words sounding out with finger tracking and proper blending. Correct any errors immediately. Although the directional arrows are no longer included, *make sure the child still uses finger tracking.*

tip	pup	that	top	this
pop	dim	mop	sin	dock
fat	Kim	fan	back	but
fin	sick	had	not	and
ask	kid	ship	lock	fill
bus	dock	than	run	dish
tick	sun	kin	sock	muck
rock	said	mash	kick	fed
tub	shut	fish	met	hush
dish	lash	shop	elk	shin
kiss	neck	bell	toss	bib
bash	fell	led	math	shell

Tim	vet	Bill	rut	fib
set	rush	miss	net	luck
shock	dip	pack	thin	us
hid	moth	duck	top	shin
dull	math	mash	thick	him
let	this	sit	rob	ran
hint	bless	help	sped	must
skip	rust	brick	trash	desk
track	skin	plan	milk	snuck
shock	held	fresh	black	lump
hush	shift	shell	brush	band
soft	best	slush	vest	still
plot	dump	stick	skim	last
said	picks	sand	left	that

- - - 5 sounds - - -   Remember to take a breath and blend smoothly.

stomp	trust	plant	drums	blocks
blast	stand	print	bland	helps

Lesson 15:

Teach Sounds:

c

>

This letter has 2 sounds. The sounds are /k/ and /s/.

We always say /k/ fast. The > under **c** reminds us we always say /k/ fast. At first you will practice the /k/ sound.   Later you will learn how **c** has the /s/ sound whenever **e i** or **y** comes after the **c** and practice reading words these where the **c** steals the /s/ sound. You will learn both the /k/ and /s/ sound for **c**.

g

>

This letter has 2 sounds. It has the sound /g/ and sometimes the /j/ sound.

The > under the g reminds us to always say /g/ fast. At first you will practice reading words with the /g/ sound. Later you will learn how the g can have the /j/ sound when it is followed by **e**, **i** or **y**.   We will practice words when the g steals the /j/ sound a little later.   You will learn **g** has 2 sounds /g/ and /j/.

Practice Sound Cards: Add the new sound cards to your collection and **practice the sound cards for: c, g,** + **previous sounds**. Make sure your child follows under the letter with his finger and says the sound correctly.

Write and Say Sounds: Have the child write (or trace) each letter. Make sure your child forms the letter correctly and says the sound as he writes. **Please write and say each of the sounds 5 times: c   g   ck   k   sh   u   b   + any other sound the child needs to practice.**

Word Making Game: As the child makes words with the sound tiles, ensure he says the individual sounds and uses smooth blending skills. After he completes the word, have him read the word using finger tracking. Correct any errors. **"Please make the word _____ "**
Use tiles.... a i o u   b c d g l m n p r s t
  cat bag   can big dug   cab bug cap   mug bog cub cob pug clip clap camp
  clod   crab grab   plug   crop grub scum slug claps clasp scrub clamp clump crisp

Use tiles..... a i(2) o u   c d f g h n r s t sh
  fig fog tug hug lag gob tag hog got act gush shag scan frog glad gust grub
  shut scat   grip   drag rust gift shrug crush grunt grand crust crash finish

Use sound tiles... a e i   d f g k l m n p r t (2)
  pig elm kid get elk land tilt flag melt left gift raft rift milk lift
  grid   felt   film   grin glad drag flat   grip   graft plant grant glint

Sound Changing Game: Remember with the sound changing game you listen and make changes to the word to make a new word.
Use sound tiles ...... a i   b d f g l r ck sh
  fish> dish > dash > lash > bash > gash > rash > rack > shack > back
Use sound tiles.... a i o   b c d g p r t
  grin > grip > trip > trap > crap > crop > drop > drip
Use sound tiles..... a e i u b c d g l m p r s t
  crisp > crimp > cramp > clamp > clump > glump > grump
  crust > crest > crept
  clap > clam > cram > crab > grab > grad > glad

82

Reading Words: Have your child read the words with proper blending skills. (Although the directional arrows are no longer included, *make sure the child still uses finger tracking.*)

a	it	us	up	am
ash	in	is	at	kit
an	if	had	its	that
I	on	than	cot	him
cut	get	leg	doll	fill
nut	pig	mug	but	fog
dug	cop	bug	and	hug
this	to	can	rug	back
fig	gum	hog	did	got
not	thug	ask	the	kid
lock	do	peg	get	cub
cap	cob	dog	act	big
shut	beg	cat	shop	elk
shin	kiss	said	fuss	bag
tag	gut	hush	gap	can
log	thin	gash	dig	cash
clap	gust	milk	best	skin

clock	snag	cast	must	skit
gimp	hunt	clip	camp	plug
grub	long	frog	sunk	gift
grip	crop	grab	clam	cram
glad	crash	flag	grill	truck
brick	glass	crush	shrug	clod
crab	glob	crib	slug	snack
grin	fled	cloth	grid	clash
cross	drag	click	floss	class

- - - 5 sounds - - - Remember to take a breath and blend smoothly.

crept	grump	plugs	grits	craft
crisp	clump	graft	crest	grand
shrimp	grant	clamp	crust	grunt

Writing (Spelling) Words: Select some of the listed words for your child to write.

Reading Sentences: Have your child read with finger tracking. Make immediate corrections. After the child reads a sentence, ask him a few specific questions.

The red bug is on the grass.

The flag is up on the big stick.

Mom got skim milk and buns at the snack shop.

I can toss a rock at the stump and hit it.

I can smell the skunk.

The cat had a bath in the tub. The cat is a grump.

Sam held the fish up on a long stick.

Mom said, "I left the gift on the desk".

The red brick fell and hit the cat. The cat got its leg stuck. I got the brick off the cat's leg. The cat is glad.

The dog can stomp in the mud. The mud is on the dog. Sam can scrub the mud off the dog. The dog is mad at Sam.

The frog can get up on the log.

I fed the fat black cat.

The red and black bug is on the plant.

Kim can pick up the cat and pet him.

The truck got stuck in the mud.

Dad did not get a big fish. I got the big fish. Dad can grill up the big fish that I got. Then Dad and I can munch on the fish.

Lesson 16:

Teach Sounds:

j
>

This letter has the sound /j/. We always say the /j/ sound fast.

The > under the j helps remind us we need to always say /j/ fast.

w

This letter has the sound /w/.

Practice Sound Cards: Add the new sound cards to your collection. **Practice the sound cards for: j, w** + previous sounds the child does not know automatically. Make sure your child follows under the letter with his finger and says the sound correctly

Write and Say Sounds: Have the child write (or trace) each letter. Make sure your child forms the letter correctly and says the sound as he writes. **Please write and say each of the sounds 5 times: j w c g ck k sh** + any other sound the child needs to practice.

Word Making Game: As the child makes words with the sound tiles, ensure he says the individual sounds and uses smooth blending skills. After he completes the word, have him read the word using finger tracking. Correct any errors. **"Please make the word _____"**
Use sound tiles...a e i(2) o   b j k l m s t w   sh th
　　kim   with   jim   wish   ask   jam   jet   jab   jot   job   jot   lot   shed   welt   mast   best   shag
　　lost   wilt   jest   task   last   mask   within
Use sound tiles... a e i o u   c g j   m n p   r s t(2) v w
　　jig   wet   jog   win   wig   van   jug   wag   vet   west   vast   swim   twig   swam   just   twin   jest
　　test   gust   swig   jump   trust   grump   twist   panic   inject   topic   project   invest   tropic

Sound Changing Game: Remember with the sound changing game you listen and make changes to the word to make a new word.
Use sound tiles....... a i e o b j k l m t
　　kim > tim > jim > jam > jab > job > jot > jet > met > let
Use sound tiles..... e i u   d j l s t w
　　just > jest > west > welt > wilt
Use sound tiles ... a o i   g l m n s t w
　　swam > slam > slim > swim > swig > twig > twin

Reading Words: Have your child read the following words to you, sounding out with finger tracking and proper blending. Immediately correct any errors.

get   in   is   us   it

wig   job   will   can   do

jack	had	its	that	wet
less	than	cot	him	win
cub	elk	act	with	Jim
jug	web	to	wag	cut
this	off	gum	cog	jig
back	but	jog	wish	and
jet	got	did	not	ask
the	luck	well	wick	jock
wed	wit	web	fuss	said
win	Jess	toss	mud	can
jam	dish	Josh	shell	Jill
kin	cup	lick	get	duck
bell	hog	pick	shag	will
drag	west	swim	twin	jump
swish	best	scat	nest	must
glad	fast	brag	trip	spell
just	gust	cluck	cast	camp

grub	frog	weld	gift	swig
crash	flag	with	swell	junk
plug	hand	gasp	kept	hunt
grin	hint	glad	welt	plug
romp	pluck	skip	flip	wilt
clog	jobs	class	wept	cross
twig	band	wins	shrug	swill

- - - 5 sounds - - - Remember to take a breath and blend smoothly.

glint	swung	twist	skunk	stand
swift	stump	plant	grasp	plunk
clump	grunt	stamp	grand	frost

Writing (Spelling) Words: Select some of the listed words for your child to write.

Reading Sentences: Have your child read with proper blending and tracking. Make immediate corrections. After the child reads a sentence, ask him a few specific questions.

Jess will camp and hunt elk with Dad.

Hand the wet rag to Jack.

Jill is swift. Jill will run fast on the track. Jill will win.

Jim just set the gift on the desk. I will pick it up.

I wish I had a pet red frog.

The sun sets in the west.

The big dog can jump in the pond. The dog will swim and splash and get wet. The pup can jump in the pond and swim with the big dog.

The big cat sits up on the rock.

Lesson 17:

Review Sounds: Quickly practice the sounds you learned!

m	t	a	s	d
i	f	r	th	l
o	n	p	e	h
v	sh	u	b	k
ck	c	g	j	w

Great job! Look how many sounds you know! Use the review to see what sounds your child may need additional practice with. You want the child to know these automatically.

Reading Irregular Words: We are going to learn a new word. This is another 'silly' or irregular word that we say somewhat differently than it should sound out.

was   /w//a//z/ is how this word should sound out but this word is a little "silly" or irregular.

We say **was** /**wuz**/. Let's read **was** together. Finger track and say **was** with the child. Then have the child track and say it alone. If the child sounds out **was** as /w//a//s/ say something like "Stop, that's how we should sound out the word but do you remember how we say it? We say **was** /**wuz**/.

Great job SAYING the word **was** correctly. I'll use our new word in a few sentences so you can hear the word. These sentences are strictly for the adult to read to the child as they contain sounds the child has not yet learned. When you read emphasize **was**: --Grandma **was** happy she got to come and see you. --Mike **was** a good basketball player.   -Jessica **was** kind to her classmates.

89

Now practice reading **was** correctly. Have the child finger track as he says the word correctly.

was   was   was   was

Reading Sentences: Ok, now it's your turn to read our new word in a sentence. Have child read the following sentences. Immediately correct any errors. If the child makes an error on the irregular words simply say "oops… do you remember how we say that word".

Mom **was** glad that I got the big fish.

Sam **was** a fun dog to pet. Sam **was** soft.

The bug **was** red and black.

I **was** sad.

The cat got wet. The cat **was** mad.

More Practice Reading Words: Have your child read the following words sounding out with finger tracking and proper blending. Correct any errors immediately.

us	up	if	its	did
wet	not	got	this	mud
fish	it	get	I	on
an	can	wig	Jim	him
will	had	cup	that	net
cat	thin	hot	nut	jug
fib	but	and	jam	well
tub	dull	wag	cut	mop
red	sip	sick	fed	dock
dim	hit	sin	wish	puff

gut	met	fish	shop	dash
with	back	deck	dish	bet
win	shut	gap	than	cash
lash	job	mesh	bed	jog
beg	rush	bell	jig	cop
west	black	camp	slip	twin
jump	pest	grub	past	glob
plum	trick	step	kept	lost
grin	clog	snag	cross	shelf
twig	risk	mask	grip	spell
best	hulk	mist	help	plug
lump	bless	clap	brag	swish
plan	left	junk	swim	stop
crash	stub	shred	lift	just
stuck	frog	shrub	fresh	crush

- - - 5 sounds - - - Remember to take a breath and blend smoothly.

jumps	twist	print	melts	grand
craft	stand	swift	stamp	crust
clamp	frost	shrimp	trust	drift

91

Lesson 18:

Teach Sounds:

ch

These buddy letters have the sound /ch/.

>   Say /ch/ quickly, just like when you chop with an axe /ch/ /ch/.
(Note to instructor: In a few words the ch has the /k/ sound. The child will learn about this later. For now just practice the /ch/ sound.)

tch

These buddy letters also have the sound /ch/.

>   These buddy letters are a little silly because the **t** is 'silent'. It does not have any sound or change the /ch/ sound.

Good job noticing. The **ch** and **tch** do have the same /ch/ sound! Most of the time the /**ch**/ sound is spelled with '**ch**' buddy letters. The '**tch**' spelling is not used in many words. You are going to learn when we use the 'ch' spelling and when we use the silly 'tch' spelling.

Practice Sound Cards: Add the new sound cards to your collection and **practice sound cards for: ch, tch** + previous sounds the child doesn't know automatically.

Write and Say Sounds: Have the child write (or trace) each letter. Make sure your child forms the letter correctly and says the sound as he writes. **Please write and say each of the sounds 5 times: ch tch j w c g + any other sound the child needs to practice.**

Word Making Game: Make words with the sound tiles. Make sure your child says the individual sounds and uses proper blending skills. After he completes the word, have him read the word using finger tracking. Correct any errors. **"Please make the word _____"**
Use sound tiles..... a e i o u   b f   g   m   n   p   r s   t   ch
     inch chat fib much chop chip bug chug fig such chin rich punch grin brag finch
     bunch chant ranch champ chest munch chimp chum branch brunch pinch grinch

Use sound tiles   a   e   i   o   u   b   d   h   l   m   n   p w tch
     latch hitch itch   match pitch notch witch hutch etch batch ditch patch

Sound Changing Game: Remember to listen and make changes to the word.
Use sound tiles..... a i   o   b   c h p t th ch
    chip > chap > chat > that > hat > hit > hot > cot > cat> bat > bath

Use sound tiles.... u m ch s b h n
    much > such > sum > chum > chub > hub > hum > bum > bun > sun

Practicing Reading Words with the 'ch' spelling for the /ch/ sound: Tell the child the 'ch' is the most common spelling for the /ch/ sound. Directly show and teach the 'ch' is always used when the /ch/ sound begins a word..

chop	chin	chip	chill	chat
chap	chuck	chug	chess	chick
chum	chomp	chunk	chant	chimp

champ   chest   chips   check   chop

The 'ch' is also used at the end of a word when there is a consonant right before the /ch/ sound. (Later the child will learn how 'ch' is also used after all the vowel and r-controlled vowel combinations)

inch   bunch   belch   finch   punch

ranch   pinch   branch   grinch   crunch

Show how these common words are spelled with the 'ch'.

*much   *such   *rich

Practicing Reading Words with the 'tch' spelling for the /ch/ sound:
Tell the child the 'tch' is NOT used very often. Directly teach and show how the 'tch' spelling is ONLY used when the /ch/ sound is at the end of a word (or syllable) immediately following a single short vowel sound. Point out the pattern as the child reads through the list. (note that much, such and rich are exceptions and use the 'ch' spelling)

itch   etch   fetch   pitch   latch

batch   ditch   catch   twitch   match

switch   stitch   clutch   stretch   Dutch

Writing (Spelling) Words:
Specifically teach the 'ch' and 'tch' spelling patterns described above and have the child practice writing words with these patterns. Don't mix spelling patterns in the early learning stages. Teach and practice spelling the 'ch' words first. Tell the child in these words the /ch/ sound is spelled with 'ch' and then give words from the 'ch' list. Explain the pattern. Directly teach much, such and rich. After the child has learned the 'ch' spelling, directly teach and practice spelling pattern for the 'tch' words. Do not mix words or test at the learning stages. Teach and practice the expected patterns. The child needs to learn that most words with a /ch/ sound are spelled with 'ch' and you only use the 'goofy tch' at the end of a word with a single short vowel sound. See spelling lesson # 10.

Reading Mixed List of Words:
Have your child read the following words to you, sounding out with finger tracking and proper blending. Immediately correct any errors.

to   get   is   this   not

fed   chip   can   such   got

than   him   do   had   catch

said	will	chin	with	much
on	chat	was	wish	chug
gut	shop	chill	shell	patch
that	wick	gum	thin	sip
cut	ditch	chuck	sick	chop
jog	ship	catch	kid	puff
nut	wet	shut	batch	chess
pitch	tub	notch	chap	latch
sun	fetch	fish	itch	back
inch	jack	check	well	chum
twin	lunch	fast	swim	clap
punch	glitch	fresh	finch	clock
grass	ranch	hand	match	chunk
west	jump	skin	stick	camp
bunch	chest	grin	chomp	wilt
hunch	chimp	chant	class	champ
slug	plum	frog	just	pinch
chop	rich	much	ask	winch
jug	must	glass	skip	cups

- - - 5 sounds - - - Remember to take a breath and blend smoothly.

crunch	twist	clamp	trust	jumps
branch	helps	flinch	brunch	stilt
French	drift	clump	crisp	swift

Reading Sentences: Have your child read with proper tracking and blending. Make immediate corrections. After the child reads a sentence, ask him a few specific questions.

Tom said, "I had hot dogs, milk and chips at lunch". "This is the best lunch!"

Dad can pitch to us. The kids will hit and catch.

The red bug was on the branch.

Can the frog jump an inch?

The thin ranch cat was with the dog. Toss the stick. The dog will fetch the big stick. But, the cat will not run with the dog. The cat will not catch a stick. It will just sit in the sun.

Chop up the branch. Cut it to 6 inch sticks.

Shut the lid on the big chest.

Do not chomp on gum in class.

The cat hid in the ditch.

The dog had mud on its chest and chin. The dog was a mud pup. It had such fun.

Lesson 19:

Teach Sounds:

qu → These buddy letters have the sound /kw/.

x → This letter has the sound /ks/

z → This letter has the sound /z/

Practice Sound Cards: Add the new sound cards to your collection. **Practice the sound cards for: qu, x, z** + previous sounds the student does not know automatically.

Write and Say Sounds Have the child write (or trace) each letter. Make sure your child forms the letter correctly and says the sound as he writes. **Please write and say each of the sounds 5 times: qu x z ch tch j w** + any other sound the child needs to practice.

Word Making Game: Make words with the sound tiles. Make sure the child says the individual sounds and uses proper blending skills. After he completes the word, have him read the word using finger tracking. Correct any errors. **"Please make the word _____"**
Use sound tiles...... a e i u   d g l n p qu s t z ck sh
    zip zap zig   quit   zag zest quick shut quack squid zest   stick squish
    plug   glad   stuck   gust   quilt   squint
Use sound tiles.... a e i o u   b d f l m n p t(2) w x
    ax ox fix win max web mix tax fox wax tux fax box next   test   text west
    flex must   expand   exit itself

Sound Changing Game: Remember to listen and make changes to the word.
Use sound tiles..... a i i o qu t ck x f b
    quit > quick > quack > tack > tax > fax > fix > fox > box
Use sound tiles..... e i   b l m n s t(2) w x
    text > next > nest > west > test > best > belt > melt > welt > wilt > silt > tilt

Reading Words: Have your child read the following words to you, sounding out with finger tracking and proper blending. Immediately correct any errors.

fix	can	am	do	ax
was	ox	box	in	this
wet	cut	this	web	zip
fox	tax	is	zig	buzz
get	off	not	that	got

wish	quit	sock	had	zap
and	the	chip	chill	such
him	said	will	zip	wax
max	pitch	job	much	six
inch	Zack	fuzz	chop	van
with	chess	max	quit	fax
quick	zag	quack	Rex	quiz
pitch	jazz	ditch	mix	switch
west	flex	swim	chest	hand
champ	brat	jump	twig	next
mask	swig	cram	plus	quits
gulp	belt	swell	drag	help
test	dwell	chant	plum	dusk
squish	text	crop	skip	hunt
quilt	zest	quick	squid	lunch
flax	plop	bulk	jest	ranch
weld	zips	chomp	pinch	flush
drug	cross	chest	wilt	fled
left	munch	gust	winch	crash

squint	branch	twist	quilts	blunt
brisk	stunt	plump	slept	blast

Writing (Spelling) Words: Select some of the listed words for your child to write.

Reading Sentences: Have your child read with proper tracking and blending. Make immediate corrections. After the child reads a sentence, ask him a few specific questions.

Tom said, "I had six hot dogs".

Dust off the chest and I will wax it.

The vet will fix the cat's leg.

The vet was in the van with a sick fox.

Zack got a gift in a box. It was a red and black quilt.

It is fun to run, jump and zig-zag on the grass.

Dad said, "Do not quit".

Quick Mom! Pack up the lunch bag with milk and chips. Drop the lunch box in the back-pack and zip up the top. Jim must run to catch the next bus. Jim will not drop the lunch if Mom zips the top shut.

Quick! Toss the stick. The pup will get the stick.

Mom will fix us a snack and pack it in the lunch box.

The duck said "quack".

Lesson 20:

Review Sounds: Let's quickly practice a few of the sounds you have learned!

p	e	h	v	sh	u
b	k	ck	c	g	j
w	ch	tch	x	z	qu

Reading Irregular Words: We are going to learn a new word. This is another 'silly' or irregular word that we say differently than it should sound out.

of ⟶

/o//f/ is how this word should sound out but this word is really "silly". We say **/uv/**.

Let's read **of** together. Finger track and say **of** with the child. Then have the child track and say it alone. If the child sounds out **of** as /o//f/ say something like "Stop, that's how we should sound out the word but do you remember how we say it? We say **/uv/.**

Great job SAYING the word **of** correctly. I'll use our new word in a few sentences so you can hear the word. These sentences are strictly for the adult to read to the child as they contain sounds the child has not yet learned. When you read emphasize **of**: --This is one **of** the best cookies I've ever eaten.   --You are one **of** the best readers!

Now practice reading **of** correctly. Have the child finger track as he says the word correctly.

of   of   of   of   of

Reading Sentences: Ok, now it's your turn to read our new word in a sentence. Have child read using finger tracking. Immediately correct any errors. If the child makes an error on the irregular words simply say "oops... do you remember how we say that word".

The frog hid in the back **of** the box.

This fish is the best **of** the batch.

Six **of** the pups ran to the pond.

The dog was in a bunch **of** mud.

Jim left a bunch **of** junk on the rug.

The cat can get up to the top **of** the rocks fast.

Lesson 21:

Teach Sound:

wh⟶ These buddy letters have the sound /wh/. This is the soft whisper sound /wh/.

Practice Sound Cards: Add the new sound card to your collection. **Practice the sound cards for: wh, qu, x, z + previous sounds** the child does not know automatically.

Write and Say Sounds: Have the child write (or trace) each letter. Make sure he forms the letter correctly and says the sound as he writes. **Please write and say each of the sounds 5 times: wh qu x z ch** + any other sound the child needs to practice.

Word Making Game: As the child makes words with the sound tiles, ensure he says the individual sounds and blends smoothly. Correct any errors. **"Please make the word _____"** Use sound tiles...... a i o u   k l m n   p(2) r s t   ch wh
    which whip chop ranch whisk print   punt lunch chip chimp lamp pump stump

Reading Words: The child reads with finger tracking & proper blending. Correct any errors.

am	us	did	if	up
get	in	zap	him	said
is	can	box	tax	zip
this	not	than	will	do
that	and	to	such	mix
when	on	was	with	rush
quit	which	much	whip	zig
six	luck	buzz	math	whiff
chin	whim	was	inch	Zack
ask	jazz	box	fox	of
next	plan	left	frog	melt

lost	felt	pest	plum	shred
quilt	squid	quick	shrub	quack
whisk	wind	squish	text	lots
track	which	best	plug	twig
bunch	camp	lunch	gift	brick
west	flex	quits	champ	crop
just	crash	when	fresh	shrub

- - - 5 sounds - - - Remember to take a breath and blend smoothly.

branch	twist	brand	grasp	craft
print	swift	trunk	stunt	crisp
stump	slept	drift	slant	squint

Writing (Spelling) Words: Select some of the listed words for your child to write.

Reading Sentences: Have your child read with proper tracking and blending. Make immediate corrections. After the child reads a sentence, ask him a few specific questions.

Tom said, "When can I run on the track?"

Which is the best of the batch?

When can I whip up the egg with the whisk?

When did Dad get such a big box?

Which man will run fast and win the sprint?

When can we help Mom with the big job?

Which pup can I pet?

Lesson 22:

Review Sounds:
Quickly practice the sounds you have learned! Use this review to determine which sounds your child knows automatically. When the student knows the sounds automatically (without hesitation), you can eliminate these sounds from isolated practice (the sound cards and sound writing activities). If a sound is not automatic, the child needs to continue practicing the sound in isolation until mastery is achieved.

m	t	a	s	d	i
f	r	th	l	o	n
p	e	h	v	sh	u
b	k	ck	c	g	j
w	ch	x	z	qu	wh

Reading Irregular Words:
We are going to learn a few more new 'silly' or irregular words that we say differently than how they should sound out.

what   /wh//a//t/ is how this word should sound out but this word is "silly" or irregular.

We say **what** /**whut**/. Let's read **what** together. Finger track and say **what** with the child. Then have the child track and say it alone. If the child sounds out what as /wh//a//t/ say something like "stop, that's how we sound out the word. Do you remember how we say it? We say /**whut**/."

Great job SAYING the word **what** correctly. I'll use our new word in a few sentences so you can hear the word. These sentences are strictly for the adult to read to the child as they contain sounds the child has not yet learned. When you read emphasize **what**: --**What** book is your favorite? --**What** would you like for lunch? --**What** game are you going to play at recess?

Please practice reading **what** correctly. Have the child finger track as he says **what** correctly.

what   what   what   what

We are going to learn another irregular word we say differently than how it should sound out.

who   /wh//o/ is how this word should sound out but this word is "silly" or irregular.

We say **who** /**hoo**/. Let's read **who** together. Finger track and say **who** with the child. Then have the child track and say it alone. If the child sounds out the word as /wh//o/ say "stop, that's how we sound out the word. Do you remember how we say it? **who** /**hoo**/ is how we say it."

Great job SAYING the word **who** correctly. I'll use our new word in a few sentences so you can hear the word. These sentences are strictly for the adult to read to the child. The child should not read these as they contain sounds not yet learned. When you read emphasize **who**:   --**Who** is becoming an awesome reader? YES YOU! --**Who** likes ice cream?   --**Who** likes to paint pictures?

Let's practice reading who correctly. Have the child finger track as he says **who**.

who   who   who   who

Reading Sentences: Now it's your turn to read our new words in sentences. Have child read the sentences with finger tracking. Immediately correct any errors. If the child makes errors on irregular words simply say "oops… do you remember how we say that word".

What is the gift in the box?

What did the fox do?

What can I do to help Mom?

What do I do next?

Who is that kid in the red vest?

Who can run to the top of the hill?

Who can pet the cat?

Who can shut the lid on the chest?

Who can mop off the deck?

What is on top of the desk?

What can Dad fix? Dad can fix the crack in the doll. Dad can fix the strap on the back-pack. Dad can fix the lock that was stuck shut. Dad can fix the rip in the map. Dad can fix this and that. Who can fix lots of stuff? Dad can!

Lesson 23: Review and Practice

Review Sound Cards: Quickly practice the stack of sound cards for all the sounds your child does not know automatically. Remember when the child automatically knows a specific sound you can remove it from the stack of sound cards for practice. If there is any hesitation (not automatic knowledge) keep the card in the stack for further practice. At this point, with the practice and repetition many of the sounds will be automatic for your child and there is no need to continue to practice them as sound/flash cards.

Write and Say Any Sounds that need additional practice: If sounds are not automatic, have the child write or trace the sound. Make sure he forms the letter correctly and says the sound as he writes. Write wh, x, z, qu & any other sounds not automatic.

Mixed Practice with Sound Changing Game: Now it's time to play some sound changing games with all the sounds you know. Remember to listen carefully to the word so you can make the changes to make the new word. "Ok, please make the word _____"
Use sound tiles.. e i u b f k l m n s t x
   next > nest > best > belt > felt > melt > milt > milk > silk > sulk
Use sound tiles... a i u   c g l m s w sh
   swish> swim > slim > slam > clam > clash > slash > slush > slug > slum >glum
Use sound tiles a i o u   b c l r s t ck
   block > black > slack > stack > stick > slick > click > cluck > clock > clack > crack > crick > brick
 Use sound tiles... a u   b d g l n r s t
   gland > grand > grant > grunt > brunt > blunt > blant > slant
Use sound tiles...... a u   c g l m p r s t
   stamp > stump > slump > glump > grump > gramp > cramp > clamp > clump

Reading Mixed List of Words: Have your child read the following words to you, sounding out with finger tracking and proper blending. Immediately correct any errors.

a	if	am	at	I
us	up	it	add	is
on	in	get	did	can
and	than	to	let	not
him	this	do	got	that
said	with	such	of	dash
zap	was	pet	zip	quit

wag	jug	fox	vet	much
but	ask	back	who	miss
what	which	inch	catch	chill
elk	will	job	wet	doll
chip	such	six	bed	match
gab	when	ship	kid	whip
dim	its	math	mesh	van
win	check	shop	path	quit
fish	pig	act	bug	shell
chin	kick	wish	shock	dull
drip	step	hand	cast	hunt
next	camp	gust	lift	bask
land	lost	wilt	club	slug
flat	mask	swam	twig	glob
held	must	jump	west	left
milk	flag	skip	clock	swig
clap	trip	grab	snap	swish
just	twin	best	clip	vest

spill	nest	junk	still	crab
spell	flip	slim	swim	felt
crack	stun	shock	shred	nuts
tint	gulp	crush	belt	stuck
task	kept	text	whisk	trap
chest	pitch	quilt	help	crop
brush	next	champ	block	hulk

- - - 5 sounds - - - Remember to take a breath and blend smoothly.

graft	swift	twist	grand	squish
clump	shrimp	crisp	stump	crust
splat	tramp	stilt	draft	grasp

Writing (Spelling) Words: Select some of the listed words for your child to write.

Reading Sentences: Have your child read with proper tracking and blending. Make immediate corrections. After the child reads a sentence, ask him a few specific questions.

Quick! Help us grab the fast pig.

This is a fun math class.

Pick up the trash that is on the grass.

Snap the lid shut on the chest.

The frog can swim fast and then jump up on the rock.

Kim's doll was lost. Then Mom said, "The doll was in the quilt on the bed". Kim got the doll back and was glad.

Much of Jim's big trip was in the west.

I can run a lap on the track. I will run fast.

Can I get the lunch box with the cats on it? It is the best!

Pick up the red pen that fell off the desk.

Mom let us catch fish at the pond.

What crop can I plant in the back plot?

Tim and I can rest when we get to the top of the hill.

Six of us fit in the van.

The slug was on the grass.

The pug can jump up on the bed.

The cat can gulp the milk in the pan.

I can stand on top of the big rock.

The nest was in the shrub.

Quick! Rush to the back of the class.

Who will help us with this math?

What can I do to fix the clock?

Lesson 24: Developing Additional Skills with Blended Consonants

Blended consonant sounds, 2 or 3 consonant sounds together, need specific work and practice. You have been practicing words with 2 consonants. Now you will begin reading words with 3 consonant sounds blended together.

Warm up with blended consonants by reading this review list of words with blended consonants.

sop → stop	fat → fast	sap → snap
sum → slum	cam → cram	cap → clap
cod → clod	gab → grab	gasp → grasp
dill → drill	sick → slick	sit → slit
fog → frog	gill → grill	tip → trip
cab → crab	dip → drip	bunch → brunch
fat → flat	sub → stub	cash → crash
band → bland	pan → plan	back → black
sack → smack	sand → stand	lad → land
cash → clash	sash → stash	tap → trap

Practice Making Words with Blended Consonants:
Making words is more difficult than reading the words. If the child misses a sound; have the child read/sound out the word he wrote and then say you made ___. You need to make ___. Can you hear what sound is missing? (example…you give him "slick" and he makes "sick". Have him read the word making sure he is pointing at the sound tiles as he reads. "That says sick, you need to make slick." *Help the child to learn to hear and distinguish the differences in the words.* **Please read directions on page 33** for information on correcting children who have difficulty distinguishing blended consonants.

Use sound tiles… a i o   b d l m n p r s t w ck
    past drat stab strip   trap twin smack stand strand pond click plant blast
    black brick damp trip drop strap drip slick slack stack print swim strap brand
    stamp   twist   stomp
Use sound tiles… a e i u   b c d g m n p r s t(2)   ch
    grasp grab   branch scrunch ranch scrap strap   brat grub grin trip crab drum
    dump glad smug cramp crest sprint clasp grump strand   crust chest
    brunch stump pinch print strip strap scram script stunt

Reading Words: Have the child read the following list of words. If the child misses a sound, stop the child and have him re-read the word. (oops you missed a sound, please try that again) If the child misses the sound again, point at the sound he missed, tell him the sound, and then have him re-read/sound out the word.

grab	frog	plant	clamp	crib
slap	drum	crab	snap	left
stub	frill	brat	brim	pact
clasp	stand	shrimp	crisp	crash
crunch	brand	drip	slant	blast
skunk	swept	shrill	grant	clump
slick	pinch	drab	crust	branch
cramp	frost	clam	twin	lunch
shred	blond	dress	graft	stunt
black	drift	dump	ranch	blunt
brisk	print	spend	crest	trust
strap	sprint	strong	splash	strand
splish	strip	scrap	split	strict
struck	script	stretch	scratch	scram
stump	grand	craft	swift	splint
stash	drop	scrub	flung	slips

*****Writing/Spelling Words with Blended Consonant Sounds:** Dictate selected words from the list above for your child to write/spell using paper and pencil.

Lesson 25: Developing Skills with Reading 2 Syllable Words

The child is going to begin developing a new skill of reading 2 syllable words. Lessons begin including some 2-syllable words for the child to read. Directly teach the child how to handle 2 syllable words. Explain syllables to the child then directly help the child learn how to handle these words. See page 37 for directions on teaching the important skill of handling multisyllable words.

Tell the Child: Now that you have learned all your basic sounds and are such a good reader, you are now ready to learn a more advanced skill. You are going to start learning how to read two syllable words. Syllables are chunks of sound within a word we say with a single puff of air. Two syllable words are said with two puffs of air. (See the introduction for Section 6 if your child does not understand syllables.) You will practice tackling these longer words. If you need help, I will help you break these longer words into parts with a pencil slash. If necessary, I will also help you pronounce these words. Let's get started!

Have your pencil ready and when necessary break the word with a pencil slash at the syllable break. (For example... with/in, fin/ish, in/sect, ex/pand, un/til, van/ish, in/sist) When necessary, directly help the child with pronunciation and then have him reread the word.

within	finish	insect	expand	until
vanish	insist	exam	children	unjust
himself	select	inspect	picnic	punish
exit	rocket	limit	robin	setup
rapid	plastic	radish	laptop	invest

The class had an exit plan.

Jill had to finish the math test.

The red and black insect was on the plant.

The children ran up the hill.

Practicing 'le' endings:

The 'e' at the end of some words is silent (it doesn't make any sound). One of the times you find this is when the 'e' comes right after an 'l' on 'le' endings on some multi-syllable words. You are going to practice a few of these 'le' ending words. When you sound out this word remember the 'e' is silent.

little   little   little

I got the big fish. Dad just got a little fish.

The **little** pup was soft.

Pick up the **little** rock and toss it into the pond.

Practice with other words that have the 'le' ending. 'Little' is just one of the words that have this 'le' ending. Let's practice a few more of these 'le' ending words. Remember the 'e' at the end of these words is silent. I'll help you with a pencil slash mark if you need help breaking these words apart and remember the '**e**' at the end of the words is silent.

simple	middle	riddle	battle	triple
pickle	jungle	cattle	fiddle	apple
chuckle	buckle	cripple	cuddle	middle
candle	scribble	tickle	uncle	crackle

Can I sit in the middle?

Set the plant in the middle of the shelf.

Pack a pickle in the lunch box.

The big cat hid in the jungle.

Sam hit a triple.

The laptop is on the desk.

The class had hot dogs at the picnic lunch.

Set the apple on top of the pan.

This math is simple. I just had to add six and six.

Uncle Tom fed the cattle grass.

Lesson 26: Review and Practice Basic Sounds

Review Sound Cards: Quickly practice the sound cards for any of the sounds your child does not know automatically.

Write and Say Sounds: If sounds are not automatic, have the child write or trace the sound multiple times. Make sure he forms the letter correctly and says the sound as he writes.

Reading Mixed List of Words: Have your child read the following words to you, sounding out with finger tracking and proper blending. Immediately correct any errors.

is	get	did	can	was
ask	who	well	has	this
fix	but	sell	add	hot
tell	let	and	had	got
map	said	tax	will	him
off	job	get	than	quit
man	wish	bad	not	six
up	cut	fish	web	act
run	box	sun	red	dog
lot	inch	ship	pass	rock
miss	top	sit	less	bed
shut	fill	wish	math	net
mix	much	zap	whip	van
shed	lick	bat	pick	shell
fast	stop	must	hand	grass

test	song	flip	west	slam
twin	last	cross	quick	skin
just	long	self	land	spell
list	plan	rest	fact	class
band	jump	left	black	swim
vest	flag	gift	hint	fresh
press	drag	track	grab	twig
snap	chant	pitch	clap	shrug
trip	soft	melt	trap	drum
chest	flash	shrub	smell	lost
best	flex	lunch	stick	skip
grill	pest	clock	grip	shift
still	hunt	flick	mint	drip
flat	snip	pluck	scum	trick
brush	wilt	dress	rust	swell
plant	trust	stand	blast	print
splash	drift	stamp	twist	frost
swift	strong	crunch	slept	squish
children	little	until	simple	exit

magnet	credit	banish	middle	within
panic	inject	valid	conflict	himself
finish	limit	jungle	topic	invest
insist	fabric	congress	rapid	catfish
laptop	traffic	pocket	pickup	solid

I got the big catfish in the net.

The little cat was in the middle of the soft bed.

I will mix up the egg with a little milk and add it to the pan.

The children sat on the bench.

With a quick chop, Kim split the middle of the log.

The robin was on the branch next to the nest.

The kitten can jump and do a back flip.

Dad had to stack up the logs in back of the shed.

I had an apple muffin with lunch.

I left the little lunch box on the bench.

The children will finish the math fact test.

I ran to the top of the hill. Then I had to rest.

Section 2: Learning Alternate & Additional Sounds

Since you are doing such a great job reading, you are ready to start learning some of the complexities or 'tricks' of the English language. You have already learned how some letters can have more than one sound. For example, you learned and have practiced s= /s/ and /z/, or a= /a/ and /ay/. In this section you are going to start reading words that use these 'other sounds'. Let's get started!

Please see instructions on page 37 Reading Alternate Sounds/Handling Complexities.

Lesson 27:

Sound:

S →   You already know the letter **s** has 2 sounds, /s/ and /z/.

You have been practicing the /s/ sound. Now you are going to read and practice words using the 2nd sound /z/. Did you know that most of the time the /z/ sound in English words is spelled with **s not z**.

Write and Say The Sound: Have the child write or trace **s** multiple times. Make sure the child says the /z/ sound as he writes the letter.

Reading Words that have the /z/ sound for s: The /z/ sound of s is used in lots of plural words. Do you know what a plural word is? It is when there is more than one (1 kid - lots of kids, 1 frog - 5 frogs). You usually say these plural words without even noticing how you pronounce or say the **s** as /z/. Go ahead and read these words. Remember **s** has the /z/ sound.

frog – frogs	dog – dogs	hill – hills
bun – buns	can – cans	kid – kids
jam –jams	rib – ribs	bug – bugs
tub – tubs	dig – digs	tag – tags
pig – pigs	pill – pills	ham – hams
hand – hands	drum –drums	bag – bags
drill – drills	hug – hugs	pin – pins

The /z/ sound of s is also used in many other common words. (Note: Many of the s=/z/ words contain code not yet taught such as use, rose, close, wise, please, choose, wisdom. Words will be systematically added into the lessons as the code necessary to read these words is learned.)

You already have been reading these words where **s** has the /z/ sound:

is   was

Reading More Words where s = /z/: Remind the child **s** has the /z/ sound. If the child reads a word using the /s/ sound for **s,** simply say, "this word uses the /z/ sound" and have your child read the word again.

as	has	his	is	was
visit	risen	closet	present	has

Making Words: Make words with the sound tiles. "Please make the word _____"
Use sound tiles...... a i(2) o u   b d f g h l n p r s t v
        is   as   hugs   has   his   bags   tags   pads   grubs   frogs   flags   visit

Reading Words: Have your child read the following words to you, sounding out with finger tracking and proper blending. Immediately correct any errors. If the child doesn't say the /z/ sound for **s**, say, "this word uses the /z/ sound for **s**" and have your child read the word again.

I	us	get	was	do
his	if	as	bags	this
pigs	has	than	is	who
six	not	cans	that	to
such	said	as	tags	hands
drums	best	left	hills	much
swims	hits	sums	stiff	digs
drip	such	was	flip	camp
self	long	spell	fins	fact
dogs	has	runs	hugs	his

116

claps	flags	west	step	grab
next	swims	songs	which	frogs
jump	lands	trust	clams	strip
plugs	stands	little	until	slams
closet	risen	children	visit	middle

Writing (Spelling) Words: Select some of the listed words for your child to write. Include 'his' and 'has' so the child learns these common words. Remind the child the /z/ sound is spelled with **s**.

Reading Sentences: Have your child read with proper tracking and blending. Make immediate corrections. After the child reads a sentence, ask him a few specific questions.

Tom has a lot of children in his class.

Fred will visit his uncle at the cabin.

Kim is as quick as a rabbit.

Jess got to visit Liz. It was lots of fun!

His fast dogs ran to the pond.

Tim has six insects in the box.

The red and black bug is his pet.

The gift bag was hidden in the back of the closet.

His little black dog was in his bed.

I can help the little kid buckle his belt.

His present was in the middle of the closet shelf.

Tim left his lunch box on the bus.

Lesson 28:

Sound:

e

→

You know the letter **e** has 2 sounds, /e/ and /ee/.

You have been mostly practicing the /e/ sound. Now you are going to work with and practice words with the 2nd sound /ee/. You are also going to see how the /e/ sound changes to almost an /i/ sound when /e/ comes right before /m/ or /n/.

Write and Say The Sound: Have the child write or trace the **e** multiple times. Make sure the child says the /ee/ sound as he writes the letter.

Reading Words that have the /ee/ sound for e: The /ee/ sound of **e** is used in quite a few words. Usually when **e** is the only vowel it makes the /e/ sound you have already practiced. But sometimes it does say /ee/, especially when the **e** is the only vowel and it comes at the end of the word or syllable. Point out this pattern to the child. Also you will begin to notice the /ee/ sound in the common prefixes **de-, re-** and **pre-**. Go ahead and read these words. I will help you break the longer words with my pencil if you need help. Remember the **e** has the /ee/ sound.

he	be	she	we	me
evil	even	secret		
began	belong	begin		
depend	demand	detect	detest	debug
refill	relax	reject	regret	respect
redraft	refit	reflect	rehash	rerun
resell	restrict	result	resist	refresh
prefill	prevent	prefix	preset	predict

Pronouncing /e/ with e+n and e+m:

e+n   e+m

You are also going to learn something funny about /e/. When /**e**/ comes right before /**n**/ or /**m**/ it sounds almost like the /**i**/ sound because of the way we pronounce these sounds together. Usually in speaking and reading we don't notice /e/ comes out sounding like /i/, but it helps to remember this when you spell words! Listen carefully as I say a few of these words…. hen, pen, hem, end, spend. Can you hear how the /e/ sounds almost like /i/? Now you try to say the /e/ sound with /n/ and /m/ and hear how it comes out sounding like /i/. This is why 'pen' & 'pin', 'hem' & 'him', and 'den' & 'din' sound so similar!

Reading Words that have e+n and e+m :

Ok, now you are going to read a few of the words where the **e** comes before **n** or **m** and almost sounds like the /**i**/ sound.

when	hem	pen	hen	end
ten	them	send	went	sent
then	lend	vent	bend	den
rent	bench	lent	mend	trend
spend	tent	blend	stench	tense
bends	dent	mitten	ends	rents
defend	ended	pretend	absent	kitten
hidden	sudden	problem	seven	happen
gotten	seven	chicken	extend	rotten

Making Words:

Make words with the sound tiles. "Please make the word _____"
Use sound tiles...... e o   b d g h l   m n p s t w   sh
    he we be she me belong hem pen hen went bent sent end dent spend spent

Reading Words:

Have your child read the following words to you, sounding out with finger tracking and proper blending. Immediately correct any errors. If the child says an alternate sound incorrectly, say "Oops, this word uses the /--/ sound" and have your child read the word again.

am	us	end	as	it
hem	not	do	we	is
he	was	she	pigs	has
them	me	be	to	his
send	rent	sent	belt	quit
lift	shell	who	what	help
inch	went	said	bent	dogs
dent	plugs	lend	tent	bend

gift	best	rent	chest	when
trust	blend	next	spend	even
belong	sudden	relax	problem	begin
visit	began	pretend	result	evil
reflect	secret	demand	prevent	refresh

Writing (Spelling) Words: Select some listed words for your child to write. Include 'he', 'she', 'be', 'we', 'when', 'then', 'went', and 'end' as the child needs to learn these common words.

Reading Sentences: Have your child read with proper tracking and blending. Make immediate corrections. After the child reads a sentence, ask him a few specific questions.

We went to the end of the path.

Send the rest of the class to me.

He can catch the fast chicken.

The math problem was simple.

He bent the stick to prop up the tent.

His pen was on the desk.

She went to sit at the end of the bench.

Seven pens belong to me.

The little kid will pretend to be a kitten.

She set up the big tent on the grass.

His next class began at six.

We began to refill the cups with milk.

Lesson 29:

Sound:

o → You already know the letter /o/ has 3 sounds, /o/, /oa/ and sometimes /u/.

You have been practicing the /o/ sound. Now you are going to work with and practice words that use the /oa/ and /u/ sounds.

Write and Say The Sound: Have the child write or trace the **o** multiple times. Make sure the child is saying the /oa/ and /u/ sounds as he writes the letter.

Reading Words that have the /oa/ sound for o: In some words **o** has the /oa/ sound. Go ahead and read these words. You will begin to notice some patterns where the single **o** has the /oa/ sound in '**old**' words and '**ost**' words and also where **o** has the /oa/ sound when is the only vowel at the end of a syllable. Read these words and remember **o** has the /oa/ sound.

go	no	so	most	post
old	cold	sold	fold	told
hold	gold	bold	scold	stroll
roll	colt	volt	bolt	open
bonus	total	focus	protect	program
protest	prolong	coldest	retold	posted
boldest	untold	oldest	folded	golden

Reading Words that have the /u/ sound for o: Sometimes **o** has the irregular or 'silly' /u/ sound. In fact, the second most common way to spell the /u/ sound in English is with the letter **o**. Many words where **o** has an /u/ pronunciation are with the unstressed syllables of multisyllable words. (See Appendix A for notes on the schwa pronunciation). When we read we often do not notice how we change to the /u/ sound. However, it helps to remember this for spelling. Go ahead and read these words. Remember **o** has the /u/ sound.

from	son	front	ton	month
won	common	random	compass	custom
second	oven	lesson	seldom	collect
construct	control	dragon	from	son

121

Making Words: Now it's time to make some words using the /oa/ or /u/ sound for **o**. "Please make the word _____"   Use sound tiles...... e o   d f g l m n p r s t v   th
go from no old most gold son sold ton front mold post fold open month oven

Reading Words: Have your child read the following words to you, sounding out with finger tracking and proper blending. Immediately correct any errors. If the child says an alternate sound incorrectly, say "Oops, this word uses the /--/ sound" and have your child read the word again

am	us	no	as	go
ton	not	do	son	is
he	was	she	we	has
most	so	them	me	old
his	send	to	went	said
front	ton	mold	chat	shop
host	from	with	gold	kids
most	no	fold	frogs	sent
did	that	hold	task	bend
post	hills	from	this	gift
glass	bolt	get	so	he
bold	from	has	cold	his
scold	stroll	spend	next	bench
slept	won	sold	stand	such
even	seven	collect	golden	protect
total	lesson	bonus	common	program
problem	control	began	rotten	ended

Writing (Spelling) Words: Select some of the listed words for your child to write. Include the common words 'go', 'no', 'so', 'open', 'most' 'old', 'told', 'from', 'son', 'front' and 'month'.

122

Reading Sentences: Have your child read with proper tracking and blending. Make immediate corrections. After the child reads a sentence, ask him a few specific questions.

Dad will go to the shop with me to get lunch.

Mom told me to fold up most of the rags.

This present is from Kim. She told me to hold the box. What is it?

Set most of the lemons in front of the glass.

Last month we got to go visit Uncle Sam. He has an old black dog. I fed the dog lots of snacks.

She told us to stand up in front of the class. We got to do a math problem. It was fun.

Dad said that we can go to the pond to catch fish.

His little son was with him in the truck.

The tag on the gift box said "To: Jess, From: Mom".

Can I hold the little kitten?

It was cold last month.

Can I open up the lid on the picnic basket?

The math lesson will begin at six.

A total of seven frogs swam in the pond.

The program began at six and ended at seven.

The roll of red ribbon was on the middle shelf.

Lesson 30:

Review Sounds: Let's quickly practice a few of the sounds you have learned! Have the child write and say any of these sounds that are not yet automatic.

a   s   i   o   e   u

w   ch   x   z   qu   wh

Reading Irregular Words: We are going to learn some new irregular words. The **o** in these words has the /u/ sound and **e** has no sound at all. You know, I'm not sure why **e** is there either! Go ahead and read these words. Remember, **o** makes the /u/ sound and **e** is silent.

some   come   done   none

Practice saying these words correctly. Be sure child is finger tracking.

some	come	done	none
come	some	none	done

Reading Sentences: Now it's your turn to read our new word in a sentence. Have child read the following sentences. Immediately correct any errors. If the child makes errors on irregular words simply say "oops… do you remember how we say that word".

Some of the kids had lunch with them.

Come with me on the trip.

I am **done** with the pen.

None of the kids had a red belt.

Some of us went on the class picnic.

Come to the back of the bus and sit with me.

None of us won the golden ribbon.

I am not **done** with the long problem.

Lesson 31:

Sound:

i →

You know the letter **i** has 2 sounds, /i/ & /ie/. You've been practicing the /i/ sound. Now you are going to work with and practice words that use the /ie/ sound.

Write and Say The Sound: Have the child write or trace the **i** multiple times. Make sure the child is saying the /**ie**/ sound as he writes the letter.

Reading Words that have the /ie/ sound for i: Most of the time when **i** is the only vowel in a word it has the /i/ sound you already practiced, but sometimes it has the /**ie**/ sound. You will start to recognize the common pattern of '**ild**' and '**ind**' where **i** has the /**ie**/ sound. Also when **i** is the only vowel and it comes at the end of the syllable, **i** usually has the long /**ie**/ sound. Go ahead and read these words. Remember **i** has the /**ie**/ sound.

wild	kind	child	bind
pint	find	grind	mind
mild	rind	wild	blind
remind	unkind	childish	wildest
virus	silent	Bible	behind
bridle	pilot	rifle	kindest

Making Words: Now it's time to make some words that have the /ie/ sound for i. "Please make the word _____"
Use sound tiles...... i e   b d f g h k l   m n   p r t   w   ch
wild   kind   child   bind   mind   pint   mild   find   grind   blind   remind   behind

Reading Words: Have your child read the following words to you, sounding out with finger tracking and proper blending. Immediately correct any errors. If the child says an alternate sound incorrectly, say "Oops, this word uses the /--/ sound" and have your child read the word again

do	us	no	as	go
is	he	was	his	wild
from	find	them	we	child
most	front	she	end	the

125

went	some	send	told	come
old	most	then	has	ton
kind	mild	pint	fist	gasp
find	done	cold	month	went
roll	blend	kick	brush	left
sold	go	child	mind	its
will	grind	bind	fold	blind
behind	begin	remind	program	wildest

Writing (Spelling) Words: Select some of the listed words for your child to write. Include 'wild', 'child', 'find', and 'kind' as the child needs to learn these common words.

Reading Sentences: Have your child read with proper tracking and blending. Make immediate corrections. After the child reads a sentence, ask a few specific questions.

Can Dad find the lost doll?

The wild cat is up on the rock.

It is kind to help a little child.

The frogs hid behind the rock.

The oldest child in his class was seven.

Remind Mom to get the pan from the hot oven.

We must focus and finish the last problem.

The old blind dog sat in the grass behind the bench.

I must find the little lost kitten.

Lesson 32:

Sound:

a

⟶

You know the letter **a** has 2 main sounds, /a/ and /ay/. You have been practicing words using the /a/ sound. Now you are going to work with and practice words using the /ay/ sound. You are also going to learn how '**a**' is sometimes pronounced differently with a funny /aw/ or /ah/ sounds.

Write and Say The Sound: Have the child write or trace **a** several times. Make sure the child is saying the /**ay**/ sound as he writes the letter.

Reading Words that have the /ay/ sound for a: Most of the time when **a** is the only vowel it has the /a/ sound you have practiced, but sometimes it has the /ay/ sound. You will start to recognize the common patterns where a single **a** has the /ay/ sound in '**ank**', '**ang**' and '**able**' words. Also when **a** is the only vowel in a syllable and it ends the syllable, **a** often has the /**ay**/ sound. Go ahead and read these words. Remember **a** has the /**ay**/ sound.

rang	sank	bang	tank	sang
bank	fang	crank	hang	blank
drank	clang	frank	thank	plank
able	table	stable	fable	cable
basic	native	blanket	bank	thanks

Pronouncing a when it is a + l, a + ll: We are also going to practice the different way we sometimes usually say (pronounce) **a** when it comes before **l** or before **ll**. You are going to learn how some letters can change or modify the sounds of other letters. '**L**' is one of those letters. When **l** stands right behind the letter **a** it often changes the way we say the **a** sound.

a + l

a + ll   When the /a/ sound comes right before l or ll we usually pronounce it /aw/ as in 'all'.

I am going to say a few words where the **l** modifies or changes the **a** to /aw/. Listen carefully! Emphasize the 'all' sound so the child can hear easier... all, ball, call, always, almost, salt.

Reading Words that have a+l or a + ll: Ok, go ahead and read a few of the words where **l** changes the sound and we pronounce the **a** with the /aw/ sound.

all	tall	ball	talk	call
balk	stall	calm	walk	small

hall	salt	fall	stalk	mall
halt	chalk	malt	all	talks
also	install	almost	called	tallest
fallen	smallest	walks	calls	halted

Pronouncing a when it is w + a:
w is another letter changes how we say **a**. We are going to practice the different way we usually pronounce **a** when it comes after **w**.

w + a   When the a comes after w we usually pronounce **a** differently as /aw/. I am going to say a few words with **w + a** where we pronounce the **a** differently Listen carefully! Emphasize the /aw/ sound so the child can hear easier… wasp, waffle, wand, wad, watch, wash. We say "please wash your hands" not "please 'w/a/sh' your hands"

Reading Words that have w + a:
Let's read a few of the words where **a** comes after **w** and we pronounce **a** with an /**ah**/ sound.

wad	wasp	wand	wash	watch
swap	swan	swamp	wallet	walrus
watched	waffle	wash	watch	wasps

Other times we say /aw/ or /uh/ for a:
There are also some other words where the /a/ is said with more of the /aw/ or /uh/ sound. Listen to me say a few of these words…across, about, father, adapt, attack. Many of these 'funny' pronunciations for the /a/ sound are in multisyllable words. When we say multisyllable words we get lazy and say /uh/ for the vowels in unstressed syllables. Most of the time, as you read you change the word to the correct pronunciation without even noticing this lazy pronunciation (*see notes at end of Appendix A on schwa). Now it is your turn to read some of these words where we pronounce **a** with an /aw/ or /uh/ sound. I'll help you with breaking words apart and pronunciation if you need help.   If you help with pronunciation, have the child re-read the word correctly.

adapt	attach	extra	tundra	adopt
attack	across	among	pasta	compass
affect	attend	attempt	ultra	

Making Words:
Now it is time to make some words that have the /ay/ and /aw/ sound for a. "Please make the word _____"

Use sound tiles…… a i   b c g k l m n p r s t w sh

rang   sang bank sank tank blank crank walk talk swan calm salt wash wasp basic

128

Reading Words: Have your child read the following words to you, sounding out with finger tracking and proper blending. Immediately correct any errors. If the child says an alternate sound incorrectly, say "Oops, this word uses the /--/ sound" and have your child read the word again

rang	all	sank	fall	tank
bank	bang	tall	salt	wasp
ball	wad	wash	call	calm
mall	hang	wand	has	walk
crank	blank	who	plank	stall
kind	watch	sang	ball	went
talk	wash	said	this	from
small	chalk	halt	stalk	malt
she	end	me	old	which
child	some	wild	front	most
who	done	all	hall	next
balk	that	snap	grind	told
cold	swamp	find	spend	thanks
blanket	table	almost	basic	across
into	also	wallet	within	native
able	even	pretend	absent	visit
relax	begin	ended	liquid	unless
problem	children	happen	walrus	little

Writing (Spelling) Words: Select some of the listed words for your child to write. Include 'all', 'call', 'small' (be sure to teach/tell child to use double **l** for spelling these words), 'also', 'walk', 'talk', 'watch', and 'wash' as the child needs to learn these common words.

Reading Sentences: Have your child read with proper tracking and blending. Make immediate corrections. After the child reads a sentence, ask him a few specific questions.

Some of the kids sang the song.

Mom told all of us to wash up.

The wasp almost stung me.

Watch the walrus swim fast.

Pass some salt to me.

He almost lost his wallet.

Find the tall kid with the black pants. He has the ball. When I ask him, he will hand it to us.

The colt was in the stall with his mom.

The bell rang. We must go back to class and do the math problems.

I can watch the small frog in the tank.

I drank a pint of milk. A pint holds 2-cups of liquid.

She can walk across the grass. She can also skip back.

The little child must wash his hands.

We must walk in the hall. We can not run.

I will open up the blanket and set it on the grass. Then Dad can set the lunch basket on the blanket. We will all be able to get lunch.

Lesson 33:

Teach Sounds:

y Y is a unique letter. It can be a vowel or a consonant. **Y** has 3 sounds! /y/ /ee/ & /ie/.

When **y** is a consonant, it usually starts a word (or syllable) and has the sound /y/. When **y** is a vowel, it is usually the final **/ee/** sound in multi-syllable words. This **/ee/** sound is by far the most frequent use of **y** in the English language. If **y** is the only vowel ending a 1-syllable word and in a few other words it has the /ie/ sound. You will learn the letter **y** has 3 sounds .. /y/ when it starts a word and usually /ee/ but sometimes /ie/ at the end of a word.

*For older children - you can mention the letter **y** also has an uncommon 4th sound of /i/. This does not need to be taught to young children at this time. Only a few words of Greek origin contain this unexpected use of y. You can explain these as irregular words. Later it is beneficial to learn the uncommon sounds for reading and for improved spelling. (see lesson 89)

Practice Sound Cards: Practice cards for: y + previous sounds not automatically known.

Write and Say Sounds: Please write and say **y**, **all vowels**, **+** any other sound the child needs practice with. Make sure the child forms letters correctly and says sounds as he prints.

Reading Words that have the /y/ sound for y: If the y is at the beginning of a word it is a consonant and the sound is /y/.

yes	yell	yet	yap	yelp
yuck	yum	yam	yip	yak
yank	beyond	yoga	yo-yo	yes

Reading Words that have the /ee/ sound for y: When **y** is found at the end of a multi-syllable word it usually has the /ee/ sound. This final /ee/ sound is by far the most frequent use of **y** in the English language.

fifty	foggy	sixty	gravy	lucky
sadly	kitty	only	dizzy	snappy
cozy	muddy	lady	puppy	hungry
very	baby	Billy	messy	sticky
hilly	buggy	picky	misty	snappy
slimy	sloppy	baggy	skinny	dressy
fussy	holy	yummy	flashy	sunny

pony	pesky	nasty	silly	happy
daddy	navy	rusty	quickly	calmly
candy	nosy	Lilly	dusty	salty
tricky	thickly	thinly	tasty	gladly
crusty	only	funny	windy	chunky
twenty	crafty	simply	kindly	stiffly
boldly	crunchy	sloppy	mostly	gusty
empty	entry	shaggy	fondly	jumpy
softly	swiftly	trusty	lumpy	study
sixty	smelly	angry	grumpy	only
body	very	squishy	twisty	crispy

Reading Words that have the /ie/ sound for y:
If **y** is the only vowel at the end of a short (1 syllable) word it usually has the /ie/ sound. Y also has an /ie/ sound in a few other words.

my	by	try	why	sky
shy	cry	fly	my	try
fry	dry	sly	retry	deny
python	my	why	try	by

- - - - - - - - - - - Note: Help the child break the following 3 syllable words if necessary - - - - - -

| *satisfy | justify | classify | notify | modify |

Making Words:
Make words with the sound tiles. "Please make the word _____"

Use sound tiles... a e o u y   b c f l m n p r s t ck sh wh
      yes   yum   yet   yap   yelp   yuck   yep   yam   beyond
      my   cry   shy   try   fly   why   by   sty

Use sound tiles ....a i u y   b(2)   c d f g h l(2) m n r s t z
      baby   crazy   hungry   sadly   madly   misty   nasty   gladly   crusty   nifty   dusty

Writing (Spelling) Words: Select some of the listed words for your child to write.

Reading Sentences: Have your child read with proper tracking and blending. Make immediate corrections. After the child reads a sentence, ask him a few specific questions.

Yes, my silly 'y' is very tricky!

Why did the baby cry? He was very hungry. The baby will be fussy until he gets his milk. When he gets his milk, he will be happy.

The candy is not yucky. It is very tasty. Yummy!!

Yes, I will try to do my best.

Only some kids got to go on the trip to the pumpkin patch.

When I sit on my pony, she will walk, trot and run.

Then my hungry pony will get some grass.

I will try to get the little kitty to come to me.

It is sunny but cold and very windy.

Jim said "Yes, I will gladly help pick up the big mess".

My only watch fell off and got lost in the tall grass.

The skinny puppy drank lots of milk.

I am very hungry. Let's go get some lunch.

Why is he so messy?

I am lucky. My daddy got me a little puppy. The puppy is very silly. He yips and yaps at me.

Lesson 34:

Review Sounds: Let's quickly practice the sounds you learned! Use the review to check which sounds your child may need additional practice with.

m	t	a	s	d	i	f
r	th	l	o	n	p	e
h	v	sh	u	b	ck	k
c	g	j	w	ch	tch	x
z	qu	wh	y			

Write and Say Sounds: Have the child write (or trace) **y** + any previous sounds.

Reading Irregular Words: We are going to learn a new irregular or 'silly' word. We say it differently than it should sound out. Note: **You** is completely decodable when the child learns the 'ou'=/oo/ combination in Lesson #58. However, for use in reading text this common word is introduced early as an irregular word.

you   The **y** starts the word with the /y/ sound. The 'ou' are buddy letters. You haven't learned their sound yet. In this word, 'ou' has the /oo/ sound. We say **you**. Let's read you together. Finger track and say **you** with your child. Have the child track and say it alone. If the child sounds out the word /y//o//u/ simply say "stop, that's how we sound out the word, do you remember how we say it? We say **you**."

Practice reading **you** correctly. Have the child finger track as he says the word.

you   you   you   you   you

Reading 'you' in sentences: Ok, now it's your turn to read our new word in a sentence. Have child read the following sentences. Immediately correct any errors. If the child makes errors on irregular words simply say "oops… do you remember how we say that word".

Can **you** pet the cat?

You can catch a big fish in that pond.

All of **you** will get to catch the ball.

Can **you** hand this mop to the tall man? Thank **you**!

If **you** study, **you** will do well in math class.

Reading Irregular Words: We are going to learn another irregular word. We say this irregular or 'silly' word differently than it should sound out.

want

In this word all the letters sound out except for **a**. Remember you learned **w** can change or modifies the **a** sound. That happens in this word. We say **a** differently. We say **want**. Let's read **want** together. Finger track and say **want** with your child. Then have the child track and say it alone. If the child sounds out the word /w//a//n//t/ say "stop, that's how we sound out the word, do you remember how we say it? We say **want.**

Practice reading **want** correctly. Have the child finger track as he says the word.

want   want   want   want   want

Reading 'want' in sentences: Ok, now it's your turn to read our new word in a sentence. Have child read the following sentences. Immediately correct any errors. If the child makes errors on irregular words simply say "oops… do you remember how we say that word".

Do you **want** to go with me?

I **want** to get chips with my lunch.

Do you **want** to hold the kitten?

I **want** to send you this gift.

Reading Mixed List of Words: Have your child read the following words to you, sounding out with finger tracking and proper blending. Immediately correct any errors.

try	yes	all	was	no
she	call	has	he	yet
find	go	end	by	come
watch	be	went	from	why
so	old	my	some	mind
you	dry	want	yell	tall
both	small	only	very	relax
behind	study	open	begin	total

135

Lesson 35:

Teach Sounds:

ing These buddy letters work together to have the sound /eeng/.

Note: Even though 'ing' is actually the /ee/+ nasal /ng/ sounds, we learn 'ing' as a unit. Not only does **ing** operate together as a unit but this **ing** is one of the most common endings in English. Children need to quickly identify and process **ing** as a unit.

ink These buddy letters work together to have the sound /eenk/.

Practice Sound Cards: Practice cards for **ing, ink, y, vowels** and any previous sounds the child needs work on.

Write and Say Sounds: Please write and say **ing, ink**, **y**, **all vowels, +** any other sound the child needs to practice. Make sure the child forms letters correctly and says sounds as he prints.

Making Words: Make words with the sound tiles. "Please make the word _____"
Use sound tiles... a i o   ing   ink   b   d   f g   k l   r   s   t   w   sh
    sing   ring   king   bring   swing   string   fling   wing   sting   sling
    going   fishing   wishing   lashing   blasting   flashing   folding
    sink   rink   blink   dink   drink   stink   wink   link   slink   brink   blinking   drinking

Sound Changing Game: Remember to listen and make changes to the word.
Use sound tiles..... ing   ink   b   d   l   r   s   t   w   sh
    stink > sting > swing > sling > slink > blink > brink > bring > brink > drink > shrink
    wink > wing > ring > rink > sink > sing > ding

Reading Words with 'ing':

ring	sing	wing	string	sling
bring	ding	king	fling	ding
sting	swing	cling	standing	lasting
going	banking	smelling	slanting	jumping
shifting	smashing	gusting	backing	flipping
sagging	asking	hugging	spinning	tapping
chanting	swimming	camping	shutting	slipping
stopping	blocking	bringing	passing	holding

testing	singing	drilling	telling	setting
yelling	catching	pinching	blending	yelping
running	sitting	fishing	standing	wishing

Reading Words with 'ink':

sink	wink	link	brink	rink
slink	shrink	blink	pink	clink
stink	drink	blinking	trinket	drinking
sprinkle	preshrink	sinking	inkjet	sprinkles
uplink	twinkle	blinked	shrinking	winking

Writing (Spelling) Words: Select some of the listed words for your child to write.

Reading Sentences: Have your child read with proper tracking and blending. Make immediate corrections. After he reads a sentence, ask him a few specific questions.

The pink ring is on the desk.

Sam is on the swing with his cat. The cat is mad and is going to scratch him.

Let us go fishing at the pond with Dad.

We must bring the long string.

We will wash off the mud in the sink.

She is going to run up the hill to the big swing.

We had fun tossing and catching the ball.

We set the lemons on the table. Can you squish them?

Lesson 36: Review and Practice

Practice Sound Cards: Practice **ing, ink, y** & **any previous sounds** not automatic.

Write and Say Sounds: Please write and say **ing, ink, y** + any previous sounds the child needs practice with! Make sure he forms the letter correctly and says the sound as he writes it.

Reading Mixed List of Words: Have your child read the following words to you, sounding out with finger tracking and proper blending. Immediately correct any errors.

I	a	we	can	am	the
at	if	did	it	and	on
its	that	this	is	in	not
had	us	up	but	to	than
said	do	can	get	got	him
will	with	was	of	which	me
what	shop	as	has	his	when
met	back	plan	left	shut	cup
old	from	he	son	all	she
post	hot	land	red	drop	no
sled	next	list	band	crash	try
nest	stop	run	shed	rash	be
drum	hunt	deck	lock	kiss	chin
skin	shop	cast	gift	camp	much
clap	west	jump	gust	flag	catch
fix	buzz	was	from	which	lunch

138

six	quick	whip	what	chest	quit
inch	who	crash	send	dogs	sing
come	most	from	wild	mind	sink
some	rang	blind	crank	stall	chess
watch	calm	next	wasp	walk	rink
you	bring	yet	fly	clock	quack
tall	yell	chalk	dry	fall	grind
walks	squish	jack	frogs	crept	print
bent	front	child	strip	crash	skunk
bunch	find	string	yes	walk	swim
stamp	plant	math	shrub	thump	luck
twist	stump	shrimp	trunk	felt	track
very	cozy	baby	only	insect	also
candy	silly	exit	pony	going	navy
almost	vanish	punish	crunchy	protect	extra
children	visit	select	angry	tallest	washing

Reading Sentences: Have your child read with proper tracking and blending. Make immediate corrections.

Can you smell the stinky skunk? I can smell it, Yuck!

The red frog is in the big tank and the black frog is in the little tank.

He sent the child to get the box from the desk.

My pup can fetch. If you toss up a stick, she will bring it back to you. She will also fetch a ball.

Did you find the red and black lady bug on this plant?

Can you bring us a bunch of sand in that bucket?

We will walk to the shop with my Mom. Then we can pick up a little snack. I will get some candy.

Who can help me find my lost wallet?

Can you help me find my cat? She is hiding from that big shaggy dog.

Yes, my uncle is bringing us lunch.

I had twenty small pink rocks in my cup.

The black pony ran quickly across the grass.

The colt is standing in his stall.

The wasp nest is in the shrub by the little shed. I will not go by the shed. I do not want the wasps to sting me.

The muddy dog is on the deck. Do not let him in. He must dry off and then you can brush him.

The empty cup was left on the table. I want you to pick it up and bring it to me.

The man was running with the big red dog.

Lesson 37: Practice with Silent Letters

Practice Sound Cards: Practice the sound cards for: ing, ink, y and any previous sounds.

Write and Say Sounds: Please write and say **ing, ink, y** + any previous sounds the child needs practice with! Make sure he forms the letter correctly and says the sound as he writes it.

This lesson is going to explain another one of the complexities or 'tricks' with reading our crazy English. Sometimes a letter in a word will be silent. It doesn't make a sound. Back in lesson # 25 you learned how sometimes the 'e' at the end of a word is silent and doesn't have a sound. You practiced this with the 2-syllable words that ended in 'le'.

Review 'silent e' endings with 'le':

little	simple	middle	able	riddle
battle	triple	pickle	jungle	cattle
stable	apple	buckle	candle	scribble
tickle	table	uncle	bottle	puddle

You will continue to read other words that have a 'silent-e' ending. In lesson #30 you learned the words 'some', 'done' and 'none'. Now you are going to read other words that also have a similar silent-e ending. When your read these words, remember the **e** at the end of the word is silent.

Practice other 'silent e' endings:

some	dense	rinse	done	pulse
none	glimpse	tense	sense	some

Another time you find the silent-e is in words that end in the /v/ sound. English words never end in the letter 'v' so if a word ends in the /v/ sound an **e** comes right after the **v**. The **e** does not have any sound. It is only there to keep the **v** from ending the word. The letter v is like the kid who will not stand at the end of the line. The **e** has to stand at the end of the line just to keep **v** from being last in line. "*Words do not end in the letter v*" is just one of those silly things about the English language. Remember when you read these words the **e** at the end of the word is silent.

Practice 'silent e' endings with 've':

have	give	live	love	solve
dove	shove	above	active	passive

141

The letter **e** is not the only letter that is sometimes silent. Other letters can also be silent at times. You already learned about the letter **t** being silent in the **tch** buddy letters. Well the letter **t** is silent in a few other words. After a bit, we usually don't even notice the silent letters when we read but it is good to pay attention for spelling. Let's look at a few of these common silent t words. Remember t is silent in these words.

Practice 'silent t' words:

listen   often   soften   kitchen   catch

Reading Sentences: Have your child read with proper tracking and blending. Make immediate corrections.

I have six red apples in my bucket.

Can you give me some muffins?

Set the muffins on the kitchen table.

I love my little fluffy puppy.

I must listen to my mom.

We can rinse the dust off my dad's truck.

Listen to Miss Smith. She will tell you what to do next.

We must solve the math problem.

We have to tell him to rinse the mud off his puppy. His puppy fell in the puddle.

We will often watch the robins fly to the nest.

I love to go camping with my uncle.

We will hang the shelf above the small table.

Lesson 38: Review and Practice

Practice Sound Cards: Practice sound cards for **ing, ink, y** and **any previous sounds**.

Write and Say Sounds: Please write and say **ing, ink, y** + any previous sounds the child needs practice with. Make sure he forms the letter correctly and says the sound as he writes it.

Reading Mixed List of Words: Have your child read the following words to you, sounding out with finger tracking and proper blending. Immediately correct any errors.

tell	by	old	yes	she	come
much	my	who	six	lick	yet
was	dry	chess	quit	chug	such
this	map	dim	bed	log	red
hid	rash	path	web	cot	tax
them	try	his	why	ask	what
when	all	both	which	box	said
luck	some	wash	bring	quick	wing
wild	sent	hang	skip	belt	plan
went	small	plum	swing	swell	step
track	sing	sold	bunch	fling	rinse
find	desk	wasp	plugs	crush	kept
pinch	long	flip	thank	talk	just
cross	most	told	must	watch	west
bless	vest	raft	flash	click	black
flinch	splash	plant	grand	plank	blind

spend	drift	clasp	solve	tense	trick
brush	drop	spell	yelp	drink	squid
swift	clump	sprint	stunt	stump	slept
front	month	hunts	soft	trust	fresh
basic	fifty	able	mostly	angry	behind
only	going	also	table	even	focus
begin	study	total	very	middle	hundred
belong	across	finish	solid	active	hidden
respect	children	protect	oldest	prevent	tallest
watching	native	triple	control	beyond	dripping
almost	standing	discuss	puzzle	secret	candle

Reading Sentences: Have your child read with proper tracking and blending. Make immediate corrections.

She will sing us a silly song when we get done.

My cat is sitting on the big rock by the shed.

Mom said we must not drop the eggs. The eggs will crack if we drop them.

My kitten is very silly. She ran fast and then did a flip.

His gift from Dad was a bat and a ball.

Can you swim across the pond?

My lunch is in the bag. Do not step on it and squish it.

We had a big math test. I had to add and subtract.

We can walk to the pond and then go swimming.

Do not run in the hall. You can crash into a little kid.

She is going to skip and hop with the little kids.

A big gust of wind can rip the flag.

My grandpa's old black dog was blind.

What kind of rocks did you find? Kim has six small pink rocks and seven black rocks. Tom got the biggest rock of all. It is six inches long and lumpy.

I am hungry. I must get a snack. Can I get some extra crunchy chips?

When will we get to go elk hunting with Dad?

Billy got to go fishing with his Mom. He got six big fish. Mom will fry the fish in a big pan. Yum!

Peggy is helping Mom with the muffins. She can mix the milk with the eggs. She can also add the apples. But only Mom can open the hot oven.

All the kids went on the class trip. We went on a bus. Jack sat in front of Sam and me. We had a picnic lunch. We had hot dogs and chips. When we finished lunch Miss Smith rang the bell to call us back to the bus. We all had to get back on the bus.

Section 3: Vowel Combinations

Lesson 39: General Information on Vowel Combinations

This section starts a new group of sounds, the vowel combinations. Children need to learn these complexities that are so prevalent in our English language. The child already knows th, ch, sh and wh. Therefore, the child is familiar with the concept that letters can work together as 'buddies'. This section systematically teaches the child the various vowel combinations or 'vowel-buddies'.

Explain to the Child: We are going to start some new sounds called vowel combinations or vowel buddies. These vowels are buddy letters that work together to make a sound. You will learn:

1. The vowels are a, e, i, o, and u and sometimes y.
2. These vowels often pair up as buddies and work together to make certain sounds. Just like when two buddies get together they sometimes make certain sounds, these buddy vowels work together to make certain sounds.
3. It is helpful to know "When 2 vowels go walking (paired together) the 1st vowel frequently (but not always!) does the talking" This means when 2 vowels are together the first vowel will often 'talk' by saying its name.
4. Sometimes the vowel combinations try to be tricky but you'll learn their tricks and practice so they won't fool you!

Let's get started with the vowel combinations!

Lesson 40:

Teach Sound:

ee   These buddy letters have the sound /ee/.

Practice Sound Cards: Practice the sound cards for ee, ing, ink, y and any previous sounds the child needs work on.

Write and Say Sounds: Please write and say the sounds ee, y, ing + any other sound that the child needs to practice.

Noticing How the 'ee' works: Read the following pairs; specifically point out and 'see' how the sound changes from /e/ to /ee/ with the 'ee' vowel combination.

ned -- need   met--meet   sped -- speed   fed--feed

ten -- teen   pep -- peep   bet -- beet   wed - weed

Making Words:
Make words with the sound tiles. "Please make the word _____ "

Use sound tiles.... ee o u i d(2) g k l n p(2) r s t(2) w sh th ch ing

see need seen keep tree deep seed week three speed teeth green sweet sheet
speech sleep greed street greet indeed keeping unseen greeting upkeep treetop
sweeping needing

Sound Changing Game:
Remember to listen and make changes to the word.

Use sound tiles..... i o ee   b d f l p s t w sh

deep > weep > sheep > shop > bop > beep > beef > beet > sheet > feet > sheet > feet > feel
flip > slip > slop > sleep > sleet > fleet > sleet > sweet

Reading Words with 'ee':

see	bee	tree	need	eel
deep	meet	seed	feet	feed
keep	teen	weed	sheep	teeth
green	jeep	greed	queen	seem
feel	seen	peep	free	screen
beef	creep	sleep	weep	peel
breed	speed	sweep	week	sheet
three	sweet	wheel	deed	creep
street	keeps	cheek	sleeps	breeze
meek	speech	tweed	steep	freeze
seep	screech	cheese	bleed	sheets
deeds	tweet	greets	seems	sneeze
beet	steel	reel	spree	beep
free	fleet	reef	green	sleet
wheel	keep	needs	feeds	bees

147

between	indeed	unseen	agree	coffee
canteen	deeply	keeping	needy	sweetly
greedy	freezing	asleep	greeting	freedom
needing	weekly	bleeding	upkeep	feeding
sleepless	weeding	sweetest	freely	degree
weekend	speeding	sleepy	sweeping	treetop
teething	sixteen	agrees	beetle	feeling
duckweed	fifteen	preteen	deepest	

Writing (Spelling) Words: Select some of the listed words for your child to write.

Reading Sentences: Have your child read with proper tracking and blending. Make immediate corrections. After the child reads a sentence, ask him a few specific questions.

We need to keep the bees in the tree.

The sheep is asleep on the green grass.

Can you see if the end of the string was cut off?

Mom can drink three cups of coffee.

Dad said you need to sweep off the deck.

The sheet was flapping in the breeze.

We need to sweep the street.

We had beef and cheese at lunch.

Meet me by the tree next to the street.

This canteen is empty. We need to fill it up.

I see three green seeds that I need to plant.

The sheep is hungry. We need to feed the weeds to the sheep.

The stick was three feet long.

The baby was sleeping in his crib.

She keeps fifteen pens in the can on top of the desk.

The green truck went speeding past the exit.

We can dry off the wet sheet by hanging it in the sun.

The black lab puppy was only sixteen months old. She was still wild and crazy.

If you want to find frogs we will need to go to the pond. I can see a big green frog sitting next to the tall weeds. If you creep up behind the rock the frog will not see you. You can catch the frog. Then we can set it free.

We can catch lots of fish in the big deep pond. Grab the fishing rods. We need to catch six fish. Let us see if you can get three fish and I will try to get three fish also. This will be a fun fishing trip! Let's go get some fish!

We need to keep the little puppy between us when we walk by the street. We do not want him to run into the street and get hit.

Lesson 41:

Teach Sounds:

oa   These buddy letters have the sound /oa/.

oe   These buddy letters also have the sound /oa/.

I bet you noticed both these buddy letters make the same /oa/ sound. The 'oa' spelling is much more common. The 'oe' spelling is only used in a few words.

Practice Sound Cards: Practice **oa, oe, ee, ing, ink, y** and **any previous sounds** the child needs work on.

Write and Say Sounds: Please write and say **oa, oe, ee, y**, plus any other sound the child needs to practice.

Making Words: Make words with the sound tiles. "Please make the word _____"
Use sound tiles... e u oa b c d f g l m n p r s t(2) th ch ing
       oat   boat goat foam goal coat coast loaf roast goal float boast soap foal
       groan   throat toasting   unload   foaming   reload coaching encroach
Use sound tiles .... oe h t f d
       hoe toe foe doe

Reading Words with '**oa**':

oat	loaf	coat	goal	float	foal
soak	coal	roam	moat	poach	foam
boat	boast	goat	coach	oak	groan
cloak	soap	croak	float	toast	goal
moan	throat	groan	roast	goad	roach
load	coast	road	loan	toad	stoat
goals	shoal	bloat	coats	soapy	foamy
toasting	reload	floating	unload	roasted	loaned
coaching	roaming	coastal	soaking	boasting	encroach
freeload	soapbox	uncloak	afloat	roadless	bloated

Reading Words with 'oe': **Notice: the 'oe' buddy letters are not very common.** (In the word shoe, the 'oe' has an unexpected /ew/ sound)

doe woe toe hoe foe roe

Writing (Spelling) Words: Select some of the listed words for your child to write.

Reading Sentences: Have your child read with proper tracking and blending. Make immediate corrections. After the child reads a sentence, ask him a few specific questions.

It is cold. You need to bring a coat so you do not freeze.

The doe was asleep by the oak tree.

The rock fell and hit his toe.

Load up the box in the back of the old green truck.

The little foal was with his mom.

You need to float the boat in the tub not the sink.

She kicked a goal and we won.

Can we go on a trip to the coast next week?

We had roast beef at lunch.

We can not walk on the road.

The little goat was munching on the grass and weeds.

We got to go on the fishing boat.

Hang up your coats in the hall.

You need to soak the coat in the tub with some soap.

If you need a snack, I have some apples and roasted nuts.

Lesson 42:

Teach Sounds:

ai   These buddy letters have the sound /ay/.

ay   These buddy letters also have the sound /ay/.

I bet you noticed the **ai** and **ay** have the same sound. Directly point out the spelling pattern to the child as he makes and reads the words. The 'ai' buddy letters are used more frequently than the 'ay' buddy letters. Point out how the 'ai' is found at the beginning or middle of a syllable and the 'ay' buddies are usually found at the end of a word or syllable. Teach the child that NO English words end in the letter 'i'. Therefore, the 'ai' buddies are never used at the end of a word. Since English words can't end in 'i', the 'ay' buddies or another spelling must be used if the word ends in the /ay/ sound.

Practice Sound Cards: Practice the sound cards for: **ai ay oa oe ee ing ink y** and any previous sounds the child needs work on.

Write and Say Sounds: Please write and say **ai, ay, oa, oe, ee** plus any other sound the child needs to practice.

Making Words: Make words with the sound tiles. "Please make the word _____"
Use sound tiles e o ai   b c d f g l m n p r(2) s t w x
    aim rain paid wait main bait train pain braid stain waist   paint drain faint
    strain   brain grain saint   braid explain retain refrain remain regain reclaim retrain
    repaid   complain complaint   proclaim
Use sound tiles… e i ay   b c d h l m   n p r s t w   ing
    say   hay play day way lay pray ray stay clay bray stray maybe praying
    inlay   delay saying midway stingray decay repay betray replay staying

Reading Words with **ai** spelling for the /ay/ sound:

aim	aid	rain	wait	rail	gain
bait	main	paid	jail	chain	maid
sail	pain	waist	faint	grain	plain
stain	raid	train	hail	drain	snail
praise	strain	slain	trait	brain	pail
saint	braid	quaint	mail	faint	laid

faith	raise	gains	Spain	claim	trail
vain	fail	strait	aims	maize	rains
frail	waits	sprain	taint	traits	daisy
raisin	rainy	contain	afraid	refrain	plainly
reclaim	explain	unchain	detail	retain	derail
retrain	maintain	faithful	waiting	regain	detain
draining	maiden	unpaid	mainly	aiming	engrain
raining	fainted	baiting	abstain	aided	gained
complain	ailment	proclaim	domain	dainty	prepaid
abstain	remain	braided	unpaid	sustain	braiding
mainland	daily	waitress	painful	training	rainfall
mailed	detain	claimed	saintly	exclaim	complaint
acclaim	acquaint	sprained	faithful	constraint	

Reading Words with 'ay' spelling for the /ay/ sound:

way	may	bray	play	ray	bay
clay	pay	pray	say	stay	day
slay	tray	stray	hay	sway	lay
spray	fray	jay	pays	days	always
today	playpen	delay	prayed	relay	display

maybe	replay	prepay	decay	hallway	praying
delay	staying	pathway	away	midway	essay
subway	roadway	railway	decay	mainstay	inlay
layoff	payment	saying	playoff	daylong	hayloft
halfway	swaying	always	playful	paying	stingray
freeway	ashtray	spillway	essay	haystack	weekday
mislay	repay	betray	byway	away	holiday

Writing (Spelling) Words: Select some of the listed words for your child to write. Directly teach the child the spelling pattern when you give him the words to spell. Tell the child the 'ai' spelling pattern is used most often and give him 'ai' words. Point out this 'ai' is usually found at the beginning or middle of a syllable. Also point out NO words end in the 'ai' spelling. Next point out how the 'ay' buddy letters are usually found at the end of a word or syllable. Tell him the /ay/ sound in these words will be spelled with 'ay' and then give him 'ay' words.

Reading Sentences: Have your child read with proper tracking and blending. Make immediate corrections. After the child reads a sentence, ask him a few specific questions.

Maybe he can stay with us and play.

We need to drain the sink.

He was from Spain.

We only got six inches of rainfall in the last six months.

What day can you come see me play?

We will go see the train pass by.

Why is he afraid of the frog?

I will explain that three plus three equals six.

We will wait and see if the stain will come off.

Lesson 43: Review and Practice

Practice Sound Cards: Practice the sound cards for: **ai ay oa oe ee ing ink y** and any previous sounds the child needs work on.

Write and Say Sounds: Please write and say **ai, ay, oa, oe, ee** plus any other sound the child needs to practice.

Reading Mixed List of Words:

wait	three	boat	play	speed	soak
went	green	gain	roast	goal	teeth
rain	seem	faint	tray	fleet	small
bring	chain	way	keep	braid	need
brain	small	watch	loan	faith	black
coast	month	grind	strong	twist	sleet
faint	spray	sweet	squish	pray	talk
rail	when	cold	wheel	deep	days
coach	long	sleep	both	yes	speech
bait	weep	stay	fail	from	free
away	finish	almost	freedom	exit	between
quickly	today	maybe	always	problem	going
beyond	sudden	only	walking	thankful	agree
feeling	belong	oldest	explain	very	sixteen
floating	study	bleeding	asleep	maintain	among

Maybe we can go to watch them paint the trains.

We always get to go fishing when we visit my uncle.

May we run to the big tree?

The raft went floating by us.

I need to find a canteen. Then I can bring it with me to get a drink.

I need to whack the weeds with the hoe.

I almost hit my toe when I dropped the big rock.

I am going to feed some grain and a little hay to the pony.

Today is the day that we get to go swimming.

Is this the day that we travel to the coast? I can not wait to go. We get to play in the sand. We also will be able to dig up clams.

Which way did my dog go? He ran away and I need to catch him. He needs to stay with me and not run away.

I will stay and wait by the tree. Mom will find me sitting on the bench. Then we will go play.

My mom will bring the mail in to me. I am waiting to see if I got a box from my uncle. He said he sent it to me last week.

The wasp nest is in the tall tree. I will stay away from the nest. The wasps may sting me. I am afraid of them.

Lesson 44: The vowel-consonant-e combinations

The next vowel combinations are slightly different than the other vowel combinations you learned. These vowel buddy letters have another letter between them. Although these vowels are not standing right next to each other these 2 vowels are absolutely still buddies working together. The 1st vowel and the **e** work together as buddies. The **e** makes the first vowel say its name (the long sound). The vowel-consonant-e combinations are some of the most frequent combinations found in English so child must learn to master them.

Explain this concept to the child in a manner he can understand. I usually make an analogy of the vowels to friends or buddies. Even though the two friends may have another kid standing between them these friends are still buddies. Just like kids standing in line, one of the friends can still reach around another kid and poke his buddy to make his buddy holler. In the same way the **e** and the first vowel are buddies and **e** reaches around the other letter and pokes his buddy (the first vowel) to make him squawk. So the **e** and **the first vowel** work together. Even though **e** remains silent he is making his buddy say his name.

There are 5 vowel-consonant-e combinations. The blank line represents the consonant.

a__e	These buddy letters have the sound /ay/.
o__e	These buddy letters have the sound /oa/.
i__e	These buddy letters have the sound /ie/.
u__e	These buddy letters have the sound /oo/.
e__e	These buddy letters have the sound /ee/.

Use the following examples to overview the vowel-consonant-e pattern with the child. Read each word to the child pointing at the sounds as you go. *Show how the e buddy letter changes the sound* from /a/ to /ay/, /o/ to /oa/, /i/ to /ie/, /u/ to /oo/, and /e/ to /ee/. (Sometimes it helps to underline **e** as you read the word to show how **e** makes the a,i,o,u or e change its sound.)

a_e	at--ate	tap--tape	mad--made
o_e	hop--hope	not--note	con--cone
i_e	tim--time	hid--hide	bit--bite
u_e	cub--cube	cut--cute	tub--tube
e_e	pet--Pete		

Tell the child he will see exactly how these buddies work in the work making activities in the next lessons. The tiles are wonderful for demonstrating how these combinations work.

Directions for Teaching vowel-consonant-e Combinations:

The child needs to learn to recognize the important and frequently occurring vowel-consonant-e combinations. It takes practice as the child needs to not only understand how the first vowel and **e** work together but also has to distinguish this combination when reading words. The interfering consonant does make this vowel combination more challenging for the child to distinguish.

Word making with sound tiles is effective in helping children learn to identify and recognize the relationship between the first vowel and **e**. Make words in pairs. Have the child make the first word and read it. Then have him add **e** to the end and point to the first vowel and say the long sound and then read the new word. *Physically seeing the addition of the* **e** *and how it causes the sound to change helps the child learn the pattern of how the first vowel and e work together.*

When making other vowel-consonant-e words, tell the child the word is made with the vowel-consonant-e buddies and then after he reads the word specifically point out this relationship to the child. The tiles allow the child to 'see' how this combination works.

When first reading words containing these vowel-consonant-e words the child will frequently apply the short vowel sound instead of the long vowel sound for the first vowel. When this occurs, give a quick "oops" or tap the word with your pencil for the 'stop-look again' signal. Do *not* tell the child the correct sound. Simply reach over with you pencil and quickly point at the **e** and draw an arrow from **e** to the first vowel. At first you can also use the verbal cue "poke" when you draw the arrow to remind the child how 'buddy-e is poking the first vowel'. After a few corrections, you generally can drop the verbal "poke" cue and just silently draw the arrow from **e** to the first vowel. This correction technique not only helps the child understand the relationship between the first vowel and the buddy **e** but also helps the child learn to 'see' and recognize this relationship within words. This technique is illustrated below. Use this correction with all vowel-consonant-e combinations. Remember after making the correction, the child must always re-read the word correctly!

Example: The child reads 'hid'. Stop the child with 'oops' or a pencil tap. Then point at **e** and draw a line back to the first vowel **i.** If needed, give the child the verbal cue "poke". Then have the child read the word correctly.

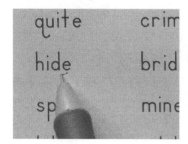  

Remember, the child must always re-read the word correctly!

These vowel-consonant-e combinations are challenging for some children. When necessary, repeat lessons, add supplemental word making, and include additional practice decoding these words.

Lesson 45: Learn and Practice a-consonant-e Combination

a__e   These buddy letters have the sound /ay/. Although they are not right next to each other,
a and e work together as buddies. The e makes the a have the /ay/ sound.

Practice Sound Cards: Practice **a_e**, **ai ay oa oe ee** + any previous sounds.

Write and Say Sounds: Please write and say **a_e, ai, ay, oa, oe, ee** + any previous sounds not automatically known.

Making Words: Make the words as pairs - Have the child say sounds as he builds the word. Have him make the first word and read it. Then have him add the e to the end and point to the a and say the /ay/ sound. *Physically seeing the addition of the e and how it causes the sound to change helps the child learn the pattern of how the a and e work together.*
Use sound tiles... a e c d f g h l m n p r s t v

pairs: at--ate   man--mane   tap--tape   mad--made   fat--fate   hat—hate
       rat--rate   can--cane   dan--dane   van--vane   plat--plate   cap--cape

other words: late cape game name trade gate crate grade grape spade slate safe scrape

Reading a_e Words:

game	ate	lame	trade	make
shade	same	made	rate	base
cake	lane	brake	rake	crate
crane	cave	gate	shape	late
ape	grape	plate	safe	make
graze	made	lake	tape	name
slate	trade	plane	daze	fade
gave	tame	hate	cane	fake
take	crate	flake	skate	quake
blade	spade	snake	shake	blaze
shave	made	save	jade	scrape
grade	blame	vase	glaze	late

159

drape	date	case	haze	fate
male	vane	chase	state	brave
behave	safest	inflate	escape	locate
ashame	mistake	rotate	latest	invade
safely	rename	debate	gateway	reshape
amaze	awake	enslave	relate	landscape

Writing (Spelling) Words: Select some of the listed words for your child to write

Reading Sentences: Have your child read with proper tracking and blending. Make immediate corrections. After the child reads a sentence, ask him a few specific questions.

We will travel to the same cave that we went to in second grade. We will take the bus on the class trip.

We need to save some cake on this extra plate.

I had some red grapes in my lunch.

Can you trade with me?

When can we go see the basketball game?

We all had lots of fun playing a game of tag.

I will save you a snack. The extra grapes will be on this plate.

I made a clay snake to play with.

Mom told us it was not safe to cross the street.

The red candy cane was sweet and minty.

I can rake up the cut grass.

We can not be late getting to the bus stop.

Lesson 46: Learn and Practice o-consonant-e Combination

o_e   These buddy letters have the sound /oa/. Although they are not right next to each other, **o** and **e** work together as buddies. The **e** makes the **o** have the /oa/ sound.

Practice Sound Cards: Practice **o_e**, **a_e**, **ai ay oa oe ee** + any previous sounds.

Write and Say Sounds: Please write & say **o_e, a_e, ai, ay, oa, oe, ee** +previous sounds.

Making Words: Make the words as pairs. Have the child say sounds as he builds the word. Have him make the first word and read it. Then have him add the **e** to the end and point to the **o** and say the /oe/ sound. *Physically seeing the addition of the e and how it causes the sound to change helps the child learn the pattern of how the o and e work together.*

Use sound tiles..... o e   b c d g h l m n p(2) r s t(2) v th

pairs: hop--hope   not--note   con--cone   tot--tote   cop--cope   mop--mope

pop--pope   cod--code   rob--robe   rod--rode   lob--lobe

other words: vote hose home nose hole those stole slope stove globe drove stone throne

Reading o_e Words:

home	joke	dome	rode	hope
note	cone	those	cope	rode
mope	code	vote	robe	hole
rope	hose	mole	choke	stone
stroke	stove	broke	prose	zone
rose	slope	grove	smoke	globe
tone	stole	spoke	dome	poke
pole	throne	dote	doze	tote
shone	froze	those	quote	lone
poles	scope	drove	strobe	nose
bone	mode	choke	clone	home
remote	frozen	homerun	broken	hopeful
alone	spoken	noted	tadpole	hopeless
stolen	quoted	erode	decode	sunstroke

Writing (Spelling) Words: Select some of the listed words for your child to write

Reading Sentences: Have your child read with proper tracking and blending. Make immediate corrections. After the child reads a sentence, ask him a few specific questions.

Mom left me a note that said "We will go home and play a game of chess."

The old rope broke when we gave it a tug. I am glad we did not swing on it.

Sandy rode the pony up the grassy slope. Then she rode the pony home and fed it some hay.

The green snake went into the hole by the big stone.

Lots of smoke came up from the big blaze.

Jane has a globe on the desk. She can find Spain.

The small mole dug a long hole.

The smoke came from the hot stove.

My dog has a choke chain on his neck.

When can we go home?

We hid in the grove of apple trees. It was fun playing in the shade of those old trees.

Jess hit a homerun to win the game.

The red rose was sitting in the vase on the kitchen table.

Hand me the hose so I can rinse the soap off the dog.

Mom drove us to the game.

Lesson 47: Learn and Practice i-consonant-e Combination

i__e   These buddy letters have the sound /ie/. Although they are not right next to each other,

i and e work together as buddies. The e makes the i have the /ie/ sound.

Practice Sound Cards: Practice **i_e, o_e, a_e, ai ay oa oe ee** + any previous sounds.

Write and Say Sounds: Please write and say **i_e, o_e, a_e, ai, ay, oa, oe, ee** plus any other sound the child needs to practice.

i_e **Making Words:** Make the words as pairs. Have the child say sounds as he builds the word. Have him make the first word and read it. Then have him add **e** to the end and point to the **i** and say the /ie/ sound. *Physically seeing the addition of the e and how it causes the sound to change helps the child learn the pattern of how the i and e work together.*
Use sound tiles i e   b d f g h k l m n p r s t w sh
pairs: tim--time   hid--hide   bit--bite   rid--ride   fin--fine   grip--gripe
          rip--ripe   slim--slime   kit--kite   dim--dime   pin--pine   spin--spine
          twin--twine   grim--grime   sit--site   strip--stripe   din--dine   shin--shine
other words: like mile wide bike pride smile spike slide stride swipe unlike

Reading i_e Words:

time	hide	bite	ride	dime
fine	ripe	kite	mile	tide
smile	tile	pine	twine	grime
wide	lime	chime	quite	crime
stripe	swine	spite	hide	bride
gripe	dive	Mike	spike	mine
like	glide	wife	hike	while
wipe	chide	trite	slime	file
side	shine	slide	dine	bribe
spine	drive	strike	bike	stride
five	pile	pipe	vine	swipe
kite	scribe	pride	size	prize

bite	white	wise	line	strive
inside	online	define	timely	offline
lifetime	sidewalk	daytime	beside	pastime
sunshine	provide	unlike	bedtime	sunrise

Writing (Spelling) Words: Select some of the listed words for your child to write

Reading Sentences:

Dad had to hide the bike in the shed. It was a secret gift. Mike will like it a lot.

Did you see the walrus dive into the tank?

I like to fly my kite. It makes me smile.

Let us sit in the shade of the pine tree.

We can wait to see if the doe comes up to get a drink in the creek. I hope we see the doe when she comes.

The pony ride costs a dime.

I need to go back inside the class to get my back-pack.

My old red dog likes to doze in the sunshine.

Can you see inside the shed?

We can ride the bike five miles.

When we play hide and seek we can hide behind the trees.

She can spike the ball.

What time is it?

Lesson 48: Learn and Practice u-consonant-e Combination

u _ e   These buddy letters have the sound /oo/. Although they are not right next to each other,

u and **e** work together as buddies. The **e** makes the **u** have the /oo/ sound.

Practice Sound Cards: Practice **u_e, i_e, o_e, a_e, ai ay oa oe ee** + previous sounds.

Write and Say Sounds: Please write and say **u_e, i_e, o_e, a_e, ai, ay, oa, oe, ee** plus any other sound the child needs to practice

u_e Making Words: Make the words as pairs. Have the child say sounds as he builds the word. Have him make the first word and read it. Then have him add the e to the end and point to the u and say the /oo/ sound. *Physically seeing the addition of the e and how it causes the sound to change helps the child learn the pattern of how the u and e work together.*
Use sound tiles... e i u   b c d f l m n p r s t
pairs: cub--cube   cut--cute   tub--tube   us--use   crud--crude   plum-plume
other: rule rude mule mute prune dune fuse flume include

Reading u_e Words:

use	cute	June	duke	rude
tube	rule	mule	Luke	tune
crude	lute	prune	flute	cube
flute	cube	mute	tube	dune
flume	fuse	plume	abuse	include
excuse	volume	costume	amuse	consume
ruled	cutest	misuse	exclude	use

Writing (Spelling) Words: Select some of the listed words for your child to write

She can play a tune on the flute.

It is a rule that you may not use the ball inside.

I got to go see the big sand dunes.

We can use the spade to dig a hole. Then we can plant the tree. It is a cute little white ash sapling.

Lesson 49: Learn & Practice e-consonant-e Combination

e_e   These buddy letters have the sound /ee/. Although they are not right next to each other, **e** and **e** work together as buddies. The **e** makes the **e** have the /ee/ sound.

.

Practice Sound Cards: Practice **e_e, u_e, i_e, o_e, a_e, ai ay** + previous sounds.

Write and Say Sounds: Please write and say **e_e, u_e, i_e, o_e, a_e, ai, ay, oa, oe, ee** plus any other sound the child needs to practice

e_e Making Words: Make the words as pairs. Have the child say sounds as he builds the word. Have him make the first word and read it. Then have him add the **e** to the end and point to the **e** and say the /ee/ sound. *Physically seeing the addition of the e and how it causes the sound to change helps the child learn the pattern of how the e and e work together.*
Use sound tiles... e(2) p m n s t v th
      pair: pet--pete   other words: these theme even eve

Reading e_e Words:

these	Pete	eve	theme	even
complete	concrete	compete	delete	deplete
supreme	obese	stampede	athlete	extreme
scalene	these	even		

Writing (Spelling) Words: Select some of the listed words for your child to write

Reading Sentences:

We will compete in the ball game. I hope we can win.

Pete will finish his painting by June.

This back step was made from concrete.

We can use these cubes to play the game.

I need to delete these old files.

We will complete this job by the end of the day.

The cute puppy even wagged his tail at me.

166

Lesson 50: Review & Practice all vowel-consonant-e combinations

Practice Sound Cards: Practice **e_e, u_e, i_e, o_e, a_e, ai ay oa oe ee** + previous sounds.

Write and Say Sounds: Please write and say **e_e, u_e, i_e, o_e, a_e, ai, ay, oa, oe, ee** plus any other sound the child needs to practice.

Making Words: Make words with the sound tiles. "Please make the word _____"
Use sound tiles... a e i o u   b d f g k l m n p r s t
    use plate rude game poke stone stripe tune rode rule trade strike broke shake skate
    time line stride glide pride drape strike spade unsafe mistake beside intake
Use sound tiles ......a e(2) i o   c d f g l m n   p r s v z   sh
    size vote line shape graze drove grape shame shine shrine gaze prize glaze drive
    spine game shave grave   grime decode compete confine locate complete confide

Reading Mixed List of vowel-consonant-e words:

game	plate	poke	stone	rule	these
hide	gave	note	save	rode	crane
stripe	tune	use	time	line	spoke
nine	flute	five	spade	graze	prize
slope	tube	stone	dime	cope	plane
smoke	doze	note	cute	made	pile
twine	brake	choke	trade	snake	quote
grape	wide	use	rude	make	tile
close	skate	vote	blade	plate	cone
white	spine	trade	file	shake	eve
fine	home	safe	stoke	spade	mile
tide	mule	glide	fade	hole	slide
dine	June	late	chase	same	size

sale	wise	code	tale	grade	globe
shave	doze	while	sale	name	bike
mine	gate	pole	state	smile	theme
rope	ride	jade	vase	froze	lane
broke	cave	ripe	dive	wife	hive
blaze	stride	drove	slate	throne	slime
shine	strive	bake	swine	pine	Mike
stole	grove	swipe	strobe	glaze	stroke
liked	volume	divide	decode	escape	beside
include	delete	remote	complete	hopeful	unsafe
latest	inside	behave	unlike	broken	even
safely	tadpole	homeless	sidewalk	amuse	compete
bedtime	rename	locate	awoke	lifetime	sunrise
alone	inflate	mistake	extreme	rotate	cupcake

Writing (Spelling) Words: Select some of the listed words for your child to write.

Reading Sentences: Have your child read with proper tracking and blending. Make immediate corrections. After the child reads a sentence, ask him a few specific questions.

We ate grapes, beef and milk.

We had to walk a mile.

The snake was by the stone.

Dad told us a funny tale.

The ape was up in the tree.

We need a rake and a spade to finish up the job.

The kite got stuck up in the tree.

We must always behave.

The plate broke when it fell.

Give this box to Mike. His name is on the tag.

We had to give the white dog a bath. She was a muddy mess.

We will take a trip to the west coast next June.

We can use the rope to get the bucket to the bottom of the hole.

He tossed the ball into the strike zone three times.

The kid likes to watch his dad shave.

It is not safe to dive into the lake in this spot. You may hit a log or a rock.

The athlete slid into home plate. The ball came late and he was safe.

He made cupcakes with his mom. He also ate them up. Yum!

Mom gave me a note. The note said we can go to the ball game with Pete. We will get to watch the baseball game. It will be lots of fun to see them play ball. I hope it does not rain on the game.

Lesson 51

Teach Sound:

c   You already know the letter **c** has 2 sounds /k/ and /s/.

You have been reading words with the /k/ sound. Now you are going to practice the 2nd sound /s/. The **c** *always* makes the /s/ sound whenever **e, i** or **y** comes after **c**. Yes **c** is naughty, it <u>always</u> steals the /s/ sound when **e, i** or **y** comes after it. You always know **c** has the /s/ sound when **e, i** or **y** comes after it!

$$c+e \quad c+i \quad c+y = /s/ \text{ always}$$

g   You already know the letter **g** has 2 sounds /g/ and /j/.

You have been reading words with the sound /g/. Now you are going to practice reading words with the 2nd sound /j/. The **g** *sometimes* has the /j/ sound when **e, i** or **y** comes after the **g**. Yes **g** is <u>sometimes</u> naughty and steals the /j/ sound when **e, i** or **y** comes after **g** (but NOT always!). However, if the **g** has the /j/ sound, it must have an **e, i,** or **y** after the **g**

$$g+e \quad g+i \quad g+y = /j/ \text{ sometimes}$$

Write and Say the Sound: Have the child write or trace **c** at least 5 times saying the /s/ sound and write or trace **g** at least 5 times saying the /j/ sound + other sounds needing practice.

Making Words: Please make words where **c** has the /s/ sound and **g** has the /j/ sound. ****** *Specifically point out and use the tiles to teach the pattern with c+e, c+i or c+y making the /s/ sound and the pattern with g+e, g+i making the /j/ sound.* "Please make the word _____"
Use sound tiles...... a(2) e(2) i o u y   b c(2) d f g l m n p r t ch
   city nice mice race dice   trace   trance place prance price chance dance   fancy
   practice   reduce   notice nicely replace bicep induce placemat graceful
Use sound tiles..... a e i(2) o u   c d f g l m n p r s t ch
  age rage strange gel change page range stage angel agent rigid logic tragic upstage magic

Directly teach the relationship of when c=/s/ and g=/j/ to the child. Specifically point out and use the tiles to teach and help the child 'see' and understand this pattern. When the child first makes words with tiles, remind him **e, i,** or **y** has to follow **c** to get the /s/ sound or **g** to get the /j/ sound.

When first reading words with c=/s/ or g=/j/ the child often applies the incorrect 'hard' sounds. When this occurs, give a quick "oops" or tap the word with your pencil for the 'stop-look again' signal. Initially, do *not* tell the child the correct sound. Reach over with you pencil, quickly point at **e** and draw an arrow from **e** to **c** or **g**.   You can use the verbal cue "steal" when you draw the arrow to remind the child how **e** makes **c** steal the /s/ sound or **g** steal the /j/ sound. After awhile, drop the verbal cue and silently draw the arrow from **e** to **c** or **g**. This correction technique helps the child understand and 'see' the relationship of c+e, y or i & g+e, i or y.

Remember after making corrections, the child must always re-read the word correctly!

This c+e, i, y and g+e, i y can be challenging for some children. When necessary, repeat lesson, add supplemental word making, and include additional practice decoding these words.

Reading Words with the /s/ sound for c:
Remember the **e**, **i**, or **y** after the **c** tells us **c** must have the /s/ sound. POINT THIS PATTERN OUT TO THE CHILD (especially if he is saying the incorrect /k/ sound). Correct to help the student 'see' and understand these patterns.

cent	pace	cell	chance	face	rice
nice	lace	race	mice	cinch	dice
since	space	ice	dance	grace	fleece
spice	prince	trace	price	glance	spruce
splice	brace	twice	place	trance	fence
ace	slice	prance	cent	since	nice
lacy	city	acid	icing	Nancy	pencil
recent	civil	Cindy	faced	decent	balance
replace	placemat	fancy	nicely	central	recess
produce	decide	enhance	office	silence	biceps
census	cement	sentence	concept	except	tracing
entrance	reduce	practice	lettuce	notice	convince
exceed	precise	process	succeed	success	citrus
distance	graceful	finance	proceed	absence	justice
necklace	advance	disgrace	advice	embrace	office

Reading Words with the /j/ sound for g:
Remember the **e**, **i**, or **y** after the g tells us the g could have has the /j/ sound. POINT THIS PATTERN OUT TO THE CHILD. If the child says the incorrect /g/ sound underline the e or i. Correct to help the child 'see' and understand this pattern.

age	gem	page	gel	sage	range
rage	change	cage	lunge	stage	plunge
wage	strange	huge	change	page	hinge

angel	agent	gentle	vintage	logic	arrange
engage	tragic	postage	agile	gently	magic
package	manage	village	rigid	fragile	teenage
luggage	voltage	changed	upstage	giraffe	savage
cottage	aged	hostage	rampage	image	changing

Writing (Spelling) Words: Have the student write/spell some of the listed words. Specifically teach the c+e c+i and c+y =/s/ and g+e = /j/ pattern. Before you start tell the student the /s/ sound is going to be spelled with 'c' or the /j/ sound will be spelled with 'g'. Help the student learn these patterns.

Reading Sentences: Have your child read with proper tracking and blending. Make immediate corrections. After the child reads a sentence, ask him a few specific questions.

Can you place the nice cake on the table?

What page do we need to study?

We will race to the end of the line.

Did you notice that Cindy was the angel in the class play?

We must change the time on the clock.

A tasty spice was on the muffins.

She had to practice the dance steps twice.

My nice red dress has some pretty white lace on it.

My old shaggy dog is very gentle with little kids.

You can trace the shape with this pencil.

I like to drink an ice cold milkshake on a hot day.

The little kid likes to dance and play on the stage.

I had to finish my spelling sentence.

You must be nice and gentle when you pet the little kitten.

We got the chance to go visit my uncle in the city.

I have to finish this page of math problems.

Do not shake the box. It is fragile. Gently set it on the table.

We need to go shopping. We need to get some lettuce, cheese, rice and also some milk.

My Dad had to go to his office. I had the chance to go with him. We even had time to get lunch. It was a nice day.

The price of a pencil is ten cents. Since we need five pencils, it will cost us fifty cents to get these pencils.

I like to practice adding with dice. If I roll a six and a three, I say "six plus three is nine". Mom rolls a three and a three. She says "three plus three is six". Six is less than nine so I won this roll of the dice game.

We can find lots of rocks. We will use the rocks to make a stone fence. It will be a huge job. But when we get done, this rock wall will keep the dogs from running away.

This ball game is lots of fun. We all get to play. We get to run fast and kick the ball. Can you play with us?

Lesson 52 Review and Practice

Review Sounds: Quickly practice some of the sounds you have learned! Have child follow under with their finger and say the sounds. Use the review to see what sounds your child may need additional practice with. The child needs to know these automatically.

a	s	i	o	e	u

c (ce ci cy)   g (ge gi gy)

ch	y	ee	oa	oe	ai

ay	a_e	i_e	o_e	u_e	e_e

Write and Say the Sound: Have the child write or trace any sounds that are not automatic.

Making Words: Make words with the sound tiles. "Please make the word _____"
Use sound tiles... a e(2) i o u y   b c(2) d f g l(2) m n p r t ch
    panic   price place crime grace direct change notice frolic glance directly prince
    candy brace public glance admit profit chance gladly   crafty tragic graceful produce
    practice credit beyond   retold remind nifty inflate
Use sound tiles.... a e i(2) o u y   d(2) g k l m n p r s t v ch
    strange   page range   strike chime stove angel   gusty vastly result change pesky invade
    kindly   mostly simply rusty invite visit almost unlike   mistake provide   divide
Use sound tiles... ee oa c d f g k l m n p r s t(2) w ch sh th
    street   sheep roast sweet toast green coach speech croak foam speed
    throat groan three shoal freed coal cloak greed

Reading Mixed List of Words:

a	me	I	am	at	you
as	his	not	has	this	by
it	my	did	if	that	an
is	what	in	on	which	and
than	the	was	him	had	of
with	but	us	can	up	do

will	to	said	who	we	from
went	while	smash	wait	end	coach
no	she	go	come	all	make
like	who	both	cent	use	done
nice	some	plant	page	home	strange
shut	back	catch	bring	meet	made
coat	hoe	rain	take	play	time
grape	note	child	choke	speed	way
test	teeth	call	seem	late	since
trace	speech	change	so	try	size
quote	trade	these	twice	same	keep
blink	seen	place	rule	talk	see
walk	smile	yet	inch	while	wild
gift	milk	face	melt	chance	three
why	dress	need	frogs	chin	life
child	green	soap	slice	blank	chain
yes	print	vase	goal	praise	string
coast	snake	globe	ride	think	small
next	find	tell	quick	last	spell

much	left	self	help	shape	race
very	away	maybe	sleepy	willing	seven
almost	hungry	afraid	today	tricky	running
lucky	going	pony	explain	only	silly
into	city	complete	simple	also	sentence
begin	study	always	behind	little	happen
nothing	inside	include	hopeful	behave	beyond
central	exit	unkind	sixteen	hundred	volume
common	fifteen	smallest	problem	softly	weekend

Reading Sentences:

He is afraid of the snake. I will tell him that it is just a nice grass snake.

We will go visit a big city next week.

We can only make three things with the clay.

He said he can print off the page we need.

My hungry frogs ate six crickets today.

She said that you need to trace the line.

Today is the day that we get to go to the coast. I hope it will not rain. If it is nice we get to go swimming.

Can we go play on the slide?

I will paint a green stripe on my bike. You can paint a white stripe on the red bike.

We will help Dad plant a small pine tree by the back fence.

I hope we can find the dime I lost. It fell off my desk. Do you see it? I was going to spend the ten cents on some gum.

This pink milk is sweet. Do you like it this way?

Mike likes to play with his train set. He can arrange the tracks lots of ways.

Lesson 53:

Teach Sound:

u   You know the letter **u** has 2 sounds /u/ & /oo/.
In a few words **u** has a silly /uu/ sound. You have practiced the /u/ sound and also the /oo/ sound in the u-consonant-e buddy letters. Now you are going to work with and practice the /oo/ and the /uu/ sounds.

Write and Say the Sound: Have the child write or trace **u**. Make sure the child is saying the /oo/ and /uu/ sound as he writes the letter.

Reading Words that have the /oo/ sound for u: Notice the patterns. Most of these are the u-consonant-e buddy letters or words where 'u' is the only vowel at the end of a syllable in a multisyllable word. The /oo/ is pronounced slightly differently in a few words. For example in cute it is almost a /you/ sound. If the child needs help with pronunciation, help him! Then have him re-read the word correctly.

use	tune	flute	rude	lute	cube
mute	cute	mule	tube	dude	rule
truth	pupil	unit	tuba	music	student
stupid	include	muted	reduce	volume	

Reading Words that have the /uu/ sound for u:

put	pull	full	push	bull	bush
pudding	bullet	pulling	bushy	pushing	fullest
bully	pulling	pushed	put	pull	bush

Making Words: Make words with the sound tiles. "Please make the word _____"
Use sound tiles...... a e i u   b c d f l m n p r t sh th
tune cube flute put bush tuba rude mute push truth

Reading Words:

rude	put	tuba	up	bull
tub	tune	flute	cube	cup
pull	tube	full	rule	mute
bush	rude	tune	push	duke
mule	pupil	pulling	bullet	bully

Writing (Spelling) Words: Select some of the listed words for your child to write.

Reading Sentences: Have your child read with proper tracking and blending. Make immediate corrections. After the child reads a sentence, ask him a few specific questions.

The cup is full of milk.

It is rude to pull his hand like that.

You need to stop putting ice cubes in the full cup. Put them in the empty cup.

He can play both the tuba and the flute.

Can you push me up the big hill?

The students rode the bus to the game.

Lesson 54:

Teach Sounds:

oi   These buddy letters have the sound /oy/.

oy   These buddy letters have the sound /oy/.

Good job noticing! Both **oi** and **oy** have the /oy/ sound.

Directly teach the expected spelling pattern. Both **oi and **oy** have the /oy/ sound. The 'oi' spelling is used more frequently and comes primarily at the middle of a syllable (occasionally at the beginning as in 'oil'). The 'oi' is NEVER used at the end of a word (remember no English words can end in 'i'). Therefore, the 'oy' spelling must be used for the /oy/ sound at the end of a word. The 'oy' spelling is found at either the end of the word or sometimes at the end of a syllable. Help the child learn this expected spelling pattern in making, reading and spelling words.

Practice Sound Cards: Practice new sounds **oy**, **oi**, plus previous sounds that need work.

Write and Say the Sounds: The child writes or traces **oy** and **oi** multiple times. Make sure the child says the /oy/ sound *as* he writes.

Making Words: Make words with the sound tiles. "Please make the word _____"
Use sound tiles...... e u oi   b c f   h j   l   m   n   p   r s   t
oil soil foil   coin boil moist spoil join joint   point broil hoist coil rejoin recoil
reboil   subsoil   uncoil
Use sound tiles ..... oy   a   e   b   c d j l(2) m n p r s t
boy toy joy enjoy employ royal loyal coy destroy deploy decoy

Reading Words with the 'oi' spelling for /oy/:

oil	coin	noise	foil	moist	soil
boil	oink	coil	spoil	join	voice
point	toil	joint	hoist	void	broil
choice	poise	moist	joist	voice	noise
avoid	recoil	pinpoint	spoiled	boiling	hoisted
subsoil	toilet	tabloid	exploit	rejoin	uncoil
poison	topsoil	oilskin	moisten	pointless	

179

Reading Words with the 'oy' spelling for /oy/:

boy	toy	joy	coy	Roy	ploy
royal	enjoy	loyal	employ	annoy	joyful
voyage	deploy	decoy	enjoy	destroy	flyboy

Writing (Spelling) Words: Select some of the listed words for your child to write.

Reading Sentences: Have your child read with proper tracking and blending. Make immediate corrections. After the child reads a sentence, ask him a few specific questions.

The boy will enjoy playing with the toy train.

Can you point at the best choice?

The soil by the plant is moist.

The boys will enjoy seeing the coal train pass by.

The class was full of joyful noise.

We have a choice to make.

The little boy played with his toy trucks in the sand box.

The milk spoiled when we left it on the table.

The snake was coiled up next to the shed.

I drank a glass of soy milk.

We need to put some topsoil in the pot. Then we can plant the seeds.

The pot on the stove was boiling.

Mom enjoys a hot mug of coffee.

Lesson 55:

Teach Sound:

ea   These buddy letters have 2 main sounds. Most of the time the **ea** buddy letters have the /ee/ sound. Sometimes they have an /**e**/ sound. You will also learn how **ea** has the unexpected /**ay**/ sound in a few words.

Practice Sound Card: Practice **ea, oi, oy** as well as previous sounds needing work.

Write and Say the Sounds: The child writes or traces **ea** multiple times. Make sure the child is saying the /ee//e/ &/a/ sounds *as* he writes. Plus write **oi, oy** & other sound needing work.

Making Words: Make words with the sound tiles. "Please make the word _____"
Use sound tiles...... ea o   c d(2) l m n p r s(2) t ch sh ing
       meat each clean stream read   seat lead peas dream preach leash east teach
       cheat peach teaching unleash   reason reading season cheating dreaming
Use sound tiles.....ea y   b d f g h k l p r s t w   v th
       /e/ words: bread head breath death   spread wealth read breast   ready heavy steady
       /ay/ words: great break steak greatly

Reading Words with the /ee/ sound for ea: This /ee/ sound is by far the most frequent sound for 'ea'.

eat	each	lean	east	heat	sea
beat	leaf	treat	seat	steam	teach
reach	beam	least	dream	neat	heap
dream	leap	ease	bean	peak	please
jeans	tease	stream	speak	sneak	cheat
cream	scream	beach	preach	leash	crease
team	read	clean	bleak	feast	stream
peace	tease	grease	peach	wheat	bleach
breathe	steal	yeast	seal	feat	mean
real	deal	least	meal	peas	beans

181

beast	leak	squeak	meat	please	eagle
easy	release	disease	repeat	creamy	reached
eating	season	reading	peanut	reason	meanest
heating	peacock	teaching	pleasing	ideal	squeaky
beaten	daydream	speaking	increase	beaches	leaflet
unleash	defeat	neatest	peaceful	seashell	ice cream

Reading Words with the /e/ sound for ea:

head	bread	ready	spread	dread	breath
dread	death	tread	health	thread	breast
wealth	dealt	stealth	deaf	steady	heaven
heavy	peasant	ready	instead	dreadful	breathless

Reading a few words with the unexpected /ay/ sound for ea:

great   break   steak   daybreak   greatest

Writing (Spelling) Words: Select some of the listed words for your child to write.

Reading Sentences: Have your child read with proper tracking and blending. Make immediate corrections. After the child reads a sentence, ask him a few specific questions.

He is teaching each of us to spell.

Can I please eat the peach?

She is ready to go to the beach.

Please feed the extra peas to the sheep.

Please put lots of cream in my coffee cup.

Can I drink a cup of sweet tea with my lunch?

Please bring the leash with you.

We will eat bread and meat with lunch.

Please spread some jam on my bread.

It is not nice to tease the little kids.

I need to use some bleach when I wash my white socks.

Pick up all the toys. It needs to be neat and clean.

We got to hike by the stream. On the way back home we even got to see an eagle.

I like ice cream.

The rags are piled up in a messy heap. Please fold these rags and place them in a neat stack.

He can join the team and play with us.

Can you please repeat the last math problem?

Can we eat a treat with lunch? Mom said yes, but I had to clean my plate and finish my peas. I ate up all my lunch. Now I can eat my yummy ice cream treat!

My dog got a treat from the lady at the ice cream shop. My dog likes to go to the ice cream shop.

You do such a great job reading!

Lesson 56 Review and Practice

Review Sounds: Quickly practice some of the sounds you learned! Have child follow under with their finger and say the sounds. Use the review to see what sounds your child may need additional practice with. The child needs to know these automatically.

c   (ce   ci   cy)   g   (ge   gi   gy)   y

ee   oa   oe   ai   ay   a_e

i_e   o_e   u_e   oy   oi   ea

Write and Say the Sound: Have the child write or trace sounds not automatically known.

Reading Mixed List of Words and Sentences:

yet	self	life	long	name	some
use	tell	went	snack	much	heat
walk	each	hand	wait	home	both
must	make	why	full	but	keep
teach	wash	day	shake	us	change
most	read	said	bring	boy	page
get	white	please	find	speak	state
smile	real	free	thank	time	black
point	way	those	from	place	made
will	size	pull	need	great	which
brain	talk	these	with	since	voice
head	price	come	peace	health	just

leash	close	side	choice	reach	crank
string	rude	five	rule	smoke	six
grace	coach	bread	joint	push	print
note	grade	who	shut	race	stage
team	rain	dance	strange	hide	save
test	next	join	brace	clay	cage
pace	leak	play	noise	dice	sneak
only	even	saying	second	mistake	also
behind	almost	open	heaven	away	sentence
hidden	unit	inside	ready	until	complete
reading	today	simple	always	quickly	very
begin	enjoy	going	city	notice	study
wishing	freedom	angry	increase	music	delete

Please take the boiling pot off the stove.

We need to walk the long way home. It is such a nice day.

Please help me find the green leash. I need to use it to take the dog on a walk. He is waiting to go.

To find the quilt shop you need to drive five miles east on this road. Then you take a left on second street.

What time will the coach begin practice?

Lesson 57:

Teach Sound:

OW   These buddy letters have 2 sounds; /ow/ and /oa/.

Practice Sound Cards: Practice **ow, ea, oi, oy** as well as previous sounds needing work.

Write and Say the Sound: The child writes or traces **ow** multiple times. Make sure the child says /ow/ and /oa/ sounds *as* he writes. Plus write **ea**, **oi**, **oy** & other sound needing work.

Making Words: Make words with the sound tiles. "Please make the word _____"
Use sound tiles... ow e i   b c d g h l m n p r s t w sh th   ing
   -/ow/ words: now cow owl plow town down drown brown howl growl clown plowing
   midtown township drowning   growling
   -/oa/ words: snow slow grow low mow own   show   shown blown throw growth
   growing   window showing below sideshow   snowing slideshow widow

Reading Words with the /ow/ sound for ow:

now	cow	how	owl	plow	town
down	drown	brown	growl	clown	crown
gown	howl	chow	frown	growl	browse
scowl	drown	now	how	brown	plowing
township	downtown	growling		midtown	

Reading Words with the /oa/ sound for ow:

snow	slow	grow	low	mow	own
flow	show	shown	blow	blown	bowl
row	crow	throw	growth	flow	glow
tow	shallow	window	pillow	rainbow	mellow
yellow	showing	slowly	bowling	lowest	snowy
follow	borrow	meadow	shadow	below	swallow
elbow	fellow	hollow	sorrow	show	low

Writing (Spelling) Words: Select some of the listed words for your child to write.

Reading Sentences: Have your child read with proper tracking and blending. Make immediate corrections. After the child reads a sentence, ask him a few specific questions.

The wind will blow the snow in town.

The brown owl is in the top branch of the big tree.

The grass grows fast.

Jess needs to mow down the tall grass.

Now you can show me the brown cow on the milk jug.

Wait and let me clean off the desk.

Now you can put down the clay plate you made.

How old will you be next month?

We had to drive slowly into town.

The cute brown and white puppy was howling at us.

Can you please throw the yellow ball to me?

The clown had a big frown painted on his face.

We had to follow the old brown truck.

Please put the cat chow in the small bowl.

Can we use the yellow paint?

Lesson 58:

Teach Sound:

ou These buddy letters have 3 sounds. Most of the time **ou** buddies have the /ow/ sound. Sometimes **ou** has the /u/ sound and in a few words **ou** has the /oo/ sound.

Practice Sound Cards: Practice sound card for **ou, ow, ea, oi, oy** as well as previous sounds not automatic.

Write and Say the Sound: The child writes or traces **ou** multiple times. Make sure the child says /ow/, /u/ and /oo/ *as* he writes. Plus write **ow, ea, oi, oy** & other sound needing work.

Making Words: Make words with the sound tiles. "Please make the word _____"
Use sound tiles... ou o y c d f g h l m n(2) p r t ch
   /ow/ words: out loud proud noun couch clout ouch found grouch ground count pout crouch pound pouch proudly compound loudly grouchy pronounce cloudy
Use sound tiles... ou a i e y b c d f g l m n p r s t(2) w th ch
   /ow/ words: trout sprout mound outside rebound without loudest
   /u/ words: young touch cousin famous (Tell child to add silent-e for: couple trouble double)
   /oo/ words: you soup group youth

Reading Words with the /ow/ sound for ou:

out	loud	pout	oust	round	ouch
pound	cloud	mound	proud	stout	found
shout	house	clout	mouse	count	south
couch	sound	ground	hound	vouch	snout
trout	pouch	noun	grouch	spout	bounce
ounce	grouse	mount	south	scout	flounce
found	pounce	round	sprout	mouth	out
about	county	proudly	countless	sounded	rebound
loudest	around	outloud	southeast	thousand	playground
outside	loudly	without	counted	sprouted	compound

Reading Words with the /u/ sound for ou:

touch   young   country   cousin   couple   double

trouble   country   joyous   famous (and other 'ous' endings)

Reading Words with the /oo/ sound for ou:

you   soup   group   youth   croup

Writing (Spelling) Words: Select some of the listed words for your child to write.

Reading Sentences: Have your child read with proper tracking and blending. Make immediate corrections. After the child reads a sentence, ask him a few specific questions.

The boy went fishing with his Mom. He got six trout to eat. Mom just got three. Mom was proud of him.

He found a couple of toys on the couch.

Did you see the geese head south?

She can count by fives up to a hundred.

Please do not drop the glass vase on the ground. It will break if you drop it.

Now can we go outside and play with the dogs?

The group of kids found the lost hound.

She found a round white rock next to the stream.

Can we give away a couple of these toys to needy children?

The youth group went down to the playground and cleaned it up. They picked up all the trash and raked the grass.

Lesson 59 Review

Review Sounds: Quickly practice some of the sounds you have learned! Have child follow under with their finger and say the sounds.

o	c	g	y	ing
ee	oa	oe	ai	ay
a_e	i_e	o_e	u_e	e_e
oi	oy	ea	ow	ou

Reading Irregular Words: We are going to read a few new irregular words. We say these words a little differently than the sounds they should make. In these words **ou** makes an /uu/ sound. We say would, could and should. Look carefully as I point to each word and read it to you.

would   could   should

I'll use our new words in a few sentences so you can hear the words. These sentences are strictly for the adult to read to the child as they contain sounds not yet learned. When you read emphasize **would/should/could**: --**Would** you like to go to the library with me? --You **could** check out a good book on trains.   --While we are there, we **should** get a cat book for your little sister.

Reading Irregular Words: Now it is your turn to read these words. Have your child finger track and read these words. If the child sounds out the word with an /ow/ or /oo/ sound simply say something like "stop, that's how we should sound out the word, do you remember how we say it? We say **would, could** or **should**." Have the child reread the word correctly. Help the child learn and practice correct pronunciation.

would   should   could   would   could

Reading Sentences: Ok, now it's your turn to read our new word in a sentence. Have child read the following sentences. Make sure the child uses finger tracking. Have the child sound out words. Immediately correct any errors. If the child makes errors on irregular words simply say "oops… do you remember how we say that word".

Would you please feed the cat?

Could you go to the game with me?

Should we bring a snack with us?

Could you please take out the trash?

Word Making Game:

Use sound tiles... oi a e(2) i(2) o u   c d(2) l m n p r t v x sh
    point clash drive voice shade void volume notice pencil divide invite complex
    expand   excite   vanish   multiply exploit

Use sound tiles... ai ou e(2) i o   c d(2) f l m n p r(2) s t w x ch
    strain found chain mound proud chime stripe told paint twine saint sprout prime faint
    pride   refrain contain complete decode conflict wisdom retain explain   retrain

Use sound tiles... ow i y   b d g l(2) p n r s w th sh ing
    shown brown throw grown window blowing   growling windy growth rowing showy

Use sound tiles.... ea i u y   b c d h l m n p r s t v ch ing
    bread beast preach spread scream bleach simply teaching heavy heating
    creamy cleaning crusty preaching ready dusty steady richly spreading

Reading Words and Sentences:

you	coin	how	east	put	count
found	enjoy	group	each	great	now
which	said	out	down	came	strange
push	out	going	has	from	brink
stream	praise	point	loud	would	found
growl	preach	voice	group	small	these
while	teach	flow	growth	spread	most
please	grace	pray	state	give	screech
noun	stop	trot	hold	catch	round
cream	find	steal	next	brown	join
sound	blow	prime	choice	health	change
enjoy	about	amaze	annoy	helpful	away
afraid	easy	punish	infect	gentle	became
contain	wisdom	maybe	pillow	justice	cousin
ready	peanut	reading	heavy	even	coffee

Could you please close the window? It is windy outside. The dust is blowing in.

Can you please bring me a snack? I am hungry. I would like to eat some grapes or maybe a slice of cheese. I would also like to drink some milk with my snack.

We just got a lot of fresh snow. Maybe we can make a big snowman when we get out of class. I would like to put my old red hat on the snowman's head. That would be funny! Next we can slide down the big hill on the sleds. I will race you and I think I can win. What do you think of that plan?

Could you please hand me that box of toys? I need to find my old little fuzzy dog. It should be inside the box.

We had a math test today. It was not easy. I had to study for it. We had to add, subtract, multiply and divide. I practiced the problems and now I got an A. My mom was proud of me.

I like to read about ladybugs. I found out a lot about ladybugs by reading. My grandma also likes ladybugs a lot. We talk about them.

My mom is teaching me how to read. I like to read. It is lots of fun! I like to read to my mom.

Did you see the film that was playing this past weekend? It was about a boy and his dog. It was funny. The dog's name was Buddy. The dog played baseball. He could hit a home run. We got to go watch it with Dad.

Lesson 60:

Teach Sounds:

ue — These buddy letters have the sound /oo/.

ew — These buddy letters also have the sound /oo/.

ui — These buddy letters also have the sound /oo/.

Good job noticing! **ue, **ew** & **ui** all have the same /oo/ sound. The **ew** and **ue** are usually used at the end of words. The **ui** is only used in a few words and is NEVER used at the end of a word.

Practice Sound Cards: Practice cards for **ue, ew, ui, ou, ow, ea, oi, oy** as well as previous sounds not automatically known.

Write and Say the Sound: The child writes or traces **ue, ew and ui** multiple times. Make sure the child says /oo/ *as* he writes. Plus write **ou, ow, ea, oi, oy** & other sound needing work.

Making Words: Make words with the sound tiles. "Please make the word _____"
Use sound tiles... ue a e   b c   d f g   h l   r s t   v
        blue clue   hue fuel true   Sue   cue   glue   due rescue   value
Use sound tiles... ew   b c d f l   n p r s t   ch
        new   flew stew chew dew drew slew news blew crew   screw   pew
Use sound tiles.... ui   e   c f   n   r(2)   s t
        suit fruit   ruin recruit

Reading Words with the 'ew' spelling pattern:

new	flew	stew	dew	drew	slew
news	blew	crew	newt	stew	grew
few	threw	screw	pew	yew	shrew
chewing	cashew	unscrew	withdrew	outgrew	renew

Reading Words with the 'ue' spelling pattern:

blue	true	clue	hue	fuel	Sue
glue	due	flue	value	untrue	rescue
venue	fescue	blue	true		

Reading Words with the 'ui' spelling pattern:

suit	fruit	cruise	juice	bruise	recruit

Reading Sentences: Have your child read with proper tracking and blending. Make immediate corrections. After the child reads a sentence, ask him a few specific questions.

Dad likes to listen to the news when he gets home.

Jim got a new bruise on his elbow in the last game.

He grew an inch last month.

She used a can of blue paint to finish the shed.

He grew peas in a small pot out on the deck.

Could I have a few grapes with my lunch?

The robin flew up to the nest hidden in the tree.

We had a few ball games last week.

I like the new blue coat that grandma gave you. It is nice.

Let's eat some fruit with the beef stew. It will be a healthy lunch.

I would like to have some chewing gum.

It is true that the t-rex was named Sue. I think that is a funny name for a huge t-rex. What do you think?

Kayla and Jess like to play with glue. The glue got all used up in a big sticky project. Now they need a new tube of glue.

He outgrew his old coat. Now he needs a new coat.

Lesson 61:

Teach Sound:

oo   These buddy letters have 2 sounds /oo/ and /uu/. Most often **oo** has the /oo/ sound and sometimes **oo** has the /uu/ sound.

Practice Sound Cards: Practice cards for **oo, ue, ew, ui, ou, ow, ea** as well as previous sounds not automatically known.

Write and Say the Sound: The child writes or traces **oo** multiple times. Make sure the child says /oo/ and /uu/ *as* he writes. Plus write **ue, ew, ui, ou, ow, ea** & other sounds needing work.

Making Words: Make words with the sound tiles. "Please make the word _____"
Use sound tiles... oo(2)   e   b c   d f g   k l m   n p r   s   t(2) th
  words with /oo/ sound: boot pool food spoon loon broom stoop proof spool troop smooth
    soonest smoothest moonset   foolproof coolest
  words with the /uu/ sound: look took book foot hood   cook stood good hook cookbook
    footrest   bookend

Reading Words with the /oo/ sound for oo:

soon	boot	pool	moon	food	too
coon	loon	broom	boom	hoop	room
noon	roof	mood	spool	choose	drool
troop	boost	zoo	bloom	spoon	stoop
smooth	root	cool	tooth	moose	loop
proof	scoop	moo	soon	shoot	too
roomful	raccoon	uproot	moody	baboon	moonrise
rooftop	soonest	balloon	mushroom	sunroof	teaspoon
coolest	smoothly	washroom	scooping		

Reading Words with the /uu/ sound for oo:

book	hook	nook	cook	foot	look
stood	took	hoof	good	shook	wool
wood	brook	hood	cooking	textbook	sainthood
looking	football	hooking	bookend	wooly	bookstand

Writing (Spelling) Words: Select some of the listed words for your child to write.

Reading Sentences: Have your child read with proper tracking and blending. Make immediate corrections. After the child reads a sentence, ask him a few specific questions.

Please sweep the room with this new broom.

Look at the nice blue balloon she got at the zoo.

You can help me cook. We can read the cook book. It says to put a teaspoon of salt into the bowl.

It was very hot outside but the pool looked blue and smooth. It made me want to dive in and cool off.

He ate his stew in the big blue bowl with his spoon.

The basketball hoop was too tall. Dad had to bring the rim down so his little boy could reach it. Now his young son can play ball. He likes to shoot hoops.

This is a good book about trains. It is new. I just got it from my Grandpa. He likes trains too. We both like to read about trains. We also like to play with his toy trains. He has a big train room at his house. I run these trains with him when we go down to visit him.

Lesson 62:

Teach Sounds:

ie   These buddy letters have 3 sounds /ie/ /ee/ and sometimes /i/.

ei   These buddy letters have 2 sounds, usually /ee/ and occasionally /ay/.

**ie and ei are not that common

Practice Sound Cards: Practice cards for **ei, oo, ue, ew, ui, ou, ow, ea** as well as previous sounds not automatically known.

Write and Say the Sound: The child writes or traces **ie** and **ei**. Make sure the child says the sounds *as* he writes. Plus write **oo, ue, ew, ui, ou, ow, ea** & other sounds needing work.

Making Words: Make words with the sound tiles. "Please make the word _____"
Use sound tiles... ie a y   b c   d f g   k l m n p r s t   ow th ch sh
    pie die lie tie thief chief   brownie shriek yield priest brief friend field shield
Use sound tiles... ei   o   c(2)   l   n p r t v   ing th
    conceit   ceiling   protein veil rein vein

Reading 'ie' and 'ei' words: If the child says an alternate sound incorrectly, say "Oops, this word uses the /--/ sound" and have your child read the word again.

Reading Words with the /ie/ sound for ie:

pie   lie   die   tie   magpie

Reading Words with the /ee/ sound for ie:

thief   chief   siege   priest   niece   grief

shriek   brief   belief   relief   achieve   retrieve

brownie   cookie   collie   rookie   Maggie   believe

Reading Words with the /i/ sound for ie:

friend   field   shield   yield   wield

Reading Words with the /ee/ sound for ei:

conceit   receive   receipt   ceiling   protein

Reading Words with the /ay/ sound for ei:

veil   rein   vein   beige

Writing (Spelling) Words: Have the student write/spell some of the listed words. The spelling guideline "i before e except after c or sounding as /ay/ in neighbor and sleigh and a few exceptions" helps us spell these words.

Reading Sentences:

His friend made him a tasty apple pie.

Please tie up the lace so you do not trip and fall.

My best friend sent me a brief note.

My cousin is also my mom's niece.

I had a brief meeting with my coach.

I like to take my dog on a walk in the big field behind my house. She is a white and brown collie. I can throw a stick. She will retrieve it.

I would like to eat a cookie now. But my mom said I had to eat some protein and drink my milk. She said I could have the cookie when I was all done with my healthy meal.

Do not tell a lie. You must always say what is true.

My friend can come ride his bike with us. I believe he can stay until five. We should also have time to go on a hike.

Lesson 63:

Teach Sound:

ey   These buddy letters have 2 sounds /ee/ and /ay/. Usually the **ey** buddy letters follow the guideline of "when two vowels go walking the first does the talking" and have the /ee/ sound. But in a few words **ey** has an unexpected /ay/ sound.

The 'ey' does not occur in many words. The most frequently encountered **ey** word is **they**.

Practice Sound Cards: Practice cards for **ey, oo, ue, ew, ui, ou, ow, ea** as well as previous sounds not automatically known.

Write and Say the Sound: The child writes or traces **ey**. Make sure the child says the sounds *as* he writes. Plus write **ei, ie, oo, ue, ew, ui, ou** & other sounds needing work.

Making Words: Make words with the sound tiles. "Please make the word _____"
Use sound tiles... ey o   k   m   n   p   r   th
   key monkey   money   they   prey honey

Reading Words with the /ee/ sound for ey:

key   monkey   money   honey   pulley   alley

valley   hockey   kidney   volley   donkey   chimney

trolley   jockey

Reading Words with the unexpected /ay/ sound for ey: (**although the /ay/ sound for **ey** is only found in a few words you see it frequently in the very common word 'they')

they   prey   obey   osprey

Reading Sentences:

I like to spread honey on my toast.

They found the key behind the couch.

We must obey all of the class rules.

How much money do you have with you?

199

We took a hike along the valley trail.

They rode the trolley down the street.

I got to feed the donkey some hay.

Please take the trash can out to the alley.

Oh no! I lost my key to the house. Can you help me find it? I hope we find it fast. We would like to go inside.

The boy had a hole in his pocket. He lost his money. He was sad. But then some kind kids came to help him. They found the lost coins. They found all ten of his dimes. The boy was happy and they all got some ice cream with the money.

The monkey was way up in the tree. He was eating some fruit. When he was done he came down and played on the ropes. I got to watch him swing around with his friends. I like watching the monkey play.

They went to the football game to watch the Cowboys play the Rams. Jim was very happy when the Cowboys won the game. They won by seven points.

How much money do I need to get that new book about dogs? It looks like a great book. I hope it is not a lot of money.

We are going to find out what is in the big box that Joe and Molly left us last week. They said we could open the box today. We have been waiting to open it. What do you think is in the box?

Lesson 64:

Teach Sounds:

aw   These buddy letters have the sound /aw/.

au   These buddy letters also have the sound /aw/.

augh   These buddy letters also have the sound /aw/. The 'gh' is silent.

Good job noticing! The **aw**, **au** and **augh** all have the same /aw/ sound.

Practice Sound Cards: Practice sound cards for **aw, au, augh, ey, oo, ue, ew, ui,** as well as previous sounds not automatically known.

Write and Say the Sound: The child writes or traces **aw, au & augh.** Make sure the child says the sounds /aw/ *as* he writes. Plus write **ei, ie, oo, ue, ew, ui** & other sounds needing work.

Making Words: Make words with the sound tiles. "Please make the word _____"
Use sound tiles... aw ou i u   c d f h j k l n p r s(2) t w th
     law jaw hawk dawn claw lawn flaw awful sawdust withdraw outlaw southpaw
Use sound tiles... au e i o u   d(2) f g h l n p s t(2) v ing
     haul fault flaunt vault auto audit August hauling defraud default taunting
Use sound tiles... i e augh c d r s t(2)
     taught caught distraught retaught

Reading Words with the **au** spelling for /aw/:

haul	fault	auto	maul	clause	sauce
pause	Paul	cause	haunt	vault	fraud
launch	gaunt	caulk	taunt	flaunt	caused
August	laundry	faucet	hauling	defraud	vaulted
default	caused	faultless	saucepan	taunting	causeway

Reading Words with the **aw** spelling for /aw/:

saw	law	jaw	paw	hawk	lawn
pawn	claw	fawn	paws	dawn	awe

201

draw   crawl   slaw   shawl   laws   drawn

yawn   awful   drawing   sawdust   awesome   awning

declaw   outlaw   chainsaw   southpaw   whipsaw   withdraw

Reading Words with the augh spelling for /aw/:

caught   taught   retaught

Writing (Spelling) Words: Select some of the listed words for your child to write.

Reading an Irregular word with 'augh': We are going to learn a new irregular word. The 'augh' does not have the /aw/ sound you just learned. In this word 'augh' has an /aff/ sound.

laugh   We say laugh. Let's read **laugh** together. Finger track and say the **laugh** with the child.

Then have the child finger track and say it alone. If the child pronounces the word incorrectly say "Stop, that's how we sound out the word, do you remember how we say it? We say **you**." Then have the child read the word correctly a few times.

Practice reading **laugh** correctly. Have the child finger track as he says the word.

laugh   laugh   laugh   laugh

Reading Sentences:

I had to laugh at the silly puppy.

It is not my fault that I was late.

The hawk flew fast, diving down on its prey. It caught the mouse.

My Mom taught us how to play this game.

We need to haul this junk to the dump.

We saw the doe and the fawn hiding in the tall grass down by the creek. We had to pause and watch them.

When you drive you need to follow the laws of the road.

Lesson 65: Review and Practice

Practice Sound Cards: Practice sound card for **aw, au, augh, ey, oo, ue, ew, ui,** as well as previous sounds needing work.

Write and Say the Sound: The child writes or traces **aw, au, augh, oo** & other sounds not automatically known.

Reading Mixed List of Words and Sentences:

out	low	head	each	all	way
keep	yet	find	son	may	fast
hold	faith	shut	wasp	mail	true
soon	saw	grow	cause	round	tie
age	stood	wait	front	send	change
haul	game	book	like	they	great
too	nice	those	new	read	law
dime	free	walk	you	now	field
rang	find	east	count	slow	shout
stay	noise	cell	key	sale	down
need	child	hawk	soap	blue	gave
page	found	goal	foot	full	friend
point	food	hide	draw	thank	brown
threw	race	yield	rule	wash	strange
fuel	look	blind	cool	good	smile
loud	twice	drip	which	finch	frost

grind	sauce	brief	smooth	screw	proud
behind	also	today	instead	double	money
yellow	couple	obey	ready	include	empty
almost	total	program	lesson	begin	Bible
able	across	fifty	student	gentle	inside
afraid	belong	away	only	himself	within

I had to laugh at the silly monkey playing in the tree with his friends.

We found a hawk nest in the huge pine tree.

He caught seven trout last week.

You need to mow the lawn by the end of this week.

I do not like hot sauce on my meat. I just like lots of ketchup.

My dad taught me how to throw a fast ball.

Mom took us down to the lake. We found an osprey nest. We watched the osprey dive and catch a fish. Then he flew back to his nest.

We went on a long hike in the woods. We walked along a trail. We crossed a small creek. I saw lots of pretty rocks. My friend found an old elk skull. I even found a white feather on the ground. It was a great day to be out in the woods.

Lesson 66:

Teach Sound:

igh   These buddy letters have the sound /ie/. The "gh" in these buddy letters is "silent".

Sound Card Practice: Practice sound card for **igh, aw, au, augh, ey, oo, ue, ew, ui,** as well as previous sounds that need work.

Write and Say the Sound: The child writes or traces **igh, aw, au, augh** & other sounds not automatically known.

Making Words: Make words with the sound tiles. "Please make the word _____"
Use sound tiles... igh e u   b d f(2)   h l m   n p r s t(2)
    high   sigh   light   sight   right   might   fight   flight   night   bright   delight   upright   penlight
    uptight   brightest   frightful

Reading Words:

high	right	light	might	sigh	fight
bright	thigh	tight	slight	night	fright
plight	sight	blight	highest	lightning	lighten
tighten	upright	frighten	highway	tightest	lights
delight	highlight	brighten	hightail	penlight	insight
brighten	flashlight	frightful	highjack	outright	nightgown
twilight	midnight	lightest	mighty	thighbone	brightest
nightlight	uptight	daylight	backlight	sighted	moonlight

Writing (Spelling) Words: Select some of the listed words for your child to write.

Reading Sentences/Paragraphs:

Please flip off that bright light.

The book is on the right side of the desk.

He might be able to catch that high ball.

We got to stay up until midnight.

I need to bring my flashlight with me when I go camping.

She likes to watch the lightning flash in the night sky.

The cat fight woke me up in the middle of the night. I had to run outside in my nightgown and break it up. I got my cat back inside and then went back to bed.

I grew a lot since I was six. This belt fit me then but now it is way too tight.

We could see the moon shine brightly in the night sky. The moon did not go down behind the hill until dawn.

Jess liked going hiking in the woods with Dad. They walked down by the stream. Jess saw a doe and a fawn hiding behind a tree. She also saw a hawk flying high in the sky. She even found an old jaw bone from an elk. She picked up some pretty little stones to keep. It was a great hike.

We made some coleslaw with the extra cabbage. What else should we make to eat with lunch?   I think a cold ham and cheese sandwich would be great. Or maybe we could make hot grilled cheese and some soup.

We watched them paint the stripes on the highway. They used a big truck that quickly spayed the paint right down the middle of the road. I enjoyed seeing how they did that.

Lesson 67: Additional Practice with /z/ sound of s

S   You know that the letter **s** has 2 sounds /s/ and /z/. We are going to practice some additional words with the /z/ sound for s.

Reading words with the /z/ sound for s:

is	as	use	his	has	wise
please	rise	choose	pause	these	noise
those	praise	raise	was	jobs	grabs
swings	nose	peas	hose	browse	stays
news	lays	grows	keys	laws	friends
hands	wins	clams	holds	pose	glows
saves	fuse	rose	cools	dogs	cheese
tease	spoils	ease	plans	whose	prays
rains	boys	ribs	does	bruise	rides
dreams	cause	use	boils	plows	noise
close	games	clause	cruise	tease	used
easy	husband	resent	obeys	result	daisy
visit	resist	music	raisin	fused	weasel
risen	poison	disease	reason	wisdom	amuse
season	excuse	because	chosen	pleasing	abuse
revise	noisy	caused	praising	reuse	cousin
excuse	paused	result	thousand	caused	oppose
flimsy	compose	disclose	translate	expose	misuse
pleasant	enclose	rosebush	easy	result	using

Lesson 68: Developing Skills Reading Common 3-Syllable Words

The child has acquired the skill of reading 2 syllable words. This lesson will introduce a few common 3-syllable words. Directly help your child learn how to handle these longer words.

Now that you are such a terrific job at reading, you are ready to learn a more advanced skill. You are going to start reading some three syllable words. You will learn and practice tackling these longer words. If you need help, I will help you break these longer words into shorter parts with a pencil slash. Have your pencil ready and when necessary break the word with a pencil slash at the syllable break. (For example: fam/i/ly, con/tin/ue, pres/i/dent, ex/pen/sive)

family	animal	continue	example	finished
develop	possible	president	agreement	citizen
celebrate	explained	positive	enjoyed	remaining
difficult	unwilling	reminded	probably	visible
negative	included	multiply	illustrate	expensive

We had a huge family picnic last week. All my cousins came to see us. We enjoyed the family time.

Mom reminded us to continue cleaning up the mess.

We probably need to get some help lifting this box. It is really heavy. My aunt is strong. I am positive she will help us.

I like to watch the animal show on the cable channel. Last week it was about training dogs to do difficult jobs.

When you multiply three times three you get nine. Math is not difficult when you practice the facts. But, you have to be willing to spend time practicing.

I explained to my friend that my family enjoys camping, fishing and hunting.

Lesson 69: Review and Practice

Review Sounds: Quickly practice all the sounds you learned! Have child finger track and say the sound or sounds. Use the review to determine if the child needs additional practice.

m	t	a	s	d	i	f	r
th	l	o	n	p	e	h	v
sh	u	b	k	ck	c	g	j
w	ch	tch	x	z	qu	wh	y
ing	ink	ee	oa	oe	ai	a_e	i_e
o_e	u_e	e_e	oi	oy	ea	ow	ou
ue	ew	ui	oo	ey	au	aw	igh

Write and Say the Sound: The child writes or traces any of these sounds that are not yet automatic. Make sure the child says the sounds *as* he writes.

Making Words: Make words with the sound tiles. "Please make the word _____"
Use sound tiles... a e i o   y oi c(2) d f g n p r t v ch
  prance choice trade   gave pride voice drove change pave price   print grace point
  place   practice fancy   notice   candy
Use sound tiles.... ou   a e   y   c d g l   n p r s t sh th
  ground strange   count age shout   stage youth shy angel young group cloudy
Use sound tiles.... aw ew igh   c d f h l   n r s t th ing
  draw screw saw   news threw high right drew night stew lawn straw flight crawling
  thawing lightning   fighting

Reading Irregular Words: Please read these irregular words. Let's see if you can remember how we say these silly words! (call them "irregular" instead of "silly" for older children)

was	to	said	you	do	who
what	some	of	would	come	done
should	was	could	laugh	want	none

Reading List of Mixed Words: The child reads the following words, sounding out with physical tracking and proper blending. Correct any errors immediately.

well	red	new	out	make	way
why	each	need	those	how	white
all	bring	few	make	look	much
boy	use	saw	show	most	free
right	home	last	just	they	must
when	size	change	point	now	keep
great	good	same	friend	young	both
true	soon	day	town	three	voice
place	late	ten	these	read	stand
nine	shell	juice	tease	left	book
frown	from	came	food	mean	small
draw	high	find	help	spell	sound
pray	time	group	blue	grace	strange
next	clean	light	sheet	slow	black
wheel	stood	taught	call	strike	since
please	fruit	such	real	praise	wash
pie	down	close	slide	growl	head
might	found	reach	twin	house	page
caught	brief	spread	quick	wise	math
walk	child	coat	led	month	safe
chest	green	kick	wing	broom	cold

laws	clap	blank	cloud	rule	pinch
field	foot	tray	gift	clue	sleep
tank	ice	grass	throw	shine	south
fresh	road	teach	spoil	smooth	wait
deaf	moose	glue	coin	owl	oil
swift	talk	swim	glance	deep	hope
cage	sauce	threw	swing	thief	roof
life	blend	felt	stout	brown	beach
even	money	about	between	sentence	because
easy	happen	behind	fifty	became	going
very	nothing	country	ready	escape	only
value	away	music	amaze	obey	almost
unit	baby	double	sixty	angel	destroy
open	always	maybe	awesome	notice	into
quickly	also	begin	hungry	honey	today

Reading Sentences/Paragraphs:

Could you please come to my game? I am on the Braves basketball team. We play today at six. I hope we can win.

Can you find the little clip that I lost? I dropped it on the ground. I need to find it quickly.

The book that I just read was great. You should read it also. It was about a boy who went on a trip to Alaska with his grandpa. You would like it!

Please open up the top of that tank. We need to empty it and clean it out. My frogs like a clean tank.

Mom said that we need to pick up these toys right now.

A balloon expands as you blow into it.

The flag is red, white and blue.

Can you teach me how to ride a bike?

Would it be possible to go swimming down at the lake at noon? It is such a hot day and a swim would cool us off.

A simple way to keep my room clean is to not throw stuff on the ground. I put stuff away when I am done using it.

I made a note in my book reminding me to study my math. We will be taking a big test soon. I will be ready if I study.

Can you please put the book on the shelf when you finish reading it? Thank you!

Almost all the kids had a chance to see the little puppy. The cute puppy was only six weeks old. He was mostly black except the small white patch on his face, a white front foot and a white tip on his tail. It was easy to see the bright white tip on the tail wagging as the kids petted him.

Mike liked to throw rocks into the stream. He would choose the biggest stone he could lift. Then he would toss it and watch it splash.

Section 4: R-Controlled Vowel Combinations

Lesson 70: General Information on "r-controlled Vowel Combinations

Explain to the Child: We are going to start some new sounds called **r-controlled vowel combinations**. You don't have to remember that name. You just need to learn how often vowels will work together with **r** as "buddy letters" to make certain sounds. You will learn a few important things about these 'vowel-r buddy letters':

1. The **vowel or vowels and r** work together as buddies or partners to make a sound. The **r** is "bossy" and controls the sounds of vowels.

2. Sometimes "vowel-r buddies" can have more than one sound (For example the printed 'ar' can represent either the /ar/ or the /air/ sound.) You are going to learn the sounds these 'vowel-r buddy letters' have.

3. Frequently, the same sound can be spelled by different vowel-r buddy letter combinations. (For example, the /er/ sound can be spelled 'er', 'ur', 'ir', 'ear' and sometimes 'or'.)

4. Just like the vowel combinations you already learned, these "vowel(s) + r combinations" or "vowel-r buddy letters" can sometimes be tricky or complex. You will learn these tricks or complexities so they won't fool you.

Let's get started!

Lesson 71:

Teach Sound:

ar   These vowel+r buddy letters have 2 sounds.

1) most of the time **ar** has the /ar/ sound
2) sometimes **ar** has the /air/ sound.

Practice Sound Cards: Practice cards for **ar** & previous sounds not automatically known.

Write and Say the Sound: The child writes or traces **ar** multiple times saying the /ar/ & /air/ sound *as* he writes.

Making Words: Make words with the sound tiles. "Please make the word _____"
Use sound tiles... ar   e   y   d   g   k   l   m   n   p   s   t   ch
    part   march   smart   market   army   chart   garden   charge   spark   large
Use sound tiles... ar   i   o   y   c   d   h   l   m   p   r   t   sh
    /ar/ sound: dark   party   tardy   sharply   tarnish   marsh   hard   hardly
    /air/ sound: carry   carrot   carol   clarity   marigold   parish

Most of the time **ar** has the /ar/ sound. Reading Words where **ar** = /ar/ sound:

car	jar	bar	arm	tar
art	arch	part	far	mart
barn	cart	farm	mark	star
park	march	card	smart	large
Mars	dart	dark	scar	bark
chart	harsh	tart	hard	harp
lard	yarn	chart	harm	stark
tarp	ark	sharp	start	shark
march	yard	scarf	cards	charm
marsh	snarl	charge	starve	spark
Clark	parch	carve	barge	starch
sharp	Mark	carp	larch	spar
parks	large	far	hard	start
market	army	garden	hardy	garlic
artist	marble	alarm	carpet	target
tardy	scarlet	arcade	carwash	sparkle
apart	parking	garnish	margin	barked
darkroom	startle	armpit	enlarge	sparkplug
party	cartwheel	hardship	cartoon	discard
hardest	sharpest	harshly	largest	farthest
depart	starving	archway	harvest	snarling

- - - - - - - - - - - - - - - 3 syllable words - - - - - - - - - - - - - - -

| argument | article | carnival | particle | |

214

Sometimes **ar** has the /air/ sound. Reading Words with /air/ sound for **ar**:

carry	carrot	carol	Mary	marry
barren	barrel	barracks	scarce	
parent	parish	parrot		
arrow	narrow	marrow	sparrow	

- - - - - - - - - - - - - - - - - - 3 syllable words - - - - - - - - - - - - - - - - - -

caravan	caribou	clarity	marathon	marigold
marinate	paradise	parakeet	parasite	

Writing (Spelling) Words: Select some of the listed words for your child to write.

Reading Sentences/Paragraphs: Have your child read with proper tracking and blending. Make immediate corrections. After the child reads a sentence, ask a specific question.

I like to read books about sharks.

Can you play a game of cards with me?

We can harvest the peas in June.

The artist used a sharp pencil.

My parents came to watch me march in the band.

We need to start lunch right now. I think I will starve if I do not eat very soon.

We can walk to the park. It is not far. I will carry the picnic basket.

Can you carry the box and put it on the desk. Thank you!

I would like to plant some red tulips in my garden. I would also like to plant pink rose bushes.

We had a hard time finding the small coin in the tall grass.

It was hard to walk down the narrow path. I kept hitting my arm on the branches.

My friend Mark had a large green pet parrot. This parrot could even talk. He said "hello" to me.

Kim likes to go shopping with mom. She gets to put the milk and the carrots in the cart.

Grandma is a good artist. She can draw and paint very well. I hope she can teach me how to paint like that also!

She could hardly reach the top shelf. Even when she stood on the stool, it was not easy to reach.

She was tardy because the car broke down.

The large brown dog barked at us when we walked by his yard.

Since it was getting dark, we could hardly see the gray owl sitting in top of the large tree behind the old barn.

Lesson 72:

Sound:

w+ar When the **ar** comes after **w** (w+ar), **ar** is pronounced differently.
The **ar** after **w** almost sounds like the /or/ sound. Remember when we talked about how **w** changes how we pronounce the /a/ sound in Lesson #32. Well **w** also changes or modifies the /ar/ sound. This is because of way we say /w/ with the /ar/ sound. Listen as I say these words... war, warm, warn, warp.

Practice Sound Cards: Practice cards for **ar** & previous sounds not automatically known.

Making Words: "Please make the word _____"
Use sound tiles... ar e   d m n p s w
　　　warm   war   ward   warp   swarm   warden

216

Reading Words w + ar words: (when ar comes after w ...the ar is pronounced differently almost the /or/ sound (This is how we say this particular w+ar combination.. try it!)

war   warm   wart   ward   warp

wars   warn   swarm   warmth   wartime

warden   warmest   warning   warhead   warthog

Writing (Spelling) Words: Select some of the listed words for your child to write.

Reading Sentences/Paragraphs: Have your child read with proper tracking and blending. Make immediate corrections. After the child reads a sentence, ask a specific question.

A ward is a large room in a hospital.

This new scarf that Uncle Mark gave me is very warm.

I need to warn my family to stay away from the wasp nest.

When the sun came out, I got warm and had to take off my coat.

This was the warmest day of the month.

Mark shot the arrow at the target.

The yellow warning light was flashing.

She warned us to slow down and walk in the hall.

We saw a swarm of wood ants on the old stump behind the barn.

I am cold. It would be nice to take a warm bath.

I am afraid of wasps. When I saw a big swarm of them by the tree I ran away. I think a big nest must be high up in the tree. I hope they do not sting me.

The Army and the Navy fight in wars. We pray "Protect them and let peace come to all".

217

Lesson 73: Reading word 'are' and Review

Reading the word 'are':

are   We are going to learn another new word. /ar/ is how we say this word.

The first part sounds out. The **ar** has the /ar/ sound. However, **e** at the end is silent and doesn't do anything at all. I'm not sure why **e** is there either! Let's read **are** together. Finger track and say **are** with the child. Then have the child track and say it alone.

Listen. I'll use our new word in a few sentences so you can hear the word. Read these sentences to the child emphasizing **are**: -- You **are** a great reader! -- You **are** learning lots.

Practice reading **are** correctly. Have the child finger track as he says 'are' correctly.

are   are   are   are

Sentence Reading:
Ok, now it's your turn to read our new word in a sentence. Have child read the following sentences. Make sure the child uses finger tracking. If the child makes errors on irregular words simply say "oops... do you remember how we say that word".

You **are** smart!

We **are** going to go to the park with Dad.

These new boots **are** warm.

We **are** going to start the game at six.

My friends **are** going to the park.

The kittens **are** playing in the yard.

My parents **are** going to give me a new book.

The cartoons **are** funny today. You should read them.

You **are** doing such a great job reading!

Reading Mixed List of Words and Sentences:

arm	find	coin	hard	small
carve	large	would	are	spoil
warn	draw	teach	start	reach

218

stool	carp	count	when	came
far	out	warm	take	coat
wasp	swarm	tree	stripe	all
high	hope	sting	peace	fight
mind	bark	need	ground	spread
east	want	howl	tall	reach
large	wart	room	face	both
jaws	are	smart	walk	warmth
leave	chart	grind	yards	read
sharks	pray	some	charge	dark
unlike	remark	about	target	student
ugly	carry	parent	largest	garden
afraid	warning	apart	tardy	carrots
even	artist	healthy	hardship	army
sharpen	hardest	sparrow	yardage	parcel
warmest	delete	contest	harshly	display

The puzzle came apart when it fell on the ground. Now we will need to put all the pieces back. I do not mind since I like to make puzzles.

I found a good book about warthogs. A wart hog is an African wild pig. The wart hogs have warts on the face and large tusks in both jaws. Warthogs are strange animals. I think they look ugly.

We are going to start the race at noon.

Lesson 74:

Sound:

or   These vowel-r buddy letters have 2 sounds.

         1) most of the time **or** has the /or/ sound
         2) sometimes **or** has the /er/ sound. It has this /er/ sound when **or** comes after **w** and at the end of some multisyllable words.

Practice Sound Cards: Practice cards for **or, ar** & previous sounds not automatic.

Write and Say the Sound: The child writes or traces **or** multiple times. Make sure the child says the /or/ & /er/ sound *as* he writes. Also write **ar** + other sounds needing practice.

Making Words: Make words with the sound tiles. "Please make the word _____"
Use sound tiles... or a e i o y b c d f l m n r s t(2) v w th
     /or/ sound: north torn   thorn   storm   snort forget acorn   inform stormy thorny format normal formal fortify   orbit tornado forbid
     /er/ sound: worm   work worth actor favor tractor flavor   doctor

Most of the time **or** has the /or/ sound:
Reading Words with the /or/ sound for or:

or	for	torn	fort	horn
form	lord	born	cord	torch
nor	port	fork	corn	dorm
stork	thorn	ford	north	cork
force	short	horse	porch	sport
sort	pork	snort	forge	storm
cord	horde	scorch	story	forty
corny	orbit	stormy	forget	inform
glory	inform	format	shortfall	afford
normal	passport	forbid	forceful	carport
forest	shortest	forward	ordeal	northeast

acorn	forming	hornet	Morgan	forgive
formal	import	report	newborn	Nordic

-------------------- 3 syllable words --------------------

tornado	history	fortify	horrible	horrify
favorite	Florida	ordinary	organic	storybook
memory	horizon	important		

When **or** comes after w (w + or) we pronounce it with the /er/ sound: (Once again it is how you can SAY these sounds together)

Reading Words with w + or that we pronounce with the /er/ sound:

work	worm	word	world	worth
worse	worst	worship	worthy	worry
workhorse	network	workshop	worsen	worksheet

Sometimes **or** at the end of multisyllable words is said with the /er/ sound:

Reading Words with the /er/ sound for or:

odor	error	mirror	doctor	favor
motor	labor	terror	flavor	actor
tractor	sailor	traitor	tailor	razor
color	donor	rumor	vapor	tumor
mayor	minor	author	factor	vendor

-------------------- 3 syllable words --------------------

instructor	professor	contractor	conductor

Writing (Spelling) Words: Select some of the listed words for your child to write.

Reading Sentences/Paragraphs: Have your child read with proper tracking and blending. Make immediate corrections. After the child reads a sentence, ask a specific question.

We got six inches of snow from that last storm.

She likes to dig in the mud and play with the worms.

Do not forget to take out the pork chops.

Can we eat pork chops for lunch?

What color will you paint the room?

My favorite colors are blue and green.

The storm clouds blew in from the north.

The gum costs forty cents.

My friend lives on a farm forty miles north of town.

What sport do you like to play? Do you like basketball or do you like swimming? I like both.

Wow! He can read a bunch of new words.

Please read me a story. Pick out a good book! Maybe you can find a good short story about horses.

It is true that you will find a large stone arch at the north entrance to Yellowstone Park.

What flavor ice cream do you like? I like mint the best. Thinking about ice cream makes me hungry. How about a quick trip to the ice cream shop? I will get a double scoop of mint. You can pick out what kind you would like.

We enjoy sitting on the front porch and watching the storms. We can even see the lightning bolts strike the hillside.

Lesson 75: Vowel-r combinations that make the /or/ sound

There are five ways we can write the /or/ sound. You learned or in the last lesson. Now you are going to learn the other ways /or/ is written.

or	You just learned how these vowel-r buddy letters have the sound /or/.
ore	These vowel-r buddy letters also have the /or/ sound
oar	These vowel-r buddy letters also have the /or/ sound
our	These vowel-r buddy letters also have the /or/ sound
oor	These vowel-r buddy letters also have the /or/ sound

Yes you noticed! There are 5 ways to write or spell the /or/ sound. The **or** is the most common followed by **ore**.

Practice Sound Cards: Practice sound card for **or, ore, oar, our & oor** as well as **ar** and previous sounds that are not automatically known.

Write and Say Sounds: The child writes or traces **or, ore, oar, our & oor** multiple times saying the /or/ sound *as* he writes. Also write **ar** + other sounds needing practice.

Making Words: Make words that have the /or/ sound. "Please make the word _____"
Use sound tiles... ore   a e i   c d f g l   m n   p r s   t x
   store score more snore forecast ignore foreman explore implore restore deplore
Use sound tiles... oar   a i u   b c   d l p r s
   board   aboard   boar oar roar clipboard   uproar
Use sound tiles.... our   e y   c f l p s t th
   pour four   tour   court   your   fourth   yourself
Use sound tiles.... oor i y d f l n p
   poor door floor indoor poorly

Reading Words with **<u>or</u>** for the /or/ sound:

cork	or	for	torn	fort
horn	north	sport	short	force
form	lord	born	cord	storm
nor	port	fork	corn	horse
porch	stork	thorn	ford	torch
story	orbit	forget	endorse	normal

format	glory	forty	report	inform
forbid	forest	morning	forceful	forgive
reform	shortest	retort	organ	import
correct	thorny	northwest	forceful	hornet

- - - - - - - - - - - - - - - 3 syllable words - - - - - - - - - - - - - - -

history	important	horrible	favorite	memory

Reading Words with **ore** for the /or/ sound:

sore	more	core	tore	chore
snore	store	more	bore	shore
gore	score	lore	spore	swore
deplore	restore	ignore	implore	before
adore	forefront	storehouse	forehand	forepaw
explore	forewarn	folklore	forego	foreclose
foremost	foresight	foreman	forecast	forearm
shoreline	foretell	foreshadow		

- - - - - - - - - - - - - 3 syllable words - - - - - - - - - - - - - - - -

omnivore	explored	carnivore	beforehand

Reading Words with **oar** for the /or/ sound:

oar	roar	boar	board	coarse
soar	hoard	roaring	aboard	uproar
backboard	keyboard	soaring	clipboard	billboard
scoreboard	snowboard	blackboard		

Reading Words with **our** for the /or/ sound:

pour	four	tour	court	your
fourth	course	source	yourself	courtyard
contour	downpour	fourteen		

Reading Words with **oor** for the /or/ sound:

door	poor	floor	moor	indoor
backdoor	boorish	outdoor	poorest	seafloor
poorly	doormat	trapdoor		

Writing (Spelling) Words: Select some of the listed words for your child to write. Be sure and tell the child which /or/ spelling to use before giving words.

Reading Sentences/Paragraphs:

Please sweep the floor for me before you go out to play.

I read a story about a horse named Misty. It was a good book.

We had corn on the cob for lunch. I was very hungry and I just love corn. I ate mine up quickly. Then I asked my Mom nicely for some more corn. Mom said "of course you can have some more corn".

I did not forget that it is my chore to pour the drinks for lunch. Would you like milk or would you like some fresh grape juice?

I like to shoot hoops on the basketball court. If I get more practice I may score four more points in the next game.

We went on a tour of the old fort.

We read a funny short story.

Lesson 76: Review and Practice

Practice Sound Cards: Practice cards for **all** previous sounds not automatically known.

Write and Say Sounds: The child writes or traces **all sounds not automatically known**. Make sure the child says the sound *as* he writes.

read	horse	smart	good	court
corn	book	just	short	may
door	came	mine	more	coast
course	you	far	out	grape
warm	chore	drink	word	floor
work	snore	carve	war	oar
fourth	would	fresh	north	take
hoops	juice	point	shore	spark
large	board	growth	yard	store
should	like	world	four	game
score	charge	pour	space	worse
your	chart	thorn	when	poor
rise	fork	these	keys	porch
prays	cause	force	shark	for
noise	loud	light	south	done
time	thief	card	strange	toast
dark	friend	bank	form	brown
born	stream	race	bark	head

yarn	sport	frame	dart	crew
need	face	reach	sort	join
story	about	named	hungry	nicely
quickly	forget	practice	afraid	indoor
aboard	foresight	apart	forest	author
remark	hardly	forward	restore	famous
newborn	printing	contain	foremost	morning
parent	carpet	forgive	ignore	forty
expand	normal	pleased	empty	mostly
today	explore	carry	shortest	beyond
flavor	offshore	worship	labor	forecast
orbit	charged	inform	highest	value
before	network	mayor	fourteen	warning
warmest	hardship	always	cartoon	distort
cartwheel	market	propane	destroy	adore
downpour	shortfall	forceful	worksheet	report
depart	misuse	closeout	harvest	healthy

We can have grapes or plums for a snack.

Can you keep score for us when we play cards?

He was four yards short of making the touchdown.

We need some more boards before we can make the fort.

The large storm tore up trees along the shore.

Lesson 77:

Sound:

er These vowel-r buddy letters have the /**er**/ sound.

Practice Sound Cards: Practice sound card for **er, or, ore, oar, our & oor** as well as **ar** and previous sounds that are not automatically known.

Write and Say Sounds: The child writes or traces **er** multiple times saying the /er/ sound *as* he writes. Also write **or, ore, oar, our & oor** + other sounds needing practice.

Making Words: Use sound tiles... er a i u d f g h m n(2) p s(2) t w th sh
her fern term stern under miner thunder sister faster usher hermit
gather mister perhaps master winter permit hunter wander

Reading Words that have the er /er/ sound:

her	verb	herd	berg	fern
term	Bert	stern	perm	perch
germ	serve	terse	term	jerk
berm	clerk	berth	tern	verse
nerve	over	after	pepper	better
summer	perky	darker	paper	hermit
mister	order	under	sister	perfect
winter	miner	butter	wander	center
ever	corner	thunder	harder	perhaps
letter	marker	cracker	former	rubber
boxer	permit	derby	baker	diner
other	elder	water	person	ladder
intern	helper	ginger	rather	binder
vertex	barter	fever	sliver	fender

228

newer	clever	loner	nervous	river
banner	power	alert	herder	jumper
monster	partner	perplex	nicer	mother
shorter	persist	shelter	printer	plaster
expert	prosper	gather	corner	poster
usher	thermal	twister	tower	slender
master	teacher	beater	hunter	shorter
cider	temper	taller	tender	zipper
father	border	pointer	brother	northern
persist	blunder	transfer	merger	cleaner
derby	prayer	younger	number	reverse
mercy	faster	jerky	perched	percent
person	cooler	singer	stranger	modern
sticker	quicker	proper	smoker	ranger
rather	chapter	antler	hunger	blinkers
tender	charter	chopper	toaster	prouder
owner	slumber	greater	bumper	luster
shooter	players	winner	differ	pattern
member	later	anger	expert	perfect
offer	fighter	eastern	wonder	thicker
heater	western	farmer	farther	danger
layers	softer	slower	hiker	server

| dancer | driver | silver | hanger | diver |

- - - - - - - - - - - - - - - - 3 syllable words - - - - - - - - - - - - - - - - - -

remember	however	different	computer	another
forever	recover	supporter	together	discover
terminate	determine	energy	persistent	vertical
internet	general	overhead	encounter	consider
explorer	attacker	officer	property	overtime

Writing (Spelling) Words: Select some of the listed words for your child to write.

Reading Sentences/Paragraphs:

Her horse can run faster than the black pony.

She had her test on verbs today.

I like to go fishing on the river with my sister.

Can you toss that rubber ball over to me?

We need to serve salt, pepper and butter with the corn.

Do you put lots of butter on your corn? I do!

My father found a large elk antler down by the river.

Do you like the summer or the winter better? I like both. It is fun to make snowmen and go sledding in the winter. In the winter, I also like to drink hot cider with my brother. In the summer we go camping. My Grandpa visits me and we go fishing on the river. In the summer I like to play under the green leaves of the big trees. I also like to eat ice cream with my sister. What do you like to do in the summer and the winter?

Lesson 78: Vowel-r combinations with the /er/ sound

There are 5 vowel+r combinations that usually represent the /er/ sound. You just learned **er**. Now you are going to learn the other vowel-r buddy letters with the /er/ sound.

er	You just learned how these vowel-r buddy letters have the sound /er/.
ur	These vowel-r buddy letters also have the /er/ sound
ir	These vowel-r buddy letters also have the /er/ sound
ear	These vowel-r buddy letters sometimes also have the /er/ sound
or	Remember how you already learned sometimes **or** has the /er/ sound when it comes after w and at the end of some multisyllable words.

Yes you noticed! There are 5 ways to write the /er/ sound. Of the five ways to write /er/, the **er** is the most common followed by the **ur**.

Practice Sound Cards: Practice sound card for **er, ur, ir, ear** as well as the **or, ore, oar, our & oor** and previous sounds that are not automatically known.

Write and Say Sounds: The child writes or traces **er, ur, ir, ear** multiple times saying the /er/ sound *as* he writes. Also write other sounds needing practice.

Making Words: Make words with the sound tiles. "Please make the word _____"
Use sound tiles..... er a i o ea b c d f l m n r s(2) t v w th
    master weather river faster sister cleaner feather other brother mother reader
    bother winter streamer silver sliver blinder
Use sound tiles... ur e i y b h n p r s t ch(2) ing
    hurt burn church turnip turn return burst hurry burping urgent
Use sound tiles... ir i y b d f g l m n s t th
    bird girl flirt third stir thirty dirty thirsty firmly infirm dirty
Use sound tiles ..... ear y d h l n p s th ch ing
    earn learn earth search pearl earl heard early learning earning

Reading Words with <u>er</u> for the /er/ sound:

her	serve	verb	herd	fern
term	jerk	stern	perm	perch
nerve	terse	term	berg	stern
berm	clerk	berth	tern	verse
center	over	sister	winter	order

marker	letter	other	after	greater
ever	power	water	newer	perfect
under	darker	summer	person	harder
fever	helper	rather	river	mother
gather	shorter	nicer	printer	corner
paper	winter	perhaps	thunder	teacher
gather	number	reverse	younger	chapter
mister	percent	border	brother	fighter
prouder	nervous	winner	differ	partner
danger	layers	driver	slower	server
dancer	persist	shelter	father	temper
taller	northern	zipper	pointer	older
expert	twister	tower	hunter	mercy
prayer	owner	anger	eastern	winner
cleaner	cooler	western	singer	stranger
antler	perfect	hunger	modern	later

- - - - - - - - - - - - - - - - - 3 syllable words - - - - - - - - - - - - - - - - -

remember	however	different	forever	together
discover	energy	general	consider	explorer

Reading Words with **ur** for the /er/ sound:

fur	cur	blur	urge	burr
nurse	turn	hurt	burn	furl
hurl	curb	curl	burp	surf

lurch	murk	churn	lurk	purge
yurt	curve	turf	surge	purse
spurt	burnt	slurp	lurch	burst
church	curve	curse	blurb	splurge
purple	curly	burned	concur	unhurt
urban	burden	furnish	murder	purpose
hurry	purchase	murky	turmoil	burping
surface	recur	turtle	furry	turnip
curfew	curved	gurgle	sulfur	turkey
uncurl	cursive	burner	survey	urgent
yogurt	survive	curtail	disturb	surfing
current	surpass	curling	turning	return
hurtful	burnable	furnace	bursting	murky
turnpike	surname	purchase	turned	purple

- - - - - - - - - - - - - - - - 3 syllable words - - - - - - - - - - - - - - - - - -

currency	surgery	surgical	turbulent	hurricane
resurface	surrender	turtleneck	survival	

Reading Words with **ir** for the /er/ sound:

fir	bird	firm	girl	stir
sir	dirt	chirp	girth	thirst
first	shirt	skirt	third	birch
birth	flirt	smirk	squirm	mirth
squirt	swirl	circle	thirty	dirty

| birthday | affirm | firmly | infirm | confirm |
| circus | thirsty | birthright | birdbath | birthmark |

Reading Words with **ear** for the /er/ sound:

earl	earth	search	pearl	earn
learn	heard	hearth	early	research
learning	earthquake	earning	searched	earthworm

Reading Words with **or** for the /er/ sound: w+or and or at the end of some multisyllable words. You've already learned these, but let's practice some of these again.

work	worm	word	world	worth
worse	worship	worst	worry	tractor
odor	error	mirror	doctor	favor
color	visitor	actor	color	worker
sailor	traitor	worldly	working	flavor

- - - - - - - - - - - - - - - - - - 3 syllable words - - - - - - - - - - - - - - - - - -

| contractor | instructor | professor | navigator | workable |

Writing (Spelling) Words: Select some of the listed words for your child to write.

Reading Sentences/Paragraphs:

Please stir the butter into the bowl.

She woke up early in the morning.

The girl wore her new purple skirt.

My friend's birthday party will be on the third day of the month.

We have to hurry so we are not late for church.

My brother likes to squirt water at me.

We are learning how to draw perfect circles.

We need to turn right at the next corner.

I was thirsty after running four laps on the hot day.

We can learn a lot about how they make paper by reading this book.

First, you must wash the dirt off your hands. Then you can come eat dinner.

She finished cleaning her room faster than her sister did. She got extra time to play before going to bed.

Have you heard what we will get for lunch? I hope we get corn dogs and French fries for lunch.

My aunt is a nurse at a large hospital in Denver. She takes care of sick and hurt children.

I did my report on the earth. The earth is the third planet from the sun. The earth is between Venus and Mars. Mars is farther away from the sun. It is cold on Mars. Venus is closer to the sun. It is hot on Venus. It is just perfect on Earth.

The kids like to play hide and seek. Kim was looking for her sister, her brother and a friend. First she found her sister under the deck. Then she found her brother over behind the birch tree. The little boy from next door was much harder to find. He was hiding in the sand box. He had closed the top and Kim could not see him. It was a great hiding place. Finally Kim found him.

Lesson 79: Review and Practice, Introduce 'were'

Review Sounds: Quickly practice the sounds you have learned! The child finger tracks and says the sounds. Use the review to determine which sounds your child needs to practice.

oa	ai	ay	a_e	i_e	o_e	u_e
e_e	oi	oy	ea	ow	ou	ue
ew	ui	oo	ie	ei	ey	au
aw	igh	ar	w+ar	or	ore	oar
our	oor	er	ur	ir	ear	w+or

Practice Sound Cards: Practice sound card for **all** previous sounds that are not automatically known.

Write and Say Sounds: The child writes or traces **all sounds not automatically known**. Make sure the child says the sound *as* he writes.

Reading Irregular Word: We are going to learn a new irregular word. We say this word differently than it should sound out.

were   /were/ is how we say this word. The **w** /w/ and the **er** /er/ sound out as expected. The **e** at the end doesn't do anything at all. I'm not sure why the **e** is there either.

Listen as I use **were** in a few sentences so you can hear the word. These sentences are strictly for the adult to read to the child. When you read emphasize **were**: -- You **were** shorter last year. – You **were** happy when your team won. -- We **were** all excited about getting ice cream.

Now it is your turn to practice reading **were** correctly. Be sure the child finger tracks and pronounces were correctly.

were   were   were   were   were

Reading Sentences: Ok, now it's your turn to read our new word in a sentence. Have child read the following sentences using finger tracking. If the child makes errors on irregular words simply say "oops… do you remember how we say that word".

You **were** the fastest kid in the class.

You **were** the last kid to finish eating lunch.

We **were** happy when we finished picking up.

Reading Mixed Words:

girl	would	stir	part	right
these	more	turn	truth	hurt
four	earth	bird	large	your
under	learn	they	hard	might
heard	calls	her	score	which
blue	word	perch	born	work
world	part	north	charge	thorn
door	serve	warm	shore	both
curve	board	white	strange	nurse
slurp	first	verse	snore	church
room	draw	mark	short	please
force	clerk	yard	starve	horse
nerve	corn	fourth	poor	thirst
squirm	churn	search	verb	roar
store	teach	snarl	storm	chart
early	over	after	color	tardy
before	number	higher	carry	starting
percent	ready	forget	going	practice
chapter	starting	fourteen	clipboard	morning
purple	water	parent	explore	sentence
danger	taller	circle	research	birthday
shorter	keyboard	normal	under	forgive

Reading Sentences and Paragraphs:

They were all going to get ice cream.

We were happy when the team won the game by four points.

The parents were all waiting for the children to finish practice.

They were able to explore the new park.

We served muffins this morning.

We were full after eating the large bowls of ice cream.

I have an aunt who lives along the Oregon coast. We are going to go see her. This is the first time I will get to see the Pacific coast. We will drive from Montana to Oregon. It is a long way. I am very excited. We will get to do lots of things when we visit the coast. We will dig for clams and try to catch some crabs. I have never done that before but my aunt will show us what to do. The water is too cold to swim in. But we will spend lots of time exploring the beach. I would like to find a star-fish in a tide pool. I will tell you all about my trip after I get back home.

We watched a big storm last night. First, we could see the light flashing in the clouds far away. Then we heard the rumble of thunder in the distance. As the storm moved closer, the wind speed increased. The thunder grew louder and louder. Before long, the lightning bolts crashed around my house. We even saw a lightning bolt strike a tree on the hill. That was scary! It rained for awhile. Then the storm blew off to the east of us. We kept watching the storm until it was just light flashing in the clouds way far away. I enjoy watching storms when I am safe inside my house. Have you ever watched a storm?

Lesson 80: Vowel-r combinations with the /air/ sound

There are 4 vowel+r combinations that have the /air/ sound. Earlier you learned **ar** sometimes makes the /**air**/ sound. Let's learn the 4 ways to write the /**air**/ sound.

are	These vowel-r buddy letters have the /air/ sound (*note.. this is NOT the word "are" but the buddy letters *are* that make the sound /air/)
ar	Remember how you already learned that sometimes these vowel-r buddy letters have the /air/ sound.
air	These vowel-r buddy letters also have the /air/ sound
ear	In just a few words the vowel-r buddy letters will have the /air/ sound.

Yes you noticed! There are 4 ways to write or spell the /air/ sound. The **are** and the **air** are the most common. The **ear** is only used in a few words. Also if you notice the /air/ sound is very similar to how you would say a blend of the /ay/ sound with the /r/.

Practice Sound Cards: Practice sound card for these new sounds as well as previous sounds not automatically known.

Write and Say the Sound: The child writes or traces **are, ar, air & ear** multiple times saying the /air/ sound as he writes.

Making Words: "Please make the word _____"
Use sound tiles... are   a e o   b c   d f g l m p s t w   sh
  mare bare dare stare care spare share glare   flare share blare beware aware
  compare   software
Use sound tiles... ar   i o y   c l m   r t
  carry   carrot   clarity marigold marry parrot

Reading Words with <u>**are**</u> for the /air/ sound:

mare	bare	dare	hare	stare
care	spare	share	flare	snare
square	pare	glare	scare	fare
blare	rare	aware	stared	shared
careless	beware	compare	careful	squarely
farewell	scarecrow	bareback	dared	prepare
software	barefoot	warfare	threadbare	careless

239

Reading Words with **ar** for the /air/ sound: (remember how sometimes the ar makes the /air/ sound)

carry	carrot	carol	Mary	marry
barren	barrel	barracks	scarce	parent
parish	parrot	arrow	narrow	sparrow

Reading Words with **air** for the /air/ sound:

air	hair	stair	fair	pair
chair	fair	flair	lair	affair
dairy	airplane	despair	unfair	airbag
repair	stairway	aircraft	wheelchair	airflow
highchair	haircut	crosshair	airline	chairlift
hairband	chairman	fairground	repairs	

Reading Words with **ear** for the /air/ sound: (remember the ear /air/ sound is only used in a few words)

bear	tear (rip)	pear	wear

Writing (Spelling) Words: Select some of the listed words for your child to write.

Reading Sentences/Paragraphs:

It was very kind of you to share your snacks with the others.

Please be careful on these narrow stairs.

Can you draw a square on the top of the page?

I hope my parents are able to repair my broken bike.

You can find both black bears and grizzly bears in Montana.

We can share the plate of purple grapes.

Could you please get me a glass of water? I am thirsty.

You have to be careful when you ride bareback.

All of my pairs of jeans are dirty.

Beware of the mean dog at the corner house. Do not walk into his yard. I am afraid he might bite if you get too close.

The mare and her colt were grazing in the field. It looked like they were enjoying the nice spring day.

Mary takes good care of her flowers. She keeps the soil moist and she pulls up the weeds.

I need to do some laundry. I am down to my last pair of clean socks. I might have to wear my old pair that has the hole in them if I do not get my wash done.

Would you like to munch on a crunchy carrot or would you rather have a sweet and crispy pear?

My parents went to get my Grandma at the airport. She will be at my house before I get out of class. I can't wait to see her. She always lets me carry her suitcase up the stairs for her. I hope she did not forget. I like to do that chore for her.

Please take the toys off the stairs. Carry them to the play room and put them away. Take your coat off the chair and hang it up. A toy airplane is also on the floor of the hall. You need to pick that up too. After that you will be all done and we can go walk down to the park to play. Hurry up so we can go to the park.

Lesson 81: Introduce 'there' and 'their' & Practice

Practice Sound Cards: Practice cards for **all** previous sounds not automatically known.

Write and Say Sounds: The child writes or traces **all sounds not automatically known**. Make sure the child says the sound *as* he writes.

Reading Irregular Word: We are going to learn a few new words. These words are somewhat irregular. They both have the /air/ sound. Both these words sound exactly the same even though they are spelled differently and have different meanings. Words that sound the same but have different meanings are called homophones for 'same sounds'.

there　　/thair/ is how we say this word. The **th** sounds out as /th/. However, **ere** has an unexpected /air/ sound. This word 'there' means in a place, at a place or to a place as in "Please put the book over **there**."

their　　/thair/ is also how we say this word. The **th** sounds out as /th/. However, the **eir** has an unexpected /air/ sound. This word 'their' is a pronoun meaning done by or belonging to them as in the sentence, "**Their** hands were cold after playing outside.".

Listen as I use **there & their** in a few sentences so you can hear how the words are used. These sentences are strictly for the adult to read to the child. When you read emphasize **there & their**:
-- Please set the plate over **there** on the table.
-- The team went and sat down on **their** bench during the timeout.

Now it is your turn to practice reading **there** and **their** correctly. Be sure the child finger tracks and pronounces 'there' and 'their' correctly.

there　　　　there　　　　there　　　　their　　　　their　　　　their

Reading Sentences: Ok, now it's your turn to read our new words in a sentence. Have child read the following sentences using finger tracking. If the child makes errors on irregular words simply say "oops... do you remember how we say that word".

there (in, at, or to a place)

　　Please set the books over there.

　　The cat was sitting over there by the window.

　　There is much work for us to do today.

　　Please put the toy over there on the desk.

　　There is no way we will make it to school on time.

their (belonging to them or done by them)

The boys put **their** coats in **their** lockers.

Their new puppy was really cute.

Please give the children **their** pencils.

I like playing at **their** house.

The children washed **their** dad's truck.

The family weeded **their** garden.

there & their

Their dog likes to lie over **there** in the shade of the tree.

Put **their** favorite book over **there** on the table.

I had to wait over **there** by **their** white van.

We saw a few eagles over **there** by the lake. They were sitting in the pine tree right next to **their** nest.

Reading Mixed Words:

far	work	their	turn	star
work	earth	warm	four	board
smart	there	more	south	place
serve	harsh	dirt	world	short
curve	score	your	part	learn
stray	page	proud	north	card
which	please	her	peace	brain
circle	color	under	owner	center

Lesson 82: Vowel-r combinations with the /eer/ sound

There are three vowel-r combinations/buddy letters representing the /eer/ sound. Let's learn these 3 ways to write the /eer/ sound.

ear   Earlier you learned sometimes **ear** has the /er/ sound.

These vowel-r buddy letters also often have the /eer/ sound.
This is like the 'ear' you hear with.

eer   These vowel-r buddy letters also have the /eer/ sound

ere   These vowel-r buddy letters also have the /eer/ sound

Yes you noticed! There are 3 ways to write the /ear/ sound. The **ear** is the most common. Although the **ere** is only used in a few words, you see it often in the common word **here**. Also if you notice, the vowel combinations ea, ee and e-consonant-e that you already learned help you learn these sounds as the /eer/ sound is almost the same as blending the /ee/ sound with an /r/ … try it /ee/+/r/= /eer/

Practice Sound Cards: Practice sound card for these new sounds as well as previous sounds that need work.

Write and Say the Sound: The child writes or traces **ear, eer & ere** multiple times while saying the /eer/ sound.

Making Words: Make words with the sound tiles. "Please make the word _____ "
Use sound tiles… ear u y   b c d f(2) g l(2) n p s
    ear near dear clear year gear spear beard fear nearly fearful unclear dearly
Use sound tiles… eer o u   d l   n p s t   v ch
    deer cheer leer peer   steer volunteer

Reading Words with <u>**ear**</u> for the /eer/ sound:

ear	dear	near	clear	tear (eye fluid)
hear	year	gear	beard	spear
fear	sear	shear	rear	smear
bleary	appear	dearly	hearing	weary
yearly	nearby	clearly	fearful	nearly
clearance	unclear	yearbook	dearest	near

Reading Words with **eer** for the /eer/ sound:

deer	cheer	leer	steer	peer
sheer	sneer	career	steering	cheering

- - - - - - - - - - - - - - - 3 syllable words - - - - - - - - - - - - - - - - - -

engineer   volunteer   pioneer

Reading Words with **ere** for the /ear/ sound: (**ere** is not found in many words.. however, you do see it often in the common word 'here'.)

here   mere   sincere   severe

Writing (Spelling) Words: Select some of the listed words for your child to write. Point out that of the 3 ways to write the /eer/ sound. The **ear** is by far the most common.

Reading Sentences/Paragraphs:

Please put the box over here. I need it near that stack of paper.

Did you hear the news? My teacher is having us do a big report. We get to work with a partner. My friend Cody and I are going to work together. We are going to learn about the Oregon Trail. We need to meet here at my house so we can work together. We are making a large map of the trail. Cody is drawing a sketch of a wagon in the corner of the map. Good thing we are almost done. It is nearly time to turn it in.

I just got a letter from my aunt. I opened it up and started to read. The letter said, "Dear Molly". Then it went on and told me all about my aunt's plans to make a trip here. She is coming to see me! She will be here at the end of May. I could read most of the letter myself. My mom only had to help me with a few sounds. It is great to be able to read my own letters. I am excited to show my aunt how well I can read. I am so glad that she will be coming here in May.

Lesson 83: Review Vowel-r combination ear

ear   You learned the vowel-r buddy letters **ear** have 3 sounds!
1) It usually has the /ear/ sound
2) Sometimes the /er/ sound.
3) In just a few silly words it has the /air/ sound.

Practice Sound Cards: Practice cards for **ear** as well as previous sounds needing work.

Write and Say the Sound: The child writes or traces **ear** saying the /ear/ /er/ & /air/ sounds as he writes.

Practice Reading the **ear** buddy letters:

Reading Words were **ear** has the /eer/ sound:

ear	dear	near	clear	tear (eye fluid)
hear	year	gear	beard	spear
fear	sear	shear	rear	smear
bleary	appear	dearly	hearing	weary
yearly	nearby	clearly	fearful	nearly
clearance	unclear	yearbook	dearest	near

Reading Words where ear has the /er/ sound:

earth	learn	early	search	earl
earn	pearl	heard	learning	unearth
searching	earthquake	unearth		

Reading Words where ear has the /air/ sound:
(The ear only has the /air/ sound in a few words)

bear	pear	tear (rip)	wear

Writing (Spelling) Words: Have your child spell a few /ear/ words.

246

Lesson 84

Sound:

ire These vowel-r buddy letters have the sound /ire/. The ire /ire/ is said the same as you would read it with the i-consonant-e combination you learned earlier. We are also going also to learn it as a vowel-r buddy letter combination. You can read it either way and it has the /ire/ sound.

Practice Sound Cards: Practice the card for **ire** as well as previous sounds needing work.

Write and Say the Sound: The child writes or traces **ire** multiple times while saying the /ire/ sound *as* he writes.

Making Words: Make words with the sound tiles. Use sound tiles... ire f h s p
fire hire tire spire

Reading Words:

fire	tire	mire	hire	spire
tired	dire	wire	inspire	tired
perspire	hired	umpire	retire	rehire
entire	desire	empire	backfire	barbwire
acquire	conspire	transpire	require	wildfire
admire	crossfire	inquire	misfire	tightwire

Reading Sentences/Paragraphs!

Mike's dad is a fire fighter.

We ate the entire bowl of fruit.

The hardware store hired my brother for the summer.

He was tired after running five miles.

The wildfire burned the forest north of town.

We had to change the flat tire.

We got a flat tire after running over a nail. Mom had to stop and change the tire. She took off the flat tire and put on the spare. I helped her by holding the lug nuts. Now we need to take the flat to the tire shop so they can repair the hole in the tire.

My little sister is six years old. Her birthday was last week. Her present from Dad was a little chair. She put her chair right near Dad's big chair. She likes to sit in her chair and read books. She is just learning how to read.

Lesson 85: Review and Practice

Review Sounds: Quickly practice the sounds you learned! Have child finger track and say the sound or sounds. Use the review to determine which sounds your child may need additional practice with.

oa	ai	ay	a_e	i_e	o_e	u_e
e_e	oi	oy	ea	ow	ou	ue
ew	ui	oo	ie	ei	ey	au
aw	igh	ar	w+ar	or	ore	oar
our	oor	er	ur	ir	ear	w+or
are	air	ear	eer	ere	ire	

Practice Sound Cards: Practice cards for **all** sounds that are not automatically known.

Write and Say Sounds: The child writes or traces **all sounds not automatically known**. Make sure the child says the sound *as* he writes.

Reading List of Mixed Words: The child reads the following words, sounding out with physical tracking and proper blending. Correct any errors immediately.

new	her	search	rule	free	for
soon	near	warm	use	there	are
work	part	found	saw	fire	make

248

out	girl	far	here	count	more
grow	they	care	these	from	learn
charge	turn	need	stair	point	true
four	show	noon	year	right	large
each	threw	nice	book	draw	boys
should	close	were	short	please	earth
friend	world	news	clear	smooth	your
come	hire	great	smart	cage	share
high	stir	laugh	feast	their	youth
small	trade	north	yield	word	clean
what	pray	first	good	sharp	brown
hurt	blue	round	feel	wait	sold
carry	chapter	over	money	forget	today
number	even	enjoy	behind	always	until

I learned all about the eastern bluebird. They live in open areas, farmland or even in suburbs. The birds nest in tree holes. They also like bird houses. The male bluebird is bright blue. The females are much paler.

I was reading a book about bears. Did you know that a bear cub is born in winter? Bear cubs are very small when they are first born but they grow fast. A bear is an omnivore. That is a long word that means it eats both plants and meat. They even eat bugs. Yuck! Both black bears and grizzly bears live around here. The grizzly bears can get bigger than the black bears. I like learning about bears. I think I will go to the library and check out a few more books about bears.

Section 5: Silent Letters, Infrequent Sounds and Practice with Common Endings

Lesson 86: Silent Letter Combinations

Sounds:

dge — These buddy letters have the sound /j/. The **d** is silent and the **e** makes the **g** have the /j/ sound.

mb — These buddy letters have the sound /m/. The **b** is silent and the **m** has the expected /m/ sound.

Practice Sound Cards: Practice sound cards for these new sounds as well as previous sounds that need work.

Write and Say the Sound: The child writes or traces **dge** and **mb**. Make sure the child is saying the sound *as* he writes.

Reading Words with the dge /j/ sound:

bridge	edge	wedge	ledge	badge
dodge	fudge	lodge	fridge	grudge
smudge	hedge	judge	budge	abridge
dislodge	footbridge	porridge	dodgeball	lodgepole

Teach the pattern & EXPLAIN WHY: Notice how the dge ending is found at end of words with the single short vowel sounds /a/, /e/ /i/ /o/ and /u/. The **e** is needed after the **g** to form the /j/ sound. The **d** is added so there is a double consonant to prevent the **e** from changing the short vowel sound to a long vowel sound. For example in 'page' the **e** makes the **a** have the /ay/ long sound (vowel-consonant-e combination). But in badge the **d** prevents or blocks the **e** from changing the /a/ sound to the /ay/ sound. If the **d** wasn't there the word would be /bayj/. Even though you can not hear the **d** it has an important job. The **d** is necessary to prevent the final **e** from changing the first vowel to a long sound.

Reading Words with the mb /m/ sound:

climb	dumb	crumb	limb	comb
thumb	plumber	numb	lamb	bomb

Writing (Spelling) Words: Select some of the listed words for your child to write.

Reading Sentences:

I put the left-over fudge in the fridge.

You need to bring the comb with you so I can brush my hair.

We walked to the edge of the little bridge and tossed some rocks down into the water.

The third grade class likes to play dodge ball.   They play it every day at recess.

I learned that a beaver's home is called a lodge.

The kids like to climb to the top of the slide.

The fire chief wore a badge when he came into our class to teach us about fire safety.

Lesson 87: More Silent Letter Combinations

Sounds:

wr   These buddy letters have the sound /r/. The **w** is silent and **r** has the expected /r/ sound.

kn   These buddy letters have the sound /n/. The **k** is silent and **n** has the expected /n/ sound.

Practice Sound Cards: Practice sound cards for these new sounds as well as previous sounds that need work.

Write and Say the Sound: The child writes or traces **wr** and **kn**. Make sure the child says the sound *as* he writes.

Reading Words with the wr /r/ sound: (**write, wrong and wrote are the most commonly encountered wr words)

write	wrong	wrote	wren	wrap
wrath	wreck	wrench	wring	wrist

wreath	wrong	wrinkle	writer	wrongly
unknown	wrestle	wrangle	wrapper	wristwatch
write-up	wreckage			

Reading Words with the kn /n/ sound: (**know and knew are the most commonly encountered kn words)

know	knew	knee	kneel	knead
knife	knight	knock	knuckle	knot
knit	knob	knack	kneecap	knockout
unknown	knowledge	jackknife		

Writing (Spelling) Words: Select some of the listed words for your child to write.

Reading Sentences/Paragraphs:

I need to write my cousin a letter.

I wonder who that is who just knocked on my door?

I spelled four words wrong on the pre-test. I will study them some more so I know how to spell all the words before the final test.

There was a wren nest in the small spruce tree behind the house. We were careful to keep the cat away from the nest. We did not want the cat to know about it.

I know how to use a wrench. My dad showed me how when I was little.

When you unwrap your snack, please toss the wrapper in the trash.

My little sister wrecked on her bike. She scratched her left knee and her right knuckle. I helped her get band-aids for her scratches. Now she feels better and is back riding her bike.

Lesson 88: Learning Irregular Words 'one', 'two', 'any', 'many'

Reading Irregular Words: We are going to learn several new words. You might already know how to read these words. We say them differently than it looks like we should.

one   /won/ is how you say this word. The number 1.

two   /too/ is how you say this word. The number 2

Yes these counting numbers 1 and 2 are rather strange! Let's practice saying these words correctly. Have child finger track while saying the words.

one   two   two   one   two   one

Reading Sentences: Ok, now it's your turn to read our new words in a sentence. Have child read the following sentences using finger tracking. If the child makes errors on irregular words simply say "oops... do you remember how we say that word".

One of the dogs got out of the fence when we were gone.

That book is so good I read it two times.

One plus one equals two.

Can we have one or two cookies after lunch?

Now you are going to learn a few more irregular words. We say these words differently than you would expect. Have child finger track while saying the words.

any   This word should sound out /an.ee/ but we say /ehn.ee/. We say **any**.

many   This word should sound out /man.ee/ but we say /mehn.ee/. We say **many**.

Let's practice saying these words correctly (be sure child is finger tracking while saying the word)

any   many   any   many   any   many

Reading Sentences: OK, now it's your turn to read our new word in a sentence. Have child read the following sentences. If the child makes errors on irregular words simply say "oops... do you remember how we say that word".

Did you see **any** of the ducks that flew over the pond?

How **many** books did you read last week?

No thank you. I would not like **any** milk with my lunch.

Many of the children liked peanut butter.

Lesson 89: The 'strange' Greek sounds ph, ch, y & Review

ph   These buddy letters have the sound /f/.

ch   You learned these **ch** buddy letters have the sound /ch/. In most words **ch** has the /ch/ sound. However, in a few words **ch** has the /k/ sound. (Note: **h** is silent and **c** has the expected /k/ sound)

y   You already learned the letter **y** has 3 sounds, /y/, /ee/, and /ie/. In a few words the **y** has an unexpected /i/ sound.

The ph=/f/, ch= /k/, & y= /i/ sounds are all found in words of Greek origin.

Reading Words with the ph= /f/ sound:

phone	phrase	graph	phase	sphere
phonics	phony	nephew	prophet	pamphlet
orphan	trophy	gopher	graphic	photo
physics	phantom	pheasant		

- - - - - - - - - - - - - - - - - - - 3 syllable words - - - - - - - - - - - - - - - - - - -

alphabet	photograph	physical	telephone	photocopy
autograph	telegraph	pharmacy	elephant	

Reading Words with the /k/ sound for ch:
The /k/ sound for ch is found in relatively few words. However, you need to learn ch=/k/ because it is found in some important words.

Christ	school	ache	chrome	scheme
chord	chronic	schedule	scholar	Christmas
chemist	anchor	schooner	chemistry	chronicle

*Occasionally **ch** represents the /sh/ sound as in: chef, chateau, chivalry, chagrin, chalet, chevron, Chicago and Cheyenne. Most of these words have French origins. Despite these inconsistencies related to the unique aspects of our diverse English language, the fact remains, **ch** has the expected /ch/ sound in the overwhelming majority of words.

Reading Words with the /i/ sound for y

gym	myth	system	symbol	physics

- - - - - - - - - - - - - - - - - - - 3 syllable words - - - - - - - - - - - - - - - - - - -

mystery	typical	cylinder	syllable	pyramid

Reading Sentences/Review Mixed Sounds:

I learn a lot in school.

We are learning how to use graph paper in math.

I called my nephew on the telephone to wish him a Happy Birthday.

They changed the schedule for our games.

The school had a wonderful Christmas program.

I would like to take classes in chemistry and physics when I get to high school.

My Mom likes to take lots of photographs of my family.

Gym is my favorite class in school.

The book I just finished was a mystery.

I can read three syllable words.

I need to make two phone calls before we leave.

My friend wrote me a letter.

Many children went swimming on the hot day.

The map key shows what the symbols on the map stand for.

We learned about the solar system.

I took a great photo of my dog.

The gopher ate plants in my garden.

I wonder if we have any ice cream left in the freezer.

Moose are the largest members of the deer family. A large bull moose can be over a thousand pounds.

Lesson 90: Less Frequent Sounds

Reading Words that have the /i/ sound for ai: You learned the **ai** buddy letters have the sound /ay/. In a few words, **ai** has the /i/ sound instead of the expected /ay/ sound. This /i/ sound for **ai** is usually found when **ai** is within the last syllable of a multisyllable word.

captain   certain   again   mountain   curtain   fountain

bargain   chaplain   villain

Reading Words that have the /ee/ sound for i: The single **i** has /i/ or /ie/ sound in most words. However **i** has the /ee/ sound in some words. Note the use of **i** for the /ee/ sound in the following words. Once again this unexpected spelling of the /ee/ sound presents more of a spelling problem than a reading problem as we often read without even noticing the i=/ee/. The parent or teacher can point out these sounds and read the following words to the child. Have the child watch while you finger track and pronounce the words.

Many occurrences of i =/ee/ are found in adding suffixes to words ending in consonant-y. The **i** spelling results from changing 'y' to 'i' before adding the suffix. In these words **i** maintains the original /ee/ sound from the initial 'y' in the base word:

worry - worrier   city- cities   carry- carrier

friendly- friendliest   sorry- sorriest   funny- funniest

happy- happier   sturdy- sturdier   angry- angrier

pretty- prettiest   duty- duties   baby- babies

The -ian suffix is another pattern where i = /ee/

guardian   barbarian   custodian   veterinarian   amphibian

librarian   comedian   civilian   Indian   riparian

The -ial ending is another pattern where i =/ee/

trivial   serial   bacterial   imperial   territorial

material   editorial   controversial terrestrial

The -iate ending is another pattern where i =/ee/

defoliate   intermediate   radiate   appropriate

abbreviate   immediate   humiliate   alleviate

Other words with i = /ee/

machine   trampoline   nicotine   magazine   ambiance

barrier   brilliant   brilliance

The /ee/ in the 'ing' & 'ink' combinations was covered in Lesson 16.

Lesson 91: "Strange" vowel combinations: eigh & ough

We will not spend much time on these sounds. These "strange" vowel combinations are not used in many words. Quickly review these sounds and when you encounter a word with these sounds just teach it as an irregular word. For now you are just exposing the child to these sounds. You can point out these sounds and read the words to the child. Have the child watch while you finger track and pronounce the words.

eigh   These buddy letters usually have the sound /ay/. This combination is NOT found in many words. The gh is silent & the ei has the /ay/ sound.

eigh= /ay/ eight eighty freight weight weigh sleigh neighbor

(unexpected sound of /ie/ in height)

ough   These buddy letters are confusing. They have six different sounds. This is one of the "strange" combinations where you just have to practice reading and saying the individual word. Luckily, not many words have this confusing 'ough' combination!

1. /aw/ ought bought thought fought sought

2. /ow/ bough drought

3. /oa/ though although dough doughnut

4. /oo/ through slough(swamp;bog)

5. /off/ cough

6. /uff/ tough enough rough slough (shed;cast off)

Suggestion: Help the child learn and master one or two of these 'ough' words at a time. Pick a word and have the child practice writing the word, paying attention to the 'strange' spelling. After repeatedly writing and saying the word the child will begin to learn this word. You can group some words (though-although) but avoid teaching words with mixed sounds (thought, though, and trough) together or in sequence.

Lesson 92: Quick Overview - A Few Other Uncommon Sounds

We will not spend much time on these sounds. These uncommon sound combinations are rarely used. We will just review them quickly so that you are aware of them. Don't make sound cards or write these sounds. If you encounter a word with one of these sounds, just point the sound out individually as 'one of those silly sounds'. Students encounter few of these words until they are reading technical material in medical and scientific fields. Point out these sounds and read the words to the child. Have the child watch while you finger track and pronounce the words.

gn   These have the sound /n/. The **g** is silent.
    gnat   gnaw   gnarled   gnome

gh　　These have the sound /g/. The **h** is silent.
ghost　　ghetto

rh　　These have the sound /r/. The **h** is silent.
rhyme　　rhythm　　rhizome　　rhinoceros　　rhombus

pn　　These have the sound /n/. The **p** is silent.
pneumonia　pneumatic (derived from pneuma, the Greek word for air)

x　　The /ks/ is the most frequent sound for **x**. However, in a few words **beginning** with the letter **x**, the sound is /z/. Words that *begin with* **x** have the sound /z/.
xylophone　　xeric　　xylem

with the exception of xylophone & maybe xeric (dry/arid conditions) most words beginning with **x** are technical scientific words and will *not* be encountered by young children. Look in the dictionary for examples.

NOTE: In the word X-ray, the 'x' does not represent a sound but instead represents the letter name 'x'. In science and math the letter 'x' is often used to represent the unknown. The scientist discovered this new 'unknown-ray' therefore called he called it the "x-ray" short for 'unknown-ray'. The name 'x-ray' stuck.

Lesson 93: Review and Practice

Review Sounds: Quickly review all the sounds you learned!

m	t	a	s	d	i	f	r	th
l	o	n	p	e	h	v	sh	u
b	k	ck	c	g	j	w	ch	tch
x	z	qu	wh	y	ing	ink	ee	oa
oe	ai	ay	a_e	i_e	o_e	u_e	e_e	oi
oy	ea	ow	ou	ue	ew	ui	oo	ey
au	aw	igh	ar	w+ar	or	ore	oar	our
oor	er	ur	ir	w+or	are	air	eer	ear
ere	ire	dge	mb	wr	kn	ph		

258

Practice Sounds: The child should know all these sounds automatically. If sounds are known, the child can drop them from isolated practice. If any sounds are not automatic the child needs to continue practicing the sound card and writing or tracing these sounds.

Making Words: "Please make the word _____"

Use sound tiles... ir ore ar i e y c d f g l m n p r s t(2) x th
thirty snore shore sharp first large chore start restore explore partly implore artist
thirsty ignore largely garlic forearm army deplore infirm target firmly carpet margin

Use sound tiles... ou igh dge a e y b c d f l g m n p r s t sh ch th
ledge shout badge right flight sound touch proudly edge youth group delight
youngest outright country rebound loudest famous brightest flashlight

Use sound tiles... ow ai ie b d g l m n p r(2) s t w x sh ing
plowing saint glide shown strain rainbow window elbow remain growing raining
below township retrain slideshow explain detain waiting remaining

Use sound tiles... oo ear a e i y b c l n s t ch th wr
earth near booth learn search wrath nearly early write wrist thinly clearly
soonest smoothly

Use sound tiles.... er or oi e i u y c d f l m n p r t v x ch sh
choice coin force point shine shorter price voice torch corner under crunchy
order exploit exit shortly former devoid report inform perform reorder record

Use sound tiles.... ea er a i o y b c d f l m n p r s(2) t v w th
master weather river faster sister cleaner feather other wealthy
bother mother reader brotherly steamer printer ready stealthy transfer

Use sound tiles... ur our ey air o b d f h k l m n p s t ch th
burnt hair churn stair lurch monkey donkey burst fourth chair
honey flair surf they money four pour

Reading Sentences/Review Mixed Sounds:

He is one of the best players on the team.

The dogs were running after the cat. But the cat ran faster than the dogs. He got away because he was the quickest.

The new pillow is softer than my old hard one.

The little dog was barking much louder than the large dogs.

I am shorter than my older brother.

The students had to find the center of the circle.

My brother ate two double burgers for dinner.

Lesson 94: Practice Reading Common Endings & Review

-ing These buddy letters have the sound /eeng/. You already learned these and know how **ing** usually comes at the end of words.

-er You already learned how these buddy letters have the sound /er/. The /er/ sound is a very common ending for words.

-ly You can easily sound out this common ending. It says /lee/. The *-ly* ending is a common ending on many words. Even though you can sound it out, it helps to practice reading it because it is so common.

Practice the Common -ing ending

running	meeting	going	writing	picking	yelling
drawing	petting	walking	blasting	chewing	learning
drinking	eating	washing	cleaning	brushing	crying
watching	cooking	lasting	dancing	starting	blasting
swinging	testing	reading	making	changing	resting
shouting	sleeping	shopping	slipping	flinging	drying
speeding	toasting	grilling	pointing	snowing	passing
striking	lightning	dating	knowing	naming	swimming
earning	calling	hiking	racing	finding	surfing
reaching	pleasing	carving	coming	squirting	roasting
raining	starting	hurting	storming	riding	working
searching	forcing	spoiling	sharing	hearing	clearing

Practice the Common -er ending

writer	taller	shorter	wider	reader	teacher
toaster	player	dancer	caller	speller	sprayer
softer	harder	cleaner	waiter	longer	tester
timer	cooler	cutter	pester	shopper	jumper
nicer	faster	heater	thicker	greater	grower
singer	helper	quicker	poster	hunter	baker

bigger	herder	marker	neater	zipper	rocker
slower	farmer	layer	sticker	swimmer	server
stranger	fighter	binder	logger	braver	farther
hanger	explorer	divider	enforcer	computer	forester

Practice the Common -ly ending

nicely	quickly	shortly	gently	quietly	loudly
kindly	yearly	brightly	rudely	sweetly	clearly
sadly	thickly	bravely	wisely	hardly	partly
firmly	sternly	worldly	warmly	proudly	nearly
safely	closely	harshly	smoothly	plainly	timely
blindly	fully	poorly	worldly	largely	fairly
promptly	neatly	lightly	bravely	nearly	wrongly
calmly	costly	friendly	freely	slowly	squarely
hopefully	finally	willingly	endlessly	unfairly	alertly
suddenly	randomly	joyfully	painlessly	happily	cleverly

Lesson 95: Practice Reading Plural Endings

This lesson reviews the common plural endings of **-s**, **-es**, and **-ies** that are added to the ending of words to indicate more than one. Plural endings are very common making up approximately 31% of all suffixed words. Although these endings are phonetic, it is helpful to practice them. When plural words are written usually an **s** or **es** is just added to the end of the word.

Practice the Common plural -s ending: When reading just add the /s/ or /z/ sound

floors	keys	blasts	days	pens	pies
tests	trees	swings	toys	streets	dogs
books	snakes	files	friends	news	rocks
blankets	sisters	dinners	binders	papers	carpets

Practice the Common plural -es ending: When reading just add the /es/ sound. Note: You add -es sound when word ends with **s, ch, sh, x, z, the /s/ sound ('s' or 'ce')**, or **the /j/ sound ('ge' or 'dge')**. Instead of memorizing the list, just *listen* to determine when you need to use the 'es' plural spelling. Basically you use 'es' spelling when the word ends in a sound where you can NOT verbally add a /s/ sound to without putting in the /e/. Try saying /s/ immediately after /s/, /ch/ /sh/ /x/ or /z/. You have to say the /es/ sound. You can hear the /e/+/s/.

bench--benches	dress--dresses	ash--ashes	box--boxes
inch--inches	bus--busses	lunch--lunches	ranch--ranches
leash--leashes	brush--brushes	pinch--pinches	porch--porches
tax--taxes	couch--couches	dish--dishes	

Practice the Common plural **-ies** ending.... You read these by just adding the /z/ sound to the word. The -ies ending is found in words that end in consonant-y. Note: In words ending in consonant-y you *change the y to i and add es*. The pronunciation keeps either the /ee/ or /ie/ sound that the y represented in the original base word and add the /z/ sound. Note: You only *change the y to i and add es* for words ending in consonant-y. Words ending in the vowel-y combinations such (ay, ey, oy) are NOT changed. If **y** is part of a vowel combination, just add **s** (boys, keys, plays...)

(consonant-y words with the /ee/ sound... ..... the plural sound is /eez/)

baby--babies	city--cities	candy--candies	story--stories
lady--ladies	party--parties	gravy--gravies	army--armies
duty--duties	puppy--puppies	penny--pennies	kitty--kitties

(consonant-y words with the /ie/ sound... ..... the plural sound is /iez/)

fly--flies	try--tries	cry--cries	dry--dries

Reading Sentences/Review Mixed Sounds:

We got to go shopping for school supplies.

Two of my friends had birthday parties last weekend.

The puppies played outside.

We read three stories after lunch.

The ladies went for a long walk around the park.

How many pennies do you have in that jar?

Lesson 96: Practice Reading Past Tense -ed Endings

The past tense **-ed** ending (suffix) used for verbs is extremely common, making up approximately 20% of all suffixed words. (This is the **-ed** past tense suffix for verbs not /e//d/ as in bed, red or shed.) The **-ed** past tense ending is pronounced three different ways, /id/ /d/ or /t/, depending on the ending sound of the base word. Once again we usually say and read these **-ed** endings without even noticing the difference in sounds. However, it is helpful to recognize different pronunciations of the **-ed** past tense ending for spelling. The past tense **-ed** ending is always spelled 'ed' regardless of the /id/ /d/ or /t/ pronunciation. Specifically notice the different pronunciations as you read the following words with the **-ed** past tense suffix. Let's practice reading these –ed past tense endings.

Practice the Common past tense -ed ending with the /ed/ or /id/ sound:
(whenever a word ends in **d** or **t** the -ed ending is pronounced /id/)

ended	lasted	started	painted	petted
landed	melted	petted	seated	dusted
pointed	threaded	slanted	printed	bended
baited	speeded	netted	rested	blasted
drifted	faded	darted	hunted	pouted
granted	handed	sprouted	lifted	toasted
grinded	tempted	pouted	reminded	corrected

Practice the Common past tense -ed ending with the /d/ sound:

grabbed	tanned	tagged	sailed	sprayed
logged	slammed	played	filled	closed
poured	spooned	smoothed	timed	waved
loved	smiled	grinned	pleased	pinned
cleaned	called	learned	failed	dived
used	planned	dreamed	caused	paused
grabbed	boiled	saved	cooled	charged
fooled	crawled	carved	stirred	called
stewed	mailed	turned	cleared	shared

263

Practice the Common past tense -ed ending with the /t/ sound:

snacked	cooked	kissed	missed	raced
marched	wished	jumped	poked	typed
raked	joked	leaped	tapped	blessed
mopped	flashed	placed	danced	flipped
bluffed	gripped	poked	dripped	laced
scratched	mixed	washed	kicked	rushed
asked	baked	masked	voiced	blocked
forced	walked	braced	striped	dressed
zipped	boxed	mashed	barked	thanked
finished	escaped	practiced	erased	famished

*Note: Our wonderful English language also contains irregular past tense verbs such as ride-rode, drive-drove, eat-ate, fly-flew, speak-spoke, run-ran, and sing- sang that do *not* apply the expected past tense -ed suffix. Luckily, the majority of these words can be read and spelled phonetically based on how we say the words in oral language.

Reading Practice With a Mixed List of –ed past tense endings:

rested	flashed	jumped	poured	voiced
placed	danced	tracked	started	clapped
mended	knitted	pressed	cheered	cleared
poked	raked	sailed	speeded	shouted
shopped	grated	chopped	cooked	sliced
leaped	wished	smiled	saved	founded
cleaned	dusted	worked	missed	called
parted	snowed	helped	lasted	asked
sounded	wanted	painted	landed	headed
needed	handed	wished	neared	changed

264

traded	blinked	counted	reached	yawned
pointed	toasted	charged	praised	traded
charted	printed	waited	needed	marched
reported	completed	repaired	finished	ordered

Reading Sentences/Review Mixed Sounds:

Kim practiced her song.

My ice cream melted in the sun. It dripped all over my shirt.

We rested after lunch.

She poured me a glass of milk.

The little baby grinned at me.

We played a game of basketball with the third graders.

We missed the bus last week.

My dog jumped over the fence.

The band marched on the field at half-time.

Mom painted my bedroom white.

The teacher graded the papers for us.

Dad cooked us up French toast and ham for lunch.

We helped Mom. We washed the table, mopped the floor and dusted. Now we are finished and can go out and play.

We lifted the old dog into the back of the truck.

I missed the phone call from my cousin.

Lesson 97: Practice Reading -ve endings

English words can NOT end in the letter **v** so **e** is always added to make the word not end in **v**. Therefore, sometimes **e** is not acting as part of the vowel-v-e combination but is simply there so the word does not end in **v**.   This **e** does not contribute phonetically to the word. The **-ive** ending (suffix -ive that means likely to do or connected with) is the most frequent **-ve** ending.

Practice the following words ending in -ve /v/ where the 'e' is only preventing the word from ending in 'v' and does not influence the other sounds in the word.

have	give	love	solve	live
valve	shove	weave	sleeve	dove
serve	active	native	captive	above
passive	motive	involve	forgive	resolve
revolve	festive	massive	positive	negative
expensive	relative	directive	expansive	effective
descriptive	detective	sensitive	relative	informative
attentive	impressive	directive	offensive	defensive
suggestive	protective	elective	aggressive	productive

Of course you still do have -ve endings where e is part of the vowel-v-e combination and this buddy e makes the first vowel have a long sound.

save	gave	grave	Steve	dive
pave	hive	drove	grove	brave
drive	stove	slave	thrive	forgave
behave	survive	concave		

Reading Sentences/Review Mixed Sounds:

You need to save some cake and give it to Steve.

I would love to help you solve the math problem.

Can you please give me the wrench hanging above the work bench?

Lesson 98: Final Review and Mixed Practice of All Sounds

Reading a Mixed Word List: The student reads the following words, sounding out with physical tracking and proper blending. Correct any errors immediately.

come	your	meat	one	short
write	tray	give	care	would
more	knew	four	are	work
save	near	please	phone	grew
girl	sharp	thumb	two	push
year	bread	true	fire	sweet
have	stair	knows	they	world
large	floor	here	proof	save
warm	earth	there	court	drive
sport	from	climb	coin	charge
place	land	dense	size	noise
loud	pair	dark	graph	word
friends	first	their	crawl	learn
board	page	right	laugh	found
hope	school	shade	brown	wrong
mail	hire	taught	were	shook
preach	tooth	stripe	keep	store
chance	coach	bright	faith	bruise
many	repair	thirty	color	before
above	quickly	again	early	forgive

enjoy	away	wisely	outline	tardy
reaching	gentle	number	practice	center
trouble	carry	payment	called	forty
clearly	freedom	alarm	purple	stories
given	amount	changed	explore	rescue
remind	over	pencil	slower	ignore
behind	lightest	circle	shared	looking
shadow	searching	certain	forget	narrow
tracked	weekday	beyond	perfect	parent
recent	prepare	safely	highest	table
mountain	only	mostly	instead	contact

Reading Paragraphs/Applying All Sounds:

Rattlesnakes are venomous pit vipers. The snake uses its rattles to make a buzzing noise. They rattle when they are alarmed. A new segment is added each time the snake sheds its skin. But rattles can break off. So counting the number of rattles does not always tell you the snake's age.

Snow-shoe hares change their coat color. In the fall, the brown summer coat slowly changes to white tipped hair. When they are white it is hard to see them in the snow. Often all you can see are the tracks.

Did you know that beavers are the biggest rodents in North America? I found that out last night when I was reading the wildlife book that my aunt gave me.

I did a report on the state of Montana. It learned it became the 41st state in 1889. The capital of Montana is Helena. The state bird is the western meadowlark. The state tree is the ponderosa pine. The state flower is the bitterroot.

Did you know that the western meadowlark is the state bird for Montana, Wyoming, Oregon, North Dakota, Nebraska and Kansas? That is six states! But the cardinal is the state bird for even more states. Can you find the seven different states that have the cardinal for a state bird? If you look at some books, I bet you can!

You have worked very hard in learning to read. You have become an awesome reader. I am really proud of you!

This ends the program of direct instruction in the phonemic code and foundational skills necessary for phonologic processing. However, this is NOT the end of reading instruction. This structured direct systematic phonics program provides the foundation for proficient decoding. It is important to continue direct instruction to help the child acquire the advanced skills necessary for skilled reading. The child needs to learn to easily handle multisyllable words, build fluency, expand vocabulary, develop comprehension and enhance other advanced skills. A program of daily guided reading where the child reads outloud to an adult with feedback and instruction is essential for developing the skills for proficient reading. Section 7 (page 308-310) contains complete directions for using guided reading to improve and advance reading skills. Do not skip this critically important, highly effective and enjoyable instructional tool!

BEGIN DAILY GUIDED READING

Use direct instruction to advance reading skills!
> Handling Multisyllable Words ~ See Section 6 (pages 270-307)
> Guided Reading ~ See Section 7 (pages 308-310)
> Building Fluency See Section 8 (pages 311-312)
> Developing Reading Comprehension ~ See Section 9 (pages 313-316)
> Expanding Vocabulary ~ See Section 10 (pages 317-320)

Use direct instruction to advance spelling skills!
> Advancing Spelling Skills ~ See Spelling Section (pages 321-338)

Section 6: Reading Multisyllable Words

Multisyllable Words - General Information

The multisyllable words *are* harder to read than short words. To read multisyllable words the child needs to apply a more advanced strategy. Some students automatically develop the proper strategies for reading multisyllable words but many do not and struggle with these longer words. Direct instruction and guided practice helps the student learn how to handle these 'long' words. The majority of English words are multisyllable so it is critical to read them effectively. This section provides direct instruction and practice in handling these 'long' multisyllable words.

Syllables are simply the chunks of sound within a spoken word that are said with a single puff of air. Every syllable has at least one vowel sound with or without the surrounding consonant sounds. Multisyllable words are made up of a combination of these distinct sound chunks. In these multisyllable words it is impossible to combine all the sounds together in one puff. To read multisyllable words the student has to not only process the print phonetically but he needs to learn how to distinguish and group the appropriate sounds together to form the correct syllables and then smoothly combine these correct sound chunks with all the adjacent syllables into one fluid word. The student needs to capture *all* the appropriate sound chunks in the word without missing one or without adding one that should not be there. The syllables need to be smoothly and quickly joined into one fluid word that is accented and pronounced correctly. Reading multisyllable words is a more complex process and absolutely takes practice.

The following lessons provide direct practice in this complex skill of handling multisyllable words. This instruction is designed for students who have already acquired knowledge of the phonemic code and established correct phonologic processing. If the student is not able to decode words, he first will need to complete the initial sections of this program (Lessons 1-98). If the student is processing print phonetically, knows the complete phonemic code, and only lacking skills in easily handling multisyllable words instruction can begin with this section.

These lessons directly teach strategies and develop skills in handling multisyllable words. Activities are designed to help the student learn how to break words down into appropriate syllables, pay attention to detail, pick up all sounds and smoothly blend sound chunks. Common patterns, including the most frequently encountered affixes, are practiced. Direct guided instruction in handling multisyllable words develops necessary skills.

It is important to realize that distinguishing appropriate syllable breaks for reading instruction is based on the sound structure of the word. In other words base 'sound chunks' on how you say the word. This is NOT necessarily the official dictionary syllable splits. For example, in the word "effect" the split based on how we say the word is e-fect not the ef-fect official dictionary split. Don't get too picky about where the word is exactly split. *Base it on sound!* Sometimes we say words differently. (i.e. for puppy you can say either pup-ee or pup-pee...either split is fine for handling the multisyllable reading of the word). This is *not* learning the rules and making the official correct written syllable splits found in a dictionary but rather quickly distinguishing and handling sound chunks within a word for reading.

Explain to the Student:

- This section provides direct instruction in how to handle multisyllable words. You will learn and practice techniques for reading these longer multisyllable words.

- Syllables are chunks of sound within a word that we say in a single puff of air. ***If the student does not yet understand syllables, you MUST spend time with some oral exercises where the student says longer words and learns to hear and orally break the word into syllables.

Accomplish this by orally saying a word (any multisyllable word) and having the child repeat the word and then orally break it down into the syllables or sound chunks. Make sure the student can orally distinguish syllables. For example: running (run - ing), tropic (trop - ic), understand (un - der - stand), Washington (Wash - ing - ton), basketball (bas- ket -ball)

- To handle reading these "long" words you need to learn how to distinguish, or "see", the appropriate syllables or sound chunks within a word and then rapidly capture all sounds and smoothly put these sound chunks together. It is a more advanced skill than simply knowing and blending the individual sounds of single syllable words together. You need to combine the sounds into appropriate 'chunks', capture all these syllables which usually do not have a meaning on their own and join them rapidly and smoothly with the adjacent syllables to form the word. It is almost like reading 3, 4 or more separate nonsense words and smoothly combining them into one fluid word. Plus to top it off, you need to get the correct pronunciation and accent. This section will help you learn how to easily handle these longer words.

Directions for Activities in the Multisyllable Word Lessons:

Reading Words: Each lesson includes guided reading of lists of multisyllable words. The student reads all the words in the list. The word lists, by design, require the student to develop correct skills. As the student reads the words to you, have your pencil ready. If the student has problems with breaking words into appropriate syllables help the student by placing little light pencil mark slashes in the appropriate syllable breaks so he can better 'see' the syllables. For example:

- inconsistent → add the light pencil marks to indicate →in/con/sis/tent
- combination → add the light pencil slashes to indicate → com/bi/na/tion
- protective → → add the light pencil slashes to indicate → pro/tec/tive
- **An illustration of this technique is shown on page 38**

This light pencil slash through the appropriate breaks and maybe a comment such as 'take another look' helps the student learn how to break words. Before long the student begins to 'see' the appropriate breaks on his own. Remember to only make the slash marks *when* the student needs help. The slash marks help the student learn how to break and handle these longer words.

Once again, as with all guided reading, make sure the student reads each word accurately. Often when students tackle multisyllable words they leave out parts, add sounds that are not there or change sounds. Stop any of these errors and have the student take another look. Make immediate corrections for any error. At this point, the correction technique of tapping the pencil on the word to signal 'stop and look again' is often all that is necessary. Correction is critical to developing the attention to detail and ability to pick up all sounds within a multisyllable word that is important to accurate fluent reading. Remember to help the student by making slash marks *when* needed. Direct instruction with correction helps the student learn how to capture all the chunks and smoothly combine them into a fluid word.

In addition, you may need to help the student with pronunciation. With multisyllable words placing the accent on the correct syllable and proper pronunciation adds another level of complexity to correctly reading the word. Not only does the student need to accurately sound out the word but he needs to accent and pronounce it correctly. If the word is familiar, the student usually gets the correct accenting and pronunciation. If the word is unfamiliar, you may need to provide the correct pronunciation. Help the student with correct pronunciation whenever he needs assistance. With improper pronunciation, correct by saying "Close, but we actually pronounce the word this way _____". Then make sure the student re-reads the word pronouncing it correctly. This correct pronunciation is important in creating the 'fluent' neural model of the word so by all means help the student learn and practice correct pronunciation of new vocabulary. Guided practice reading multisyllable words is essential for developing necessary skills. If the student is not fluently reading the words in a list have him re-read the list of words at least once before moving on. If necessary, have the student practice reading previous lists. Fluency is built by practice. It is exciting to observe and note how with practice the student develops fluency on specific words.

Writing /Spelling Words: The student writes multisyllable words in each lesson.   Printing orally presented multisyllable words effectively helps students learn how to tackle and proficiently read multisyllable words. Not only does printing words phonetically by syllable directly establish and develop necessary phonologic processing but it also builds understanding of the syllable structure of words. The student learns how long words break apart into smaller sound 'chunks' and gains knowledge of common patterns and affixes. Writing spoken multisyllable words by syllable directly strengthens the converse skill of breaking words into appropriate syllables for reading.

Select some of the listed multisyllable words and read the words out-loud to the student. Have the student write the word by syllable *as he says the sound chunk or syllable*. The student should write 10 to 20 words for each lesson (or affix group within the lesson). In the beginning, the student can leave a small gap between the syllables to help him 'see' the syllable splits. Use words from any the lists in the lesson or previous lesson. You may also make your own multisyllable word writing lists. The word writing should be given to the student with specific affix or spelling patterns grouped together to help him learn and recognize common patterns in our language. Usually the writing itself is easy for older students allowing word writing to be used as a simple highly effective tool. If the physical printing process is difficult, you may need to give the student fewer words to write and instead provide additional direct reading practice.

The word writing activity is an exercise in handling and processing multisyllable words NOT a spelling test. *However*, you do not want a student to practice spelling a word incorrectly. Help the student learn the correct spelling patterns. Help the student build skills by grouping common patterns and providing direction. Help teach correct spelling by saying "these next words are going to use the ___spelling for the ___ sound". As he writes, help with spelling hints such as the /ow/ sound in this word is spelled with "ou", or "in this word the /s/ sound is spelled with 'c'". If you give a word with a 'tricky' spelling, teach the 'unexpected' portion so the student learns correctly. The following are some examples of spelling/word writing lists designed to help the student develop skills:

- List 1: "These words have the -ment ending (remind the student that the e in ment sounds like an i but we spell it -ment)" and give…. placement, pavement, statement, refreshment, adjustment, equipment, banishment, enjoyment, employment, enrichment

- List 2: "These words all start with the re- prefix" and give him…….renew, replace, return, recheck, review, repay, refill, reflect, reprint, revisit, rewind, remind, restore

- List 3: "These words have the -able ending" and give him…..washable, bendable, moveable, readable, fixable, comfortable, agreeable, mixable, breakable, changeable, punishable, questionable (don't mix -ible endings in the list when the student is practicing the -able ending)

- List 4: "These words all start with the dis- prefix" and give him …..discover, display, discharge, disturb, discredit, disrespect, dispatch, distrust, disagree, discount (if the student spells dispatch incorrectly with 'ch' instead of 'tch' give a reminder of the correct 'tch' spelling pattern).

- List 5: "These words have the 'tion' spelling for the /shun/ ending" and give him…. nation, station, action, injection, tradition, motion, creation, lotion, migration, reflection, direction, formation (don't mix in words such as confession with the -sion endings on this word writing list)

Remember, fluency is built by practice. If a specific word is difficult for the student, have the child write that individual word several times saying the sounds as he prints the word. This repetition of correct phonologic processing in 'word writing' is an excellent tool for developing fluency on a specific word.

Reading Multisyllable Words Lesson 1: Practice

This lesson provides practice reading multisyllable words. You have already been reading numerous two and some three syllable words. Remember syllables are chunks of sound and every syllable has a vowel sound. Learning and practicing how to handle these multisyllable words greatly improves your reading. *If* you need help breaking the words down into syllables, I will make a light pencil mark to help you 'see' the proper syllable breaks. If necessary, I will also help you with correct pronunciation.

*As the student reads, have a pencil ready and make slash marks to indicate syllable breaks *only* if and when the student needs assistance with a word. If necessary, help with pronunciation and then have child re-read the word with correct pronunciation.

Practice with 2 syllable words

statement	canvas	carpet	cartoon	divide
children	notice	impress	reject	install
around	number	between	almost	inside
surface	within	sudden	himself	learning
outside	always	careful	became	prevent
morning	sentence	today	behind	problem
relax	adapt	after	recess	public
raccoon	neglect	pencil	refrain	afraid
contain	receive	complete	service	inspect
magnet	mustang	extend	hidden	entrance
canteen	hundred	hostage	outside	softly
plenty	gossip	ending	frequent	include
concrete	freedom	canteen	reflect	program
safely	explode	morning	hungry	captive
remote	silver	detour	discard	native
respond	around	beside	broken	given
vintage	yearly	regain	mushroom	laundry
graphic	flavor	confront	banish	confirm
confine	conflict	baptize	complex	divine

expense	forbid	glamour	forgave	helpless
invite	observe	obtain	engage	complain
lumber	mitten	unless	slander	static
temper	teaching	vessel	charcoal	follow
chapter	bandage	beaver	basement	artist
appear	account	simply	corrupt	decent
famous	hunter	elapse	insist	intense
lightning	manner	market	skipping	higher
enjoy	prepare	contact	antler	batter
report	events	suggest	river	worker
cancel	bundle	compress	county	danger
peanut	something	nasty	swimming	common
walrus	corner	detail	complaint	deadline
rainbow	lizard	tadpole	printer	finger
respond	closely	return	sharpen	plenty
amaze	money	express	control	equate
update	ahead	rattle	propane	lawless

Practice with 3 syllable words

celebrate	testify	incomplete	terminate	similar
terminal	capital	appointment	gratefully	evidence
expected	develop	disinfect	calculate	hesitate
vitamin	hospital	simplify	reported	president
tornado	circulate	quality	qualify	relative
centipede	victory	classify	sediment	fantastic
enjoyed	dedicate	inhabit	accident	capital
important	devastate	electron	sensitive	vertical

obligate	expansive	obsolete	department	destiny
determine	disappoint	average	primitive	principal
tangible	unfriendly	indicate	latitude	charity
compensate	obstacle	camera	agenda	electric
literal	multiple	objective	pelican	secretive
accomplish	memory	investment	diminish	dishonest
document	edible	engagement	entertain	exclusive
family	fascinate	discover	fortify	gentleman
history	horizon	inspector	internal	numerous
interval	invalid	innocent	isolate	justify
minister	minimize	modify	nonprofit	powerless
rejected	animal	important	multiply	hesitate
wonderful	resistant	assistant	adjustment	monitor
constantly	reminded	difficult	enormous	however
repeated	steadily	vertical	secretly	amazement
wondered	forgotten	employer	returned	contacted
completely	interest	expected	embarrass	interview
astonish	frequently	extremely	amplify	abrasive
inspecting	ordering	effortless	company	practicing
popular	interrupt	continue	inventive	introduce
recover	adjusting	argument	fabulous	incorrect
preventive	comprehend	remember	understand	isolate
contrasted	unfaithful	different	opposite	forever
whenever	medical	objective	particle	reminder
unequal	establish	resident	populate	expanding

Writing/Spelling Words: Write some of the listed words.

Reading Multisyllable Words Lesson 2: Compound Words

In this lesson you practice reading compound words, a special type of multisyllable word. Compound words are usually easier to read because they are made up by joining other words.

laptop	landmark	overflow	mainland	sideways
runway	horseback	playground	bedroom	bathroom
tablecloth	baseball	basketball	outdoor	doghouse
underground	schoolhouse	railway	railroad	mailbox
groundhog	typewriter	flashlight	bookcase	ladybug
placemat	football	backup	hotdog	doorbell
weekend	download	copycat	waterfall	highway
highchair	expressway	hamburger	birthday	backpack
sweatshirt	starfish	makeup	jailbird	jackknife
catfish	craftsman	cowgirl	cowboy	dugout
dumbbell	downstairs	seaweed	downtown	drainpipe
seafood	online	roundup	overgrow	outline
overhead	outsmart	overall	overcast	undergo
within	windmill	underdog	windfall	bookmark
bullfrog	wingspan	bluegrass	blindfold	blacktop
blueprint	blackmail	bighorn	blackout	bedrock
billboard	bathrobe	battleship	bareback	ballgame
backbone	armpit	dogwood	outside	armchair
spacecraft	thunderstorm	toolbox	toothpaste	weekday
toothpick	touchdown	upstairs	videotape	warehouse
wasteland	wheelchair	whirlwind	whitewash	wildcat
playpen	hairbrush	earring	shoelace	bookmark
manhole	bathtub	notebook	offshore	handshake

nutcracker	outfield	outgrow	ponytail	payroll
outlaw	desktop	fireman	lighthouse	stairway
lifetime	junkyard	stopwatch	lifeboat	lightbulb
screwdriver	hacksaw	crosscut	crossroad	clockwise
crossword	crowbar	hotshot	crossbow	cookout
firefighter	crosswalk	handwriting	handbook	handshake
oatmeal	haircut	halfway	gentleman	gateway
sidewalk	overcoat	driveway	pickup	inkpad
underwear	chalkboard	headache	headline	fingernail
roadway	newborn	grasshopper	birthplace	aircraft
candlestick	nightgown	newspaper	checkup	anyone
anyplace	airstrip	warpath	soapbox	waistline
drumstick	downstream	driftwood	driveway	drugstore
homeland	horseshoe	hubcap	household	paycheck
footsteps	earthquake	clipboard	sunrise	sunset
bluebird	toothbrush	landlord	yardstick	moonlight
campsite	hallway	brainstorm	buttermilk	dishpan
shortstop	pitchfork	doorbell	blackberry	workshop
haystack	cardboard	headlight	sandpaper	loophole
sunflower	shoelace	candlestick	coastline	jellyfish
snowshoe	toolbox	wallpaper	bookcase	handbag
teammate	lunchroom	barnyard	seashell	grandson
fishhook	birdhouse	battlefield	whenever	cookbook
paperback	cupcake	bedtime	proofread	footstep
shortbread	gingerbread	greenhouse	dragonfly	keyhole
steamboat	swordfish	blackbird	handmade	railway

afternoon	Thanksgiving	moonlight	sunshine	worldwide
grandstand	overboard	shipwreck	hallway	teaspoon
waterproof	daredevil	underground	overhead	bulldog
courthouse	snowflake	keyboard	touchdown	sometime
bedside	tugboat	textbook	nighttime	daytime
stoplight	firewood	worldwide	headboard	fullback
headlong	sunbeam	underway	breakaway	manpower
backboard	wildland	firehall	crackdown	daybreak
homeland	nearby	roadside	spokesman	cutthroat
taxpayer	walkway	overstretch	dashboard	breakaway
buttonhole	greenhouse	cheesecloth	clockwise	cookout
earplug	faraway	flashlight	homework	firestorm
spacewalk	campsite	household	earmark	watchdog
outpost	crackdown	notepad	catwalk	handcuff
checkout	cloudburst	copycat	cutback	flagpole
footbridge	rattlesnake	meanwhile	junkyard	slipknot
lawmaker	buyout	viewpoint	storewide	buttermilk
chairman	classmate	clubhouse	counterpart	freehand
grandfather	deadline	folklore	wildlife	toothpaste
slashmark	cookbook	copyright	cutoff	daylight
downhill	driftwood	dropout	highlight	homestretch
everyone	keynote	mixup	lifesaver	necktie
layout	timekeeper	matchbook	pipeline	kneecap
newborn	landslide	workbook	offshore	patchwork
troubleshoot	withstand	woodland	lifeguard	workout
lookout	nowhere	makeshift	penknife	sawdust

Multisyllable Words Lesson 3: Common Prefixes and Suffixes

Prefixes are syllables or word parts with their own meaning that are added to the **beginning** of a base or root word that change the meaning of the word. **Suffixes** are syllables or word parts with their own meaning that are added to the **end** of a base or root word that changes the meaning.

Although most of the common prefixes and suffixes are phonetic it helps to quickly identify the appropriate 'chunks' of these common affixes. Direct practice in reading these common affixes helps the student quickly identify, group, and process appropriate sounds. The repeated practice builds fluency in these common affixes and greatly improves reading fluency of other words that contain the same common affixes. In addition, knowing the meaning of the common prefixes and suffixes helps students understand the word and expand their vocabulary knowledge.

There are hundreds of possible prefixes and suffixes the student will eventually need to learn. However, it is best to first focus efforts on those prefixes and suffixes that are most commonly encountered. Twenty prefixes account for approximately 97% of the prefixed words. Teaching the most frequent prefixes helps in both reading fluency and in vocabulary. A good list of common affixes is found in the Texas Education Agency publication number GE01-105-04. Page 28 of this publication contains a table "The Most Frequent Affixes in Printed School English". **www.tea.state.tx.us/reading/practices/redbk5.pdf**

RANK	PREFIX	% of all prefixed words	SUFFIX	% of all suffixed words
1	un-	26%	-s, -es	31%
2	re-	14%	-ed	20%
3	in-, im-, il-, ir-	11%	-ing	14%
4	dis-	7%	-ly	7%
5	en-, em-	4%	-er -or (agent)	4%
6	non-	4%	-ion, -tion, -ation	4%
7	in-, im-	3%	-able, -ible	2%
8	over-	3%	-al, -ial	1%
9	mis-	3%	-y	1%
10	sub-	3%	-ness	1%
11	pre-	3%	-ity, -ty	1%
12	inter-	3%	-ment	1%
13	fore-	3%	-ic	1%
14	de-	2%	-ous, -eous, -ious	1%
15	trans-	2%	-en	1%
16	super-	1%	-er (comparative)	1%
17	semi-	1%	-ive, -ative, -tive	1%
18	anti-	1%	-ful	1%
19	mid-	1%	-less	1%
20	under-	1%	-est	1%

To assist reading fluency, it is also helpful to look at the length of the affix. The longer affixes (such as inter-) are more difficult to read quickly than the shorter ones. The next lessons provide practice with the more common as well as the longer prefixes and suffixes. There are numerous other prefixes and suffixes the student will encounter as he reads. With practice the student will also begin to build fluency and quickly identify and rapidly process these common affixes.

Reading Multisyllable Words Lesson 4: Common Prefixes

Although most of these common prefixes are phonetic it helps in reading to quickly process them. Practice reading and writing these common prefixes helps the student master the complex task of reading multi-syllable words. In addition, learning the meaning of the prefixes develops vocabulary. This lesson is long and will require multiple sessions to complete. Work through reading and writing one prefix group at a time. For each prefix, have the student read the listed words. Make syllable breaks only if the student needs help. Next have the student write/spell 10-15 words from *each* prefix listing. If the student is not fluent in the words have him re-read the list of words at least once before moving to the next prefix. If necessary, include review where the student reads previous lists. Remember, fluency is built by practice. If specific words are difficult, have the student write those word several times.

*As the student reads, have a pencil ready and make slash marks to indicate syllable breaks *only* if and when the student needs assistance with a word. If necessary, help with pronunciation and then have child re-read the word with correct pronunciation.

un- (not or opposed to)

unpack	unclean	unlike	unbolt	unglue
unfold	unbound	unclear	unearth	unknown
unload	unreal	unseen	untrue	unfit
uncap	unrest	unfurl	unhook	unjust
unwell	unsafe	uncoil	undress	unwise
unclench	unwind	unfed	uncurl	uncut
unfair	unpaid	unclasp	unscrew	unburnt
unsure	unwrap	untold	untried	unclog
uncertain	unconcern	uncover	uneven	unable
unarmed	unbeaten	unchosen	uneaten	unfasten
unfriendly	ungrateful	unhappy	unselfish	untangle
untimely	unwilling	unlikely	unequal	unbroken
unwritten	unworthy	uncorrupt	uncalled	unending
ungodly	unhealthy	unbending	unbiased	uncanny
unfeeling	unscramble	uncaring	uncommon	unhelpful
unfounded	unsightly	unselfish	unwrapped	untidy
unfenced	unplanned	unfaithful	unchained	unspoken

unclogged unafraid unfinished unwilling unworthy
unbuckle unchanging unbalanced unfamiliar unadjusted
unashamed unappetizing unavailable unlimited undamaged
unconcealed undecided unprofitable unsuccessful unemployed
unpopular unprepared unconcerned undisturbed unbelieving
uncontrolled unexciting unexplained unseasoned unaffected

re- (again or back)

renew replace redo return restore
repeat remind rebuild recheck regroup
remove reload relay rename reshape
rebound recall recede reclaim redeem
reflect remit react reprint retain
retrieve review revive revise rehire
rewrite repay refill restate retie
rewind recount return reheat respond
remake report reread restart retake
reuse revolt revolve resolve refrain
retype rework remade reroute restrain
reword resend rehire retest recoil
retraced refreshing refilled reenter renumber
recopy relocate reinvent rekindle reoccur
remember recover redirect revisit reinsert
reinspect reaffirm reappoint reattach rekindle
reconfirm redefine reflective repeated reignite
reinfect reconstruct resharpen readjust rearrange
reappear reinvest reprocess reinforce recovery
repopulate reprocess reevaluate recirculate redirected

281

in- (not, without)

insane	inept	incorrect	infinite	incomplete
inexact	incorrupt	inactive	informal	inhuman
injustice	indistinct	indirect	indecent	infidel
infamous	insanity	inedible	ineffective	infrequent
incompetent	inequity	incapable	inability	inadequate
inconsistent	incredible	independent	inorganic	invisible
inconvenient	inaudible	inaccurate	inarticulate	incoherent
incombustible	incompatible	indifferent	inconclusive	inconsiderate
incurable	insecurity	indecisive	indefinite	inoperable
inequality	inconsolable	incomparable	inescapable	inflexible
intolerant	inflammable	indestructible	inapproachable	

the prefix *in-* (not, without) has spelling variations including im-, ir- & il-

im- this spelling variation is often used with base words starting with 'p' and 'm'

impart	impure	immoral	immense	imperfect
immobile	immortal	immodest	imperfect	improper
impolite	impassive	immigrate	immovable	impersonal
impassible	immobilize	immediate	impossible	immorality
immigrant	immaterial	immaterialize	imperishable	improperly
imbalance	implausible	improbable		

ir- this spelling variation is often used with base words starting with 'r'.

irregular	irreplaceable	irrecoverable	irrelevant	irresponsible
irresistible	irretrievable	irreverence	irreversible	irrefutable
irradiant	irritable	irreducible	irrevocable	

il- this spelling variation isn't as common and is often used with base words starting with 'l'.

illegal	illiterate	illegitimate	illicit	illogical

in- (in, into, within)

include	increase	induce	induct	indulge
infect	inflate	inflict	inflow	influx
inform	infuse	inhale	inlay	inscribe
inspect	inspire	install	instill	instruct
intend	institute	inherit	increasing	included
incumbent	incubate	inclusive	incorporate	incriminate

dis- (away from, apart, or the reverse of)

distract	discount	disband	discard	discharge
disturb	distrust	disgrace	dislike	disprove
displace	dispatch	distort	discreet	disbar
dismount	disown	disdain	dispense	display
disarm	displease	disguise	disclaim	disband
dissent	distance	disservice	disaffirm	disarray
disobey	disembark	disable	disenchant	disfavor
discover	disagree	discolor	discomfort	discredit
disfigure	dishonor	disorder	disregard	disrespect
disconnect	disappoint	disrepair	disorder	disgruntle
displacement	disloyal	disavow	discontent	distribute
disclaimer	disinfect	dislocate	disappear	disapprove
disengage	disrespect	distribute	discharged	disconnected
discontinue	disobedient	disorganize	disqualify	dissatisfy
discovered	disadvantage	disagreement	disgraceful	disorderly
discriminate	disdainful	discouraged	disinterested	disregarded
disruptive	disrespectful	dissimilar	distributive	disappointed

en- (to place into, to cover or surround)

enclose	enforce	engage	endure	enact
encamp	enchant	encode	enroll	enclasp
enclave	enshrine	engrave	engross	engulf
enhance	enjoy	enlarge	enlist	enrich
entrench	ensnare	enslave	entrust	enrage
engrain	endear	enfold	encode	ensnarl
enliven	enrichment	envelope	enforced	encroach
enable	endanger	endeavor	enfeeble	encircle
encompass	encumber	encourage	entangle	envelop
enjoyment	enclosure	encounter	endowment	enduring
engagement	enhanced	enlargement	enlighten	encampment

em- (to place into, to cover or surround) this spelling variation of en- is often used with base words starting with 'b' or with 'p'.

employ	embalm	embank	embark	embody
emblaze	embrace	embarrass	embattle	embellish
embitter	empower	employed	empathy	embankment
embargo	embraced	employment	embarked	embedded

non- (not)

nonuse	nonsense	nonstop	nonprofit	nonliving
nonmetal	nonbasic	nonburnable	nonlethal	nonnative
nondescript	nonstandard	nonrigid	nonverbal	nonvisual
nonfatal	noncorrosive	nonbeliever	nonviolent	noncontrolling
noncompliant	noninvasive	nonmember	nonvocal	nontoxic
nonconforming	nonreactive	nonproductive	nonresident	nonexistence
nonflowering	nonlinear	noncombatant	nondurable	nonlicensed
nonflammable	nonobjective	nonrestrictive	nonexempt	nonproductive

over- (excessive or above/on top of)

overall	overtake	overtime	overwork	overstep
overlay	overland	oversight	overboil	overcame
overdrive	overkill	overrun	overblown	overboard
overcast	overcome	overdo	overhand	overwrite
overhang	overwhelm	overhear	overlap	overturn
overthrow	overlook	overpass	overspend	overreach
overheat	overdose	overeat	overhead	overseas
overcharge	overhaul	overprice	overrate	overpay
overview	overpower	overshadow	overruled	overextend
overeager	overexpose	oversimplify	overactive	overestimate
overcrowded	overdeveloped	overcharged	overprotective	

mis- (bad, amiss, wrongly, not)

misshape	misfit	miscall	misfire	misdeed
mismatch	mislay	mislead	mistreat	misuse
misguide	mishear	misplace	misread	misjudge
miscount	misdate	misrule	misspoke	misspell
mislabel	mistrial	misprint	misquote	mistake
misdirect	misguided	misnomer	mistaken	misconduct
misbehave	mismanage	mispronounce	misapply	misjudgment
misclassify	misunderstand	misinformed	misappropriate	misprinted
misrepresent	miscalculate	misinterpret	misquoted	misdirected

sub- (under, beneath or below)

subway	subfloor	submit	subdue	subtext
subscribe	subside	subject	sublease	submerge
subgroup	subscript	subset	sublet	subtract
subsequent	subsidy	subtropics	subdivide	subcompact

subalpine	subdevelop	subsample	subzero	subtotal
subcontract	subsurface	subarctic	substandard	substitute
submarine	subatomic	subcontinent	subclassify	subordinate

pre- (before or in front of)

precede	precook	predict	preface	preset
prefer	prefix	preflight	prescribe	prevent
preview	predate	preclude	prewarn	preheat
prepaid	preschool	pretest	prejudge	presume
predawn	presoak	prepay	preplan	presale
prescribed	prearrange	preamble	predispose	prefigure
preliminary	preoccupy	preregister	preprogram	predestined
predominate	prefabricate	prehistoric	preliminary	predesignate
predetermine	preoccupied	premedical	prerequisite	preventive

inter- (together, with each other, or between two things)

interact	intercede	intercept	interchange	interview
interlock	intermix	intersect	intersperse	interstate
intercom	interlink	intercede	interchange	interdict
interfere	interject	interlay	interlude	interrupt
interval	intervene	interlink	intertwine	interlace
internet	interconnect	interoffice	intermingle	interagency
intercoastal	interlocked	intercepted	interplanetary	

fore- (earlier in time or place; or at or near the front)

forecast	foresight	forehand	foreword	foreclose
forearm	foretold	forewarn	foreground	foreseen
foretell	forenoon	foregone	foremost	foresee
foreman	foreleg	foregone	forehead	forerunner
forecaster	forefather	foreshadow	foreboding	

de- (away from; off; down; or sometimes to undo or reverse an action)

depart	decode	deflate	defrost	deplete
detach	decrease	default	destruct	debug
debrief	defend	demount	defense	debone
declaw	delist	debrief	deform	describe
defame	debase	defraud	deflect	depress
descend	decongest	demerit	devalue	demolish
decompress	deforest	depressed	depolarize	dehydrate
deactivate	deglorify	deodorize	decentralize	declassify

trans- (across, over, through)

transport	transect	transmit	transcribe	transfer
translate	transfix	transform	transfuse	transgress
transpire	transplant	transverse	transit	transpose
transcript	transarctic	translated	transpire	transported
transfigure	transparent	transcontinental	transient	transmitter

super- (above, beyond, more than)

superheat	superscript	superbusy	supercharge	supersede
superpower	supervise	supermarket	supersonic	superhighway
superimpose	superlative	superdifficult	supercritical	superscript
supervisor	supersensible	superalloy	superabundant	

semi- (partly, exactly half)

semiround	semicircle	semiannual	semiarid	semifinal
semilunar	semiweekly	semimonthly	semiprivate	semirigid
semiautomatic	semiconductor	semitropical	semiskilled	semiperfect
semidarkness	semiclassic	semidesert	semicivilized	

anti- (against, opposed to)

antifreeze	antiwar	antivirus	antidote	antiaircraft
antibiotic	antibacterial	antipolitical	antitrust	antipersonnel
antislavery	antioxidant	antitobacco	anticlimax	antiseptic
antivenom	antiperspirant			

mid (middle, amid)

midway	midnight	midland	midpoint	midwest
midrib	midriff	midship	midyear	midterm
midtown	midstory	midweek	midwife	midstream
midair	midfield	midrange	midsole	midday
midsummer	midshipmen	midwinter	midmorning	midafternoon

under- (below in position, beneath)

underhand	underact	underdog	underage	undercoat
understand	understate	underarm	underclass	underwrite
underdone	underfeed	undergrowth	underrate	undertake
underfoot	underbreath	underscore	undertone	undergo
underground	underpay	underneath	undermine	underlay
underside	undertone	underripe	underlie	underbid
undercut	underwent	underfund	underpass	underline
underway	underpin	undersea	undersign	undertow
understood	undergrowth	undercount	undercoat	underrun
undersized	underpower	underachieve	underwater	undervalue
underclassmen	underrated	underexpose	undercover	undercurrent
understudy	underestimate	understanding	underhanded	underutilize
underscored	undernourished			

Writing/Spelling Words: Write words from each of the prefix groups.

Reading Multisyllable Words Lesson 5: Common Suffixes

Although most of these common suffixes are phonetic it helps in reading to quickly process them. Practice reading and writing these common suffixes helps the student master the complex task of reading multi-syllable words. In addition, learning the meaning of the common suffixes helps the student understand the word's meaning and develop vocabulary knowledge.

As mentioned before, **-s** & **-es** (the plural endings), **-ed** (the past tense ending), and **-ing** are the most common suffixes (65% of all suffixed words). These suffixes have already been practiced in previous lessons as well as in much of the vocabulary encountered in the student's other reading. In addition, even young children regularly use these endings in their oral language, making them easier to read.

This lesson is long and will require multiple sessions to complete. Work through reading and writing one suffix group at a time. For each suffix, have the student read the listed words. Make syllable breaks only if the student needs help. Next have the student write 10-15 words from each suffix listing. If the student is not fluent in the words have him re-read the list of words at least once before moving to the next suffix. If necessary, include review where the student reads previous lists. Remember, fluency is built by practice. If specific words are difficult, have the student write those word several times.

*As the student reads, have a pencil ready and make slash marks to indicate syllable breaks *only* if and when the student needs assistance with a word. If necessary, help with pronunciation and then have child re-read the word with correct pronunciation.

-ly (suffix of adjectives & adverbs meaning like or pertaining to)

kindly	yearly	brightly	rudely	sweetly
tiredly	quickly	slowly	loudly	thinly
nicely	thickly	sadly	safely	lately
lonely	smoothly	calmly	cheaply	bluntly
blindly	neatly	partly	lowly	nearly
lastly	plainly	lately	smartly	lightly
deeply	boldly	costly	merely	bravely
softly	nightly	strongly	lively	richly
likely	mostly	rightly	wisely	newly
proudly	promptly	freely	fairly	timely
sickly	gladly	strictly	friendly	portly
silently	quietly	actively	rapidly	secretly
suddenly	easily	normally	finally	directly
brotherly	absently	hopefully	motherly	locally

mannerly	overly	quarterly	precisely	modestly
cleverly	politely	foolishly	sisterly	tenderly
unjustly	forcefully	mortally	positively	vertically
evenly	formerly	abruptly	admittedly	formally
amazingly	concisely	refreshingly	unselfishly	absolutely
nervously	alternately	perfectly	astoundingly	currently

-er with noun (person or thing that performs the action; agent)

maker	teacher	worker	mover	reader
writer	caller	speller	poster	farmer
sprayer	timer	hunter	hiker	pointer
herder	shopper	singer	grower	marker
binder	elder	driver	player	jumper
zipper	burner	toaster	sticker	swimmer
dancer	camper	logger	rocker	mixer
explorer	computer	stapler	manager	eraser
fighter	stranger	recharger	divider	officer
comforter	enforcer	employer	transporter	forester

-er with adjective or adverb (comparative)

harder	wider	nicer	darker	taller
longer	bigger	softer	cooler	cleaner
clever	later	rounder	shorter	faster
slower	braver	faster	farther	greater
smoother	richer	smarter	nearer	quicker
quieter	older	kinder	brighter	higher
later	calmer	deeper	prouder	lower
sweeter	stronger	sharper	stricter	clumsier

-able (capable of; likely to; tending to)

washable	bendable	readable	workable	moveable
loveable	solvable	fixable	peaceable	mixable
breakable	suitable	curable	changeable	teachable
payable	treatable	learnable	changeable	valuable
adjustable	achievable	adorable	presentable	predictable
reasonable	questionable	honorable	favorable	agreeable
comfortable	employable	noticeable	manageable	preventable
punishable	exchangeable	avoidable	enjoyable	excusable
excitable	supportable	serviceable	respectable	perishable
returnable	invaluable	remarkable	chargeable	available
repairable	unnoticeable	disagreeable	considerable	durable
allowable	justifiable	knowledgeable	acceptable	deliverable
forgettable	identifiable	indisputable	inseparable	invaluable
preventable	adaptable	untreatable	attainable	

-ible (capable of; likely to; tending to)

sensible	visible	possible	terrible	tangible
edible	credible	audible	forcible	feasible
defensible	detectible	reducible	digestible	collapsible
collectible	convertible	impossible	expressible	destructible
constructible	suggestible	accessible	digestible	reversible
transmissible	impossible	irreversible	plausible	indefensible

-ness (condition of; state or quality of being)

thickness	weakness	madness	sickness	quickness
paleness	goodness	wellness	illness	darkness
kindness	blindness	calmness	smoothness	dimness

softness	likeness	neatness	newness	brightness
faintness	greatness	freshness	fairness	sadness
gentleness	cleverness	wilderness	happiness	foolishness
bitterness	laziness	thankfulness	usefulness	playfulness
alertness	unhappiness	clumsiness	bitterness	forgiveness

-ment (the product or result of; the means of; the result of)

placement	vestment	statement	basement	treatment
pavement	ointment	parchment	figment	torment
easement	payment	abatement	detachment	deployment
installment	argument	experiment	equipment	filament
adornment	escarpment	engagement	enforcement	amazement
complement	government	excitement	supplement	ornament
employment	agreement	replacement	announcement	refreshment
punishment	enjoyment	enrichment	endorsement	banishment
adjustment	fulfillment	astonishment	development	appointment
confinement	document	enticement	amusement	achievement
settlement	contentment	environment	advertisement	requirement
apartment	commitment	assignment	sacrament	alignment
nourishment	parliament	assortment	disbursement	containment
astonishment	compliment	retirement	tournament	testament
embarrassment	allotment	displacement	encampment	amusement

-ive -ative -tive (having a tendency to; having nature, character or quality of)

massive	motive	passive	captive	festive
expensive	offensive	descriptive	expansive	attentive
detective	supportive	impressive	suggestive	directive
relative	protective	elective	informative	defensive
negative	aggressive	effective	positive	affirmative

| corrective | restrictive | combative | tentative | creative |
| conservative | sensitive | alternative | representative | ineffective |

-ful (full of) *note that the -ful suffix is spelled with only one l

fruitful	gainful	frightful	gleeful	handful
hopeful	armful	useful	playful	painful
harmful	careful	helpful	thankful	truthful
faithful	fearful	joyful	peaceful	dreadful
armful	skilful	watchful	cheerful	youthful
restful	wasteful	mindful	forceful	mouthful
grateful	cupful	hateful	trustful	blissful
frightful	prideful	flavorful	colorful	forgetful
wonderful	powerful	delightful	meaningful	merciful
sorrowful	suspenseful	successful	prayerful	respectful
delightful	plentiful	disgraceful	resentful	unfaithful
unmindful	neglectful	eventful	disrespectful	

-less (without)

sleepless	needless	timeless	pointless	baseless
aimless	flawless	soundless	tasteless	thornless
wordless	voiceless	stainless	boneless	classless
nameless	homeless	restless	hopeless	priceless
harmless	helpless	reckless	endless	worthless
faultless	useless	fruitless	countless	sightless
fearless	careless	speechless	painless	cloudless
meaningless	defenseless	blameless	ageless	childless
rainless	breathless	groundless	numberless	irregardless
sleeveless	sugarless	noiseless	carelessly	needlessly

-est (superlative degree of adjective)

hardest	strongest	tallest	shortest	neatest
loudest	fastest	quickest	cleanest	smartest
softest	longest	darkest	neatest	tallest
wettest	brownest	deepest	smoothest	fondest
fastest	greatest	softest	nicest	widest
safest	quietest	farthest	coldest	slowest
rudest	wildest	coolest	oldest	cheapest
youngest	highest	largest	tightest	bounciest
cloudiest	craziest	earliest	friendliest	rockiest

Writing/Spelling Words: Write words from each suffix group.

Reading Multisyllable Words Lesson 6: Practice

This lesson provides additional direct instruction and practice with multisyllable words. Remember practicing how to handle these multisyllable words greatly improves your reading. I will add a light pencil mark if you need help breaking a word apart.

*As the student reads, have a pencil ready and make slash marks to indicate syllable breaks *only* if and when the student needs assistance with a word. If necessary, help with pronunciation and then have child re-read the word with correct pronunciation.

Practice with mixed 2 and 3 syllable words

evergreen	notice	reject	neglect	victory
refrain	contain	receive	complete	electric
inspect	extend	entrance	hundred	develop
softly	frequent	included	celebrate	testify
understand	suddenly	behind	remember	anything
around	number	between	almost	inside
surface	consider	himself	learning	remotely
outside	always	careful	became	prevent

morning	sentence	laptop	behind	problem
complete	concrete	terminate	terminal	purpose
capital	hostage	freedom	entrance	adequate
disinfect	reflect	calculate	hesitate	vitamin
hospital	simplify	whatever	capital	carnival
tornado	circulate	relative	sediment	pattern
argument	adhesive	president	victory	circulate
dedicate	accident	explode	discount	enormous
prudent	excellent	proclaim	increase	insist
endure	general	introduce	combine	careful
devastate	electron	obligate	expansive	captive
obsolete	documents	destiny	determine	discarded
disappoint	average	native	primitive	inspecting
similar	unfriendly	vintage	yearly	indicate
graphic	flavor	fantastic	mushroom	confront
confirm	confine	conflict	baptize	amplify
abrasive	observe	pelican	secretive	temper
obstacle	complain	compensate	complex	camera
agenda	expensive	exploring	helplessness	charcoal
lumber	multiple	objective	sensitive	vertical
chapter	finance	artist	artistic	appear
appointment	addictive	envelope	leather	corrupt
accomplish	accident	constructed	diminish	dishonest
displacement	document	enrichment	entertain	exceed
exclusive	extreme	internet	fascinate	festival
forbid	forecast	horizon	pretend	difficult
gentleman	handful	fragile	frustrate	confirm

inspector	history	internal	narrow	element
investment	isolate	justify	lightning	monitor
canopy	minister	minimize	incentive	introduce
medium	dedicate	incomplete	recorded	replenish
forbidden	assignment	wonderful	interrupt	victory
continue	centipede	adequate	carpenter	harmony
orphanage	tornado	circumstance	remote	dentist
hurricane	illustrate	sacrifice	inhabited	hospital
statistic	adjustment	extend	forbidden	classical
satisfy	fearfully	refueling	ownership	repaired
proceeding	generally	disturbed	distribute	rewarding
converted	virus	sheltered	excitement	excited
exciting	monument	delighted	replaced	professor
replacement	internal	freedom	balance	disconnect
respectful	minimal	benefit	vitamins	mineral
difference	different	differing	related	exclusive

Practice with 4 & 5 syllable words

emergency	accumulate	ordinary	particular	identify
centimeter	certificate	humanity	intensify	considerable
capitalism	personality	confidently	academic	consequently
development	disconnecting	disadvantage	affirmative	fertilizer
enormously	universal	administer	vocabulary	equivalent
apparently	replenishing	indirectly	participate	consolidate
considering	successfully	fundamental	permanently	unhappiness
independence	indestructible	accomplishment	formative	increasingly
environment	disappointment	unexpected	elementary	understanding

Writing/Spelling Words: Write some of the listed words.

Reading Multisyllable Words Lesson 7: /shun/ Suffixes
- tion -sion -cian -cion

These special /shun/ suffixes are found in the second or subsequent syllable of a multisyllable word. These suffixes mean the action or process of, a condition or state of being, or result of. There are 4 ways to spell the /shun/ ending of a multisyllable word; -tion, -sion , -cian, and -cion. By far, the most common spelling for the /shun/ suffix is -tion. The -sion is the alternate spelling. The use of -tion or -sion is often determined by the spelling of the root word (For example for direct--direction, vacate--vacation, tense--tension, confess-confession). The --cion spelling is used for an occupation such as electrician. The unexpected -cion suffix is rarely used.

***As the student reads, have a pencil ready and make slash marks to indicate syllable breaks *only* if and when the student needs assistance with a word. If necessary, help with pronunciation and then have child re-read the word with correct pronunciation.

-tion (this is the most frequently encountered /shun/ ending)

nation	traction	station	motion	notion
action	option	function	portion	section
lotion	ration	portion	caution	junction
fraction	fiction	edition	flotation	question
rational	national	infection	subtraction	exception
adoption	eviction	eruption	fraction	solution
donation	hydration	vacation	relation	deletion
correction	convention	emotion	inspection	transition
direction	reaction	addition	prescription	invention
emotion	vibration	ignition	tuition	duration
intention	election	tradition	foundation	attraction
condition	affection	instruction	migration	attention
reflection	completion	tradition	promotion	location
position	formation	collection	digestion	construction
destruction	injection	vocation	objection	protection
rotation	suggestion	pollution	selection	projection
expedition	expectation	fascination	conversation	aggravation
obligation	organization	circulation	abbreviation	orientation
isolation	adaptation	redirection	observation	condensation

297

federation	application	institution	installation	identification
occupation	inspiration	confrontation	intuition	explanation
confirmation	investigation	activation	condensation	ammunition
contradiction	invitation	observation	illustration	intervention
saturation	recreation	preparation	conversation	population
inflation	plantation	translation	agitation	amputation
capitalization	concentration	conformation	contemplation	frustration
celebration	communication	decoration	operation	violation
salvation	starvation	situation	production	international
filtration	sanitation	inception	litigation	violation
allocation	notification	consideration	delegation	consolidation

-sion (this is the alternate spelling of /shun/ or /zhun/)

vision	dispersion	confession	aversion	mission
aggression	occasion	explosion	conversion	pension
confusion	expansion	invasion	version	omission
inversion	expression	depression	admission	division
extension	permission	collision	delusion	abrasion
dimension	suspension	decision	transgression	pension
tension	illusion	intermission	transmission	confession
confusion	erosion	explosion	decision	pension
passion	session	compassion	television	adhesion
procession	submission	conclusion	succession	transfusion

-cian (this /shun/ ending is used for an occupation)

electrician	magician	musician	physician	politician
technician	pediatrician	mathematician		

-cion (this 'unexpected' spelling of /shun/ is rarely used)

suspicion   coercion

Writing/Spelling Words: Write some of the listed words for each group.

298

Reading Multisyllable Words Lesson 8: Other "Special" Endings

*As the student reads, have a pencil ready and make slash marks to indicate syllable breaks *only* if and when the student needs assistance with a word. If necessary, help with pronunciation and then have child re-read the word with correct pronunciation.

There are 2 ways to spell the /shul/ ending of multisyllable words; -cial or -tial. Once again the root word usually determines the spelling of the ending (race--racial   part--partial   face---facial finance--financial)

-cial and -tial

special	artificial	facial	financial	social
racial	glacial	commercial	official	superficial
beneficial	crucial	partial	nuptial	potential
glacial	judicial	provincial	sacrificial	unofficial

There are 2 ways to spell /shus/ ending of multisyllable words; -tious -cious

-tious and -cious

cautious	infectious	contentious	nutritious	ambitious
fictitious	atrocious	audacious	spacious	vicious
ferocious	conscious	gracious	delicious	suspicious
precious	pretentious			

The /zhur/ ending of multisyllable word is spelled - sure.

measure	pleasure	treasure	leisure	closure

The /chur/ ending of multisyllable words is spelled -ture.

fracture	picture	nature	sculpture	future
mixture	overture	feature	denture	fixture
moisture	scripture	creature	culture	capture
posture	structure	texture	lecture	pasture
feature	departure	denture	mature	torture
vulture	indenture	recapture	signature	aperture
adventure	agriculture	horticulture	furniture	

Writing/Spelling Words: Write some of the listed words from each group.

Reading Multisyllable Words Lesson 9: Practice

This lesson provides additional direct instruction and practice handling multisyllable words.
**As the student reads, have a pencil ready and make slash marks to indicate syllable breaks *only* if and when the student needs assistance with a word. If necessary, help with pronunciation and then have child re-read the word with correct pronunciation.

upset	amazing	wonderful	article	prepare
outline	direct	passive	interested	destroy
transform	nearly	distant	exceed	exclusive
understand	between	around	important	discover
almost	several	surface	within	sentence
simple	different	another	himself	outside
always	usually	possible	however	became
example	together	today	behind	second
recently	restore	working	believe	flexible
distress	shipment	number	message	litter
connect	cancel	explore	successful	advantage
conversation	similar	events	expands	rapidly
testing	destroy	standards	students	however
requirement	agreement	processing	improved	normal
missing	debate	according	appear	shortcut
increase	completed	address	displace	request
report	multiple	intercept	largest	support
provide	defending	system	crackers	represent
parents	interview	fighting	federal	assessment
nationwide	lifestyle	balanced	contributed	electrical
combination	involved	another	reported	develop
decided	winter	eliminate	ensure	offered
alternative	member	district	responsible	contract

vending	existing	published	triple	canceled
section	delayed	southern	bitter	arctic
window	several	concerned	searched	anybody
halted	imports	expected	feeding	promise
located	another	infected	problem	assume
remain	computer	history	options	delay
presented	placement	heater	weekend	salad
several	remark	announce	entire	transfer
consider	powerful	vicinity	money	member
northern	hospital	corrupt	standoff	suspect
undercover	outside	investigate	department	protest
reserve	rewritten	disturb	conflicts	assume
doctor	away	office	faded	trouble
return	available	temporary	waiting	better
decorate	uncommon	accept	compare	updated
identify	interview	aimed	preview	demand
discuss	programs	disputed	increase	mistrust
according	unlikely	interest	finalize	return
dental	urgent	searching	difficult	principle
hardship	alter	dislike	certainly	practice
snowpack	percent	operated	assist	several
feeling	progress	reverse	deployment	unfair
actions	compete	adding	appoint	compromise
again	duration	leaving	expanding	maintains
conflict	restrict	repaint	coldest	average
driven	jackets	allowed	alert	inflame
everything	predict	prevent	constrict	inhale

clinic	replace	sudden	episode	component
infect	direct	secure	afford	policy
listen	twenty	afraid	enter	inside
wonder	material	daily	deliver	request
reward	product	thrifty	obligate	happened
monument	explain	infested	program	consult
shortest	external	camera	complete	recommend
release	become	focus	correct	select
continue	indicate	display	subject	confirm
enter	agreed	motion	activity	classroom
divide	specific	indirect	darkness	breaking
notice	practice	throughout	triple	powered
describe	basket	attention	example	border
purchase	supplies	affection	begins	details
establish	obvious	property	expansive	renewal
worshipped	traditions	government	descendents	answered
fortunately	enormous	frightening	miracle	craftsmen
considered	destroyed	convinced	mountains	completely
conquered	disgusting	unmerciful	tranquility	subpolar
explanations	peaceful	approaching	senator	conversion
introduction	elementary	civilization	victorious	triumphantly
dictator	impossible	settlements	retreated	unfaithful
servant	invaluable	invention	property	dangerously
intensity	experienced	opportunity	endurance	individuals
unexpected	challenging	approaching	supervisor	resistant
meanwhile	demonstrate	frequently	achievement	successfully

302

Reading Multisyllable Words Lesson 10: Practice

This lesson provides additional direct instruction and practice handling multisyllable words.
**As the student reads, have a pencil ready and make slash marks to indicate syllable breaks *only* if and when the student needs assistance with a word. If necessary, help with pronunciation and then have child re-read the word with correct pronunciation

extending	entrance	oversee	maintain	distress
flexible	discipline	persistent	attacking	splendid
activity	speculated	prospective	shipment	excitement
purchase	disappoint	cultivated	perfectly	different
afternoon	persistent	discovered	ownership	difficult
observe	properly	equipment	information	unexpected
underneath	beneath	around	number	several
almost	understand	suddenly	morning	another
complete	common	voyage	nothing	careful
without	together	remember	everyone	treacherous
between	learning	flexible	exploring	covered
thousand	combined	literally	deepest	planet
countless	discover	certain	remaining	trusted
sometimes	confident	insult	careful	establish
underwater	farthest	predictable	finished	clockwise
surrounded	consisting	landscape	transmit	modify
frantic	provided	difficult	comforting	internet
attach	challenge	dangerous	improving	remembering
recently	exclusive	protect	wonderful	gathering
responsible	property	containing	participate	leadership
overcast	blindfold	unselfish	investment	enjoyment
support	continue	division	concentrate	appropriate
encountering	competent	ultimately	untimely	researcher

303

determine	overheard	troublesome	creative	wisdom
universal	corrective	foundation	meaningful	avoiding
handling	practice	practical	majority	effectively
automatic	developing	condition	advocate	unfamiliar
successful	sentence	realize	classroom	existing
extensive	inappropriate	centralize	illustrate	announcing
everything	possibility	requirement	attendance	absolutely
ignorant	indicator	moment	monument	inclination
analysis	contradict	internal	consequence	progress
publisher	consultant	segments	percentage	assessment
individual	fluently	informative	acquire	mastered
increasing	performance	introducing	difficulty	manipulate
subtract	substitute	activities	towards	undergoing
processing	probability	network	particular	frequent
ordering	mistakes	department	comments	perfection
commentary	workout	organization	instructing	computer
antelope	detection	pronounced	leaving	subscribe
nutrition	escape	scraping	certificate	waterproof
difference	dependable	opportunity	average	accomplish
following	participate	community	commute	processing
donated	anywhere	remember	promptly	following
talented	reflection	afternoon	delivering	monitoring
arrangement	blessings	deflect	inspect	introduce
available	abolish	progress	highlights	emergency
experiment	belong	prescribe	decision	expected
marketed	advertise	increased	restriction	annoyance
respected	witness	dexterity	description	continued

Reading Multisyllable Words Lesson 11: Practice

This lesson provides additional direct instruction and practice handling multisyllable words.
**As the student reads, have a pencil ready and make slash marks to indicate syllable breaks *only* if and when the student needs assistance with a word. If necessary, help with pronunciation and then have child re-read the word with correct pronunciation.

transformed	behavior	predicted	remarkable	alongside
comparative	incident	commander	evacuation	consolidate
expected	narrowly	boundary	legislation	establish
connecting	engineer	responsible	construction	resident
tropical	vertical	confident	uncertain	platforms
documenting	respiratory	security	furthermore	moderate
necessary	interaction	certainty	organized	renovate
military	historical	reasonable	comprehension	incompetent
ointment	conversion	obligation	memories	injustice
fundamental	connections	prehistoric	dramatic	gentleness
amusement	destructive	majority	dedicate	principal
discovery	excitement	humorous	imaginary	sustained
elegant	capitalize	imperfect	ungracious	uniform
plastic	faithfulness	destruction	rumble	recognized
reconstruct	distant	unpublished	background	improperly
disgraceful	foreshadow	prearrange	incompatible	dealing
exchangeable	disqualify	unbelieving	irrelevant	underground
suggestible	ineffective	resharpen	independent	punishment
unadjusted	quarterly	preliminary	forerunner	interchange
avoidable	forgetful	countless	leadership	unluckily
encouraged	antibacterial	decrease	inspiration	supervisor
underestimate	disagreeable	usefulness	retirement	withdrew
meaningless	friendliest	primitive	sensitive	reformat

disrespectful	appointment	interest	managing	customize
boundless	creating	remarkable	documents	transporting
erosion	balanced	mineral	community	intensity
viewing	accomplished	navigating	behavior	security
expedition	experienced	visual	evacuation	troubleshoot
preview	assemble	renegade	searched	productive
moderate	acquainted	multimedia	increased	urgently
technology	inexperienced	treacherous	international	incorrect
updates	multiple	velocity	underline	multiple
obligation	password	reliable	highlight	encouraged
alongside	digital	harness	connection	endurance
element	desirable	mixture	dissolve	confusion
delivers	performance	automatic	dependability	advanced
streamlined	frequently	returning	throughout	hazardous
progress	systems	desktop	warnings	professional
download	noticed	retailer	homemade	broadcasts
abilities	collections	network	scanner	independence
confusion	biologic	fundamental	security	reference
section	selection	subdivided	evaporate	identifies
preview	parallel	substances	chemicals	ingredient
inactive	destructive	pollinate	percent	predictably
vertebrate	enclosed	reusable	interaction	invention
submerse	volunteer	overtake	hurricane	granite
durable	contrasting	sediment	computer	compound
properties	rotation	backup	unbalanced	decentralize
generate	friction	unequal	applying	bacteria
promptly	reinforce	earthquake	groundwater	forecast

Reading Multisyllable Words Lesson 12: Continued Practice

It is important to continue *guided* practice with multisyllable words until the student has mastered this complex skill. Repeated practice with multisyllable words helps the student not only build fluency on specific words but also develop awareness and knowledge of the common patterns in our language that will help him master reading other multisyllable words. The following are a few ideas for continued practice of multisyllable words:

Reading Word Lists: Continued practice with reading lists of multisyllable words helps develop skills. Once again word lists are effective because they force the student to use proper careful processing. They intentionally train the student to look carefully at all sounds. The student is not able to glance at portion of the word and 'guess' based on context. Word lists are a wonderful teaching tool for developing skills. Of course after the student has developed necessary skills, word lists are no longer necessary.

Reading Dictionary Entries: Another way to practice handling multisyllable words is to grab a dictionary and quickly read down the entries in the dictionary pages. The words already have the syllable breaks shown. This is not reading the entire dictionary but using the dictionary entries as an easily accessible list for practice reading multisyllable words. Some of the school/junior dictionaries (not young children editions) are preferable as the print is easier to see and also they contain fewer unusual words than a collegiate dictionary. Reading word lists with syllable breaks shown gives practice "seeing" the appropriate syllables in words and helps develop knowledge and recognition of common patterns.

Marking the syllable breaks when necessary as the student reads: Continue guided practice with reading multisyllable words. Use a combination of word lists and any printed text that contains multisyllable words. It is advantageous to have the student read material that you can write on (a copied page, newspaper, magazine or book that you can write on). As the student reads, you can help him by making light pencil marks or slashes in the appropriate break *when* he needs help seeing the syllables. Or have him make his own pencil marks at the appropriate breaks when needed. Remember with guided reading it is important to have the student read the word correctly. Stop the student if he makes an error. If the child struggles with a word, indicate the syllable breaks for him with a pencil and have the student re-read the word. As he child practices, the syllable breaks will become automatic and you will no longer need to indicate these with pencil slashes. The pencil marks are an intermediate step to assist learning how to read the multisyllable words by breaking them into appropriate parts.

Writing/spelling multisyllable words: As discussed earlier, the process of having students hear a multisyllable word and then write the word phonetically is a highly effective technique for learning to read multisyllable words. Remember this is an exercise in handling multisyllable words not a spelling test. Teach the student and make sure he is writing the words phonetically. If a student has difficulty with a specific multisyllable word, have the student write that word 5 to 10 times saying the sounds by syllable as he writes. This word writing helps build fluency on specific words.

Review New Multisyllable Words Before Reading a Passage: Another suggestion to help a student improve their handling of multisyllable words in their reading is to preview the new multisyllable words in isolation before reading the passage. Before the student reads a new chapter, go through the text and list the new vocabulary and more difficult multisyllable words. Have the student practice reading and writing these words in isolation before he tackles the entire passage. By practicing the new words in isolation ahead of time, the child will be better prepared to read and comprehend the chapter. In addition to building fluency in reading multisyllable words, this method of previewing new words before reading text is also a terrific tool for improving vocabulary and enhancing reading comprehension.

Section 7: Instructions for Using Guided Reading to Improve Reading Skills

The validated research shows that guided out loud reading has significant beneficial impact on word recognition, fluency and comprehension across a range of grade levels.[11]

Guided reading is reading out loud to an adult, or other proficient reader, with feedback. This is NOT independent silent reading. The key part to the effectiveness in developing skills is to provide 'guidance' to the child. Do not confuse this beneficial teaching tool with various independent reading programs some of which are labeled 'guided reading'. Correction and instruction are the *essential* elements to helping a child learn and improve skills.

In order to achieve *significant* beneficial impact on word recognition, fluency and comprehension:
#1 The student must read out loud to an adult (or other proficient reader) and
#2 The adult must provide correction, feedback and instruction on specific skill development.

Guided reading benefits both good and struggling readers. In contrast, silent independent reading may *not* actually improve reading skills for beginning readers. Numerous studies show the best readers read the most and poor readers read the least. However, these studies are all correlational in nature and correlation does not imply causation. It may just be the good readers just choose to spend more time reading. Although it sounds like a good idea to have children read more alone, there is *no* research evidence that shows *independent silent reading* actually improves reading skills. Think about it. If poor readers are just sitting there flipping pages or struggling with the reading and making errors, their skills will not improve, no matter how much time they sit there. In contrast, *guided* oral reading instruction is proven to help students improve reading skills. This is NOT saying students should not read on their own, or that there are no benefits for children sitting there looking at books, or that students do not need to read more. Rather, it demonstrates *to improve skills*, particularly in learning or remediation stages, the student needs to read *out loud with feedback*. At more advanced levels, silent reading does improve the higher skills of fluency, vocabulary acquisition and comprehension.

Guided reading has significant beneficial effects on helping student's develop reading skills. It is one of the most effective tools not only to improve a student's fundamental reading skills but also to help the student develop higher level comprehension skills.

With guided reading you can directly help the student:
*   establish fundamental skills necessary for proficient reading
*   identify weaknesses and strengthen specific skills
*   improve attention to detail
*   build fluency
*   expand vocabulary knowledge
*   develop reading comprehension skills

PLUS guided reading is enjoyable! This is where you sit down with your student and read. Guided reading offers a wonderful opportunity to share the joy of reading with your student.

Specific Instructions for Conducting Guided Reading:
*   Conduct guided reading with the student a minimum of 20 minutes/day (more is better!).
*   The child must read out loud to you.
*   The parent/teacher/other proficient reader must be looking at the printed text and providing immediate feedback. This careful monitoring is particularly important in the learning and remedial stages. You MUST be looking at exactly what the student is reading so you can make immediate corrections. This careful monitoring of each word is necessary

---

[11] National Reading Panel's "Teaching Children to Read" Summary Report
www.nationalreadingpanel.org/publications/summary.htm

until the student has become skilled at accurate decoding. (The rule of thumb is when the student makes no more than 2 errors per page). Either sit directly next to the student where you can both see the print OR make a copy of the material so you can follow along. Having a separate copy is sometimes preferred if you are tutoring other students or if the student does not appreciate someone 'reading over their shoulder'.

- Require the child to read carefully. Teach the student to look carefully at the words instead of rushing through with 'fast & careless' reading. Stopping the student at every mistake is highly effective in slowing down the 'fast & careless' reading. Usually, the impatient students who like to 'rush' do not like to be stopped. Therefore, when you stop the student at every mistake he begins to read more carefully. Like anything else, the careful reading is a habit. Help the student develop good habits.

- Require complete accuracy in all reading. Stop the student all errors, no matter how 'minor' they may appear. This includes skipped words as well as any mistake on accurately reading a word. Stopping the errors is critical for helping students build necessary skills. With correction on errors, often all you need to do is tap the missed word with a pencil. This signals the student to 'look again'.
    o   If the student skips a word, tap the word he missed and have the student reread it.
    o   If the student reads a word inaccurately (says wrong word or misses detail of word) have him reread the word correctly. Point to the specific sound/error if necessary.
    o   Do not let any errors slip by, no matter how 'small'. Make sure the student pays close attention to all details.
    o   If the student uses the wrong choice/alternate sound, tell him something similar to "Good try, however this word uses the __ sound" (For example if the word was 'bestow' and the student uses the /ow/ sound for 'ow' instead of the correct /oa/ sound). Have the student re-read the word applying the correct sound.

- The student needs to correct their mistake. Frequently the student has the skill to accurately read the word but either he was not paying attention or slipped back into a previous incorrect strategy (such as word guessing or visual 'whole word' processing). Often by 'looking again' the student uses the correct process and is able to accurately read the word.

- If the student is lacking a skill, you need to teach him that skill so he is able to accurately read the word. Examples:
    o   If the student does not know the correct sound (lacks knowledge of a sound within the word) tell him the sound and then have them read the word to you. This is not 'telling' the student the entire word where all he needs to do is orally repeat the word. In contrast, this is only giving the student the knowledge he is missing and then requiring him to apply this to his reading. This technique can also be used when student comes across code he has not yet learned For example reading 'vacation' before the student has learned 'tion'=/shun/ you would tell them something similar to "the 'tion' partner letters have the /shun/ sound..try sounding that out again". In addition, if the student misses a sound several times you know the student needs to practice that specific sound in isolation so it becomes automatic
    o   Focus on building necessary skill. Help the student develop necessary skills. For example often students who have previously learned phonetically incorrect 'consonant clusters' will add sounds when they are not present. (strap as stramp, clap as clamp, sting as string,) In this case you need to focus the student on looking carefully at the exact printed letters. You can say something similar to "look closely" and point at the specific sounds.

- Help the student with multisyllable words when necessary. Use a pencil to make light slash marks at the syllable breaks. If certain words are difficult, you can write these down for later practice in isolation. See Section 6 for specific instructions on handling multisyllable words.

- Help with proper pronunciation whenever necessary. New words, especially some of the multisyllable words with the 'lazy' schwa, pronunciation can be tricky. The decoding is correct but the word is mispronounced. By all means help the student learn the correct pronunciation. Tell the student how the word is pronounced. Say something similar to "Good try, that was close, we actually pronounce the word _____". Have him repeat the word and then reread it with correct pronunciation while looking at the letters.

- Require physical tracking (with finger, pencil or other pointer) when reading UNTIL the student no longer makes tracking errors. If the student is making *any* tracking errors or whole word errors, be sure the child continues to physically track. Once again this kinetic motion helps direct correct processing of each letter/sound. The tracking also helps focus the student on the details of the word and improves attention to detail.

- Develop vocabulary as the student reads. When appropriate, stop the student at new words. If he does not understand the word, explain what the word means. Then have the student re-read the sentence so he will understand it. See Section 10 for more details on developing vocabulary.

- Work on developing specific comprehension skills. This often involves questions and discussing the material as the student reads along. The depth of comprehension skills increases as the student becomes older and their skills advance. Beginning comprehension is having the student simply pay attention to what he is reading. The higher level comprehension skills have the student thinking about deeper questions such as 'why did this happen', and inferring 'what do I think this means'. See Section 9 on Developing Reading Comprehension for more detailed instructions.

Monitor the student's progress and modify the instruction to meet the student's needs. When decoding skills improve/advance to the point where he makes very few errors/page, careful attention to accurate decoding is no longer necessary and guided reading can shift primarily to the higher level skills. At this point, you no longer have to monitor each and every word. Instead you primarily focus on the vocabulary and reading comprehension skills. This level of guided reading where you shift from the 'technical skills' of decoding to the content of what you are reading is enjoyable.

Other tips and suggestions:

- If the student is 'skipping lines' as he reads or frequently losing his place, have the student use a bookmark or index card to hold under the line. The student uses the index card to mark the line he is reading. This is especially helpful in books with small print where it is easier to accidentally miss lines.

- If the student reads 'run on' sentences help him learn to make the appropriate pause at the end of sentences. Have the student take a breath at each period. If necessary, place your pencil on or tap the period to remind the student to pause. While this intentional 'stop' and conscious breath slightly exaggerates the needed pause, it helps the child begin to notice and react properly to periods. Guided reading of text is where the student develops this necessary skill of appropriate pauses and inflection.

- Help the student practice proper inflection and expression as part of the guided reading. Fiction is often the easiest material to help the student practice and develop skills in appropriate expression. Demonstrating and encouraging expressive reading helps students develop these skills. If the student reads a passage in a flat monotone voice, simply ask him to reread it with expression.

- Use high interest books for the guided reading. Have the student pick out a book that interests him or her. The high interest books help make the guided reading time something to look forward to. There is nothing like an engaging story or a fascinating subject to keep the student excited about the guided reading time.

- Increase the enjoyment by reading the book together. Share the reading by alternating chapters or pages. Not only is this shared reading enjoyable, it is useful in both demonstrating and building enthusiasm for reading.

- While you should definitely incorporate 'fun' 'exciting' reading of the students choice, some of the guided reading can and should be done with the students classroom reading material. This ability to 'kill two birds with one stone' of directly developing reading skills while studying for the next day's science test is helpful on the busy nights. The use of classroom reading material is also particularly useful with students in a classroom pullout situation. The guided reading of classroom material, whether it be the history textbook or the science unit not only directly develop reading skills but also helps the student gain knowledge in other subjects. From a time efficiency standpoint, many students prefer to do some guided reading with classroom material, especially if they have to read it anyways. It is also important to do some guided reading with textbooks so you can help the student develop comprehension skills with the textbook format.

Section 8: Building Fluency

What is fluency?

Fluency is 'fast' or 'automatic' reading. Fluent readers are able to read quickly and accurately without effort. By appearances, the student instantly recognizes words and reads the 'fast way' without slowly sounding out. It seems by simply 'knowing' the words the student is able to read easily and quickly.

We know fluency is critical to reading comprehension and skilled reading. However, it is important to realize appearances do **not** reveal the actual process involved in fluent reading. To help students become fluent readers, we need to learn specifically about the actual process of fluent reading and how fluent reading is developed. The necessary answers lie in the amazing field modern neuroscience.

The remarkable advances in neural imaging allow scientists to look closely at the process of fluent reading. Researchers have learned and discovered much about the neural processes involved with fluent reading and how fluent reading is developed. Neuroscientists learned fluent reading uses a 'fast reading area' different from the 'slow' phonologic processing pathways used by beginning readers. Fluent reading uses a neural 'expressway' to process the word. With fluent reading, a quick look at the word activates a stored neural model. This neural model allows not only 'fast' reading but also activates correct pronunciation and understanding of the word. These 'fast' pathways allow rapid, effortless reading.

How is fluency developed?

Importantly, neuroscientists are learning how fluency is developed. Fluent reading is established after the individual reads the word at least four times using accurate phonologic processing (slow accurate sounding out). Fluency is build word by word and entirely dependent on repeated, accurate, slow sounding out of the specific word. Fluency is not established by 'memorizing' what words look like but rather by developing correct neural-phonologic models of the word. Repeated accurate phonologic processing is essential for developing fluency. In simplified terms, the repeated accurate phonologic processing literally engraves a neural model of the word. This neural model is then is stored in the 'fast reading area' available for rapid retrieval. An individual's storehouse of fluent 'fast' words is built word by word and is dependent on repeated accurate print to sound (phonologic) processing.

Neuroscientists also discovered dyslexic readers do not develop these fluent or 'fast reading' pathways. Struggling readers do not convert print to sound. Because they don't sound out words, the neural phonologic 'engraving' of the word is never made and fluent reading is not developed. This is why struggling readers can see a word hundreds of times and never develop fluency on that word. Fluency is completely dependent on phonologic processing. Without express reading pathways, reading remains slow and laborious. These children may work hard and eventually learn to read accurately but they will not achieve the quick and almost 'effortless' process of skilled reading.

In summary, 'fast' or fluent reading is different than slow sounding out. However, this rapid effortless reading is entirely dependent on initial phonologic processing. Individuals build fluency one word at a time by repeatedly sounding out individual words using correct phonologic processing pathways. Phonologic processing is key to developing fluency.

How do I help a student become a fluent reader?

The critical information to keep in mind for effective reading instruction is fluency or effortless 'fast' reading is developed word-by-word based on repeated accurate phonologic processing of specific words. To develop fluency, the child FIRST has to be reading by correct, accurate phonologic processing. The child must be 'sounding out' the words correctly. THEN, the student needs to build their storehouse of fluent or 'fast' words by repeated accurate phonological processing of individual words. This expansion of fluent reading requires practice repeatedly reading individual words.

311

To help a student develop fluency:

- First you must ensure the student is **reading using proficient phonologic processing pathways.** The best way to ensure your student is reading with phonologic pathways is to teach him with an **effective direct systematic phonics program**. If the student is NOT using phonologic neural processing pathways to convert print to sound, he will be unable to develop the neural 'expressway' of fluent reading. The initial phonologic processing or 'slow sounding out' is essential to developing fluency.

- Teach the student the **complete phonetic code** (all the vowel combinations, r-controlled vowel combinations and other complexities). This gives the student the necessary knowledge to process print to sound proficiently and form accurate phonologic models of the word. If their code is incomplete the student may not be processing the word accurately. Knowledge of the complete phonetic code is a necessary subskill of correct phonologic processing.

- Teach the student to pay **attention to details** as he reads. The details are critical to form accurate neural models of the word.

- Remember fluency is built one word at a time based on repeated phonologic reading. This requires repeated accurate reading. **Practice is essential**! Repeated practice reading correctly builds a student's 'storehouse' of 'fast reader neural models'. With practice the student adds word-by-word to their fluency. Obviously, the more the student reads the more words he will repeatedly read correctly and the quicker he will build fluency. Because fluency is build word-by-word, students do not develop fluency overnight.

- After fundamental skills are established, **guided oral reading** is the single most effective way to help your student develop and build fluency. The guided reading has significant positive impact on reading skills across all age and reading levels. Guided reading works! Note: Guided reading is NOT the same as silent independent reading. With guided reading, the student reads out loud to an adult *with* feedback and correction.

- After the child has advanced to skilled reading, the time the child spends silent reading continues to add to and build fluency. The more **time spent reading** the better. This is where the 'good readers' spend significant amounts of time reading!

- Another highly effective tool for building fluency on individual words is phonologic writing/spelling of specific words. This is **spelling/writing the word by sound** (writing down as you say the sounds not spelling by letter name). For this to be effective in developing fluency, the student must repeatedly print the word by sound. Have the student print the word 5 to 10 times, saying the sounds as he prints. Then have the student read the word a few times paying careful attention to the specific print=sound relationship. The repeated writing by sound helps the student form the 'fast' neural model of the word necessary for fluency on the specific word.

Remember, fluency is build word-by-word and entirely dependent on repeated, accurate phonologic processing of the specific word. Fluency is *not* established by visually 'memorizing' what words look like but rather by developing correct neural-phonologic models of the word. **Repeated accurate phonologic processing is essential for developing fluency and practice reading is essential for expanding fluency.**

Section 9: Developing Reading Comprehension Skills

Overview of Reading Comprehension:

Comprehension or acquiring meaning from the text is a complex higher level skill. Obviously, comprehension is critically important to the development of a student's reading. Comprehension is an active process that requires an intentional and thoughtful interaction between the reader and the text. Vocabulary development is critical to comprehension.

While readers acquire some comprehension strategies informally, **explicit or formal instruction in the application of comprehension strategies has been shown to be highly effective in enhancing understanding** (from the Report of the National Reading Panel). In other words you *can* take specific actions to help a student develop comprehension skills.

Remember the student must *first* develop accurate phonological decoding skills and build fluency. This fluency that is critical to reading comprehension is accomplished word by word and is absolutely dependant on repeated accurate phonological processing. Comprehension strategies focus on teaching students to understand what they read NOT to build skills on how to read/decode. If the student struggles with accurate fluent decoding then comprehension will continue to be limited. Basically if decoding is not automatic and easy then the student has little energy left to devote to thinking about what he is reading. Remember, if the student has decoding difficulties you need to *first* establish the necessary fundamental decoding skills of proficient phonologic processing BEFORE you can develop the more advanced comprehension. This section addresses techniques for developing the higher level comprehension skills.

Specific Actions You CAN Use To Help Readers Develop Comprehension:

This summary gives specific techniques you can use to help students develop comprehension skills. These strategies will help a student think about, understand and remember what he is reading. These strategies are effective for non-impaired readers. The following reading comprehension strategies should be implemented as a part of the guided reading.

Overview material BEFORE starting to read: Use various techniques to focus the student on the material before he begins reading. Basically, you help the student think about the material before they start reading.

- Before the student begins reading, provide statements to direct the student toward what he will be reading. Quickly summarize previous text and overview the section/chapter the student is about to read. Make statements such as: "In the last chapter you already learned about ___. This chapter is going to discuss ___". For example: "The last chapter was on invertebrates, now you will be reading about vertebrates." or "You just finished learning about the Roman Empire. Now you are going to read about the fall of the Roman Empire". "You are continuing to learn about energy. This section discusses thermal or heat energy."

- Before the student starts reading, ask questions to help get the student on target. Ask questions such as: "What is this chapter about?" "What will this chapter discuss?" "What are you learning about now?" Make questions specific to the material such as: "Which region of the country does this chapter cover?" "What form of energy is this chapter discussing?"

- In non-fiction, preview the titles and headings of the sections before starting to read the chapter. Previewing the chapter outline is especially helpful with textbooks. This preview helps the student understand the overall intention of the chapter or section.

- Review key vocabulary before reading the chapter. Some textbooks highlight key words, and important vocabulary terms. Defining keywords before reading is especially critical with subject terminology. For example, knowing the definition of the term 'Axis Powers' is important before reading about WWII history. Knowing the difference between exothermic and endothermic reactions is key to understanding text discussions on chemical reactions. To comprehend basic physics of motion, students need to understand the difference between speed, velocity and acceleration.

- With fiction, you can summarize the previous chapters and ask the student to briefly review key events. Ask specific questions on the plot or key events to 'set the stage' for reading such as: "So what is going on in the story?", "What happened so far?" "Where are they at?"

- With fiction, in addition to having the student give you an overview of key events ask what he thinks may happen next. Ask questions along the lines of "What do you think will happen now?" Make questions as specific as possible: "How do you think Sarah will be able to help her grandmother?" "Do you think the old man will be able to land the fish?"

Help the student understand the structure and organization of writing: By recognizing important fundamentals about the structure and organization of writing, the student is better able to extract important material.

- Specifically point out the structure of paragraphs, sections and chapters. In informative writing most sections should have a main idea and supporting details. Most paragraphs have an opening, a middle and an end. The opening sentence usually outlines the main idea of the paragraph. The supporting points and details should be in the body of the paragraph and the concluding sentence at the end. Awareness of the structure of paragraphs, sections and chapters helps the student better understand material.

- Non-fiction can be organized differently. For example, stories usually contain a conflict with the typical plot structure of exposition, rising action, climax and conclusion or catastrophe. Awareness of elements including the point of view or voice the author uses to tell the story, situation, setting, and characterization all contribute to overall comprehension. Help the student understand key writing elements.

Help the Student Learn to Identify and Extract the Main Ideas: The ability to find, identify, extract and understand main ideas is critical to not just reading comprehension but to educational objectives. Much of the reading students do is to acquire specific information. Some students have high comprehension on fictional stories yet have difficulty extracting necessary information from textbooks and other non-fictional informational reading. These students need direct instruction on how to identify and extract necessary information. Many of the new textbooks contain a style of writing that many students need to learn how to read. The short paragraphs, numerous interruptions, interesting but irrelevant trivia, and tidbits of boxed information at various locations can sometimes make it more difficult to locate, identify and extract pertinent information. For example, if the student is reading a chapter on United States expansion, the photo of a grizzly bear and sentences about how Thomas Jefferson had a grizzly bear in a cage on the White House grounds may distract the student from the main point. For content comprehension, the student can't just relate the trivia of the grizzly bear in the cage. The student needs to understand Thomas Jefferson made the Louisiana Purchase and sent the Corps of Discovery expedition to explore this new territory. He needs to understand how Lewis and Clark mapped this new region and recorded information not just on many new plants and animals but also on the peoples that lived there. Help the student learn how to look for and identify the main idea both before reading and during the reading process.

- As discussed in the 'overview materials' techniques, introductory statements and questions can point the student in the right direction before he starts reading.

- Review the main headings and overall outline of the chapter.

- As the student reads, help him identify and focus on main ideas by asking specific questions. Stop the student at appropriate paragraphs or sections and ask targeted questions to direct the student to important information. "What was the Lewis and Clark expedition?" "What were the primary missions of the Corps of Discovery?" "What important information did Lewis and Clark gather during their expedition?" "Explain the process of oxidation?" "What happens in an exothermic chemical reaction and how is it different from an endothermic reaction?" "Why did the Greeks begin the first Olympic Games? "What weakened the Greek civilization and made is susceptible to defeat?" Ask specific questions to help the student identify and understand key concepts and learn how to focus on important information.

- By asking questions, you can help target the student toward the key concepts he does not recognize or understand. For example if you ask the student to explain complete metamorphosis and he gives you the answer 'a frog', then you would ask the student a follow up question such as "Yes, a frog is an example of an animal that undergoes complete metamorphosis, but can you explain the primary difference between complete and incomplete metamorphosis?" Do not 'give' the answers to the student, but rather help direct her toward locating and understanding the main ideas.

- If the student can not answer questions or is missing pertinent details, then have the student re-read the paragraph or section. Not only does this allow the student to find necessary information but it teaches the student the essential skill of looking back and re-reading text to find necessary information.

- Outlining can be a highly effective tool for helping students identify main points. Show the student how to make an outline. Outlining does not have to be detailed. Short bullet statements are often effective in identifying main ideas. The student can then orally explain the bullet points.

Stop or pause the student during the reading to think about and process the material. Directly encourage and develop the student's skills in processing and understanding text as he reads. These techniques help the student develop the interaction between the reader and the text that is important to comprehension. Encourage and develop skill in actively processing the material. Help the student think about what he is reading.

- Stop at appropriate paragraphs or sections and ask specific questions that make the student think about what he is reading. Once again design questions to help the student think about specific aspects of the text. Ask both direct informational as well as more advanced interpretative questions.

- As the student comes across unknown vocabulary or expressions, stop and see if he understands what they are reading. Explain or define the word or expression and then have the student re-read the paragraph or section. For example, the reader comes across the phrase "take the bull by the horns" make sure the child understands the phrase means "to tackle tough issues head on with direct action". The English language is full of many sayings and phrases that do not make sense if read literally. The student needs to not just read the phrase correctly but understand what that phrase means to comprehend the overall meaning of the text.

- Once again, if the student can not answer a question or is missing pertinent details, have him re-read the section.

- Begin helping the student develop the higher level processing skills of interpretation and inference. Ask both 'what do you think' and 'why do you think' type questions. The process of explaining "why" helps the student think through and back up their answers with reasoning.

Help Reader Learn to Summarize: Help the student learn to summarize material as he reads. In other words, teach the reader how to integrate all the various aspects of the material and give the 'nuts and bolts' of a short and quick summary of the text. This ability to summarize is a more advanced skill than simply pulling out the main points. Summarizing main points can be harder for some students because they need to understand the material well enough to be able to explain the key points in their own words.

- Have the student practice this essential skill by asking "What was that about?" or "How would you summarize that in your own words?" If the student is unable to 'pull out' and summarize important information, give guidance that teaches him how to do this. Sometimes students will remember small details but are unable to summarize the important points. Once again questions and discussions are effective in helping the student learn this important skill of understanding and summarizing important points.

Specifically Develop Vocabulary Knowledge: Vocabulary instruction leads to gains in comprehension. Please see Section 10 for specific techniques to expand vocabulary.

Develop Comprehension Monitoring: Self-monitoring is where the reader checks himself and recognizes if he understands the material. The goal is for the student to develop self awareness of his or her comprehension.

- The student needs to ask themselves at the end of each paragraph or section "Do I understand this material?". To develop this essential skill, have the student ask themselves out loud, "What was that about?" By asking and answering this question out loud, the student learns to check himself. The out loud self questioning is a temporary tool. When the student learns to automatically check and monitor their own comprehension, the out loud self questioning is no longer necessary.

- Another technique for developing self comprehension monitoring is for the student to generate questions about various aspects of the content. By coming up with their own key questions, it allows the child to review their understanding of the material. The student answers these questions himself or asks you the questions.

- If the student does not understand what he read, he needs to learn to go back on his own and re-read text. This self-directed 'going back' and re-reading is critical to comprehension. Be sure and compliment the student when you notice him going back on his own.

- Point out this self-monitoring of comprehension is a characteristic of skilled readers.

Use of Graphic Organizers: Various graphic representations of the material such as story maps, outlines and timelines can effectively enhance comprehension. The key with graphic organizers is to ensure these tools are carefully targeted to achieve comprehension goals and the tools are appropriate for the content areas.

- Maps are virtually mandatory when studying content areas dealing with geography. Maps are also critical in understanding history. For example: It is difficulty to understand the importance of the Panama Canal without looking at a map, and understanding the ancient Egyptian civilization is dependent on understanding the influence of the Nile river and the geography of the region.

- Timelines are a highly useful tool. The timelines allow students to 'see' the progression of events chronologically. Once again history is a prime candidate for timelines. The timelines are also useful in other subjects that relate to chronologic progression such as medicine, scientific discoveries, and advancement in technology.

- Sketches, illustrations, diagrams and other visual representations can be highly effective when they are properly applied. For example, sketches of the various landforms helps students define and understand geography terms. Diagrams are important in describing and understanding the physical structure and function of item such as atoms, cells, and life cycles.

- Story maps are a tool for visually outlining fiction.

- Outlining is a highly effective tool across a wide range of subjects and material context.

- Once again, all these tools need to be properly targeted to develop the necessary content objectives. It is important to realize that not all 'projects' or 'visual representations will enhance comprehension. For example spending time making a paper pirate ship mobile is unlikely to improve comprehension of 'Treasure Island'. Building a model of a pyramid out of sugar cubes is unlikely to help the student learn the importance of the ancient Egyptian civilization. Remember to target and focus graphic organizers to what the student needs to learn.

Cooperative Learning: Cooperative learning is where students learn and discuss material with others. Effectiveness of 'cooperative learning' strategies varies greatly. These cooperative learning strategies need to be properly applied and carefully monitored.

- Discussions guided or facilitated by a knowledgeable instructor are more effective than unguided discussions. Even if the instructor does not direct the details of the discussions, facilitation is important. Students who start off discussing their thoughts about "The Old Man and the Sea" can easily drift off into a series of unrelated fishing stories. Facilitation is important for keeping students on target.

- The open discussions between students are usually more appropriate for fictional text than for non-fictional informational reading. Students can learn from each other when discussing elements such as 'what do you think will happen? "Why did this character do this?" "Why do you think…" etc. These types of discussions can bring out elements of the story that the student had not previously thought of.

- Common sense dictates the effectiveness of these 'cooperative' discussion strategies with factual informational text. Obviously, it does not help students' comprehension if the 'cooperators' share incorrect or inaccurate information. Particular care and careful monitoring is essential so that uninformed students do not share misinformation with other students. Cooperative discussions among students often have limited benefit when students are learning new concepts and information. While question generation from students is helpful, the answers and factual information need to be provided by knowledgeable sources. In contrast, cooperative learning with knowledgeable individuals or subject experts can be highly beneficial. For example, if my son discusses military history with his grandfather the cooperative discussions provide incredible opportunities for expanding his comprehension and knowledge base. Obviously he would not achieve the same benefits discussing the topic with a buddy whose knowledge of WWII history was limited to a fictional TV show.

- Monitoring is always important with cooperative learning to ensure accurate information is shared and the students remain on target.

In summary, comprehension is the essential higher level skill of actually understanding the material being read. Obviously, comprehension is the goal of proficient reading. You can help students develop these critical comprehension skills with various direct instruction strategies. Most of these activities that develop comprehension skills can be effectively applied as a part of guided reading.

Section 10: Expanding Vocabulary Knowledge

Overview of Vocabulary Development:

As can be expected, vocabulary knowledge is critical to reading development. Vocabulary is beyond correct decoding. Vocabulary is understanding the meaning of the word. Expanding the student's knowledge bank of vocabulary words is important to comprehension. The greater the student's vocabulary the easier it is to make sense of and understand text. Vocabulary is generally related to understanding individual words where comprehension generally refers to understanding larger parts of the text. Vocabulary and overall comprehension are closely related.

Vocabulary knowledge is distinct from the skill of decoding print. A student can fully understand words that he is not able to read. For example a five year old has a much larger speaking and understanding vocabulary than a printed reading vocabulary. He may not be able to read the printed words 'gorilla', 'vacation' or 'chocolate' but knows exactly what the words mean. He has the necessary vocabulary knowledge even though he can't read the print. In contrast a student may be able to correctly decode a word perfectly and still now know what it means. This would be a vocabulary knowledge issue. Of course for comprehension, the student needs to both accurately decode the word *and* know what the word means.

Expanding a student's vocabulary knowledge is important to reading development. Vocabulary instruction leads to gains in comprehension (noted by the National Reading Panel). A comprehensive reading program needs to include vocabulary development. The student can learn vocabulary both incidentally and through direct instruction. Various techniques designed to directly build vocabulary are effective in expanding vocabulary knowledge and improving reading comprehension. Optimal learning occurs when vocabulary instruction involves a combination of different techniques.

Specific Actions You CAN Use To Help Readers Develop Vocabulary:

Vocabulary is enhanced by both direct instruction and incidental exposure. Techniques you can use to help your student expand their vocabulary knowledge include:

- Directly teach new vocabulary to the student. To maximize effectiveness the student should learn and practice new words both in isolation and in context. The student can practice the meaning of the words in isolation (word lists with definitions) and in context (using the word in a sentence). In other words, the old-school English teacher method of presenting a list of new vocabulary words and having students write both the full definition and writing a complete sentence using the word is highly effective in helping students learn new vocabulary. These direct methods of expanding vocabulary have beneficial impacts on reading comprehension.

- Highlight and define key words before having the student read a passage. Comprehension is improved when students to learn new vocabulary words before reading text. This strategy is especially beneficial with subject terminology that is critical for overall comprehension. Acquiring the vocabulary knowledge prior to reading the text enhances overall understanding of the material. (For example before reading a science chapter on energy, highlight and learn the meanings of kinetic energy, potential energy, thermal energy, conduction, convection and radiation.)

- As a part of guided reading, have the student stop if he does not know the meaning of the word. You can verbally explain the word and then have the student re-read the sentence. As the student reads, he will also 'figure out' the meaning of many new vocabulary words simply from context.

- Help the student learn to use a dictionary as a resource. You want to help the student learn how wonderful and informative a good dictionary is. The goal is to help the student to progress from the stage where he needs direct orders to 'go look it up' to where he voluntarily reaches for the dictionary to determine word meanings. Directly practice looking up new words in a dictionary.

- Help the student learn to notice new unknown vocabulary words. The student can either look up the word as he reads or can write down the word for later. It is helpful for the student keep a small notepad to record new words. The student can then look up and learn these unknown words at a later time. My daughter prefers the 'write down for later' method, because she does not have to stop reading a good book to look up a definition. To encourage the student, you can even come up with a system of rewarding a certain number of new vocabulary words.

- Repetition and multiple exposures to new vocabulary enhance vocabulary knowledge. In other words, teach words and have the student practice words more than once.

- Vocabulary can also be learned indirectly/incidentally through exposure. Vocabulary knowledge can be acquired through oral conversations, discussions and other verbal presentations. In general, written language contains a higher level of vocabulary than oral language.

- Because vocabulary is acquired through exposure, books on tape can be an excellent supplemental tool for exposing students not only to expanded vocabulary but also the benefits of a wide variety of literature and information. A collection of fiction and non-fiction audio books are found at most libraries. While these audio books should not replace reading, they offer an opportunity to expose your family vast wealth of literature at times where sitting down and reading a book is not feasible. These audio books can be listened to while driving in a car, preparing dinner, conducting chores or while engaged in other activities. For example, my son loves to listen to audio books while playing basketball in the driveway.

- Students can also learn new vocabulary from various word games. Fun vocabulary games, such as crossword puzzles and the vocabulary quizzes found in Reader's Digest magazine, can be used to expand vocabulary in an entertaining manner. You can also make your own games where members of the family find, learn and quiz each other on their 'new' words.

- Direct instruction in the most common affixes helps students expand their vocabulary knowledge. Learning the meaning of these common 'building blocks' helps students understand many new words. The definitions of common prefixes and suffixes are included in Section 6 (Multisyllable Words). The definitions of other prefixes and suffixes can be found in dictionaries, other lists and vocabulary programs.

- Direct instruction in the common Latin and Greek root words is highly beneficial in expanding vocabulary knowledge. Study of the Greek and Latin root words provides a strong foundation for vocabulary development. For example if the student knows the Latin root script=write he can better understand the meaning of the words scribe; transcribe, manuscript, prescription, inscription, describe, transcript.

Lists of root words are readily available through internet searches for 'common root words'. Many sources can be found on organization (.org) and education (.edu) websites. In addition, complete structured root word programs such as "English from the Roots Up" by Joegil Lundquist are also available. A partial list of common Greek and Latin root words is included on the next pages.

Greek Roots:

astron - star (astronaut, astronomy, astrology, astronomical)

auto - self (automobile, automatic, autobiography, autograph, automate, autonomy)

biblio - book (bibliography, Bible, bibliomania)

bio - life (biology, biodegradable, biography, biosphere, antibiotic)

chron - time (chronology, chronic, synchronize, chronological)

demos - people (democracy, demography, democratic)

dia - across or through (diameter, diagonal, diagnosis, diagram, dialect)

geo - earth (geology, geometric, geography, geopolitical,)

graph - to write or draw (graph, telegraph, graphic, autograph, homograph)

hemi - half (hemisphere)

homo - same (homograph, homogeny, homonym, homophone)

hydro - water (hydrant, hydrate, hydroelectric, hydrology)

logos - word study (logic, -ology = the study of biology, geology)

mega - large or great (megaphone, megapod)

meter - measure (thermometer, barometer, diameter, optometry, altimeter)

micro - small (microscope, microbe, micron, microfilm)

mono - single (monorail, monologue, monarch, monopoly)

para - beside (parallel, parable, parenthesis, paragraph, parachute)

pathos - feeling (pathetic, apathy, sympathy)

philia - love friendship (Philadelphia= city of brotherly love, philosophy, philanthropist)

phobia - fear (claustrophobia, hydrophobia)

phone - sound (phonics, telephone, symphony, microphone, phonological, homophone)

photo - light (photograph, phototropic, photocopy, photosynthesis)

poly - many (polygon, polymer, polynomial, polygamy, polyhedron)

psych - mind, soul (psychology, psychic, physics, psyche

scope - to look at inspect (scope, microscope, telescope, periscope)

sphere - ball (hemisphere, sphere, spherical, atmosphere)

syn/sym -together or with (synonym, symphony, synchronize, synthesis, symmetry)

techne - skill or art (technology, technical, technician)

tele - distant, far away (telephone, telegraph, telescope, television)

therm - heat (thermometer, thermostat, thermodynamics, thermos)

thesis - place position (thesis, theme, synthesis)

tropic -turning (tropics, phototropic)

Latin Roots:

annus - year (annual, anniversary, perennial, annuity)

aqua - water (aquarium, aquifer, aqueduct)

audio - hear (audible, auditory, audience, auditorium)

bene - well, good (beneficial, benefit)

bi - two (bisect, bicycle, bipartisan, biped, binary, binocular bicentennial, bifocal)

capitis - head (capital, captain, cabbage, capitalism)

centum - hundred (centimeter, cent, percent, century, centipede)

circum - around (circumvent, circumference, circulate)

contra - against (contrary, contradict, contraband, contrast)

dict/dictum- say or speak (dictate, dictionary, contradict, dictation, predict, verdict)

duct - lead (conduct, aqueduct, conductor)

duo - two (dual, duet, duel, duplex)

equi - equal (equitable, equator, equal)

finis - end (finish, final, finite, infinite)

fix - fix or attach (fix, affix, prefix, suffix)

fract - break (fracture, fraction, infraction, refract)

ignis -fire (ignite, igneous)

ject - throw (reject, interject, object, project)

junct or join - join or connect (join, joint, junction, rejoin)

manus - hand (manuscript, manufacture, manual, manipulate, manicure)

migrat - move (migrate, migrant, migratory)

ped - foot (pedal, pedestrian, pedestal, centipede)

populus - people (people, popular, population, republic, publish)

port - carry (portable, porter, deport, transport, import, airport, portage)

pre - before (predict, prepare, predawn, preset, preamble)

quartus/quad - fourth (quart, quadrant, quarter, quadrilateral)

scribe/script - write (script, transcribe, prescribe, scribble, inscribe, describe, manuscript)

spect - look (inspect, speculate, spectacle, perspective, introspect)

struct - build (construct, structure, destruction, instruction)

tempor - time (temporary, contemporary, temporal, tempo)

trans - across (transfer, transcript, transplant, transparent, transaction, transmit)

verb - word (verb, verbiage, proverb, verbal, verbose)

vid/vis - see (video, visible, evident, visual, visit, visitor)

ADVANCING SPELLING SKILLS ~ SPELLING LESSONS

A. General Information for the Parent or Teacher

This section helps you teach a student how to spell (correct written representation of our language). Common patterns should be taught from the beginning as a part of the direct systematic phonics instruction. In addition it is beneficial to specifically teach spelling guidelines to students. Although there are exceptions, guidelines are very useful in learning to spell correctly. While the spelling of individual words in our English language can be strange at times, for the most part it is not complete chaos. It is always much easier to learn a few general guidelines than try and memorize a vocabulary of 50,000+ words individually with no overall guidance or direction. An article summarizing effective spelling instruction is also found at **www.righttrackreading.com/howtospell.html.**

First and foremost, always **emphasize the phonetic nature of spelling**. Teaching a student how to read using a direct, systematic phonics approach, will already greatly improve their spelling ability. Help the student learn to listen to the sounds in the word. Practice spelling with common patterns. Although there is overlap with the code (more than one way that a sound can be written) and irregular and unexpected spellings, spelling is not a matter of memorizing random letters in tens of thousands of individual words. Learning accurate spelling is trickier than reading. Good phonetic knowledge is essential to proficient spelling. A strong phonetic base, awareness of frequency patterns and knowledge of spelling 'guidelines' are very useful tools in learning common and expected spelling patterns in our language.

The spelling 'guidelines' listed in this section are not a list of rules meant to be memorized but rather a tool to **teach common spelling patterns**. Teaching how and why certain patterns are used and then practicing these common patterns is more effective than memorizing a list of rules. A table summarizing expected spelling patterns for the sounds is located in Appendix G.

I will make a comment on the use of "invented spelling" that is contrary to some of the prevalent educational theory. **Do NOT use 'invented spelling'** where the student is allowed to 'discover' and write words however he would like to. Although children will obviously make spelling errors and perfection should not be expected, do *not* allow and encourage the continued, repeated use of improper spelling. Instead of letting the student continuously repeat errors, simply teach him the correct way to spell the word. This is not just a minor problem with spelling a few words wrong. The use of "invented" or "self-discovery" spelling allows the student to learn and repeatedly reinforce incorrect patterns and form improper 'neural models' of the words. You witness this in many perfectly bright older students who continue to spell they as 'thay'. Repeated writing of 'thay' for years engrained the incorrect 'thay' representation in their brain. It is a disservice to students to let them learn incorrectly. I strongly believe as parents and teachers it is our job to teach students the correct representation of our language. There are numerous things that are wonderful and necessary for students to discover on their own. However accurate representation of our written language is not one of them. Once again the corrections and teaching can and should be done in a positive manner. Acknowledging and even encouraging their phonetic spelling attempts should not preclude teaching correct spelling. ("You wrote that word how it sounds. That's a great try. But let me show you the way that we actually spell it"). It is always better to learn correctly!

Accurate spelling is not an isolated skill limited to a student's weekly spelling test or for competing in a spelling bee. Spelling is one of the fundamental subskills of effective written communication. The vast majority of spelling occurs in real life applications to achieve communication objectives. The goal of spelling instruction should not be temporary memorization of words but rather the development of skills to be able to correctly represent our written language. Help the student learn how to accurately represent our written language.

B. Specific Recommendations for Teaching Spelling: (For the parent or teacher)

Use the following tips to help your student develop successful spelling skills.

- Directly teach phonetic spelling. Base spelling on 'writing' the sounds *not* on memorizing letter names.
- In the beginning, teach spelling as a part of the reading instruction. Start with basic phonetic spelling and include only the phonetic code the student has already learned. Link spelling directly to direct systematic phonics

instruction. For example do not ask a student to spell the word 'rain' if he has not learned 'ai'=/ay/. Teach spelling in a systematic, phonetic based manner to establish strong foundational spelling skills.

- As the student masters the basic sounds and skills, add the complexities in a systematic manner. Teach one spelling pattern at a time. Directly and systematically teach specific vowel combinations, r-controlled vowel combinations and other complexities. Structure spelling instruction so that is makes as much sense as possible. *Give word lists by groups of common spelling patterns.* Teaching spelling of specific patterns and groups is much more effective than 'testing' mixed lists or phonetically unrelated words.

- Directly teach and practice common spelling guidelines. By learning these common spelling patterns, the student is better able to understand the structure of our spelling. Knowing the patterns, guidelines and expected frequency of occurrence helps children (and adults) learn how to spell. This program includes helpful spelling guidelines.

- The most effective and efficient way to have the student learn spelling words is to have the student write the word 5 to 10 times while saying the sounds. It is simple; all you need is paper and pencil. It's efficient because it directly teaches the necessary print to sound and doesn't waste time on processes that have nothing to do with spelling. It is highly effective because it directly builds knowledge in the correct printed representation of the word using multisensory processes (kinetic-forming the letters), visual (seeing the correct print), oral/auditory (saying and hearing the word). Writing the word 5-10 times provides the repetition that enhances learning. Simple, effective and efficient.

- Directly teach the 'irregular' words and 'unexpected' patterns. Teach these irregular words in a systematic manner, including them where appropriate. For example, teach the unexpected /ay/ sound in 'great', 'steak', and 'break' as part of your instruction in the 'ea' words . Have the student specifically notice these 'unexpected' spelling patterns.

- Advance skills in a systematic manner. Add complexities and multisyllable words after basic foundational skills are established.

- For multisyllable words, teach the student to sound out and spell by syllable. Writing the word by syllable helps prevent the common problem of leaving out parts of the word.

You can easily create a spelling program by selecting words from the decodable word lists in the *Right Track Reading Lessons* program. Use these lists in combination with the specific lessons on spelling guidelines to create a highly effective spelling program. Pre-made spelling lists for the initial reading lessons can be found at http://www.righttrackreading.com/spelllistsforrtr.html Teaching in a direct systematic manner helps the student learn.

When making spelling lists, remember it is best to teach spelling in common patterns. After the student has mastered and learned the common patterns you can then test for 'spelling' knowledge. In the learning stages it is important to teach by grouping spelling patterns. The following examples demonstrate how to make spelling list that teach specific spelling patterns.

If you are teaching the student to spell /ay/ words, group by spelling pattern. List 1 would have 'ai' words (rain, bait, brain, wait, grain…). List 2 would give 'ay' words (play, away, stay, pay, pray…). List 3 would give the a-consonant-e spelling pattern (gate, trade, game, make, grade…). List 4 would contain single vowel 'a' spellings (rang, bank, thank, sang…). List 5 would contain the 'unexpected' spellings of /ay/ (eight, weigh, great, …).

If you are teaching the student to spell the /er/ sound, group by common spelling pattern to help the student learn. List 1 would contain /er/ words spelled with 'er': (verb, river, under, stern, sister, hunter….). List 2 would give /er/ words spelled with 'ur'(hurt, burn, church, curl, burst….). List 3 would give /er/ words spelled with 'ir' (bird, firm, stir, dirt…). List 4 would give the words spelled with the more unusual 'ear' spelling (early, earn, earth, learn…) When teaching specifically point out the spelling pattern. Also teach that the 'er' is the most common spelling pattern for the /er/ sound.

It is preferable to give students lists of common spelling patterns grouped together because this systematic grouping helps the student *learn* how to spell. This can be contrasted to using lists of mixed spellings. Using a list of mixed spellings for a sound, especially before the student has learned all the individual patterns, contributes to confusion. The mixed lists not only make spelling difficult but they often prevent students from even recognizing the common patterns. For example if you use a mixed "long-a" list (wait, space, great, game, bang, play, they, eight) it is difficult for the student to recognize and learn the individual ways we spell /ay/. Similarly, 'theme' based spelling lists are frequently very poor tools for teaching spelling. For example a 'summer' theme that contains the words; summer, swimming, dive, pool, vacation, hot, ice cream, beach, picnic. This type of mixed list makes recognizing and learning patterns difficult. At the younger level, these lists frequently contain patterns the student had not yet learned. As a result, the student often spells by memorizing random letters instead of learning how to correctly write our phonetic language. While students eventually need to learn all the spelling patterns and know which spelling pattern to use for what word, foundational spelling skills are most effectively taught in a systematic manner grouped by common phonetic spelling patterns.

It is best to avoid all worksheet and activities that show words spelled incorrectly. You do NOT want the student to read incorrect spelling. Repeated exposure to incorrect spelling allows the student to build incorrect neural models of specific words and to actually learn combinations and patterns that do not exist in English. Check carefully! Many spelling worksheets and programs provide exposure to repeated incorrect spelling. While students do need to learn how to proofread and identify spelling errors, repeated exposure to incorrect spelling *in the learning stages* can be detrimental. If the student continually sees misspelled words he develops incorrect models of the words. In contrast, if the student learns the correct representation he is then better able to recognize incorrect spelling.

In addition, many spelling programs use inefficient activities to teach spelling. While puzzles and games such as solving codes, searching through word finds, unscrambling letters, and answering riddles, can be entertaining and provide other benefits these activities tend to be time consuming and often have limited value *in directly developing spelling skills*. Some of these activities such as jumbled letter arrangements can possibly confuse the development of correct spelling skills. At best these activities frequently consume large quantities of time on the activity itself (such as the searching process in a word find) instead of on developing a necessary skill (learning the correct written representation of words). In contrast, the highly effective and extremely efficient activity for directly developing spelling skills is to have the student repeatedly print the word correctly while saying the sound.

C. Specific Recommendations for Learning Spelling Words (For the Student)

The following tips will help you develop effective spelling skills and study spelling words.

Spell by sound! Write the sounds.

Practice spelling by common patterns.

Learn expected spelling patterns and helpful guidelines.

When learning how to spell specific words:

First look at the written word and say the word, looking at how the sounds are written. This should be done *phonetically* NOT by letter name (for example: bird is /b//ir//d/ not the letter names B..I...R..D which is said /bee/ /ie/ /ar/ /dee/). Read the word once or twice paying attention to the sounds and how they are written.

Next write the word at least 5 times (10 times is better), taking care to *write* the letters *as you say the sound*. Look at which letters represent what sounds. Pay close attention to the 'partner' letter combinations. For example when writing the word "bird" you write 'b' as you say /b/ and write 'ir' as you say the /er/ sound and write 'd' as you say the /d/ sound. Notice specifically which letters are representing the sound. This is especially critical for sounds that have multiple spellings (specifically note that in bird, the /er/ sound is made by the 'ir'). Practice by sounds not letter names.

For any multisyllable word, be sure and say and write the word by syllables. Example for the word 'consistent' you would write 'con' as you said /kun/, write 'sis' as you say /sis/, and write 'tent' as you say /tent/.

A helpful hint for learning how to spell a word is to pronounce all the sounds in the word, even if that is not how you actually say the word. We often speak 'lazy' English. This is fine in speaking and reading but it creates problems with accurate spelling. When you practice spelling completely pronounce all the sounds in the word. This often gives you a silly sounding 'proper' version of the word. Although we don't really say the word that way, it helps greatly when practicing spelling to say all the sounds. This is especially important with the 'schwa' pronunciation of many unstressed short vowels in multisyllable words where a 'proper' complete pronunciation of the short vowel sound greatly aids spelling. For example:

- for 'clothes' say /clo**th**z/ not the usual lazy /cloze/
- for 'family' say /fam- i -lee/ not the usual lazy /fam-lee/
- for 'listen' say /lis-**t**en/ emphasizing the /t/ that is normally silent
- for 'aunt' say /**aw**nt/ even if you usually pronounce it /ant/
- for 'manual' say /man-yoo-**al**/ emphasizing the /a/ of the -al ending
- for 'environment' say /en-vi-ron-ment/ instead of the usual /en-vi-ru-ment/
- for 'magazine' say /mag-**a**-**z**ine/ emphasizing the /ay/ sound for the a and saying the /ie/ sound for the 'i' in the last syllable instead of the actual /ee/ pronunciation

In summary, the most effective and efficient way to learn spelling words is write each word 5 to 10 times while saying the sounds. It is simple; all you need is paper and pencil. It's efficient because it you are not wasting time on processes that have nothing to do with spelling. It is highly effective because it directly builds knowledge in the correct printed representation of the word using multisensory processes of forming the letters(kinetic), seeing the correct print(visual), and saying/hearing the word (oral/ auditory). Writing the word 5 to10 times provides the repetition that enhances learning. Simple! Effective! Efficient!

Spelling Lessons
Helpful Spelling Guidelines and Patterns

The following spelling lessons directly teach helpful spelling guidelines and patterns. Each lesson presents and explains a guideline and includes a list of applicable words or refers to the reading lesson the words are located in. Read the guideline, look at the words and notice the specific spelling pattern. Have the student practice writing/spelling words meeting the guideline. Writing/spelling these words allows the student to 'see' and practice the expected patterns. The majority of these lessons are not memorizing a rule but rather learning the guideline or pattern and understanding how and why it works. These spelling lessons are to be conducted after the child has established the foundation of correct phonologic processing and learned the complete phonemic code (after completing reading lessons 1-98).

Spelling Lesson 1:

Every syllable has a vowel

Syllables are simply the chunks of sound within a spoken word that we say with a single puff of air. It is important to know **every syllable has a vowel.** Knowing that every syllable has a vowel is a fundamental element of spelling English words.

- Knowing every syllable has a vowel helps in spelling words where the final e is silent.

  Practice Words: little sparkle struggle handle angle apple article triple principle flexible possible table tumble riddle puzzle fiddle single grumble tumble saddle raffle simple bubble terrible brittle cattle jungle stable dazzle dribble candle scribble

- Knowing every syllable has a vowel also helps the student look at a word and 'see' if it 'looks right'. If a syllable doesn't have a vowel then something is missing.

Spelling Lesson 2:

'Silent e': Learning the 5 types of 'silent e' and knowing when to use the 'silent e'.

"Silent-e" is found at the end of many words. It is important to realize in most cases 'silent-e' is *not* randomly added to the end of words. Although the 'e' is 'silent', it has very important purposes. There are five ways the 'silent-e' occurs. Spelling is easier when you understand the important functions of 'silent e'. The five primary functions of 'silent-e' are:

- In the vowel-consonant-e combinations the 'e' is needed to make the first vowel say its name. This is the most common occurrence of 'silent e' when the 'e' is acting as a necessary partner of the other vowel. It is not 'magic'. This 'e' has a specific function. The final, silent 'e' is the hardworking partner for the vowel in the vowel-consonant-e combination. (tim-time, bit-bite, at-ate, not-note, rob-robe, cod-code, home, strike, graze, flute)

    Practice Words: See Reading Lessons 45 - 50.

- In words with 'ce' and 'ge' where the 'e' is necessary to make the 'c' have the /s/ sound (as in dance, chance, fence, justice, sentence, prance, prince, peace) or the 'g' have the /j/ sound (large, charge, manage, change, edge, fridge). This 'silent-e' is necessary to make the 'soft c' /s/ or 'soft g' /j/ sound.

    Practice Words: See Reading Lesson 51

- In words ending in **ve**: In the English language words do *not* end in **v.** Therefore, the 'e' is added to the end simply to prevent the word from ending in 'v'. This 'e' often does not change the sound of other letters in the word.

    Practice Words: have, give, love, above, live, active, native, captive, passive, massive, active, negative, motive, relative, expensive, aggressive, descriptive, detective, sensitive, informative

    See Reading Lesson 97 for additional words.

- In words with ending consonant blend and **le** ending, the 'e' is necessary because every syllable needs a vowel. This was explained in Spelling Lesson 1.

    Practice Words: See words listed in Spelling Lesson #1 on the preceding page.

- And of course, some words have a final '**silent-e**' for no apparent phonetic reason. Maybe it is just to make spelling difficult and confusing! Although the 'e' is not needed phonetically, a spelling pattern does exist for many of these words. Notice most of the 'no-reason' silent-e words end in the /s/ or /z/ sound spelled with the letter 's'. These 'no-reason' silent-e words do need to be practiced and learned. Grouping by similar spelling patterns helps the student learn these words.

    Practice Words: (house, mouse, grouse, louse);(please, crease, lease, tease, grease, decrease, increase, release); (geese, cheese); (cruise, bruise); (cause, pause, because, clause); (loose, choose, goose); (some, come, done), horse, promise, noise.

Spelling Lesson 3:

No English words end with the letter i

No *English* words end with the letter 'i'. It is very helpful to remember this in spelling because **you must spell the word in a pattern that does NOT end in 'i'.**

- The /oy/ sound at the *end* of words is always spelled with 'oy' (boy, toy, ploy, destroy) as 'oi' can never be used at the end of a word. See Reading Lesson 54 for practice words.

- In the same way the /ay/ sound at the end of a word cannot be spelled with 'ai'. It must be 'ay' (play, away, stay) or another pattern (sleigh, they). See Lesson 42 for practice words.

- In spelling the 'ie' ending of words such as brownie, collie, cookie, rookie, and auntie you know the 'i' must come first as 'e' must end the word. See Lesson 62 for practice words.

Exceptions are words from *other* languages and proper names.

1. taxi (short for taxicab);
2. macaroni, manicotti, rigatoni, (The Italian 'noodle' words)
3. radii, nuclei, (the plurals of some Latin words found mostly in math and science)
4. alkali (French from an Arabic word); zucchini (Italian); chili (Spanish); kiwi (Maori)
5. lei, Maui, Hawaii, Molokai (You guessed it; these are Hawaiian words.)
6. Proper names can always provide exceptions. For example: location names (Cincinnati, Missouri, Mississippi), personal names (Jeni, Heidi, Toni and numerous surnames). There are also a few common nouns originating from proper names ending in 'i'. For example the wildland firefighting tool, 'pulaski' was named after Edward Pulaski, a US Forest Service Ranger and firefighter hero of the 'Big Burn' that raged though Idaho & western Montana in 1910.

While this trivia on word origination and search for exceptions may be interesting, the guideline "No English words end in the letter i" remains a very useful spelling guideline.

Spelling Lesson 4:

No English words end with the letter v

As previously discussed in the 'silent e' section, no English words end with the letter 'v'. If a word ends in the /v/ sound, you *must* add the 'silent e' to the end so the word does *not* end in 'v'. This is most common in the -tive and -ive suffixes.

Practice Words: See Spelling Lesson #2 "Silent e" words ending in -ve and Reading Lesson 97.

Spelling Lesson 5:

No English words end in the letter j

No English words end in the letter 'j'. Therefore if a word ends in the /j/ sound, you must spell the /j/ ending with either the 'ge' or 'dge' ending.

Practice Words: charge, barge, rage, strange, range, edge, ledge, pledge, stage, page, fridge, change, large, cottage, savage, engage, package and words from Reading Lessons 51 and 86.

Spelling Lesson 6:

If g= /j/ then it must be spelled 'g+e', 'g+i' or 'g+y'

To have the /j/ sound, g *must* be followed by 'e', 'i' or 'y'. Remember 'g' can keep the /g/ sound if 'e', 'i' or 'y' comes after it (get, give, girl, gift, gear, shaggy). However, *if* the 'g' has the /j/ sound an 'e', 'i' or 'y' must come immediately after the 'g'. This guideline is extremely helpful when accurately spelling words that contain the g=/j/ sounds.

- This helps to know when you must add the 'silent e' to some words that end in the g=/j/ sound (change, range, charge, large, savage, package, manage, voltage) See Spelling Lesson #2 and Reading Lesson 51.

- This helps you remember how to spell words such as 'angle' and 'angel' that can be easily confused.

- This helps when adding suffixes to words ending in 'ge'. For example to add 'able' to 'change' you must retain the 'e' ('changeable') to keep the /g/ sound. (More on suffixes in later spelling lessons)

Practice Words: gym, ginger, gentle, gyroscope, giant, giraffe, geometry, general, gender, energy, gypsy, biology, ecology, other -ology endings, Spelling Lesson #5 and Reading Lessons 51 and 86.

Spelling Lesson 7

The /j/ sound: Is the /j/ sound spelled with j, g or dge?

The /j/ sound can be made by either 1) the **j**, 2) the **g+e, g+i, or g+y**, or 3) the **dge** combination.

- The 'j' is *only* found at the beginning of syllables. (joy, juniper, jungle, reject, enjoy, rejoice, inject) Note: The 'j' spelling beginning syllables is not exclusive as 'g'=/j/ also begins syllables.

- For the letter 'g' to have the/j/ sound, the 'g' *must* be immediately followed by either 'e', 'i' or 'y'. See Spelling Lesson 6. Therefore if the /j/ sound is followed by any other vowel (a, u, or o) the 'j' spelling *must* be used. Practice Words: jam, jail, jacket, jade, jagged, jacks, jab, jaguar, join, joint, journal, jog, joke, journey, enjoy, just, juniper, jump, junk, jungle, judge, juvenile, justify).

- English words do not end in 'j'. Therefore, the /j/ sound at the *end* of a word needs to be spelled with 'ge' or 'dge'. See Spelling Lesson #5.

- The 'dge' spelling is used when the extra consonant 'd' is needed to retain the short vowel sound. The'd' is necessary for 'blocking out' and preventing the 'e' after the 'g' from making the first vowel "say its name". Notice 'dge' is found at the end of words with the single short vowel sounds /a/, /e/ /i/ /o/ and /u/. (bridge, edge, wedge, ledge, badge, dodge, fudge, lodge, fridge, budge). The 'd' is necessary and added so there is a double consonant to prevent the 'e' from changing the short vowel sound to a long vowel sound. Without the silent 'd' the 'e' would act as a partner with the first vowel and change the vowel sound to a long sound (vowel-consonant-e combination). For example in 'page' notice how the 'e' both gives the 'a' the /ay/ sound in the vowel-consonant-e combination and also modifies 'g' to the /j/ sound. But the 'd' in 'badge' prevents the 'e' from changing the /a/ sound to /ay/ and retains the short /a/ sound. Badge without the 'd', 'bage' would be pronounced /b//ay//j/.

Practice Words: See Reading Lessons 16, 51 & 86.

Spelling Lesson 8

If c = /s/ then it must be spelled c + e, i or y
c+e   c+i   c+y = /s/

The important fact that '**c always has the /s/ sound whenever e, i or y comes after it**' is extremely helpful when accurately spelling words that contain the c=/s/ sounds. This dictates the spelling guideline that to have the /s/ sound the 'c' *must* be followed by an e, i or y.

- This often tells us if a word with the /k/ sound is spelled with 'c' or 'k'. (kitten could not be spelled 'citten' as the c would have the /s/ sound and it would become /s//i//t//e//n/; rake has to be spelled with 'k' or else it would be 'race' /r//ay//s/).

- This helps in knowing when you must add the 'silent e' to some words that end in the c=/s/ sound. See Spelling Lesson #2. Practice Words: dance, trance, prince, practice, glance, since, entrance, notice, furnace, balance, distance, violence, justice, juice, allowance, and Reading Lesson 51.

- This helps to correctly add suffixes to words that end in -ce. For example: change-changing-changeable and notice-noticeable-noticing. (More on suffixes in later Spelling Lessons)

Spelling Lesson 9

Spelling the /k/ sound: The following guidelines help you accurately spell the /k/ sound. This lesson explains when to use 'c', 'k' and 'ck'. Additionally, the Greek 'ch'=/k/ and the /k/ sound within 'qu'=/kw/ are addressed.

1. The beginning /k/ sound must be 'c' or 'k' (or sometimes 'ch' or 'qu'). The 'ck' spelling NEVER starts words.

2. **Always remember c+e, c+i, c+y = the /s/ sound. This guideline dictates when you must spell a word with 'k' to maintain the /k/ sound. Understanding this guideline helps you accurately spell the /k/ sound in many words. (See Spelling Lesson #8)

3. If the /k/ sound is immediately followed by e i or y, the 'k' spelling must be used. The 'k' spelling is necessary to maintain the hard /k/ sound. If you spell the /k/ sound with 'c', the 'e', 'i' or 'y' would make the 'c' have the /s/ sound. Look at the spelling of rake-race, fake-face, brake-brace to demonstrate why the 'k' must be used to maintain the /k/ sound. Carefully look at the following words to see WHY the 'k' spelling *must* be used.

kid	kind	king	keg	kitten	kite	kill
kiss	kick	kitchen	kerosene	like	rake	brake
strike	basket	parakeet	kept	keep	kennel	poke
stroke	choke	skin	skip	skirmish	skirt	sky
pumpkin	markers	snake	ketchup	key	monkey	basket

4. If the /k/ sound is followed by any other letter (NOT 'e', 'i', or 'y') the /k/ sound is usually spelled with 'c'.

The /k/ sound followed by other vowels (a, o, u) is USUALLY spelled with 'c':

cot	camp	call	cut	cover	capitol	cast
come	cap	color	computer	cart	can	car
carry	cash	cat	cave	cove	collect	code
cow	coin	count	confess	cone	curl	curve
coil	contest	cure	cover	consider	coat	copy

ALMOST ALL consonant blends when /k/ is FOLLOWED by another consonant sound, the /k/ sound is spelled with 'c': (the 'cr' and 'cl' are commonly encountered k+consonant blends)

clip	clasp	clue	crisp	class	clank	clam
clear	cloak	club	crunch	crazy	script	scream
cross	cramp	crumble	crown	clover	classic	scroll
screw	scratch	screen	scrub	scribe	act	insect
respect	inspect	strict	deflect	reject	obstruct	destruct
object	product	predict	perfect			

There are exceptions to this expected pattern of spelling the /k/ sound with 'c' when it is followed by letters other than 'e', 'i' or 'y'. The exceptions are primarily proper nouns and unusual words.

-Some exceptions to the /k/ + a, o, u include: kangaroo, koala, kayak, kudos, karate, kazoo, skunk, skull, and skate. Other exceptions are primarily proper nouns (Kansas, Koran, Kodiak, Korea, Karachi, Kabul) or unusual words (karyoplasms, kumiss, kumquat, kurbash, kapok, kana, kolinsky) Most exceptions are not everyday words unless you happen to be studying advanced cell microbiology or learning about fermented mare's milk drunk by the nomads of central Asia.

-Exceptions to the expected 'c' for /k/ + consonant words are a few proper nouns (Klondike, Klamath, Klein, Kremlin...) or uncommon (klystron, klaxon, krait, krona, kloof). There are only a few 'k+consonant words that would likely be read by most students (krill, kleptomaniac). The vast majority of blends where /k/ is followed by a consonant ARE spelled with 'c'.

5. WORDS with the /kw/ sound (/k/+/w/) ARE SPELLED with 'qu'; There are NO 'cw' spellings and NO 'kw' spellings in English. The only exceptions are a few Chinese provinces such as Kwangtung and Kweichow, and words such as kwacha, the monetary unit of Zambia. Therefore it is very helpful to teach students the /k+w/ sound IS spelled with 'qu'.

Practice words: quick, quit, quote, quest, queen, quench, quaint, squish, squid, square, squirm, quake, quail, quart

6. The ending 'k' sounds a slightly more complex:

The 'ck' is ONLY used at the END OF A SYLLABLE with a SINGLE SHORT VOWEL SOUND. *Most* 'ck' words are one syllable single short vowel words or these one-syllable base words with a prefix or suffix. (pack-unpack-packing; back-backed-backing; luck-unlucky-lucked). A few other words use the 'ck' spelling to maintain the /k/ spelling. Once again this 'ck' spelling occurs *only* at the end of a single, short vowel syllable ending with the /k/ sound. Look and you can see why the 'ck' spelling is necessary to maintain both the short vowel sound and the ending /k/ sound. (locket, picket, ticket, rocket, package, racket). Note this 'ck' spelling is only used ending single short vowel syllables. It is not used with vowel combinations, long vowel sounds, r-controlled vowel combinations or blended consonant endings.

sick	back	stick	black	rack	chuck
sock	stuck	rock	flick	deck	duck
muck	lick	track	stack	pack	crack
slick	shack	kick	pick	block	fleck
packet	rocket	sticking	packing	chucked	rocking
flicking	racket	locket	truck	unpack	package

Most SINGLE SYLLABLE words with vowel combinations or consonant clusters ENDING in the /k/ sound are spelled with 'k': Words with any combination except the single short vowel word/syllable endings.

folk	ask	walk	milk	silk	elk
balk	talk	bulk	risk	mask	task
bank	tank	thank	pink	bunk	hawk
rink	caulk	peek	beak	break	steak
pork	disc	shark	hook	look	dark
book	spark	pork	mark	peak	frisk
task	work				

The final /k/ sound in MULTISYLLABLE WORDS is USUALLY spelled with a 'c'

picnic	plastic	panic	stoic	economic	metric
periodic	politic	basic	medic	acidic	terrific
domestic	public	pediatric	frolic	historic	automatic
classic	clinic	patriotic	prolific	graphic	topic

Also note the pattern: When a prefix or suffix is added to a base word, the same 'ck' or 'k' spelling is usually maintained. (pack-repack-unpack-packed-packing; hook-unhook-hooking-hooked; mark-marked-marking-remark; walk-walking; public-republic). There are a few exceptions when the spelling of the base word is changed when suffixes beginning with 'e', 'i' or 'y' are added and would alter the sound of the word. This occurs with some of the multisyllable words ending in the 'c' spelling such as picnic and frolic. In these words the spelling of the ending is changed from 'c' to 'ck' when the suffix is added in order to maintain the /k/ sound and the short vowel sound (picnic - picnicking, frolic - frolicking, panic-panicking-panicked)

7. *To keep things interesting, a few Greek words use 'ch' spelling for the /k/ sound: You just need to learn these!

Christ	school	scheme	ache	chronic	chromosome
character	chlorine	chorus	chronicle	Christmas	Christian

See Reading Lesson 89 for additional words.

(The 'kn' spelling is NOT covered in this lesson as the 'kn'=/n/ and is not a spelling for the /k/ sound.)

Spelling Lesson 10

The /ch/ sound: Is the /ch/ spelled with ch or tch?

The 'ch' spelling for /ch/:

- **ch** is by far the most frequent spelling of the /ch/ sound

- **ch** is *always* used at the beginning of a word or syllable (chest, chimp, check, chum, chat, chip, chin, chess, chap, chant, chop, chick, chug, champ, choice, change, cheap, checkers, cheer)

- **ch** is used when there is a consonant sound immediately preceding the /ch/ sound (lunch, pinch, ranch, branch, hunch, crunch, inch, pinch, flinch, crunch, bunch, brunch, belch, mulch, trench)

- **ch** is used for the /ch/ sound following all vowel combinations (roach, reach, coach, preach, pouch, teach, touch, crouch, speech) and r-controlled vowel combinations (march, birch, church, porch, starch, larch, torch, parched)

The 'tch' spelling for /ch:

- The **'tch'** spelling is **only** used when the /ch/ sound is the end of a word or syllable immediately following a single short vowel sound. (batch, itch, fetch, match, notch, catch, ditch, latch, patch, hutch, stitch, pitch, catching, pitching, and hatchet) The 'tch' spelling pattern is limited to this syllable ending /ch/ for single short vowel words. Also note, these are primarily one-syllable words or variations of these base words with affixes added (fetch-fetching, latch-unlatch).   NOTE: such, much and rich are exceptions (these are spelled with the 'ch' spelling)

In summary, the **'ch'** spelling is used for the /ch/ sound except for the final /ch/ in a syllable with a single short vowel sound when the 'tch' is used. Practice Words: See Reading Lesson # 18

Spelling Lesson 11

Doubling consonants at end of one syllable words (f, l , s)

Sometimes consonants are doubled at the end of a word. The letters most frequently doubled are **f, l & s**. With **one syllable** words with **one vowel** that end in f, l s or z, the final letter is *usually* doubled.
Practice words:
ff: puff, gruff, stuff, off, stiff, staff, fluff, bluff
ll: ill, pill, dill, cell, tell, well, yell, still, doll, bell, tall, shell, fell, hill, grill, frill, chill, drill, ball, all,
   fall, hall, mall, wall, pull, full, kill
ss: dress, mess, miss, pass, toss, less, glass, mass, chess, bass, class, bliss, gloss, press, cross, stress

Spelling Lesson 12

These consonants are not doubled (j, k, w, v, x)

In English, the consonants j, k, w, v and x are never doubled.   The only exceptions are a few compound words such as 'bookkeeper', 'jackknife' whose parts happen to end and begin with the same letter and a few slang words ('savvy' and 'divvy'). It is not necessary to memorize this guideline. However, through reading and writing the student should recognize these letters doubled 'look wrong'. (One of the reasons the student should not practice spelling incorrectly or be exposed to repeated incorrect spelling.)

Spelling Lesson 13

Is the word spelled with 'ie' or 'ei'?

Remember **"i before e, except after c, or sounding as /ay/ in neighbor and sleigh" and a few exceptions.** I am not a big proponent of memorizing rules but it is useful to memorize this one. To this day I still use this 'i before e' rhyme my mom taught me years ago to correctly spell many 'ei'/'ie' words. This 'guideline' as well as knowing English words do NOT end in 'i' is helpful in spelling the often confusing 'ie'/'ei' words. You also need to learn the common exceptions.

- **"i before e"**:
  belief, believe, thief, brief, grief, chief, yield, relief, shield, field, friend, priest, niece, shriek
- **"except after c"**
  receive, receipt, ceiling, conceive, deceive, perceive, deceit
- **"or sounding as 'ay' in neighbor and sleigh**:
  eight, sleigh, freight, neighbor, weigh, weight
- **"and the common exceptions"**
  either, neither, height, seize, weird (As in "Spelling is so weird at times!")
- **And don't forget....words can not end in 'i'**
  collie, brownie, cookie, rookie

Spelling Lesson 14

"When 2 vowels go walking the first usually does the talking (but not always!)"

It is important to know and understand that usually when vowels are together (BOTH when they are standing right next to each other and also often when they are separated by only one consonant) the first vowel will usually 'talk' or 'say its name' (make the long vowel sound). Although there are exceptions, understanding this vowel 'guideline' helps greatly with spelling many words.

- This helps with remembering how to spell the basic vowel combination words. (For example: boat is spelled 'oa' not 'ao' because the first vowel does the talking.)
- This helps in spelling the vowel-consonant-e words in understanding when to add the 'silent e' (for 'time' you add the e to make the 'i' say /ie/, without the 'silent e' the word would be /tim/).
- This knowledge helps in accurately adding suffixes. Many of the lists of 'rules' and directions for handling the addition of suffixes to words can be explained and understood with this single fundamental 'when two vowels go walking' guideline. For example, this explains why you must add the 2nd 'p' to 'hop' when you add the '-ing' suffix to correctly spell 'hopping'.
- This knowledge helps you understand when you must spell words with the 'dge' ending to maintain the short vowel sound (ledge, badge, fridge) or spell words such as 'package' with the correct 'ck'.

It is critical for the student to understand this fundamental concept of two vowels working together. It is not memorizing the little 'when two vowels go walking' rhyme in isolation, but fully understanding how vowels impact each other. The way I explain the concept to younger students is to make an analogy between the 2 vowels and 2 buddies poking each other in class. When the buddies poke each other, one of them will squawk. For vowel buddies, the first vowel usually 'says' its name or the long sound when its buddy 'pokes' it. I use this analogy because it is helpful not only with reading but also in explaining how to handle consonants with spelling. When the two students are in line 'poking' each other and making noise, the teacher splits them apart. If the teacher splits them with only one other student they can still reach around and poke each other. This is why the vowels in the vowel-consonant-e combinations can still impact each other. They can still 'reach around' the single consonant and poke their buddy. To keep the students or vowels 'quiet' the teacher must split the troublemakers by 2 people. Or in the case of vowels, you need to split the vowels by 2 consonants so they are too far apart to reach around and 'poke' each other. Use your own explanation, but insure the student fully understands this important concept.

Lesson 15 - 27 give the detailed explanations of adding suffixes under certain situations. Don't try to memorize all the variations. Simply look at and try to understand how they work and practice the patterns.

Spelling Lesson 15

Adding Plural Endings: How do you spell words with plural endings?

- For **most words** just **add s.** (cat-cats, tiger-tigers, table-tables, tree-trees, train-trains, storm-storms)

- If the words **end in s, ch, sh or x,** you need to **add es.** These are the words that you can *not* verbally add or say the /s/ sound without adding the /es/ syllable. You do not need to memorize this guideline. Simply, *listen* to how you say the word! (class-classes, watch-watches, dish-dishes, tax-taxes, fix--fixes)

- If the words **end in vowel-y combination** (ay, oy, uy) just **add s.** These are the same as most regular words. (boy-boys, toy-toys, play-plays, key-keys)

- If the words **end in consonant-y** need to **change the y to i and add es.** (city--cities, fly-flies, pony--ponies, party--parties, cry--cries)

- In *some* words that **end in f** you need to **change the f to v and add es.** (leaf-leaves, shelf--shelves, calf--calves, half--halves)

- There are exceptions with irregular words that have their unique plural form (mouse-mice, goose-geese, child-children, foot-feet, man-men, ox-oxen). These irregular words just need to be learned. Luckily once you verbally know the correct plural form of the word, most are spelled phonetically.

Practice Words: See Reading Lesson #95.

Spelling Lesson 16

Adding the -ed past tense ending to verbs: How do you spell past tense verbs?

- The past tense suffix for verbs is spelled **'-ed'.** This '-ed' suffix is pronounced three different ways depending on the ending sound of the base word. It is pronounced either: 1) /id/ (graded, blasted), 2) /d/ (loved, climbed), or 3) /t/ (baked, hopped). In reading and speaking we usually do not notice these variances. However, in spelling it is important to realize the past tense verb ending is spelled '-ed' regardless of the pronunciation.

- Notice when words end in **'silent e'** you drop the original 'silent-e' when adding '-ed' as the 'e' in the '-ed' ending takes over the 'silent-e' duty. Or you use the existing 'e' and just add 'd' to the make the '-ed' ending. Either explanation results in only one 'e' for the '-ed' suffix. (Don't create a double 'ee' in the word (create--created, waste--wasted, bake--baked, race--raced).

- With the words that end in **consonant-y** (cry, try, spy, baby, party, hurry)... **change the y to i and add -ed** (cried, tried, spied, babied, partied, hurried..). This still keeps the '-ed' spelling of the past tense, except you must first change the y to i before adding the -ed.

- With 'short vowel' words you often need to double the final consonant so that the 'e' in the 'ed' ending does not change the sound of the first vowel (hop--hopped, bat-batted, grab--grabbed, grip-gripped). More on this in the next guideline!

- English contains irregular words that have their unique past-tense form. These must be learned. The good news is that most of these are commonly used in oral language and once you verbally know the accurate past tense form, most are spelled phonetically. (run-ran, fall-fell, write-wrote, fly-flew, grow-grew, make- made, ride-rode, eat-ate, fly-flew, speak-spoke, sing-sang, draw-drew...)

Practice words: See Reading Lesson 96

Spelling Lesson 17

General patterns for adding suffixes to words that have a short vowel sound and one consonant at the end:

When you add suffixes that begin with vowels (such as -ed, -ing, -y, -er, -ous, -ish,) to the end of words that have a short vowel sound and end with only one consonant, you need to take care to ensure the sound of that short vowel is NOT changed by the addition of the suffix. (Remember your understanding of "when 2 vowels go walking"). How you handle this *depends* on if it is a one-syllable or multisyllable words. If it is a multisyllable word, the syllable accent determines how you handle adding the suffix.

When you add suffixes that begin with vowels (such as -ed, -ing, -y, -er, -ous, -ish) to **one-syllable words** with short vowel sounds that end in single consonants (run, hop, drop, kid, bug, sun, hit) you first need to double the consonant so that the short vowel sound is maintained (running, hopped, dropping, kidding, sunny, hitter). With this understanding you will realize that if the one-syllable word already ends in two consonants, then simply add the suffix (fast--fastest, gift--gifted, grant--granting).

Of course it can't be too simple. So with **multi-syllable words** that have the short vowel sound, the consonants are ONLY doubled when you add suffixes that begin with vowels **if** the last syllable short vowel sound is the accented syllable. If last syllable is *not* accented no doubling is necessary (as in... exit--exiting; visit--visited; profit--profiting; happen--happening) If the last syllable *is* accented then the doubling of the consonant is necessary to maintain the short vowel sound (forgot--forgotten, permit--permitted, admit--admitting). This takes listening to the word, practice and yes, some memorization and checking with a dictionary.

Spelling Lesson 18

General Patterns for adding suffixes to words with "silent e' at the end:

When suffixes that begin with a vowel (-es, -ed, -ing, -er, -y , -ity,) are added to words with a 'silent e' at the end, the silent e is often dropped because the vowel in the suffix provides the 'partner' vowel to maintain the proper sound in the first vowel. Check to see if you are maintaining the proper sounds. (rake-raking, bake-baking, save-saving, vote-voter, smoke-smoker, dance-dancer-dancing, give--giving, replace--replacing, grade--grading, safe--safer--safest, trade--trader--trading, brave--bravest).

Spelling Lesson 19

General Patterns for adding suffixes to words that end consonant-y:

When you add suffixes that begin with a vowel (-es, -er, -ing, -ed, -ish, -est) to the end of words that end in the consonant-y:
1. Most often you change the 'y' to 'i' and add the suffix the same as was previously discussed in spelling past tense -ed and plural endings. For example cry-cried-cries, dry-dried-dries, baby-babied-babies, fly-flies-flier, candy-candies, silly-silliest, foggy-foggiest, hungry-hungriest-hungrier, happy-happiest-happier.
2. However, you can *not* have a double 'i' (ii). So in the suffixes that begin with 'i' (such as -ing and -ish) you just add the suffix without changing the y. (dry-drying, baby-babyish, fly-flying, cry-crying, try-trying, carry-carrying)

Spelling Lesson 20

General Patterns for adding suffixes to words ending in -ce /s/ or -ge /j/ sounds:

Remember the c+e, c+i, or c+y is necessary in order to create the c=/s/ sound. (Spelling Lesson 8)
Remember that g+e, g+i, or g+y is necessary in order to have the g=/j/ sound. (Spelling Lesson 6)

When adding suffixes to the end of words that have the -ce /s/ sound or the -ge /j/ sound, just remember the important fact that for 'c' to have the /s/ sound or for the 'g' to have the /j/ sound it MUST be followed by 'e', 'i' or 'y'. Knowing and understanding this important guideline helps explain many spelling patterns with suffixes:

If the suffix does NOT begin with 'e', 'i', or 'y', you must keep the -e before adding the suffix in order to maintain the soft /s/ or /j/ sound. This is often with the -ous, -able suffixes because the 'a' or 'o' would not keep the 'soft' /j/ or /s/ sound. In the following examples notice how the 'e' is necessary to maintain the /j/ or /s/ sound:

change---changeable	courage-courageous	notice--noticeable
outrage--outrageous	embrace--embraceable	enforce-enforceable-enforcing
service--serviceable	knowledge--knowledgeable	replace--replaceable

If the suffix begins with 'e', 'i' or 'y', you usually drop the 'e' because the 'e', 'i' or 'y' in the suffix maintains either the /s/ or /j/ sound. In suffixes such as '-ing', '-y', '-ed', and '-er' the leading 'e', 'i' or 'y' vowel in the suffix maintains the /s/ or /j/ sound. Notice how dropping the 'e' does not alter the sound.

change--changing--changed	replace--replacing--replaced	dance--dancing--dancer
fleece--fleecy	place--placing--placed	practice--practicing-practiced
race--racing--racer--raced	service--servicing-served-server	

Spelling Lesson 21

Adding Suffixes to many other words

When you add many suffixes to most other words (words that do not contain short vowel sounds in the last syllable, do not end with the ge/j/ or ce/s/ sound, or do not end in 'silent e') or when adding suffixes that start with consonants (such as -ly, -ness, -ment, -ful, -less) you usually add the suffix with no changes to the base word. For example:

join-joining; park-parking; punish-punishable; deep-deeper; disagree-disagreeable; short-shortest;
lone-lonely; quiet-quietly, year-yearly, bright-brightly, pay-payment, place-placement, rest-restless; fear-fearless;
speech-speechless; grow-growing; perfect-perfectly; high-higher; strict-stricter

Practice Words: Multisyllable Section Lesson 5 contains word lists grouped by common suffix.

Spelling Lesson 22

Spelling with -able or -ible suffix

The -able and -ible suffixes (which both mean capable of or likely to) often sound the same. So which one do you use to correctly spell a word? There are a couple of patterns that can help. First, based on frequency, the '-able' is used more often than the '-ible'. Secondly, although this does not always work, often **if the base word is complete or when the only change is dropping the 'silent e'** before you add the -able you spell the suffix '-able' (bendable, agreeable, favorable, manageable, readable, punishable, notable, desirable, escapable, comfortable, profitable, reasonable, laughable). If the base word is **incomplete (Hint: i=incomplete)** without the suffix then often the "-ible" spelling is used (terrible, edible, reducible, visible, tangible, horrible, possible, visible, reducible, accessible, sensible, plausible, feasible, divisible). Also notice the pattern with the '-ible' spelling: many of the base words that are spelled with '-ible' end in the /s/ or /z/ sound.

Practice Words: See Multisyllable Section Lesson 5 for a list of words with the '-able' and '-ible' endings.

Spelling Lesson 23

Spelling the -ful suffix

The word "full" is spelled with two ll's. *However* when the "full" is used in multisyllable words as a suffix to mean full of or characterized by, the suffix is spelled -ful with only one l.
Practice words: See Multisyllable Section Lesson 5

Spelling Lesson 24

Spelling with the suffix -ist or -est

The suffix -ist & -est sound the same when saying a word. How do you know which one to use to correctly spell a word?

The **-est** spelling is by far the more common and **means the superlative degree** (longest, quickest, fastest, highest, greatest, slowest, tallest). A list of words is found in Multisyllable Section Lesson 5.

The **-ist** is **someone who does something** (druggist, artist, pianist, typist).

Spelling Lesson 25

Spelling with 'ant-ance-ancy' OR the 'ent-ence-ency' endings

The suffixes -ant & -ent; -ance & -ence; -ancy & -ency sound the same. So which one is the 'correct' spelling?

•   Frequently by looking at the spelling of the base word you can determine which suffix to use. Although it does not always work, the following examples show the usual pattern:

ent-ence-ency:

absent - absence	adhere - adherence	affluent - affluence
confident - confidence	confluent - confluence	decent - decency
delinquent - delinquency	different - difference	fluent - fluency
independent - independence	frequent - frequency	negligent - negligence
potent - potency	resident - residency	solvent -solvency
turbulent - turbulence	urgent - urgency	violent - violence

ant-ance-ancy:

abundant - abundance	brilliant - brilliance	distant - distance
expectant - expectance	fragrant - fragrance	jubilant -jubilance
ignorant - ignorance	observance - observant	reluctant - reluctance - reluctancy
redundant - redundancy	significant - significance	truant - truancy
tolerant - tolerance	vagrant - vagrancy - vagrancy	variant - variance
vibrant - vibrancy	vigilant - vigilance	

• Another tool for determining the correct spelling is to apply the guidelines for 'g' = /j/ and 'c'=/s/. If the base word ends in the 'g' = /j/ or 'c' = /s/ the '-ence or -ency' spelling must be used so the 'e' maintains the /s/ or /j/ sound. (See Spelling Lessons # 6 and #8). For example:

agent - agency	converge - convergence	emerge - emergent - emergence
intelligent - intelligence	translucent -translucence	insurgent - insurgence -insurgency

• Finally, if you know how to spell one variation of the word you can often determine the correct spelling of the other endings. For example, if you know how to spell 'tolerant' you could correctly spell 'tolerance' by applying the consistent 'ant-ance' pattern.

Spelling Lesson 26

Spelling the /tion/ endings:

There are 4 ways to spell /shun/ endings (-tion, -sion, -cian, -cion). These special suffixes are found in the second or subsequent syllables of a multisyllable word. There are a few patterns to help you spell these words.

- First, consider frequency of occurrence. The **-tion** spelling is by far the most common spelling of the /shun/ ending. The **-sion** spelling is next in frequency. This frequency pattern is helpful because thousands of words use the '-tion' spelling compared to only about 200 words that use the -sion spelling. The **-cian** occurs only in a limited number of words referring to a person or occupation. The unexpected **'-cion'** spelling is rarely used, found only in two words (suspicion and coercion).

- Although it doesn't always work, often the use of **-tion** or **-sion** can be determined by the spelling of the root word.
  Root word spelled with 't', use -tion:

create--creation	direct--direction	decorate--decoration	pollute -- pollution
edit -- edition	promote--promotion	violate--violation	frustrate--frustration

  Root word spelled with 's', use -sion:

tense--tension	confess--confession	express--expression	televise--television
confuse--confusion	process--procession	transgress--transgression	

- The **-cian** is limited to words for person or occupation: electri**cian** physi**cian** musi**cian**   techni**cian**

- The **-cion** is *rarely* used. You just need to learn this unexpected spelling in 'suspicion' and 'coercion'.

Practice Words: See Multisyllable Section Lesson 7

Spelling Lesson 27

Spelling the /shal/ and /shus/ endings:

- **cial or -tial:** There are 2 ways to spell /shal/ at ending of multisyllable word, **-cial** or **-tial.** The -cial is more common and often can be determined by the spelling of the root word,
  cial: race--racial   finance--financial   glacier-- glacial office-official
  tial: part -- partial

- **tious or -cious:** There are two ways to spell the /shus/ ending, **-tious** or **-cious**. The spelling of the root word often helps you spell these words.
  tious: infect-infectious   or   **cious:** grace - gracious   space-spacious

Knowledge of how other variations of the word are spelled helps in spelling these unusual /shal/ and /shus/ endings: For example: If you know 'caution' it helps you spell 'cautious' correctly. If you know 'ambition' it helps you spell 'ambitious'.

Practice Words: See Multisyllable Section Lesson 8.

Spelling Lesson 28

Spelling Words When Adding Prefixes:

Prefixes are usually just added to the base word with no change.

    dis + appear = disappear, dis + continue = discontinue, dis + agree = disagree
    un + happy = unhappy; un + clear = unclear;
    re + turn = return, re + place = replace, re + make = remake,
    pre + arrange = prearrange, pre + test = pretest, pre+school=preschool, pre + historic = prehistoric

Practice Words: See the lists of common prefixes in Multisyllable Section Lesson 4.

Spelling Lesson 29 ~ Spelling "all" when it is used as part of other words:

The word "all" (the entire substance or every) is spelled with two l's. However, when "all" is used as a part of another word, it usually is spelled with only one l.

Practice Words: almost, always, almighty, altogether, already, although

Spelling Lesson 30 ~ Other 'unique' aspects of English effect accurate spelling.

English contains a number of homophones (Greek for same-sound). These are words that sound the same but have different meanings for the different spellings. Students simply need to learn the correct spelling that matches the definition. The following lists some of these homophones:

ate - eight	bear - bare	be - bee	beat - beet	blew - blue	bread - bred
by - buy	course - coarse	dear - deer	do- due - dew	fair-fare	feet - feat
flee - flea	flour - flower	for - four - fore	grown - groan	guessed - guest	heel - heal
here - hear	heard - herd	hare - hair	hire - higher	horse - hoarse	I - eye
its - it's	know - no	load - lode	loan - lone	made - maid	mail - male
main - mane	mall - maul	meat - meet	new - knew	need - kneed	night - knight
pail - pale	pain -pane	pause - paws	peace - piece	peak - peek	pear -- pare
peer - pier	pen - pin	poor-pore-pour	pray - prey	rain - rein	rap - wrap
red - read	principal - principle	ring - wring	road - rode	sale-sell-cell-sail	scent - cent
see - sea	seen - scene	sight - site - cite	so- sew	some - sum	sore - soar
stare - stair	sun - son	tail -tale	there - their	tin - ten	to - too - two
through - threw	so - sew	steal – steel	waive - wave	stationery-stationary	wait - weight
way - weigh	week - weak	whole - hole	won - one	write - right	you - ewe
would - wood	your - you're				

The English language also has homographs (Greek for same-writing). A homograph is a word that is spelled the same as another word with a different meaning and often pronunciation. While spelling remains consonant, the only way to determine the meaning and pronunciation of the word is from context.

bear (Grizzly bears live in Montana. He wasn't able to bear weight on his sprained ankle.)

bow (I tied a red bow on the package. Take a bow at the end of the performance).

close (Please close the door. He needs to sit close to the front so he can see the board.)

dove (The white dove flew by the window. The boy dove into the water.)

lead (My pencil lead broke. The teacher will lead the children to the bus.)

live (I live in Montana. We fished with live bait.)

minute (We'll leave in one minute. You need a microscope to see the minute organisms.)

present (I got a birthday present from Dad. Please present your idea to the class.)

read (I read the book last year. You need to read this book.)

record (She broke the state record in the 3000 meter race. Can you record this song for me?)

right (Turn right at the corner. You got the right answer.)

sow (A mother pig is called a sow. The farmer needs to sow the seeds.)

tear (Tear drops help clean dirt out of your eyes. Don't tear up the paper.)

wind (The wind is blowing. Please wind up the clock.)

wound (Cover the wound with the bandage. She wound up the clock.)

Spelling Lesson 31 ~ There will be exceptions to the guidelines and expected patterns. At times spelling will be tricky and frustrating! Although phonetic spelling and knowledge of the guidelines are very helpful for *most* words, there will be exceptions to the guidelines and expected patterns. In other words, while these guidelines can greatly improve spelling, at times the only strategy is to simply learn the word. The solution for improved spelling is to make it easy as possible by spelling phonetically, learning expected patterns, practicing correct spelling and keeping a dictionary handy to look up words.

Final Review Helpful Spelling Tips:

Tip #1   ~ Spell phonetically ~

Base spelling on writing the sounds of the word instead of memorizing random letters.

Tip #2   ~ Learn guidelines and expected spelling patterns ~

Learning and understanding the structure of our written language and the fundamental guidelines of 'how it works' and 'why it works' is always easier than memorizing thousands and thousands of individual words. Learning the expected spelling patterns is a valuable tool for improving spelling. Spelling Lessons 1-31 provide direct instruction in spelling guidelines and expected patterns. A table summarizing the spelling patterns for specific sounds is located in Appendix G.

Tip #3   ~ Practice correct spelling ~

Read and write words correctly. Avoid all incorrect representations. The more often you read and especially write words correctly the better your spelling becomes. Writing words, paying careful attention to the correct sounds as you write, is especially helpful in developing correct neural models of the word. Always practice accurate representations of our written language.

Tip #4   ~ Use a dictionary ~

The vast majority of spelling does not occur during a spelling test but rather in real life applications. If you are not sure how to spell a word, LOOK IT UP! A dictionary is a valuable tool. Looking up the word in a dictionary allows you to write the word correctly. Not only does this make your writing accurate at that point in time but it also develops and strengthens the knowledge bank of accurate representation of our written language.

Tip #5   ~ Note words you misspell and practice those specific words ~

Keep a list of the words that you frequently misspell and practice those specific words. Pick a few at a time and write them in isolation. Write the individual word five to ten times paying attention to the sounds and spelling patterns used.

Tip #6   ~ Make a 'cheat sheet' of words you frequently find yourself looking up ~

Most individuals have a few troublesome words that they continually misspell. It seems, no matter how many times you look up and write the word you still seem to forget how to spell it correctly. If you wear out the pages of your dictionary repeatedly looking up the same words over and over, make yourself a quick reference 'cheat sheet' and tape it inside the front cover of your dictionary or in some other convenient location. (I have restaurant and museum on my list.)

Tip #7   ~ Remember, spell check programs are only a tool ~

While useful, do not depend entirely on automatic spell check programs. These programs have definite limitations. They do not find all errors. In addition, the automatic features will often make inaccurate adjustments.

APPENDIX A
Sound Pronunciation Table and Notes

The following table explains correct pronunciation of the sounds and provides the key for how sounds are indicated throughout this book. This table is a reference for the parent/instructor. (Student directions are in the lessons.) *Speech difficulties are briefly addressed following the pronunciation table. This discusses the speech developmental issues where a student has difficulty saying certain sounds.

It is critical to teach these sounds to the student correctly from the beginning.

- Make sure you can say the isolated sound correctly before instructing the child.
- Take care to not add sounds that do not belong (for example 't' is a quick /t/ not /tuh/, r is /rr/ not /er/ or /ruh/).
- Teach the sound the letter represents in our language NOT the letter name. For most letters these are not the same thing, (the letter t is pronounced /t/ not /tee/, m is /m/ not /im/.) Students need to know the letter names for other reasons but *to read* the student must link the printed letter(s) directly to the sound the letter represents in our language.
- Some sounds must be said quickly. If these 'fast' sounds such as t, d, p, k , are not said quickly, a vowel sound is usually erroneously added (t becomes /tuh/). Always say these sounds quickly.
- Some sounds are more difficult for some students to say (such as h, r). Other sounds are more difficult to distinguish (/t/-/d/, /b/-/p/, /k/-/g/, and /f/-/v/-the soft /th/) Pay extra attention to these sounds and be sure the student is pronouncing them correctly and distinguishing them correctly. For example, this is why in speaking some children say 'baff' for bath or 'haf' for have. They do not distinguish and say the sounds correctly. This type of error needs a little work on speech/pronunciation.

The sound pronunciation table on the following pages shows:

1) The phonogram (letter or 'buddy letters'): These are listed in the same order as they are presented in the lessons.

2) The sound(s) for each phonogram: the sound is shown between slashes /_/ (for example /m/). This pronunciation key shows how sounds are indicated throughout the book.

3) An indicator if the sound must be said quickly: The sounds specifically listed as a 'fast' sound *must* be said quickly to prevent distortion. These 'fast' sounds such as /t/ and /d/ can NOT be said slowly. If they are said slowly, the student usually adds an additional vowel sound (/t/ becomes /tuh/). If the sound is not listed as 'fast', it can be stretched out without distorting the sound. (such as /mmmm/ or /sssss/).

4) Notes or explanation of any pertinent information to help describe the sound. This includes descriptive notes and examples of the sound in a few words. These words can be used to check if you are saying the sound correctly and as a tool to help you determine and isolate the individual sound the letter makes.

5) An additional note of caution is included for some of the sounds that are commonly mispronounced when said in isolation. This serves as a heads up to help avoid common pronunciation errors on these sounds. Helpful tips for teaching students to pronounce the sounds correctly are included.

*Speech difficulties where a student has a difficulty saying certain sounds are briefly addressed following the pronunciation table (see page 347).

Sound Pronunciation Table

letter	sound	note if sound 'fast'	any pertinent explanation and example of the sound in words	notes of caution
m	/m/		am, mat, me	not /muh/ or /im/
t	/t/	'fast' >	this is a quick /t/ as in sit, at, tag	not /tuh/
a	1. /a/ 2./ay/ -------- (3)/ah/		1. the /a/ sound is the 'short' vowel sound as in..... at, apple, rat 2. the /ay/ sound is the 'long' vowel sound as in...... ape, late, navy (3rd pronunciation /ah/ as in father about)	
s	1. /s/ 2. /z/		1. /s/ as in ... sit, miss, Sam, 2. /z/ is the same sound as the letter z as in.... is, as, his, use, boys	
d	/d/	'fast' >	this is a quick /d/ as in..... did, dad, mad, drop	not /duh/
i	1. /i/ 2./ie/ ------- 3./ee/		1. /i/ sound is the 'short' vowel sound as in...it, pig, if, 2. the /ie/ sound is the 'long' vowel sound as the word 'I' and as in ...... pint, time, (3rd pronunciation /ee/ as in machine, trivial)	
f	/f/		if, for, flat, off	not /fuh/
r	/r/		/r/ as in rat, run, rip note: /r/ is tricky for some children. So they don't say /er/... have them start saying an easy word like 'rat' holding the /r/ to say /rrrrrraaat/. Have them cut off before they start the /a/ sound. Practice with them until they get the hang of it.	not /er/ or /ruh/
th	1./th/ 2./th/		1. /th/ is the 'hard' /th/, the tickle the tongue sound as in.....this, that 2. /th/ is the 'soft' quieter /th/ sound that does not vibrate the tongue as in..... bath, three, thin	not /thu/
l	/l/		pill, tall, lid, lap	not /luh/ or /el/
o	1./o/ 2./oa/ 3./u/		1. /o/ is the 'short' vowel sound as in... odd, top, lock 2./oa/ is the 'long' vowel sound as in..... old, no, most 3. this is the 'short' vowel /u/ sound as in... son, love, from, some	
n	/n/		no, not, fin, nest	not /in/
p	/p/	'fast' >	this is a quick /p/ as in....... up, pig, lap, play (It is harder for some children to say /p/ fast, have them try quickly popping their lips like popping popcorn.../p//p//p/)	not /puh/
e	1. /e/ 2./ee/		1. /e/ is the 'short' vowel sound as in.. get, egg, set, best 2. /ee/ is the 'long' vowel sound as in... me, he	
h	/h/	'fast' >	this is a quick /h/ as in..... hat, him, hold /h/ is a harder sound to say. It needs to be said quickly. In reading is linked directly to the next sound. If difficult, have the child practice feeling the short puff of air with their hand in front of their mouth as he quickly says /h/	not /huh/
v	/v/		van, vote, give Notice how the /v/ vibrates your lower lip	not /vuh/

letter	sound	note if sound 'fast'	any pertinent explanation and example of the sound in words	notes of caution
sh	/sh/		/sh/ as in… **sh**ip, di**sh**, **sh**ell, ma**sh** Teach proper pronunciation of /sh/ by using the standard 'be quiet', finger signal /shshshshsh/	not /shuh/
u	1./u/ 2./oo/ (3./uu/)		1. /u/ is the 'short' vowel sound as in…**u**p, t**u**b, f**u**n 2. /oo/ is the 'long' vowel sound as in…r**u**de, t**u**be (3rd pronunciation /uu/ the same sound as oo in look. Found in few words…p**u**t, p**u**sh, b**u**ll,)	
b	/b/	'fast' >	this is a quick /b/ as in…. **b**at, **b**ig, cu**b**, cra**b**	not /buh/
k	/k/	'fast' >	this is a quick /k/ as in…. **k**id, see**k**, s**k**ate, ba**k**e	not /kuh/
ck	/k/	'fast' >	this is a quick /k/ as in…. ba**ck**, si**ck**, du**ck**	not /kuh/
c	1. /k/ 2. /s/	1.'fast' >	1. this is a quick /k/ as in…. **c**at, **c**rab, **c**ap 2. this is the /s/ sound (when the c steals the /s/ sound) it is sometimes called the 'soft c' sound as in….. **c**ity, ni**c**e, ra**c**e	not/kuh/
g	1./g/ 2./j/	1.'fast' > 2.'fast' >	1. this is a quick /g/ as in ba**g**, bi**g**, **g**o, (this is sometimes called the 'hard g' sound) 2. this is a quick /j/ sound (when the g steals the /j/ sound) This is sometimes called the 'soft g' as in… pa**g**e, **g**iraffe, ener**g**y	not/guh/ not/juh/
j	/j/	'fast' >	this is a quick /j/ as in….**j**am, **j**ob, **j**ill	not /juh/
w	/w/		**w**in, **w**ish, **w**oke s**w**ish	not/wuh/
ch	/ch/	'fast' >	the /ch/ is always said quickly **ch**in, **ch**urch, mu**ch**	not/chuh/
tch	/ch/	'fast' >	this is the alternate /ch/ spelling la**tch**, ca**tch**, i**tch**	not /chuh/
x	/ks/	'fast' >	this is the quick /ks/ sound as in a**x**, fo**x**, fi**x**, ta**x**	not /ex/
z	/z/		**z**oo, **z**ipper, ama**z**e	
qu	/kw/		this is a tight joining of the quick /k/ with /w/ sound to make /kw/. The 'qu' partner letters make the sound /kw/ as in…. **qu**een, **qu**ilt, **qu**ick, equ**a**te	
wh	/wh/		the /wh/ is very similar to the /w/ except it is 'whispered'. as in… **wh**isper, **wh**en, **wh**ite, Have the child practice the quiet whispering of /wh/	not /whuh/
a+ll	/ah/ +/l/		when a short a is followed by an l or ll, the a pronunciation is modified to say /ah/ as in… **a**ll, c**a**ll, **a**lmost, **a**lways, w**a**lk	
w+a	/w/+ /ah/		when short a comes right after w the pronunciation is modified to say /ah/ as in…. w**a**sp, w**a**d, w**a**sh *There are also some other words that have the /ah/ pronunciation such as in…f**a**ther	
y	1./y/ 2./ee/ 3./ie/		1. the beginning consonant /y/ sound …**y**es, **y**ou, **y**et 2. this is the final /ee/ sound in multisyllable words (this is the most common sound for y). as in… bab**y**, stor**y**, sill**y**, quickl**y** 3. this is the final /ie/ sound when y is the only vowel ending a 1 syllable word as in.. m**y**, b**y**, sh**y**, tr**y** (and also found in a few other words such as. p**y**thon, W**y**oming, t**y**pe)	not /yuh/

	sound	any pertinent explanation and example of the sound in words
ing	/eeng/	this /eeng/ is actually the combination of the /ee/ with the nasal /ng/ sound but it is taught as a single unit because it is so common. as in.... s**ing** r**ing** str**ing** go**ing**
ink	/eenk/	this is actually the combination of the /ee//n//k/ sounds but is also taught as a single unit.. as in....**ink**, r**ink** s**ink** br**ink**
ee	/ee/	these partner letters have the sound /ee/ as in b**ee**, tr**ee**, n**ee**d
oa	/oa/	these partner letters have the sound /oa/ as in... **oa**t, b**oa**t, r**oa**d
oe	/oa/	these partner letters have the sound /oa/ as in....h**oe** d**oe**
ai	/ay/	these partner letters have the sound /ay/ as in....r**ai**n, w**ai**t, p**ai**d
ay	/ay/	these partner letters have the sound /ay/ as in...pl**ay**, st**ay**, pr**ay**
a_e	/ay/	in this combination, the e works with the a to make the a have the /ay/ sound as in .... **a**t**e**, t**a**p**e**, pl**a**n**e**
o_e	/oa/	in this combination, the e works with the o to make the o have the /oa/ sound as in .... r**o**p**e**, h**o**m**e**
i_e	/ie/	in this combination, the e works with the i to make the i have the /ie/ sound as in .... t**i**m**e**, h**i**d**e**, **i**c**e**
u_e	/oo/	in this combination, the e works with the u to make the u have the /oo/ sound as in .... r**u**d**e**, fl**u**t**e**
e_e	/ee/	in this combination, the e works with the e to make the e have the /ee/ sound as in .... **e**v**e**, compl**e**t**e**
oy	/oy/	these partner letters have the /oy/ sound as in...b**oy**, t**oy**, enj**oy**
oi	/oy/	these partner letters have the /oy/ sound as in...b**oi**l, **oi**l, c**oi**n
ea	1. /ee/ 2. /e/ (3. /ay/)	1. /ee/ is the most common sound for these partner letters as in... **ea**t, t**ea**m, **ea**ch, 2. these partner letters sometimes have the /e/ sound as in h**ea**d, br**ea**d, r**ea**dy (3. In a few words 'ea' has the /ay/ sound as in... gr**ea**t, st**ea**k)
ow	1./ow/ 2./oa/	1. the /ow/ sound as in... n**ow**, br**ow**n, pl**ow**, 2. the /oa/ sound as in .... sn**ow**, kn**ow**, shad**ow**
ou	1. /ow/ 2./oo/ 3./u/	1.the /ow/ sound is the most common as in...**ou**t, l**ou**d, h**ou**se 2. the /oo/ sound as in ....y**ou**, s**ou**p, y**ou**th 3.the /u/ sound as in.. y**ou**ng, c**ou**ple & -ous endings like nerv**ou**s,fam**ou**s
ue	/oo/	the long u /oo/ sound as in.... bl**ue**, cl**ue**, tr**ue**
ew	/oo/	the long u /oo/ sound as in....n**ew**, st**ew**, fl**ew**
ui	/oo/	the long u /oo/ sound as in....s**ui**t, fr**ui**t
oo	1./oo/ 2./uu/	1. the /oo/ is the long u sound as in..... m**oo**n, c**oo**l, b**oo**t 2. the /uu/ sound is softer oo sound found in ....c**oo**k, b**oo**k, f**oo**t
ie	1. /ie/ 2./ee/ 3./i/	1. the /ie/ sound as in.....p**ie**, d**ie**, 2. the /ee/ sound as in th**ie**f, bel**ie**f 3. the /i/ sound as in fr**ie**nd, sh**ie**ld
ei	1./ee/ 2./ay/	1. the /ee/ sound as in rec**ei**ve, c**ei**ling 2. the /ay/ sound as in r**ei**n, n**ei**ghbor
ey	1./ee/ 2./ay/	1. these partner letters usually have the /ee/ sound as in... k**ey**, mon**ey** 2. In a few words ey has the /ay/ sound ... th**ey**, ob**ey**
au	/aw/	the /aw/ sound as in....f**au**lt, h**au**l, c**au**se
aw	/aw/	the /aw/ sound as in... **aw**ful, l**aw**
augh	/aw/	the /aw/ sound as in..... c**augh**t, t**augh**t
igh	/ie/	the /ie/ sound as in..... h**igh**, r**igh**t
ar	1./ar/ 2./air/	1. the sound /ar/ as in......c**ar**, st**ar**, f**ar**m 2. the sound /air/ as in .....c**ar**ry, p**ar**adise
or	1./or/ 2./er/	1. the usual /or/ sound as in...c**or**n, f**or**, t**or**ch 2. after w (w+or) and at the end of multisyllable words the or has the /er/ sound as in..... w**or**k, w**or**m, flav**or**, doct**or**

	sound	any pertinent explanation and example of the sound in words
or	/or/	There are 5 combinations that have the /or/ sound
		or, f**or**, n**or**th
ore	/or/	m**ore**, st**ore**, ch**ore**
oar	/or/	b**oar**d, **oar**, r**oar**
our	/or/	f**our**, c**our**se, y**our**
oor	/or/	d**oor**, fl**oor**
er	/er/	There are 5 combinations that have the /er/ sound
		h**er**, broth**er**, pap**er**, t**er**m
ur	/er/	h**ur**t, ch**ur**n, b**ur**p, t**ur**n
ir	/er/	d**ir**t, g**ir**l, st**ir**, b**ir**thday
ear	/er/	**ear**th, s**ear**ch, l**ear**n
or	/er/	w+or and or at end of multisyllable words…as in w**or**m, w**or**k, doct**or** flav**or**
are	/air/	There are 3 combinations that have the /air/ sound
		d**are**, sh**are**, sc**are**
ar	/air/	c**ar**ry, p**ar**rot, p**ar**ent
air	/air/	**air**, h**air**, ch**air**, p**air**
(ear)	/air/	(*not common only a few words such as b**ear** and p**ear**)
ear	/eer/	There are 3 combinations that have the /eer/ sound
		ear, h**ear**, d**ear**, n**ear**
eer	/eer/	d**eer**, ch**eer**, p**eer**
ere	/eer/	h**ere**,
ear	1./eer/	1.the ear partner letters usually have the /eer/ sound as in…..**ear**, h**ear**, d**ear**,
	2./er/	2. sometimes the ear partner letters have the sound /er/ as in… **ear**th, s**ear**ch, l**ear**n
	3./air/	3. in a few words the ear partners have the /air/ sound … b**ear**, p**ear**
dge	/j/	these letters have the /j/ sound as in… bri**dge**, e**dge**, ba**dge**
mb	/m/	du**mb**, cli**mb**, thu**mb**
wr	/r/	**wr**ite, **wr**ong, **wr**ap
kn	/n/	**kn**ow, **kn**ew, **kn**ee
ph	/f/	**ph**rase, **ph**one, gra**ph**

Additional notes on sound pronunciation:

*There is no need to teach the terminology "short", "long", "soft" or "hard" when teaching the sounds. Although it is sometimes helpful to learn these to help in describing what sound to use, it is not necessary especially with beginning reading. In fact teaching these labels can just add additional processing steps if the terminology is used as a "middle man" in learning the sounds. Students need to learn direct letter=sound relationship not letter = label to describe the sound=actual sound. Keep the sounds direct to the letter without having to first recall some label like 'short'. If the student says the wrong sound option, simply say something like "do you remember the other sound that it makes?"

*Although comprehensive, this list does not include every possible alternative pronunciation or spelling that is encountered in our language. This list includes the majority of the phonogram spellings and sounds based on frequency. For example, the printed representation of the /u/ sound is given for 'u' (run, up), for 'o' (son, from), and for 'ou' (young, couple, nervous) but not for the unusual oo spelling (flood). The infrequent 'oddball' sounds and spellings are not included. If you look you can always find exceptions, pronunciation variances and unexpected spellings.

Variations in Pronunciation (schwa, accents, regional differences, modifying sounds)
There are variations in pronunciation that occur in speech. These therefore, are encountered when reading. In fact, dictionaries often show these variations in pronunciation.

- Some variations are due to the differences in accents (how we say the word) that vary by region or preference. For example, someone saying /dawg/ instead of /dog/).

- Many of the pronunciation differences occur with the "schwa", the unstressed short vowel sound in many multisyllable words. The schwa (shown as /ə/) is the "lazy" pronunciation of the short vowel sounds /a/ /e/ /i/ /o/ & /u/. The pronunciation varies greatly depending on the vowel, the specific word and how the individual says the word. For example, notice the sound of the schwa /ə/ in the following words: a (banana, about, mineral, tradition); e (sicken, pocket, element); i (clarity, ability, hurricane); o (button, melon); and u (focus, peanut) and how these words are often pronounced differently by different people. Although is important to realize that there are differences in pronunciation and accenting of the short vowel sounds, these 'schwa' pronunciations do not have to be taught as separate sounds. You will find students unconsciously modify the pronunciation to how they say the word. If new words vocabulary words are encountered, teach the student the correct pronunciation for the specific word as 'this is how we say the word'. The schwa, lazy pronunciation does need to be specifically addressed with advanced instruction in spelling. However, for reading, it is highly effective (and far simpler) to teach straightforward short vowel sounds and then let the student adjust pronunciation appropriately as he reads specific word. In other words, don't worry about these slight differences in pronunciation. Teach the short vowel sound and you will find the student automatically and appropriately adjusts the pronunciation to how he says the word.

- Pronunciation modifications occur when we say certain sounds together (how these sounds orally blend together). These are automatically incorporated when we speak. For example, how the short /e/ sound is automatically modified to /i/ when it comes before /m/ or /n/ (hen, pen, hem). When we read we make these type pronunciation changes without even noticing (although it is helpful to point these out for accurate spelling).

- Slight variations in pronunciation of certain sounds occur in some words. If you go to split hairs, the long u sound is pronounced /oo/ in some words (rude, tune) and a slightly different /yoo/ in others (use, cute). Instead of confusing the student with numerous slightly different pronunciations give the child one good solid pronunciation /oo/ and then you will notice that on their own the student makes those slight changes/appropriate adaptations.

- Speakers of other languages are likely to pronounce words differently than English speaking students. Accenting and proper pronunciation is more challenging for students whose primary language is not English or who are in the process of learning the language.

Pronunciation Difficulties due to Speech Difficulties: Some students have limitations in their ability to say certain sounds. These are speech development issues, not reading issues. This is where the student, for various reasons, is not saying specific sounds. These types of speech difficulties in correctly pronouncing a certain sound are NOT considered reading errors. See the next pages for additional information on speech difficulties.

Speech Difficulties

Some students have limitations in their ability to say certain sounds. These are speech development issues, not reading issues. This is where the student, for various reasons, is not saying specific sounds. Some of these children have physical limitations and others are physically capable but just have not learned to say certain sounds automatically. If a student is facing speech difficulties he needs to be evaluated by a professional. Most school districts have screening processes and speech specialists who help identify and assist students with speech difficulties or recommend necessary assistance. Background information on speech development issues can be found on the internet. The National Institutes of Health NIDCD "Speech and Language Developmental Milestones" fact sheet provides general information and links to other resources. It is found at www.nidcd.nih.gov/health/voice/speechandlanguage.asp or you can order a hard copy of this free government publication (NIH publication No. 00-4781). Another source of information is the website www.helpforkidspeech.org established by a non-profit Scottish Rite Masonic organization under a program to help children with speech and language disorders. This parent-friendly website contains general background, informative articles and links to resources. The article *Speech Language Home Activities: Teach Specific Sounds to Your Child* and additional articles on individual sounds provide activities you can do at home to develop specific sounds.

Reading instruction does *not* replace the need for speech assistance. However, the individual attention and work on specific sounds provides an opportunity to supplement and assist students. As you work on specific sounds both in isolation and with reading words, you can sometimes help the student learn and practice correct pronunciation. Obviously this informal work on sounds is most helpful for students who do not have physical limitations and just need to learn how to make the sound. When you are working with a student with speech difficulties, the best option is to talk with the speech specialist about recommendations for helping the individual student. These specialists can usually provide specific tips. In addition, the following list shares some general information and tips that a parent or reading tutor may be able to use to help a student say specific sounds.

General Information and Tips:

- Use a small hand mirror, so the child can 'see' how he is making the sound. For example, to make the /th/ sound the student needs to 'stick out' their tongue. With the mirror, they can see the correct position.

- Face the student and make sure he is looking at you and can see your lips move as you say specific sounds. By looking carefully the student can sometimes 'see' the difference between sounds. For example, it is difficult to hear the difference between /f/ and the soft /th/. That is why many children say "It is time for a /baf/ instead of the correct /bath/. However, by looking at the lips you can 'see' the difference between the 'tongue sticking out' for soft /th/ and the teeth on the bottom lips for /f/.

- You can use the 'feel' of the sounds to help children distinguish and say specific sounds. This is helpful for distinguishing some of the sounds with vibrations (such as /v/, hard /th/, /z/) and those with 'puffs' of air (such as /h/, /p/), and the voice on-voice off differences that can be felt in the Adam's apple area between the similar 'sister sounds' (such as /t/ & /d/ or /p/&/b/).

- There are specific 'sister sounds' that have the same formation. The only difference is one sound is 'voice off' and the other is 'voice on'. With the closely related sounds you can feel the difference between 'voice off' and 'voice on' by touching the Adam's apple area. These closely related 'sibling' or 'sister' sounds include: /s/-/z/, /t/-/d/, /f/-/v/, /th/-/th/, /p/-/b/, /k/-/g/, /ch/-/j/

- Demonstrate to the student! Show the student how to make the sound. Let the child listen, look and feel the differences between sounds. When necessary, exaggerate specific elements of position.

- There is a progression of difficulty in making specific sounds. Some sounds are more difficult to make. Talk to you speech specialist for specific details. In general the sounds /k/, /g/, /ch/, /j/, /th/ /sh/ /r/ /l/ /y/ /s/ blends and /l/ blends are more difficult.

- **/s/ and /z/:** "Keep the tiger in the cage". Both these sounds are made by keeping the tongue inside/behind the teeth. The /s/ and /z/ are 'sister sounds' made with the same tongue/mouth position. However /s/ is 'voice off' and /z/ is 'voice on'. Teach the child to make /s/, then tell him to say /z/ 'make the tiger rattle the cage'. The /z/ sound is a vibration, 'voice on' sound. The child can feel the difference in the Adam's apple & in vibration on the tongue/teeth.

- **/th/ and /th/:** "Stick your tongue out!" For both the hard /th/ and the soft /th/ sound the student needs to stick their tongue out. Exaggerate sticking the tongue out to teach the sound. A mirror is particularly helpful so the student can see their tongue sticking out between the teeth. Both the /th/ and /th/ sounds are made by sticking the tongue out. The only difference is the 'voice on' 'voice off'. With the hard /th/ the student vibrates the tongue. You can feel the vibrations 'tickle the tongue'. With the soft /th/, the 'voice off' makes the quiet /th/ that does not tickle the tongue. The student can feel the difference on their tongue and also by touching their Adam's apple area.

- **/t/ and /d/:** The /t/ sound is made by 'tapping' the tongue on the roof of the mouth right behind the top of the teeth. Teach /t/ as a fast 'tapping' sound. Demonstrate and let the student use a mirror to see the tongue tapping. The /d/ is made the same as /t/ except for it has 'voice on'. The student can feel the difference by touching their Adam's apple area. Also remember both of these sounds are 'fast' sounds that must be said quickly. If you say slowly you distort the sound. The /d/ and /t/ are difficult for some students to orally distinguish. The phonemic awareness of the 'fast' sounds is particularly difficult when they are blended with other consonants.

- **/k/ and /g/:** These are both 'back' sounds made with the back of the tongue almost pulled back to the throat. /k/ and /g/ are also 'fast' sounds that must be said quickly. The /k/ is made with the 'voice off' and the /g/ is made with the 'voice on. The child can feel the difference on their Adam's apple.

- **/r/:** The /r/ sound is difficult for many students. The /r/ is made by having the tongue curl up with lips apart. (If the lips are together the sound is /w/). The /r/ is a 'lift' sound where the tongue is lifted up. A mirror is helpful for teaching this sound. For speech you can exaggerate the /r/ to /er/. To say /r/ for reading have the student start to say a word such as 'run' or 'race' slowly /rrrrun/ and then have him cut off at the /rrr/. The /r/ is a tricky sound!

- **/ch/ and /j/:** The /ch/ is an 'explosive' sound. Start in the /t/ position (tongue up touching the roof of the mouth right behind the front teeth). Have the student drop their jaw as he blows out. Demonstrate and teach with an exaggerated jaw drop. Also, thanks to a little boy I worked with who loved to watch his dad chop wood, I came up with a helpful analogy. Chopping wood can effectively explain how to make this sound. An analogy between the quick force of an raised ax falling to chop the wood compares to the quick force of the tongue dropping to make the /ch/ sound /ch/ /ch/ - raise the ax (tongue) and /ch/ 'chop' (drop quickly). Also if the student has difficulty saying the /ch/ sound, start practicing with 'nch' blend words such as 'lunch', 'pinch', 'ranch' as the tongue is already raised for the /n/ sound so the /ch/ is then easier to say correctly. The /j/ is the 'voice on' sister sound for /ch/. The student can feel the /j/ in the Adam's apple area.

- **/p/ and /b/:** The /p/ is a quick sound made by 'popping' the lips together just like 'popcorn popping'. The student can also feel the air puff at each 'pop'. Once again this is a 'fast' sound that must be said quickly. Demonstrate and use a mirror to help the student see how to make the /p/. The /b/ is the 'sister sound' made with 'voice on' that can be felt in the Adam's apple area. Both sounds are said 'quickly' with the lips and puff of air.

- **/l/:** The /l/ is a 'lift' sound that is made by lifting the tongue up behind the teeth. Exaggerate and have the student curl their tongue up, placing the tip behind the front teeth (in the /t/ position). Make sure the child keeps the tip of their tongue up behind/inside the teeth. Demonstrate and then have the student use a mirror to 'see' the position.

- **/f/ and /v/:** These sounds are made by the top teeth resting on the bottom lip and blowing. Exaggerate to teach how to make the sound. Demonstrate and use the mirror. The student can see the top teeth on the bottom lip. The /f/ sound is the soft sound of gently blowing. The /v/ sound is the 'voice on' sister sound. The /v/ is the 'vibration' sound (/v/=vibration). The student can feel the vibrations on the lower lip as well as feel the 'voice on' in the Adam's apple area. Also note that the phonemic awareness between /f//v/ and soft /th/ is often difficult for younger children. (Why children say 'baf' for bath, 'haf' for have and cute sayings like "My mom is a votographer') Help the child develop an 'ear' for the difference by having them look at the formation differences as he hears the sounds.

- **/sh/:** This is the 'quiet' /sh/ sound. The child needs to keep their teeth together and lips rounded as he blows the air out. Demonstrate and use a mirror. The standard 'quiet' /sh/ symbol can help, except drop your finger lower towards the chin so the child can see the teeth together and rounded lips.

- **/h/:** The /h/ can be a tricky sound to make. Have the student feel the 'hot' puff of air on their hand. This is a 'fast' sound that must be said quickly. Also make sure the child says the sound quietly as /h/ is a 'voice off' soft sound.

APPENDIX B

Lesson Progress Chart

1	27	53	79
2	28	54	80
3	29	55	81
4	30	56	82
5	31	57	83
6	32	58	84
7	33	59	85
8	34	60	86
9	35	61	87
10	36	62	88
11	37	63	89
12	38	64	90
13	39	65	91
14	40	66	92
15	41	67	93
16	42	68	94
17	43	69	95
18	44	70	96
19	45	71	97
20	46	72	98
21	47	73	99
22	48	74	Begin guided reading
23	49	75	
24	50	76	
25	51	77	
26	52	78	

APPENDIX C ~ Letter Formation Instructions

Correct letter formation is important in helping children develop both reading and printing skills. Learning how to form the letters correctly in the learning stages is critical. It is much more effective and efficient to take the time to directly teach and help the child learn correct formation in the beginning than to try and correct poor formation practiced over and over. Use direct instruction to teach correct formation. The following notes and tips on letter formation are for the parent to review before teaching the child so you can help your child learn correctly!

Attention to correct formation helps prevent common problems and makes writing and reading easier for the child. Focus on correct formation over 'neatness'. There is a natural developmental progression for fine motor skills in young children with differences between individuals. Emphasize correct formation and neatness will improve with practice and as fine motor skills develop with age.

Use a standard block print manuscript style and lower case letters for reading instruction. Do not use cursive, italics or any of the loopy script crossover styles. This program uses the Zaner-Bloser manuscript print but other comparable styles are similarly effective. Please see page 28 explaining the purpose and importance of using standard manuscript styles and lower case letters for teaching reading skills.

Use tracer letters if your child needs help learning correct formation. Tracer letters are highly effective in reading instruction. I highly recommend using pre-dashed tracer letters for young children who are just learning their letters and developing fine motor skills and for children who have difficulty with accurate letter formation. It is much more effective for a child to trace letters and learn correctly than it is for the child to independently write letters incorrectly. Tracer letters help the child learn correct formation form the beginning! Free pre-printed tracer letter pages for all the basic sounds are available at **www.righttrackreading.com/tracerletterpages.html**

Important Notes and Helpful Hints on Letter Formation:

The following shows how to form each of the letters. The dot • indicates where to start the letter and the directional arrow → shows which way to write. On the letters that require picking up the pencil a number 1 is given to show which part you write first. Other letters are made without lifting the pencil.

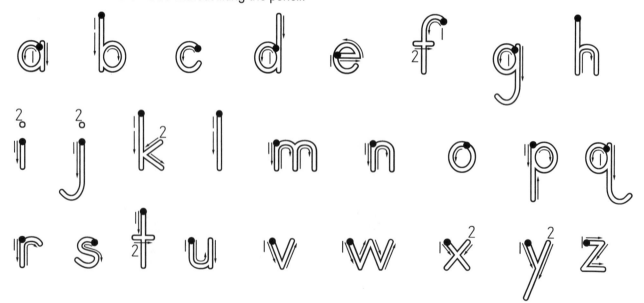

- First, ensure your child is holding the pencil and sitting correctly! Directly teach the child proper pencil hold and the correct sitting position for writing. Children need to use the correct 'tripod grip' where they gently hold the pencil between their thumb and first two fingers. It is important to establish proper grip from the beginning. A complete description of proper finger grip and correct sitting and paper position can be found in the *Zaner-Bloser* manuscript handwriting program.

- Letters sit on the line or "stand on the ground". I tell young children that letters do NOT like to jump up in the air or float around. "Letters like to stand on the ground." Children need to learn to print using lined paper so the child has a 'ground line' to print the letter on and learns from the beginning the importance of writing letters 'standing on the ground'. All letters sit on this ground line!

- Often it is helpful to use lined learning paper that has the light dashed 'midline'.

  This dashed paper helps the child see the midline or 'hill line' that is halfway between the bottom or ground line and the top or 'skyline'. If the child learns using standard lined paper that does not have dashed midlines, the child has to understand the imaginary midline or 'hill line' that sits halfway between the lines.

- Letters are made up either tall parts or short parts or a combination of tall and short parts. The tall parts go almost up to the top line or 'skyline'. The short parts are half the size of the tall parts and go to the midline or 'hill line'. If you are not using the dashed learning paper, you need to directly teach the child to imagine the 'hill line' and make these parts half the size of the tall parts. Letters with tall parts include b, d, f, h, k, l, t. All other letters are made up of short parts that are half as tall. Help the child learn correct sizing from the beginning!

- A few letters have parts that go below the ground line: g j p q y

- For most letters, you write the entire letter without picking up the pencil. You need to pick up your pencil for the letters with crosses (f, t) with dots (i, j) and for k x and y. Other letters are made without lifting the pencil.

- It is important to begin writing the letters starting with curves/circles (a, c, d, f, g, o, q, s) at the correct position. These letters begin at the 2 o'clock position and go around counterclockwise. To explain the correct position to young children who do not understand '2 o'clock' or 'counterclockwise', show the child to picture a little smiley face and tell the child to start the letter where the right ear would be and go around 'this way'. Point and show the child where to start and which way to go. When making 'round' letters, remind the child to start at the 'monkey's ear' and go around. Demonstrate where to start and which direction to move and use tracer letters to help the child learn. Letters starting with curves must begin at the correct starting point and formed in the correct direction.

  a c d f g o q s

  *For a, c, d, f, g, o, q & s... start at the ear and go up and around!

- Letters are formed from the top to the bottom. Help the child learn to start at the top.

- Many letters start with a straight line going down. Teach the child to start at the top & go down.

  Letters that start tall and go straight down include b h k l t

  Letters that start short at the midline and go down include i j m n p r u

- For letters starting with a slant, directly teach the child the starting point and to make a straight slant down from top left to bottom right.

  Letters starting with a slant include: v w x y

- For letters starting with a horizontal line, directly teach the child the starting point and to make a straight line across to the right. Only two letters start with a horizontal line.

  Letters starting with a horizontal line include: e z

- Correct letter formation is especially important for the visually similar letters b, d and p. These letters, (b, d, and p) are different orientations of the same shape. Therefore, they are visually similar and easily confused by many children. Explicit instruction and careful attention to how these letters are formed helps the child learn to distinguish the difference between these visually similar letters and prevent the common confusion that occurs in both reading and writing. Proper formation helps student learn to differentiate these letters. A highly effective technique for both preventing and overcoming letter confusion is to focus on correct formation.
  - ➤ d - Write the letter with the 'round part' first. Start at the 2 o'clock position (or monkey's ear) and go around and then up. A fun way for young children to learn this is 'donut for dad' /d/ make the 'donut' or round part first
  - ➤ b - Start at the top and make the full down stroke first, then go up and around. A fun way to help young children learn the correct 'b' formation is 'big board for the big building'; make the big tall board first
  - ➤ p - Start at the top and go down below the line and then up and around. A fun way for young children to remember this is 'pony tails hang down' so go down first.

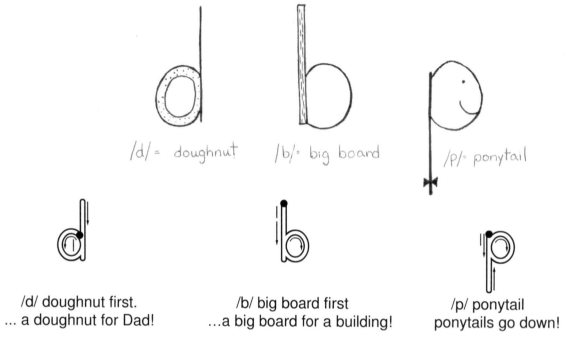

/d/ = doughnut   /b/= big board   /p/= ponytail

| /d/ doughnut first. | /b/ big board first | /p/ ponytail |
| ... a doughnut for Dad! | ...a big board for a building! | ponytails go down! |

Notice the distinct formation of correctly printed letters d, b, & p. The kinetic motion of correct formation engrains the proper shape and gives the student a way to differentiate these visually similar letters. d = /d/ doughnut first, b= /b/ big board first, p=/p/ ponytails go down. It works!

- If you are looking for an effective handwriting program, I recommend the *Zaner-Bloser* manuscript handwriting program. This effective handwriting program teaches the specific steps involved in correct penmanship from how to hold the pencil, to correct position, formation and spacing. I would like to thank Mr. Clint Hackney for introducing and sharing this effective handwriting program with me. The step-by-step instructions illustrating details such as how to correctly hold the pencil and proper paper position are fantastic. Many students have difficulty writing because they never learned 'how' to write. Often students who struggle with writing do not even hold the pencil correctly and lack other basic skills. Direct instruction in the exact skills of skilled writing is highly beneficial and effective in helping children improve penmanship skills. A single student workbook cost approximately $12 and is suitable for individual tutoring situations. Classroom programs which include the teacher materials are also available. More information on the *Zaner-Bloser* program can be found at their website **www.zaner-bloser.com/html/hwgen.html**.

APPENDIX D ~ Teaching/Learning Capital Letters

Aa Bb Cc Dd Ee Ff Gg Hh Ii Jj Kk Ll Mm Nn Oo Pp Qq Rr Ss Tt Uu Vv Ww Xx Yy Zz

Frequently children will have already learned capital letters through other instruction. However, if a child does not know the capital letters or if he has gaps in this knowledge, he absolutely will need to learn these important versions of the letters of our alphabet. The *Right Track Reading* program emphasizes and utilizes lower case letters in the reading instruction program because the vast majority of reading occurs with lower case letters. Please see page 28 to learn why lower case letters are used for effective reading instruction. This appendix provides supplemental information on directly teaching capital letters if your child needs to learn this important component of our English language.

Use direct instruction to systematically and explicitly teach the child capital letters. This can be done in conjunction with the *Right Track Reading* direct systematic phonics program. Simply incorporate direct instruction of each capital letter into the reading lesson for the associated lower case letter. To help your child acquire knowledge of the capital letters:

- First, introduce and explain the concept of capital letters and lower case letters to the child in understandable terms. Explain how we have two different ways to write the same letter. Most of the time we use the regular lower case letter. But when we start a sentence or start a proper name we always use capital letters. These 'capital' or upper case letters show the letter is important. The first letter of a name is special so we use capital letters. Show the child how you write their name and other family members' names with capital letters. The first letter of a sentence is important. Pick up a book and show the child how capital letters start each sentence.

- Directly teach each of the capital letters and link the capital letter to the lower case letter. Systematically introduce the capital letters. Explicitly tell the child this is the capital letter for this sound. Luckily over half of the capital and lower case pairs are similar. The child easily recognizes the larger version as the capital letter (Cc, Kk, Oo, Pp, Ss, Uu, Vv, Ww, Xx, Yy, Zz) and quickly learns other fairly similar pairs (Ff, Jj, Ll, Mm, Tt).

- Directly teach the child correct formation for each of the capital letters. The following shows how to form each of the letters. The dot • indicates where to start the letter and the directional arrow → shows which way to write. On the letters that require picking up the pencil a number 1 is given to show which part you write first. Other letters are made without lifting the pencil.

- Directly teach print = sound for the capital letters. Use the sound card and sound writing techniques described in the *Right Track Reading* program. Make a distinct sound card for each individual capital letter. Don't combine upper and lower case letters together as a unit. For example, the child needs to learn M = /m/ so make a sound card for 'M', not the combined unit 'Mm'. Use sound writing as an effective technique to help the child learn the sound for these capital letters. For example, the child would practice printing 'M' while saying /m/. With capital letters, it is only necessary to practice the basic alphabet not the entire phonemic code.

- Matching games are a terrific tool for helping children learn the capital letter and associated lower case letter. However, once again be sure and make distinct/separate cards for the lower and upper case letters. For matching you need a 'M' card to pair with the separate 'm' card or 'G' card to match to the 'g' card. You can play games with matching cards. You can make your own games. In addition, many puzzles and games are commercially available for matching capital and lower case letters.

- Writing matching sets is a highly effective technique for learning the lower case-capital pairs. Again, have the child print single letters. For example the child prints R R R & r r r on adjacent lines while saying the /r/ sound (not 'Rr').

Appendix E
Supplemental Activities ~ Oral Sound Blending Exercises

Smooth blending is an essential subskill to proficient reading. Some children automatically and easily learn how to blend sounds together smoothly. However, others need specific work to master this essential skill. *It is essential the child masters smooth blending in the initial stages.* If the child can not blend smoothly it will handicap his ability to process print phonologically and to develop fluency. Please see page 27 for information on the importance of smooth blending. Ensure the child understands and develops correct smooth blending. If the child has difficulty blending sounds, immediately stop and work on this critical skill with some oral blending practice. The following oral blending activities help the child learn how to smoothly blend sounds together.

These oral activities help the child develop smooth blending skills. Tell your child you are going to play some fun sound games. Say: "First I will say some sounds slowly. Then you say the same sounds slowly by yourself and say them at regular speed. Let me show you how we are going to do this." Demonstrate an example:

> I will say "mmmmoooooommmm", Then you would repeat 'mmmmoooommm'.
> Next I ask you to "say it regular" and you would say "mom".

Important NOTES for all oral blending activities:

➢ Do NOT let the child 'chop' or segment sounds when blending. He must keep the sounds 'hooked together'.

➢ Ask the child to 'say it regular'. I avoid asking children to say it 'fast' as they tend to shout and distort sounds. Demonstrate examples if the child does not understand how to 'say it regular'.

Tell the child "Let's play a few of these sound blending games together" and demonstrate by working through several example rounds with your child.

> Parent: "Say mmmeeee"
> Child repeats: "'mmmeee"
> Parent: "Now say it regular"
> Child says: 'me' at normal speed
>
> Parent: "Say sssaaaammmm"
> Child repeats: "'ssssaaammm"
> Parent: "Now say it regular"
> Child says: 'Sam' at normal speed

"Now it is your turn" and give the child words to 'stretch out' and then say at regular speed.

The format is:
Parent: "Say ____ " -the parent slowly says the stretched out word ("wwweeee")
Child: -the child repeats the stretched out sounds slowly ("wwweeee").
Parent: "Now say it regular"
Child: The child says the sounds/word at regular speed (we)

For this blending skill development activity, use simple single syllable words. Begin with the 'slow stretchy' sounds and avoid 'fast' blended consonant combinations until the child first masters the basic blending technique. Some appropriate words include:

> me, am, if, we, in, is, see, sam, sun, fan, fun, run, rim, ram, this, mom, his, math, fuss, mess, nut, met, red, fin, fed, mop, shop, ship, net, will, with, seed, road, that, seat, meet, lap, flip, top, bus, flag, vest, wish, mast, slam, last, was, team, look, swim, flat, reach, high, must, swill, shag, off, at, not …

APPENDIX F
Supplemental Phonemic Awareness Activities

Phonemic awareness (PA), the ability to hear, distinguish, recognize and manipulate sounds within words, is critical to reading success. We know that phonemic awareness training has a significant positive effect on reading and spelling. We can directly teach children how to hear, recognize and manipulate sounds within words to intentionally develop the phonemic awareness skills necessary for proficient reading. Specific information on phonemic awareness and how to help your child develop phonemic awareness can be found in the following locations:

Background Information on Phonemic Awareness:

- Explanation on page 10.
- *Phonemic Awareness Explained; What Phonemic Awareness Is, Why Phonemic Awareness is Important and Linking Phonemic Awareness to Print* **www.righttrackreading.com/whatpais.html**

Specific Activities to Develop Phonemic Awareness:

- *Free Activities to Develop Phonemic Awareness Skill* **www.righttrackreading.com/morepaactivities.html**

- *Fun Activities to Help Your Child Develop Phonemic Awareness* **www.righttrackreading.com/paactivities.html**

Informal Phonemic Awareness Evaluation Tool:

- *Quick Evaluation of Phonemic Awareness* **www.righttrackreading.com/phonemicevaluation.html**

Information and details on phonics phones including instructions for making and using this simple yet highly effective tool for enhancing PA instruction:

- *Phonics Phones Explained* **www.righttrackreading.com/phonicsphones.html**

Additional Phonemic Awareness Activities:

Sound Identification PA to Print Game "What Sound Starts the Word?": This activity helps children both in developing phonemic awareness to distinguish the beginning sounds of a given word and in developing skills to link this PA directly to print as they begin to develop print=sound knowledge.

Activity Directions: Lay out tiles or cards with the print for several sounds (3 to 5 sounds). Orally give the child a word starting with one of the available sounds. Say the word slowly and repeat if the child needs help hearing sounds. The child listens and can repeat the word into their phonics phone if necessary. The child listens to the word, distinguishes the beginning sound, says the starting sound out loud and points to the appropriate printed letter (tile or card).

Introduce and rotate sounds as skills develop. Mix up the words and give new and different words to the child must actually listen to the word and distinguish the sounds. In other word, don't use 'sun' every time where the child can bypass skill development by remembering 'sun' is the 's' letter. Instead mix up many different /s/ words (sun, swim, sat, sad, soft, sick, sack, salt, sand, saw, soap, snake, snow, slug, salamander, sink, skunk…). Remember the progression of difficulty for phonemic awareness. The 'slow/stretchy' sounds are easier to hear (s, m, a, f, l, r, n, o, sh..) than the 'fast/quick' sounds (t, d, b, k, g, p). Also blended constant clusters are more difficult especially blends with 'fast' sounds. A few blends are especially tricky for younger children ('dr').

In this example tiles 'm', 's', 'd', 'i' and 'th' have been set on the table. You orally give the word 'soap' and the child says /s/ and points to the letter 's'. Then you give the child the word 'milk' and she says /m/ and points to the letter 'm'.

Activities to help students build skills in distinguishing the short /e/ and /i/ sounds

The ability to distinguish the short vowel sounds /e/ and /i/ can be difficult for some students as these sounds *are* very similar. In general, when a child has difficulty distinguishing certain sounds you need to help him develop or 'fine tune' their PA to recognize the difference between these similar sounds. The following PA activities directly build skills in distinguishing /i/ and /e/. Before beginning activities to develop PA for the /e/ and /i/ sounds, tell the child the /e/ and /i/ sounds ARE tricky. These activities will help you develop 'an ear' for these sounds. The secret is to listen carefully.

Practice identifying /e/ and /i/ sounds in isolation: This initial drill provides practice hearing and distinguishing the /e/ and /i/ sounds in isolation. Place a sound tile or sound card on the table for both 'e' and 'i'. Say either the /e/ sound or the /i/ sound and the child points to the correct letter when you say the sound. Be sure to mix up the sounds so the child has to listen and not just point to the 'other one'. The student can use a phonics phone to help him hear the difference.

Practice identifying sounds within single /e/ and /i/ words: Orally say a word with either the /e/ or the /i/ sound. The child then points to either the printed 'e' or 'i' on either a sound tile or a sound/letter card. Randomly mix up the /e/ and /i/ words so the child has to listen carefully. If the child makes an error, repeat the word prompting the child to listen carefully. Slow down and 'stretch out' the sounds when possible (without distorting the sounds) to help the child hear.

Use single syllable short vowel words containing /e/ or /i/ within the word. Most short vowels sounds are found in the interior of words so the child needs to learn to distinguish the /e/ and /i/ sounds within words. If the child can not yet distinguish beginning sounds you need to back up and work on beginning phonemic awareness skills. See the article phonemic awareness explained for information. www.righttrackreading.com/whatpais.html

A sample list is provided below. However, you can use other simple short vowel /e/ and /i/ words. CAUTION! – Do NOT use words with the short /e/ before an 'm' or 'n' as we often pronounce these with an /i/ sound. This is why 'pen' and 'pin' sound the same. For example don't use: hem, them, end, send, dent, stem...etc. Avoid multisyllable words as our 'lazy' schwa pronunciation changes vowel sounds. Keep it simple!

/e/ words: net, fed, tell, get, bet, beg, sell, mess, set, press, met, let, net, red, deck, step, Fred, help, mesh, smell, spell, ledge, best, fled, test, sped, mesh, belt, self, sled, speck, felt, rest

/i/ words: big, pill, wish, fin, mid, miss, mill, lit, rim, kit, tip, kill, mitt, kid, win, hill, rid, tip, did, dip, dish, bill, rich, fish, fist, flip, brim , trip, mist, spin, list, prim, strip, sniff, risk, film

Practice identifying sounds using pairs of /e/ & /i/ words: This activity uses pairs of words (similar except for the short vowel sound). Say one of the words. The student identifies either 'e' or 'i' and points to the correct letter on a tile or card. Once again be sure and mix up the order of the words. Don't always list the 'e' word first. Make the child listen.

| pet-pit | set-sit | fell-fill | mess-miss | bet-bit | red-rid | bell-bill |
| bed-bid | let-lit | red-rid | peg-pig | beg-big | sled-slid | tell-till |

Practice making words with 'e' and 'i' sounds: Making 'e' and 'i' words with sound tiles is a terrific way to develop PA skills in distinguishing these sounds. See pages 32-33 for word making directions. Make single words or make words in pairs. Orally give the child a word. The child listens, distinguishes the sound, translates print to sound, and makes the word. Use words from the lists given above. You can also play 'sound changing games' with the word pairs. For example, "Please make the word 'pit'". The student makes the word. Then ask, "What sound would you change to make that word say 'pet'?". Or have the child make the word 'peg' and then ask, "If you changed /e/ to /i/ what word would you have?".

If the student makes an error, have the child stop, read the word he made and then listen for the difference. For example if you gave him 'red' and he made 'rid', have him stop and read the word 'rid'. Then say "you made the word 'rid'" (point at word as you read it to him), "Please make the word 'red'". Help him hear the difference. Repeat the word and slow the word down if necessary. And then just practice!

These techniques and activities can be modified and used with other sounds to build phonemic awareness.

APPENDIX G
~ Summary of Spelling Patterns for Specific Sounds ~

The following table provides the different phonograms or spelling patterns for each sound. The spelling patterns for each sound are listed in general order of frequency of occurrence with the more common ways of writing a sound listed before the less frequent spelling patterns. The 'unexpected' spellings are indicated with an asterisk (*). The list is organized with the consonant sounds listed first, followed by vowel, vowel-combinations and then r-controlled vowel sounds. A few special endings are listed at the end. Although this list covers the most common spellings it does not include all the possible spellings for every sound. Also pronunciation can vary for some of the sounds.

Sound	Spelling Pattern (Examples) The spellings alternatives for each sound are listed in order of frequency with * = unexpected pattern
/b/	**b** (bass, bring, grab)
/d/	**d** (did, drop, sad, wild)
/f/	**f** (fun, draft, flip, gift) **ff** (off, stiff, staff) used to end single-syllable short-vowel words ***ph** (phrase, graph, photograph, phone, orphan)
/g/	**g** (gum, grip, bag, tangle)
/h/	**h** (hum, hold, help, hide)
/j/	**j** (jump, jug, job, enjoy) **g+e** (age, angel, strange, lunge) **dge** (ledge, badge, fudge, bridge) used to end single-short-vowel words **g+i** (giraffe, giant) **g+y** (gym, energy)
/k/	**c** (cold, came, scare, act, class) **k** (kid, soak, keep, kite, rake) **ck** (back, sick, luck, sock, racket) used at end of syllables w/ single short vowel ***ch** (school, Christmas, ache, scheme)
/l/	**l** (learn, love, cold, slap, clam) **ll** (all, call, roll) used to end single-vowel, single-syllable words
/m/	**m** (map, mark, mom, storm, smear) ***mb** (dumb, climb, comb, lamb)
/n/	**n** (not, ran, nothing, never, land, went, snap) ***kn** (know, knew, knee, knife)
/p/	**p** (puppy, plug, gulp, spell, space)
/kw/	**qu** (quick, quilt, quiet, equal)
/r/	**r** (run, ride, rest, brick, string) ***wr** (write, wrong, wrote, wrap)
/s/	**s** (sun, see, swing, mist) **c+e** (cent, race, cell, nice, space, price, trace) **c+i** (city, cinnamon, Pacific, Cindy) **c+y** (bicycle, cylinder, cyst, lacy) **ss** (pass, toss, miss, mess, boss) used to end single-syllable short-vowel words
/t/	**t** (told, tip, tall, stop, test, last, kitten)
/v/	**v** (vest, vent, have, love)
/w/	**w** (west, wild, winter, swell, swat)
/y/	**y** (yes, you, yellow, beyond) when 'y' is a consonant beginning syllables
/ks/	**x** (fix, box, exit, expand)

/z/	**s**	(is, was, has, rose, use, risen, raisin and numerous plural words)
	z	(zoo, zipper, zebra)
	zz	(buzz, fizz, jazz) used at end of single-syllable short-vowel words
	***x**	(only in a few Greek origin words starting with x, xylophone, xeric, xylem)
/ch/	**ch**	(child, chop, choke, munch, reach)
	***tch**	(watch, latch, itch, match) used ending single syllable single-vowel words
/sh/	**sh**	(shut, ship, wish, mash)
	***ch**	(only in a few French origin words machine, chivalry, chalet, Cheyenne)
/th/	**th**	(this, that, those, mother)
/th/ (soft)	**th**	(math, bath, thin)
wh	**wh**	(whisper, when, whip)
/a/	**a**	(had, at, am, as, mad, apple)
/ay/	**a_e**	(ate, made, rate, space, grace, page, game, bake)
	ai	(rain, pain, wait, aid, aim, waist, train)
	a	(rang, bang, bank, navy, thank, gravy)
	ay	(play, stay, may, pay)
	***ei**	(vein, rein, veil)
	***eigh**	(eight, sleigh, weigh)
	***ea**	(great, steak)
	***ey**	(they, obey)
/e/	**e**	(egg, set, check, elk, felt, west, mess, wet)
	ea	(bread, head, ready, instead, health, tread, steady, heaven)
/ee/	**ee**	(bee, see, green, need, deep, street, meet, sheep)
	ea	(eat, team, seat, leap, peach, reach, heat, seal)
	y	(baby, silly, candy, picky, quickly) Used for /ee/ end of multisyllable words
	e	(he, she, be, me, and in the prefix pre- , re- and de-)
	***e_e**	(eve, Pete, precede, concrete)
	***ie**	(grief, brief, brownie, collie)
	***ey**	(key, money, monkey, honey, turkey)
	***i**	(machine, brilliant, material, radiate)
/i/	**i**	(hid, it, is, if, grip, instead, hit, sit)
	***y**	(gym, typical, system, syllable, mystery, symbol)
	***ie**	(friend, shield, yield)
	***ai**	(again, captain, mountain, certain)
/ie/	**i_e**	(pine, fine, time, nice, ride, hide, ice)
	i	(wild, child)
	y	(shy, cry, by, fly, my, try)
	igh	(high, tight, right, sight, night, fright, might, sigh)
	***ie**	(pie, die, lie)
/o/	**o**	(not, mop, hop, sob, sock, hog)
/oa/	**o_e**	(vote, home, hope, tote, shone, globe, rode, choke, hose)
	o	(no, go, so, old, told, most)
	ow	(snow, glow, own, show, blow, owner)
	oa	(boat, oat, goat, roam, shoal, coal, loan, soap)
	***oe**	(toe, foe, doe, hoe)
	***ough**	(dough, though)
/u/	**u**	(up, us, cup, fun, must, hung, until, under)
	o	(son, from, love, some, contain, money, month, front, of)
	***ou**	(couple, cousin, famous, nervous) often found in 'ous' ending multisyllable words

/oo/ or /yoo/ (long-u is pronounced as /yoo/ in some words such as cute)	**oo**	(moon, soon, cool, hoop, boot,
	u_e	(use, rule, tune, flute, cube, mule, bugle)
	ew	(stew, drew, chew, threw, few)
	***ue**	(blue, blue, true)
	***ou**	(you, group, youth)
	***ui**	(fruit, suit, bruise, cruise)
	***u**	(music, tuba, pupil)
	***ough**	(through)
/uu/	**oo**	(cook, book, took, foot,)
	***u**	(put, push)
/ow/	**ou**	(out, pound, ground, stout,)
	ow	(now, how, owl)
	***ough**	(plough)
/oy/	**oi**	(choice, coin, oil, boil, moist)
	oy	(boy, toy, employ,
/aw/	**aw**	(law, paw, lawn, crawl)
	au	(haul, cause, fault)
	a+l & **a+ll**	(almost, all, call, also, talk) pronunciation of a+l
	***augh**	(taught, caught)
	***ough**	(bought, thought)
/ar/	**ar**	(arm, car, star, artist, market)
/er/	**er**	(her, term, sister, over, hunter)
	ur	(nurse, turn, lurch, curve)
	ir	(stir, bird, thirst, shirt, girl)
	or	(w+or as in work, word & ending some multisyllable words visitor, doctor)
	***ear**	(early, learn, earth, heard)
	***ar**	(dollar, collar, solar, lunar, orchard)
/or/	**or**	(or, for, torn, north)
	ore	(more, tore, snore, score)
	oar	(oar, roar, board)
	***our**	(four, pour, tour, your)
	***oor**	(door, poor, floor)
/air/	**are**	(mare, dare, share)
	ar	(carry, parent, barren)
	air	(air, hair, stair, chair)
	***ear**	(bear, pear, wear)
/eer/	**ear**	(ear, dear, near, clear)
	eer	(deer, cheer, peer)
	***ere**	(here, mere)
	Special endings for multisyllable words	
/shun/	**tion**	(nation, station, motion, correction)
	sion	(vision, confession, mission)
	***cian**	(electrician, magician, technician) used for an occupation
	***cion**	(suspicion, coercion) rarely used
/shul/	**cial**	(special, artificial, financial)
	***tial**	(partial, potential)
/shus/	**tious**	(cautious, infectious, nutritious)
	cious	(precious, spacious, ferocious)
/chur/	**ture**	(fracture, picture, nature, future, mixture)
/zhur/	**sure**	(measure, pleasure, treasure, closure)

~ Free Reading Information ~
~Supplemental Free Resources~
~ Comments & Questions ~
~Ordering Information ~

www.righttrackreading.com

Free Information on Teaching Children to Read:

Informative articles
Useful resources
Effective activities
Links to other resources and research

Questions & Comments:

The author welcomes any questions or comments on *Right Track Reading Lessons*. Please contact Miscese Gagen at **mail@righttrackreading.com** if you have any questions about the program or need additional information on helping your child or student achieve reading success. In addition, feedback on the program is appreciated as this information helps the author fine tune and improve the program.

Please send any questions or comments to mail@righttrackreading.com or to Right Track Reading, PO Box 1952, Livingston MT 59047.

Ordering:

To order additional copies of *Right Track Reading Lessons* or to order *Back on the Right Track Reading Lessons* please go to the website.
1. The book can be directly ordered and purchased from www.righttrackreading.com using the PayPal ordering and payment system.
2. Print off a hard copy of the order form and include a check or money order for full amount payable to Right Track Reading LLC. Mail the order form with payment to: Right Track Reading LLC, PO Box 1952, Livingston MT 59047
3. The book is available in some bookstores. See the website for a list of bookstores where you may directly purchase the book.

Shipping details and additional contact information are located on the website.

Empowering parents and teachers.
The tools to achieve reading success, one child at a time!

Key Elements Reference Card

✂ Cut out & use as a bookmark and handy reference guide

Reference Key Elements for Effective Reading Instruction

Right Track Reading Lessons' targeted multisensory activities directly build skills and establish proficient reader phonologic processing. **Key elements to apply in reading instruction to help children achieve reading success include:**

📖 Establish Phonologic Processing (read print by 'sounding out')
  *read by 'sounding out'   *decodable text   *practice integrating & applying skills

📖 Direct Printed Letter = Sound Knowledge of Complete Phonemic Code
  *direct print-to-sound   *correct pronunciation   * practice until automatic

📖 Left-to-Right Tracking in All Reading
  *use physical movement with finger or pointer   *engrain proper tracking

📖 Smoothly Blend Sounds Together
  *keep sounds hooked together/don't chop apart   *take a breath   *sing

📖 Pay Attention to the Details
  *read carefully   *process all sounds   *read accurately

📖 Immediately Correct All Errors – Always Learn Correctly!
  *Stop all errors (oops)   *require correct skills   *help the child learn correctly

📖 Use Direct Instruction
  *explicitly teach the child all necessary skills

Free Resources for *Right Track Reading Lessons* are located at
www.righttrackreading.com/resourcesforrighttrackreading.html
